DESIGN DYNAMICS

Integrating Design and Technology

Joyce S. Hertzson

Eileen Feeney Bushnell

Stephanie Kirschen Cole

Karen Sardisco

Bruce Wenger

Rochester Institute of Technology

Prentice Hall

Upper Saddle River, New Jersey 07458

Library of Congress Cataloging-in-Publication Data

Design dynamics / Joyce S. Hertzson ... [et al.].
p. cm.
Includes index.
ISBN 0-13-098350-0
1. Design—Technique. 2. Computer graphics. I. Hertzson, Joyce S.
NK1510 .D4725 2002
741.6—dc21
2002070213

Editorial Director: Charlyce Jones Owen
Publisher: Bud Therien
Assistant Editor: Kimberly Chastain
Editorial Assistant: Sasha Anderson
Director of Production and Manufacturing: Barbara Kittle
Production Editor: Judy Winthrop
Project Liaison: Louise Rothman
Prepress Manufacturing Manager: Nick Sklitsis
Prepress and Manufacturing Buyer: Sherry Lewis
Marketing Director: Beth Mejia
Marketing Manager: Chris Ruel
Cover Design: Kiwi Design
Art Director: Jayne Conte

This book was set in 10/12 TNR by Lithokraft II
and printed and bound by von Hoffman.
The cover was printed by Phoenix.

Prentice Hall

Printed in the United States of America

10 9 8 7 6 5 4 3 2 1

0-13-098350-0

Pearson Education Ltd., London
Pearson Education Australia Pty, Limited, Sydney
Pearson Education Singapore, Pte., Ltd.
Pearson Education North Asia Ltd., Hong Kong
Pearson Education Canada, Ltd., Toronto
Pearson Education de Mexico, S.A. de C.V.
Pearson Education—Japan, Tokyo
Pearson Education Malaysia, Pte., Ltd.
Pearson Education Upper Saddle River, New Jersey

CONTENTS

PREFACE

Design forms the basis of a universally utilized visual language. It transcends differing cultures, generational experiences, changes in technology, and advances in scientific knowledge. The computer—originally engineered as a toolbox for the mathematician, scientist, and business person—has in recent years become the media and tool of choice for many artists, designers, and visual thinkers. Though the media and methods of approach used to make visual products have broadened to include digital technology, the basic principles that govern design do not change.

As committed participants in the process of integrating technology into the study of design, the faculty of the Foundations Department in the College of Imaging Arts and Sciences at Rochester Institute of Technology have been "surfing the digital wave" for almost two decades. The two-dimensional design faculty has been experimenting with and using the personal computer and its attendant technologies as a teaching tool in Freshman Design courses. Though not always easy, it has always been a valuable experience for students and faculty alike. Our explorations have resulted in an innovative program of study that utilizes the computer to promote creative problem solving as a primary approach to learning. Although the origins of our curriculum lie in a traditional studio approach to design, the computer has become for us a flexible tool through which ideation, project development, and finished visual solutions may be accomplished.

Because we recognize that not everyone has had the same opportunity to explore the technology or exploit its creative potential, we have collectively worked on this book to share our experience and provide a framework that integrates digital technology and its creative applications with the more traditional realm of basic design. This is a project-based exploration of concepts and ideas, providing a variety of options for teaching and learning. We offer a diversity of ideas for independent study or curriculum enhancement in the classroom setting. The projects chosen for inclusion are those that most closely illustrate the premise of the book. Although inclusive and extensive, the book differs significantly from the comprehensive courses we each teach on site.

Design Dynamics demonstrates how the computer may be used as a tool to enhance visual vocabulary in an increasingly digital and web-connected culture. Our emphasis here at RIT is to explore the fundamentals of design through hands-on projects that teach design concepts and the incidental technical skills of art making. We have organized this book to explore structures in and of design through various options and themes of investigation. The projects generally progress from simple to complex both in underlying fundamental concepts and possible technological complexity. Most offer computer and noncomputer alternatives, as well as suggestions for other solutions to investigate. In fact, the digital portions of most of the projects evolved from their traditional counterparts when the computer provided a more efficient working method.

As imagemakers, we recognize that the transitions in identity, society, and technology causing great cultural shifts are occurring at a tremendous pace. Our excitement and experience in navigating the changing cultural landscape have led to the creation of this book. It is our hope that a broad range of visually interested persons will find this book stimulating and useful.

CHAPTER 1

DESIGN ESSENCE

WHAT IS DESIGN?

What is "design"? Is it the newest sports car on the market, wallpaper patterns, or the latest in fashion magazines? Design is all of these and more. It is everywhere we look, from the structures in which we live, work, or play to what we read or wear.

While design might fill our environment, recognizing and appreciating good design is a learned skill. We grow up observing changes in fashion and style. What we like is often instilled in us by our surroundings; the cultures in which we live, both geographic and chronological. The particular taste of the people who influence our environment can be positive or negative. How do we separate design from the whims of fashion and taste? We focus on the aesthetics of forms and images combined with their intended function for the purpose of communication. Design centers on what we desire to communicate and how that affects the balance of form and function.

Design also comprises a complex and intricate set of issues including elements and principles that can be learned and applied two-dimensionally or three-dimensionally. Though the issues are similar, intrinsic differences appear when you add a third dimension.

A chair is a chair is a chair. Whether a comfortable easy chair or a drafting stool, we can measure the length, the width, and the depth. Two-dimensional design has length and width, remaining flat. Depth, the third dimension, creates objects that occupy space.

So how do we know when a chair, whether in two dimensions or three, is well designed? When form and function intertwine. The Form consists of more than surface decoration; it is the quality of line, the curve of a seat, the grace of the total object. As to function, a chair must provide seating, so it needs to support weight and be comfortable and appropriate for the chosen placement and purpose. "Appropriate" for a classroom likely differs from "appropriate" for in the living room. The overstuffed chair with ottoman does wonders for relaxation at the end of a long day, but proves a death knoll for the classroom environment, where students should remain active and alert. The appropriate studio chair must take into account the height of the desk or drafting table and a need for mobility. Any stool of the right height would work, but a stool with a back to lean against and a padded seat—ah, comfort as well as suitability for the purpose!

One additional aspect of function is cost. The stool with added attributes for comfort will certainly cost more. While cost does not change the intrinsic beauty of an object or how well it functions, the price may determine whether something is ultimately produced or purchased. If it is not made, can it be well designed? If a tree falls in the forest with no one there to hear, does it still make a sound?

Three-dimensional design is tangible—we can view it, touch it, and sit on it. If it looks good, feels good, and supports our weight, we deem it successful. What do we consider well designed in two dimensions? When the design is aesthetically pleasing and if it serves the necessary purpose—that being to communicate in the best way possible. Measurement of success in two dimensions is somewhat more difficult because you can't sit in a drawing of a chair. So, how do we know when a drawing is balanced or whether it supports "weight"? What makes a painting the "best of show"? Is it the prettiest picture, with colors you like? If you were looking for that perfect painting to fill the space above the couch, then personal taste and purpose satisfy function.

But what if this flat image needs to do more than look good? What if it needs to "speak"? Two-dimensional design provides the vocabulary needed to speak in the complexity of visual imagery.

TO SEE, OR, THE ELEMENTS OF VISUAL LANGUAGE

If we use the same criteria for two dimensions that we have for three, we still need to look at

- Aesthetics—is it visually pleasing?
- Function—does it serve the necessary purpose?

Before we start learning how to design, maybe we should learn how to see. What exactly do we look for in an effective visual? If we look at the beautiful scene in Figure 1.1, do we stop and think about whether it is well designed? Does Nature do a good job? If we change our view, or our frame of reference as demonstrated in Figures 1.2a, b, c, does it change the success of the image?

Nature's success in the form of a tree or the cut of the horizon is not in question. In fact, we are not really examining nature, but a photograph of nature, a two-dimensional representation. To measure the success of the photograph,

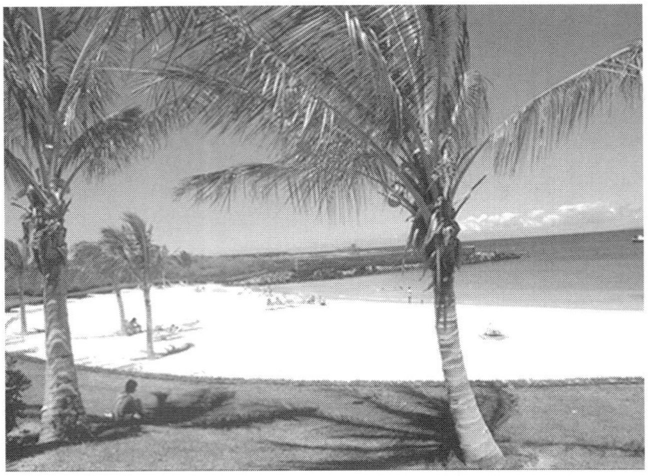

Figure 1.1

we look for the same elements we would measure in any two-dimensional creation, whether a photograph (Figure 1.3a), representational drawing (Figure 1.3b), or other abstract organization (Figure 1.3c).

So, what are those elements? To understand a photograph as a design, we must look for the ***elements*** of design that exist in the image. Let's start with the ***horizon line,*** where the sky meets the sea, and the graceful curved line we see in this view, where the sand meets the green of the grass in Figure 1.4.

Although clearly visible, some of the elements are truly visual while others are merely conceptual. In Figure 1.5, we see the horizon as line because the value of the sky contrasts with the darker value of the water, creating an edge or conceptual line element. There is, however, a dark band formed between the sand and the grass, in Figure 1.6, making this a visual line element. Our eye is drawn to the ***point*** where the land juts into the water, a point being the smallest, conceptual element of design (Figure 1.7).

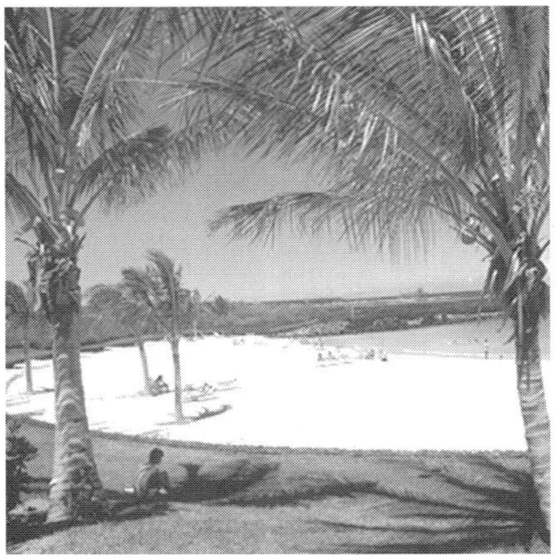

Figure 1.2(a)

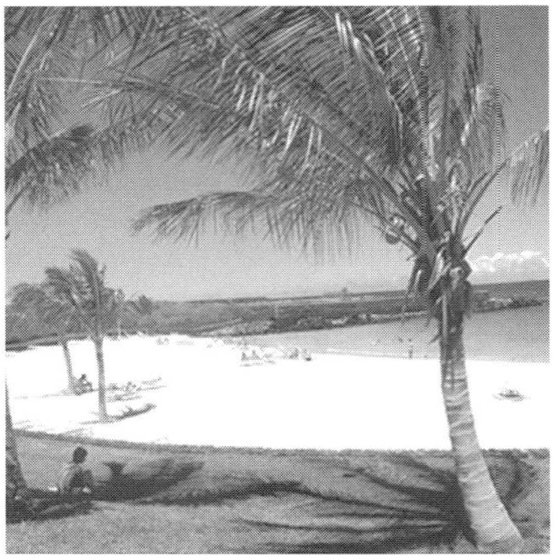

(b)

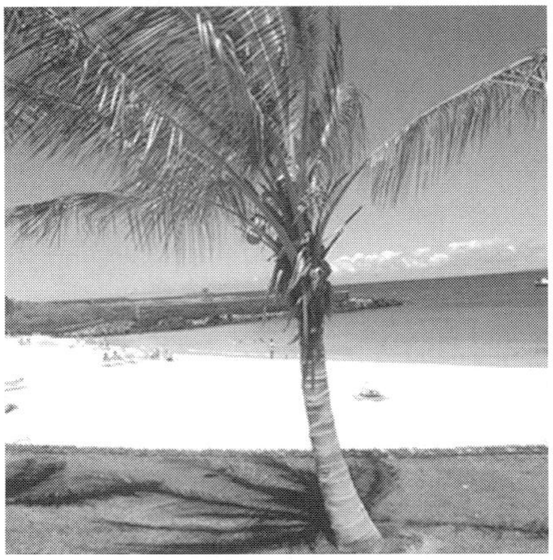

(c)

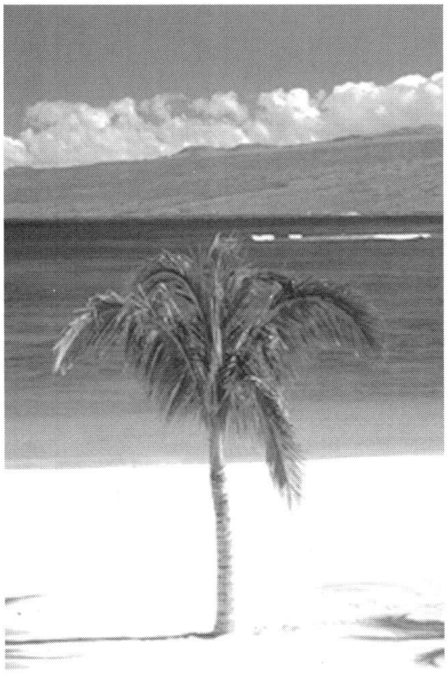

Figure 1.3(a) Photograph

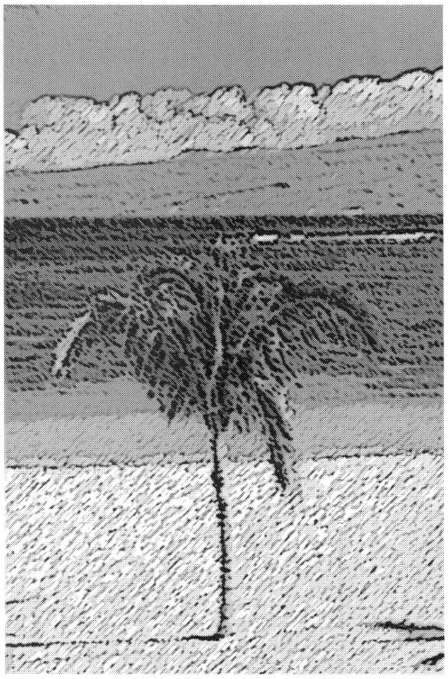

(b) Representational Drawing

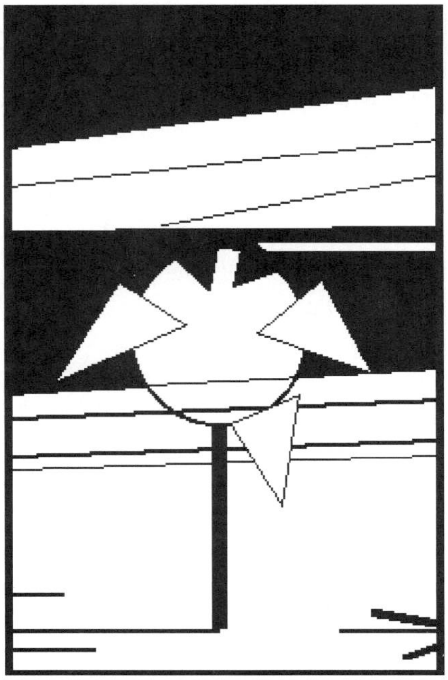

(c) Abstraction

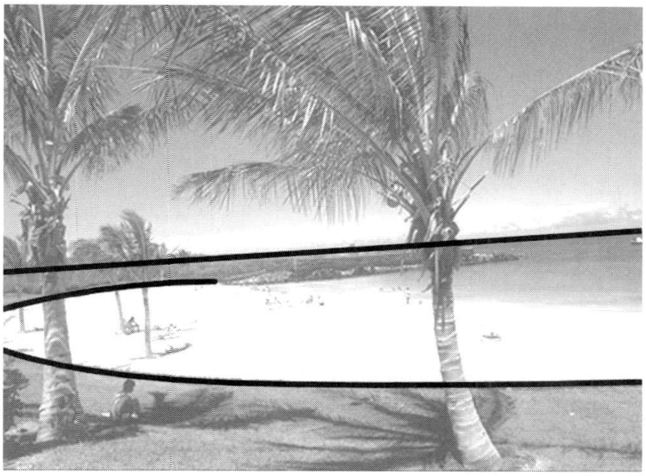

FIGURE 1.4

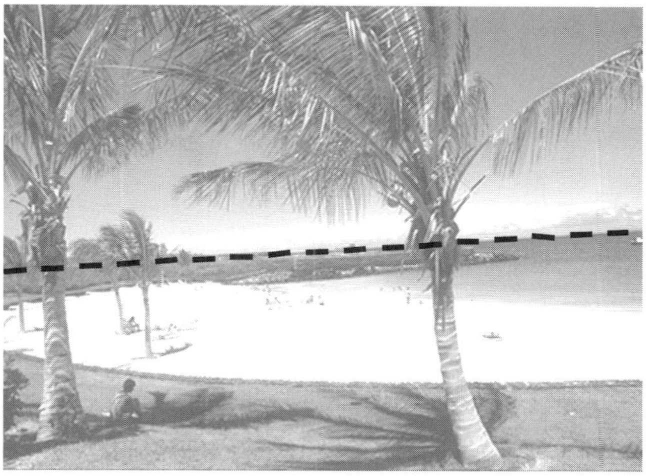

FIGURE 1.5

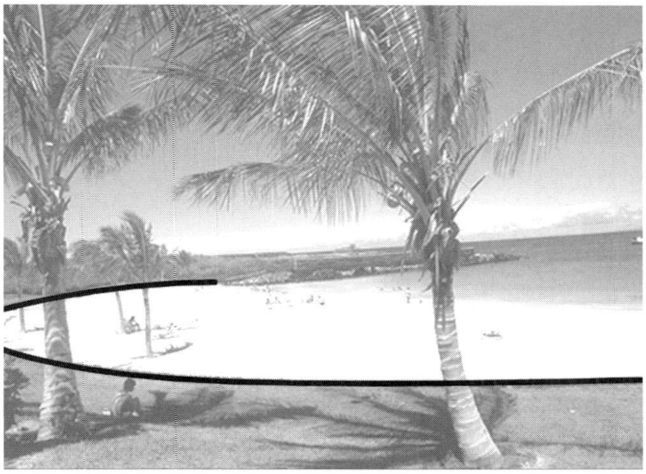

Figure 1.6

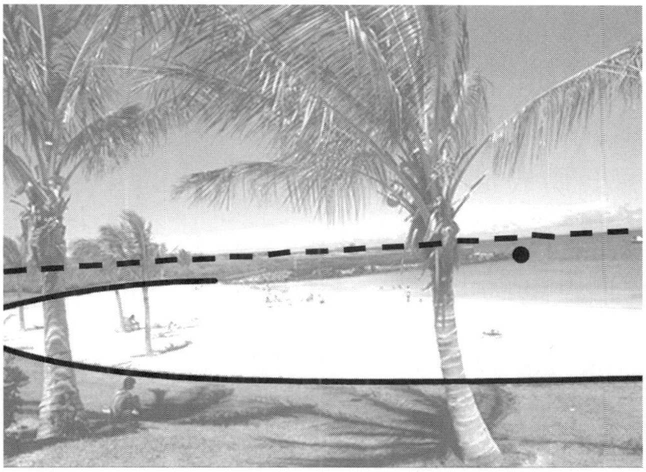

Figure 1.7

From the point where the land ends in the water, in Figure 1.8, our eye is drawn to the white dot of a sailboat, forming a conceptual line from the point of land to the edge of the page. In Figure 1.9, the coconuts in the tree, though small and point-like, are examples of visual design ***elements,*** having definite ***shape, size, color,*** and ***texture.*** The trees, reduced to a basic expression as line, are angled, establishing direction and position by the relationship of their placement (Figure 1.10). Large or small, they convey a sense of weight, which helps their stability. The contrast in ***scale*** helps to create the ***illusion of depth*** within the ***space*** they occupy.

Like an arrow, the meeting of two edges forms a point in Figure 1.11, that directs our eyes and creates a shape with direction. As the movement of a point along a path creates a conceptual line, so the repetition of a line within a boundary creates a plane. In Figure 1.12, a few simple arcs convey the essence of the palms blowing in the wind, casting shadows on the ground, while the outlined circles help to isolate the visual space they occupy.

If we remove the photograph from Figure 1.13 to clearly view the graphic elements that have been established, we can evaluate the design on the successful relationship of the elements to each other. Adding a border to Figure 1.14 shows how the elements relate to the image area or page within the frame of reference. While not necessarily visible, the frame of reference marks the boundaries of a design. How the created elements and remaining space work together within the frame is the essence of ***composition.*** (Figure 1.15). Therefore, the basic elements of design can be visual or conceptual and are relative to the context or environment in which they are placed.

NON-VERBAL COMMUNICATION, OR, LEARNING TO DO IT VISUALLY

While an "object d'art" can be aesthetically pleasing or serve as the personal expression of the creator, a design is creation with a purpose.

Three-dimensional design is tangible. With the well-designed chair, we can touch it or sit on it to know how it feels, whether it is balanced, and if it supports weight. We have tangible evidence of when the object satisfies its purpose.

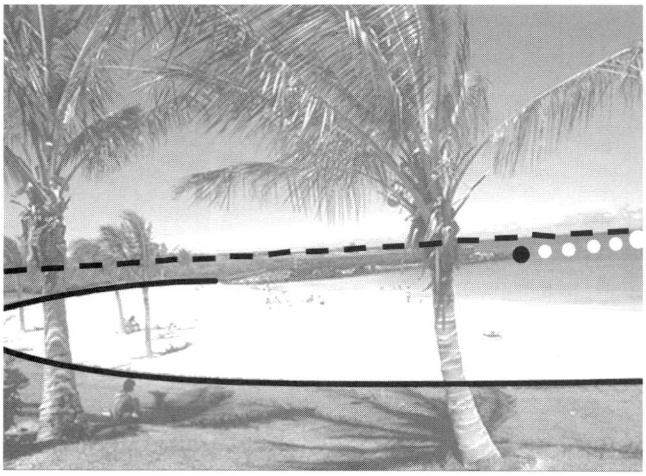

Figure 1.8

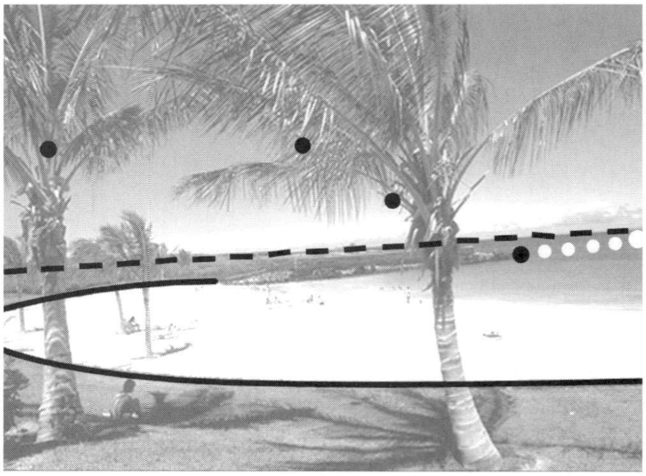

Figure 1.9

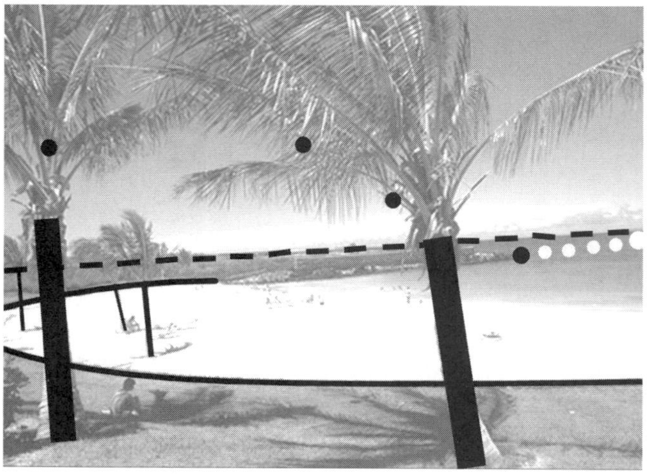

Figure 1.10

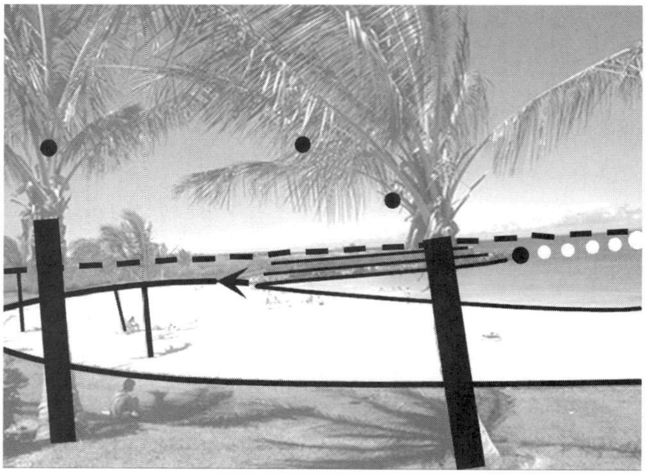

Figure 1.11

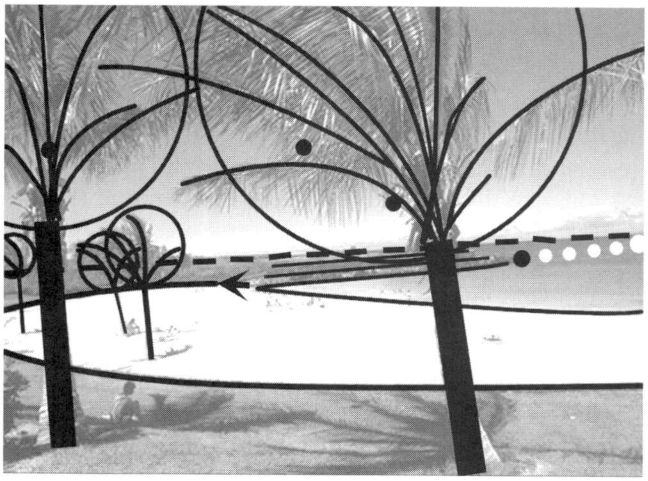

Figure 1.12

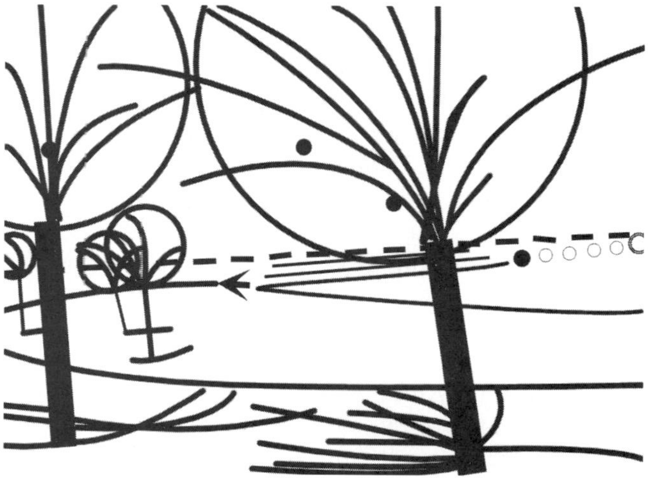

Figure 1.13

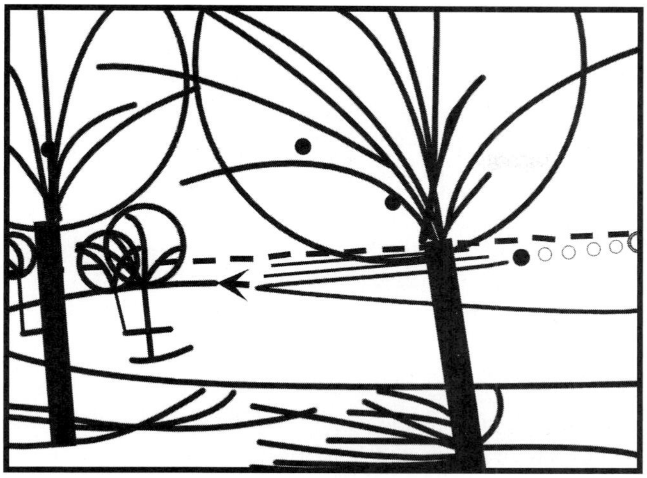

Figure 1.14

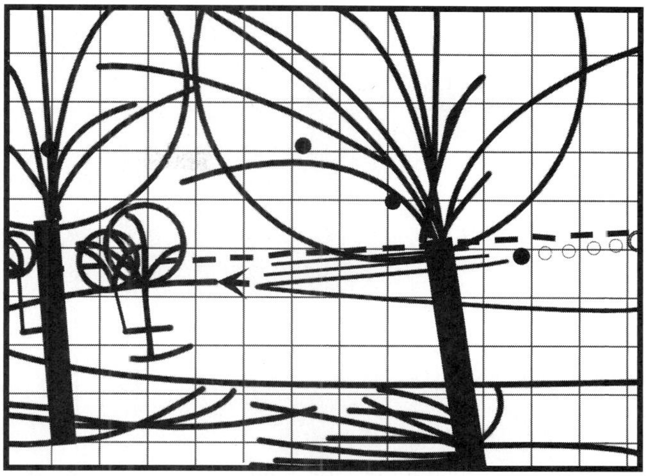

Figure 1.15

If we use the same criteria for two dimensions as we have for three, we still need to look at

- Aesthetics—is it visually pleasing?
- Function—does it serve the necessary purpose?

What is the purpose? To communicate in the best way possible.

But how do we communicate? We are raised with language, using words to express our ideas, our needs, and our wants. To design, we must now learn a visual language.

Let's start by analyzing a classic cigarette advertisiment that might be found in our popular culture. Imagine

- A good looking man with a tan
- Portrait, head and shoulders view
- The character fills the page, bringing him closer to the viewer
- White cowboy hat
- Blue shirt collar
- Background out of focus
- Dramatic lighting, with half of the face in light, the other half in shadow
- A general projection of warmth
- A pack of cigarettes, with a strong color drawing the eye

All of this creates "the icon of American masculinity." What does it say? Smokers are rugged individualists, like the cowboys who tamed the American West. We have become so familiar with this *icon* that no more is needed to convey the message.

Now let's analyze an advertisement for a menthol brand of cigarette. What would you expect to see?

- A young couple walking along the beach
- Street clothes, not bathing attire
- Figures small in contrast to the environment, increasing our sense of space
- A blue sky and blue water crashing on the sand
- Pine trees in the distance
- Bright sunlight casting shadows on the wet sand

What does it say? If you too smoke a menthol cigarette, you too can be part of a couple, enjoying the clean, refreshing air and water with the pine scent.

Both of these avertisements convey a message that appeals to our senses through the manipulation of carefully selected elements. Issues of gender, age, attire, location, and quantity are coordinated to appeal to the appropriate audience. If we analyze the image characteristics and translate them into representative visual terms, we are looking at

- Shapes, their size, texture or color
- Position or placement on the page and the sense of space conveyed and the relationship to you, the viewer
- The quality of light and the time of day or temperature we perceive and how that makes us feel.

We have been manipulated by various elements and principles of design, those that are visible as well as those that are conceptual, perceived as opposed to seen, and the relationships they have to each other and to the page.

CHAPTER 2

SEEING AND PERCEIVING: OBSERVATION

LINE

Line is a basic two-dimensional ***element*** that can be described as a continuously moving point drawn across a surface. Defined and altered by weight, value, texture, and direction, line is often thought of, within the context of design, as a purely visual form. Like all of the elements, however, the genesis of line is found in the natural and human-made environment that surrounds us. The visual perimeters of forms, their contours, are considered to be linear (Figure 2.1)

These lines emerge as a result of ***value contrasts*** between forms and their surroundings. Trees, houses, horizon lines, edges of mountains, and even the human form are thought of as having an edge that we perceive as being linear. Modified by decreasing scale or extended length, forms themselves become lines within the environment. Branches, vines, veins, painted lines on the road, telephone poles, and telephone wires are all perceived as linear forms (Figure 2.2).

Additionally, lines emerge at the intersection of planes as they meet in space. The edges of tables, the corners of houses, and the intersection between the back and seat of a chair, are all places where lines emerge within our environments (Figure 2.3).

Line as an actual element—visible and having the two dimensions of width and length—does not, however, exist within the external world. In the process of mediating the space between the actual environment and the two-dimensional picture plane, we abstract transitions between values and surfaces and "see" lines in the environment. Very few if any three-dimensional forms are actually outlined, and those forms that we "see" as lines, (branches, paint, poles, etc.) inevitably have a third dimension.

Lines are also seen when separate but visually related forms align within our surroundings. A line of people, a line of cars, a line of music, or a credit line are all examples of series of individual elements that we coalesce into a single form that we think of and see as a line.

These ***implied lines*** emerge as a function of the ***gestalt principle of closure,*** which is our mental and visual ability to finish or close forms when given even a limited amount of visual information (Figure 2.4).

Lines may even emerge or be sensed where there is no physical evidence of their existence. These ***psychic lines*** are perceived between two pairs of staring eyes, between a finger and a face (Figure 2.5) and behind a flock of geese as they move across the sky. Their presence as indicators of

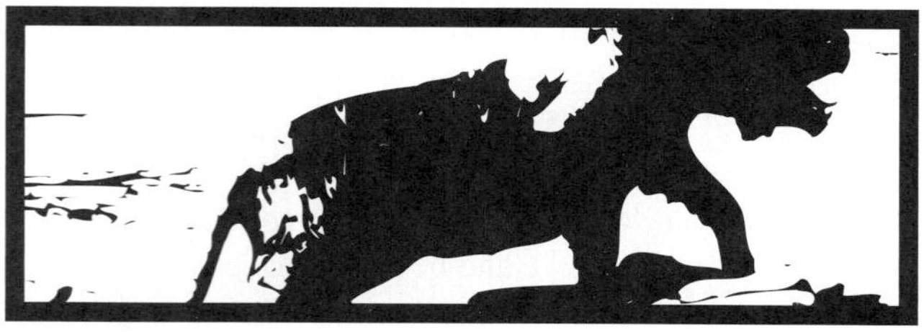

Figure 2.1(a)

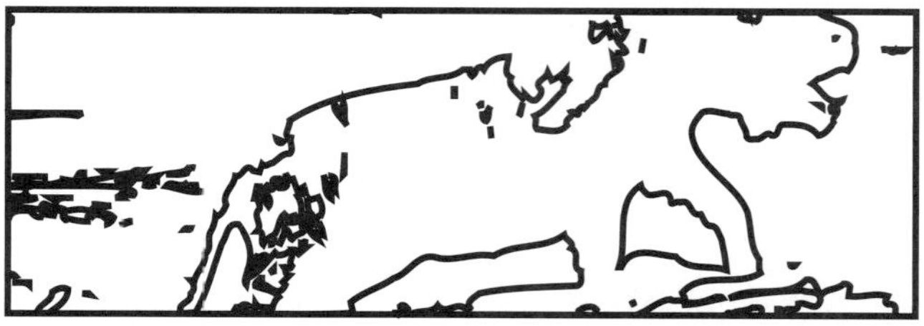

(b)

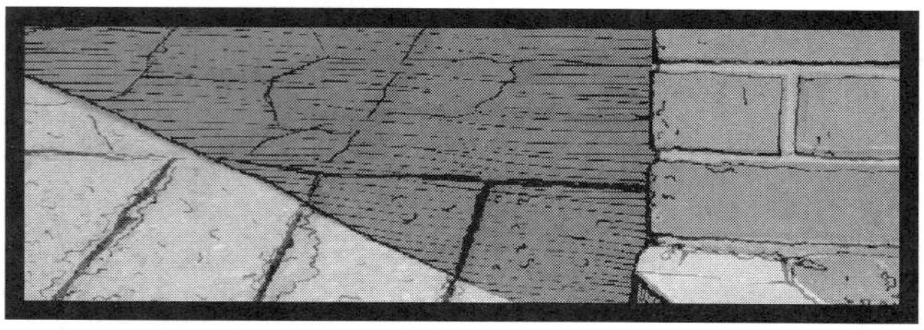

Figure 2.2(a)

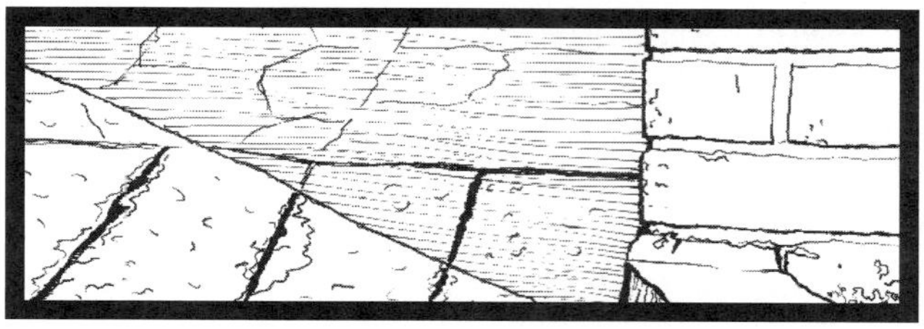

(b)

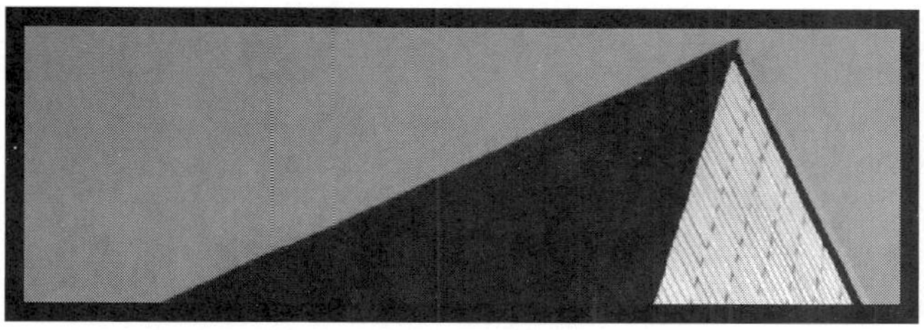

Figure 2.3(a)

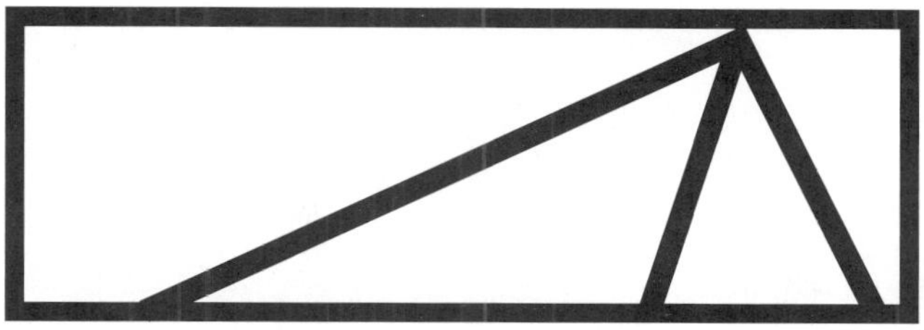

(b)

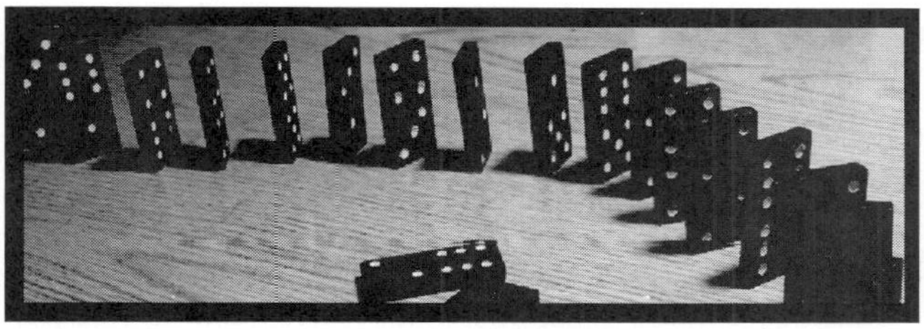

Figure 2.4

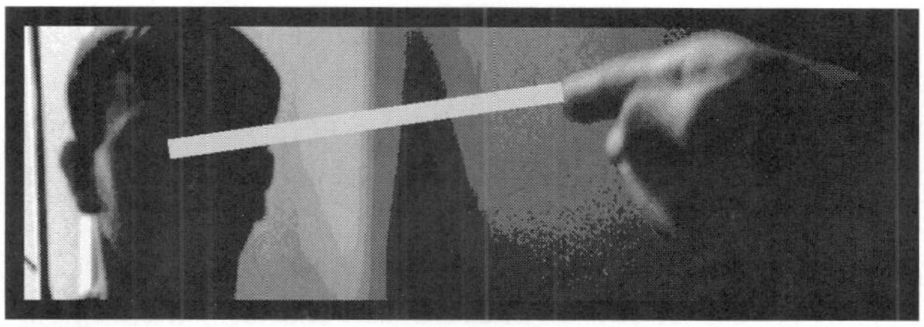

Figure 2.5

direction is indicative of the critical role of forms that point and therein govern movement within two-dimensional compositions.

On a two-dimensional surface, line functions to define edge. ***Shapes*** emerge as lines close on themselves, in turn creating positive and negative spaces within the picture plane. Directional movement is dependent on linear movement, either by the element itself as it moves through space or through the alignment of forms along linear paths.

Seen in parallel groupings, lines become purveyors of ***rhythm*** and ***sequence*** within a composition (Figure 2.6). Lines can change in terms of their ***value,*** (Figure 2.7) ***texture*** (Figure 2.8) and ***weight*** (Figure 2.9).

Perhaps the most dynamic quality of line, however, is its ability to convey emotional, visual, and even physical ***movement*** on a two-dimensional surface (Figure 2.10). This quality is best understood when referenced to the movement lines in the environment around us. Horizontal lines are found on the horizon, in architectural forms, in the movement of waves, and in the sleeping posture of people and many animals. They are therein associated with quiet, calm, and stasis. Lines and aligned forms that move along horizontal paths reference these associations and can lend quiet, calm, and static qualities to the compositions in which they function. Vertical lines are found in trees, architectural elements and the path of growth of many living things. Quiet, strong, and stable, their association with growth makes them slightly more dynamic linear forms than horizontal lines. Their presence in a two-dimensional composition, like their presence in architectural forms, is indicative of the stability and strength that they lend to an image (Figure 2.11).

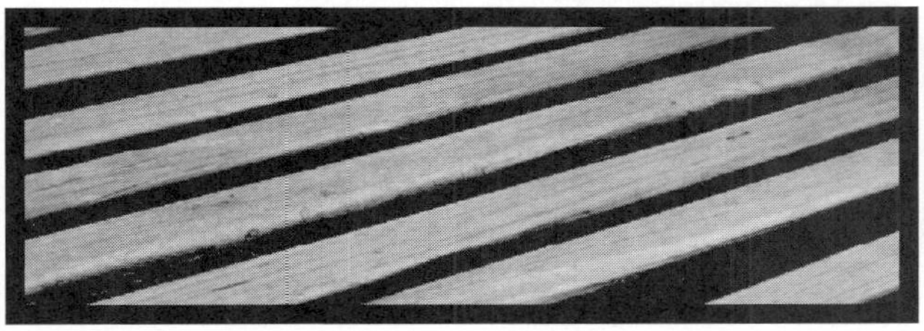

Figure 2.6

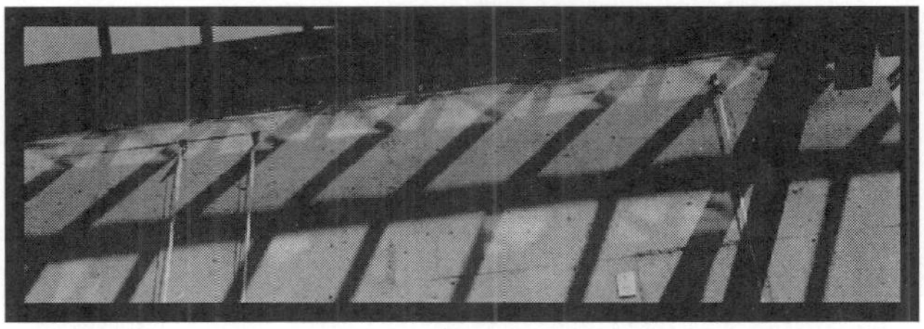

Figure 2.7

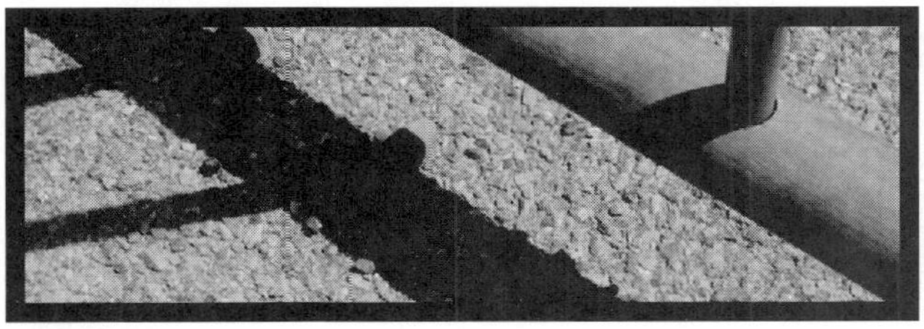

Figure 2.8

Figure 2.9

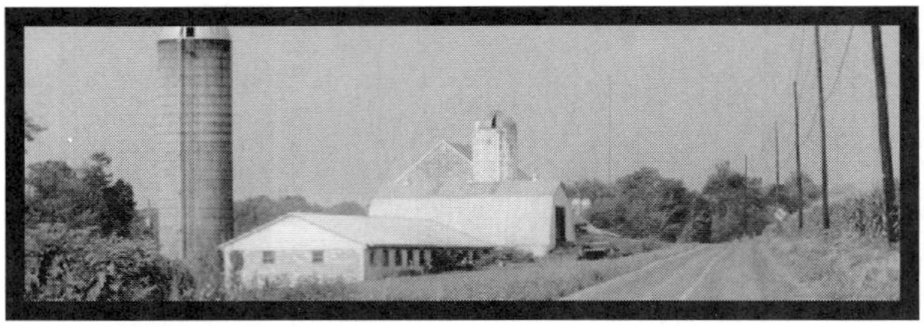

Figure 2.10(a)

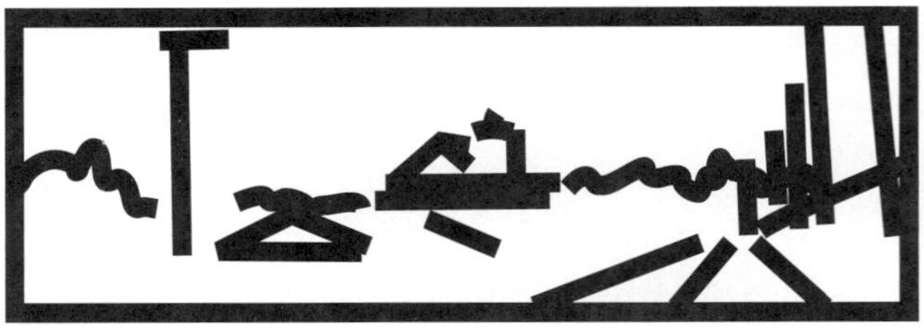

(b)

Curved lines are found along the edges of many organic forms and patterns in nature. Water, coursing through a river or creating a pattern of erosion through the earth, travels in curved paths. Animals, moving within their immediate environments, tend to utilize repetitive movements that also create curved paths. Even the migratory flight patterns of birds take the form of curved spatial routes. These occurrences indicate the more dynamic and active nature of curved lines, which may be thought of as being lyrical, sensual, and flowing (Figure 2.12). Diagonal lines, found along the edges of mountains and volcanoes, and in the paths of lightning, are logically associated with action and energy.

The presence of both of these types of lines within a two-dimensional image creates a much greater level of motion and activity. As with all elements within compositions, these associations are generalized and their impact can only be truly assessed in the context of the entire design.

Perceptually, line has the ability to delineate edge and space within both two- and three-dimensional environments. Conceptually, line can convey emotional and psychological content and meaning. From a formal point of view, line is the most basic of all of the visual elements, defining edge and movement within two-dimensional compositions and bridging the chasm between the three-dimensional fact of our environment and the two-dimensional reality of the picture plane.

Divine Inspiration, or, Line Rhythms in Nature

How do we know when a page is balanced, when the weight is well distributed? What keeps our interest and moves our eye around the page? We may now recognize the elements of design in an established composition, but how do we begin to design? How do we apply those elements to communicate most effectively?

We discussed in the section in Chapter 1 on nonverbal communication that it is successful expression of intangible emotions that communicates to us. Our next step is to understand how to appeal to those senses with basic, visual elements—building an intuitive understanding of the effect of a line or the correct placement of a shape is the next order of business. Once again we will look to a natural environment on which to build our understanding.

If we take a look at this single surfer moving diagonally across the page, (Figure 2.13(a)) we can choose to represent this graphically in many ways. We might want to identify those things we feel important to our understanding of the composition. While we see the diagonal trail of spray

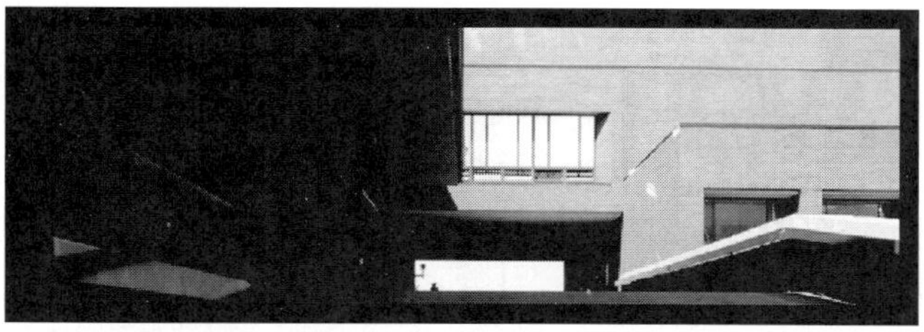

Figure 2.11(a)

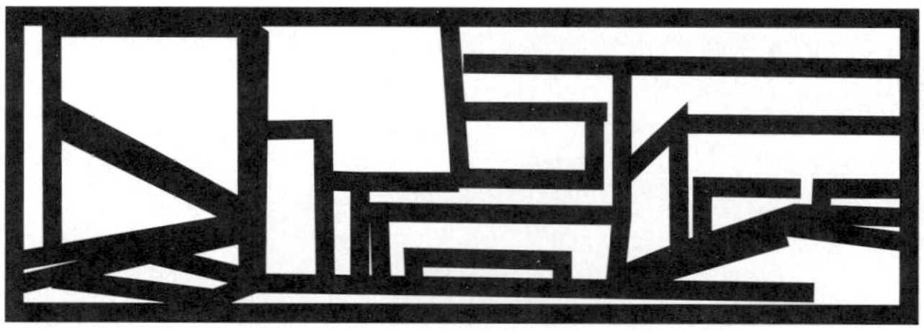

(b)

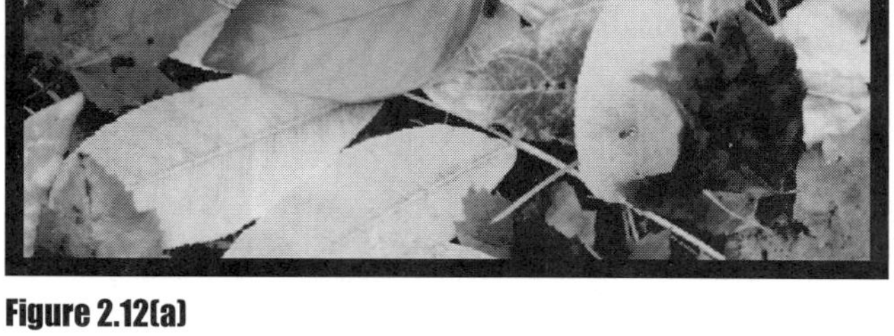

Figure 2.12(a)

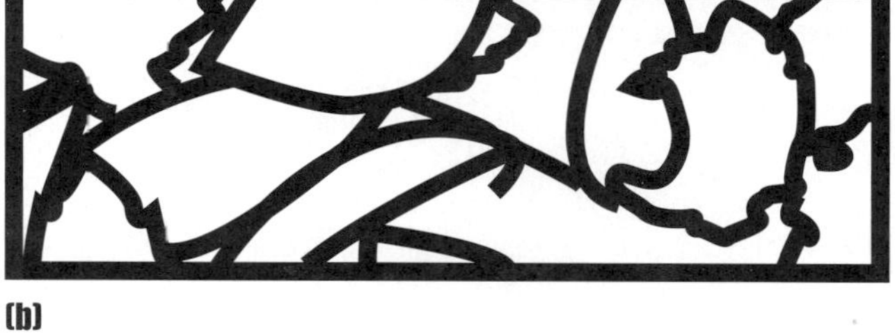

(b)

left by the water (Figure 2.13(b)), what is the dominant element that draws our eye into the composition? It is the surfer who is forever frozen right in the middle of the page like a bullseye (Figure 2.13(c)). Whether we see the surfer as a single dot, or the triangle he forms in his relationship to the surfboard, it is the central focus that is important.

To stay focused on the substance of our search for design, the first step is to identify the key elements in a composition as we look for the patterns or rhythms they create by their placement. We will take a visual leap here, as we translate the surfer in (Figure 2.13(a)) into a single line of sufficient weight to represent the mass of the figure. (Figures 2.14(a, b))

This flag picture (Figure 2.15) is certainly easier to visualize as a line in relationship to the picture plane, demonstrating the asymmetry of the composition.

In Figure 2.16, the trees in the foreground are easy to identify as strong vertical lines (Figure 2.16(b)). The trees in the distance (Figure 2.16(c)) and the figures on the beach (Figure 2.16(d)) are less obvious, but can also be represented by lighter-weight lines, still running from the top to bottom of the page. (Figure 2.16(e))

We will continue to look for ***line rhythms in the environment,*** using vertical line as a means for identification and representation.

As we view this stand of trees at a distance (Figure 2.17(a)), the lines are lighter weight. We must not be distracted by the swell into shape of the palm leaves at the top (Figure 2.17(b)). Our focus is on the rhythm created by the repetition of trees (Figure 2.17(c)).

When our view moves closer to the trees (Figure 2.18(a)), the composition changes. We identify different line weights as the trees move forward (Figure 2.18(b)), and the balance of the page changes as the interval between trees appears to increase. We also lose the quantity of negative space on the right side, changing the balance of the composition (Figure 2.18(c)).

We will continue to look for interesting relationships by the placement of elements in various compositions (Figures 2.19 and 2.20).

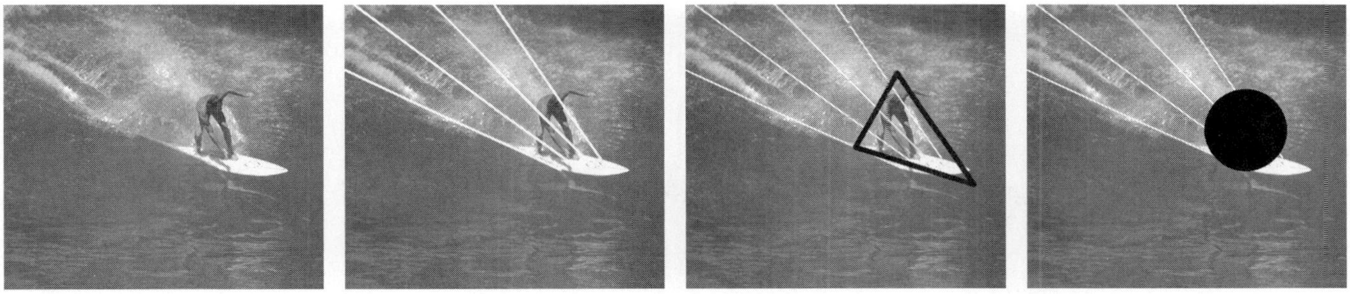

Figure 2.13(a) **(b)** **(c)** **(d)**

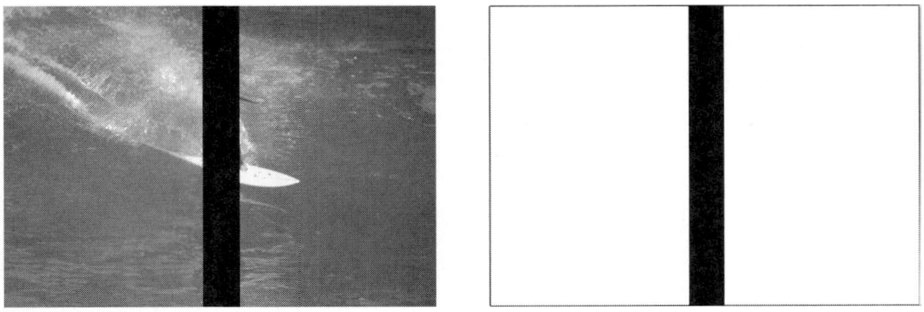

Figure 2.14(a) **(b)**

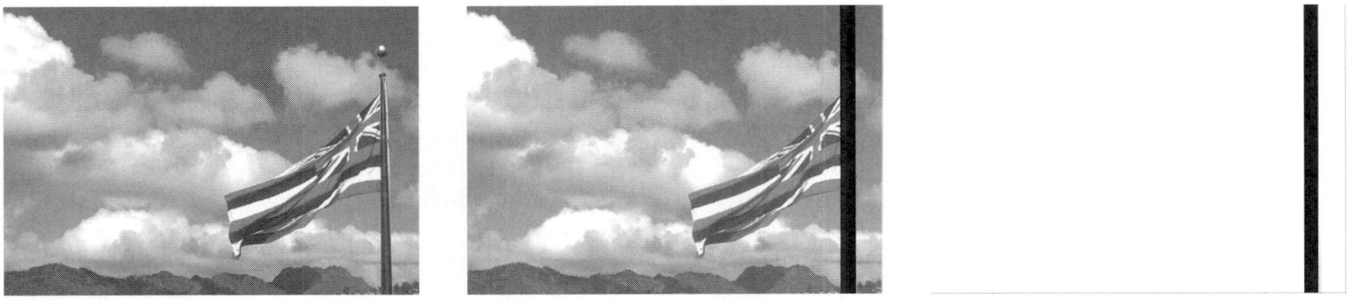

Figure 2.15(a) **(b)** **(c)**

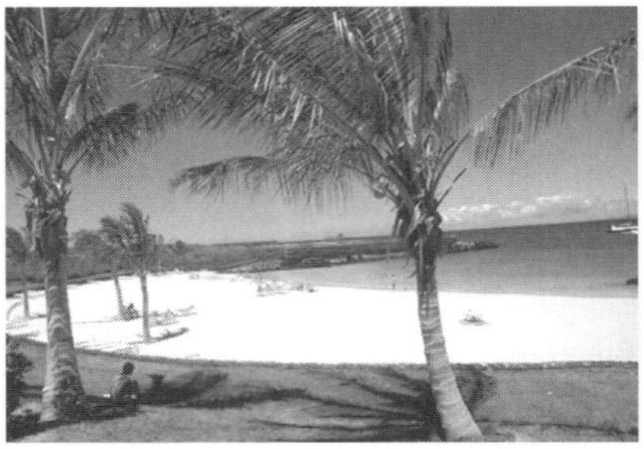

Figure 2.16(a)

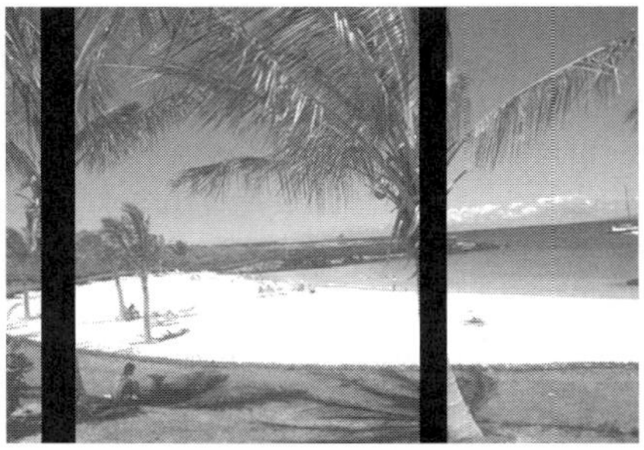

(b)

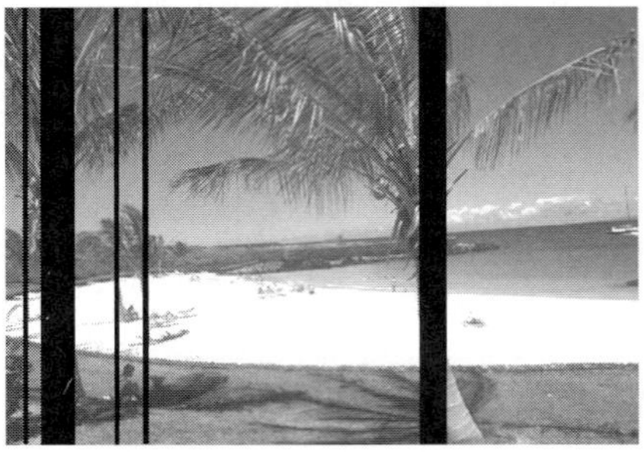

(c)

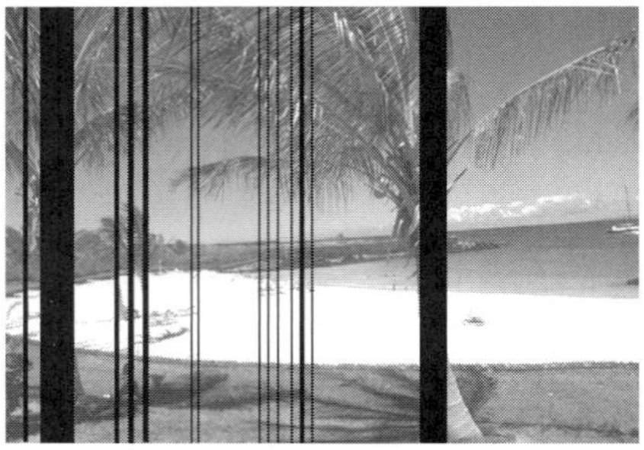

(d)

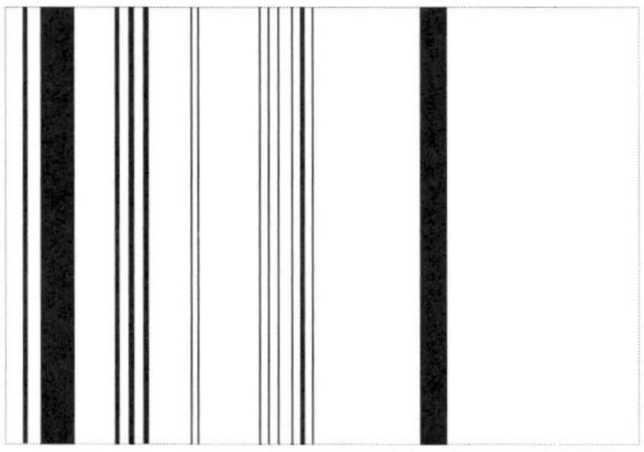

(e)

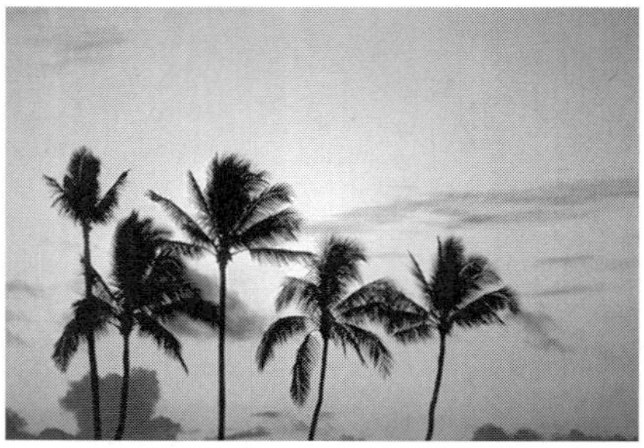

Figure 2.17(a)

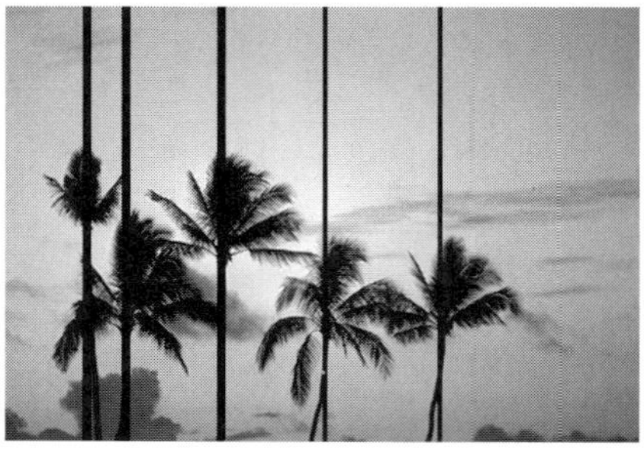

(b)

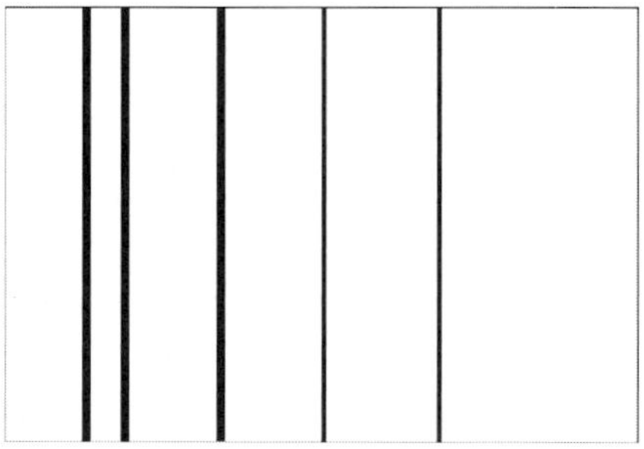

(c)

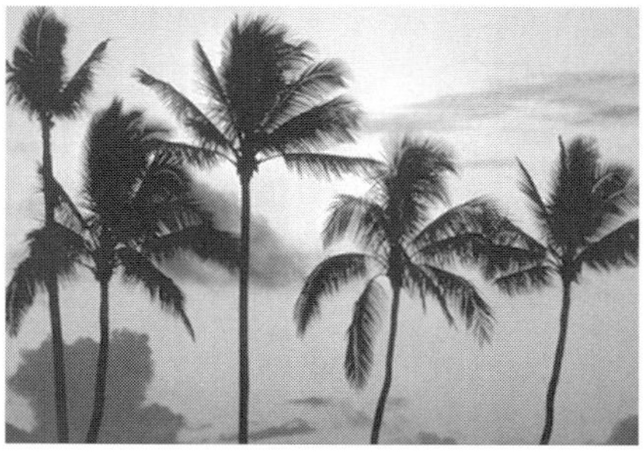

Figure 2.18(a)

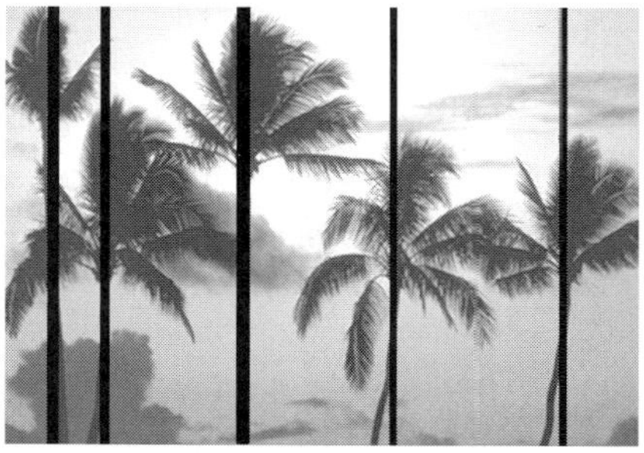

(b)

(c)

A photograph, as in the case of this thatched hut (Figure 2.21), can have variables, allowing you to make choices as to what is line versus what is interval. Which of the following line rhythm solutions most closely represents not only the divisions in the image but the sense of weight and balance?

Notice the effect that perspective plays on the movement of line and interval in Figure 2.22.

Looking for clarity in this mass of trees (Figure 2.23), we can easily identify the many verticals of the tree trunks at a distance. The diagonals in the foreground add a dynamic emphasis (Figure 2.23(b)). To satisfy the requirements of this exercise, allow the crossing lines to fill in and become the weight implied on the left side (Figure 2.23(c,d)).

This white monument is striking in the stand of trees. Fine lines that trace over tree trunks and fence posts are one possible line rhythm solution, as we saw previously.

But lines do not always have to be black. How much stronger is the solution when we invert the values, allowing the lines to be white while the shadows create strong, black negative space? (Figure 2.25)

The stark contrast created by the waterfall in Figure 2.26, is easily represented by a white line of appropriate weight in a field of black.

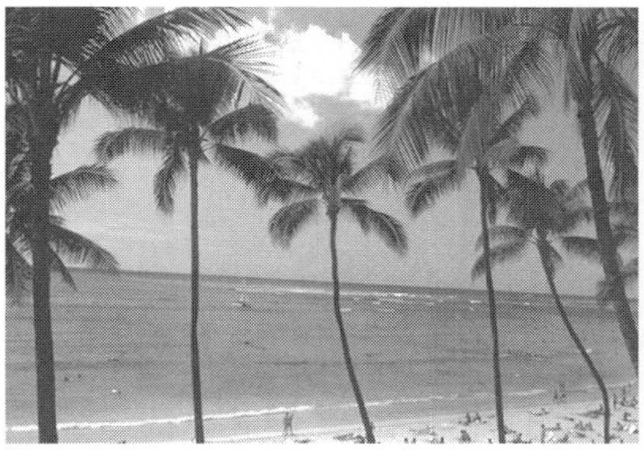
Figure 2.19(a)

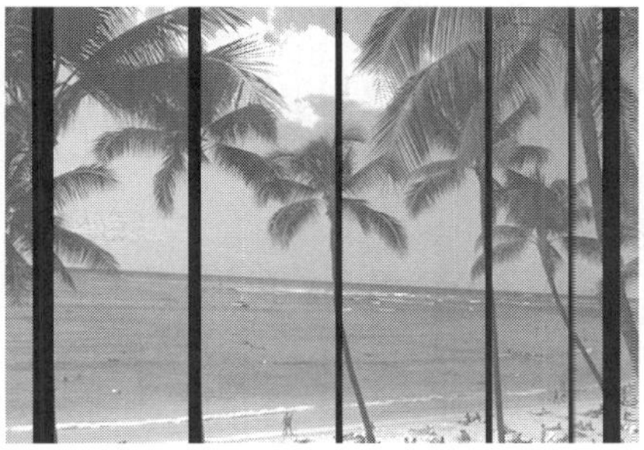
(b)

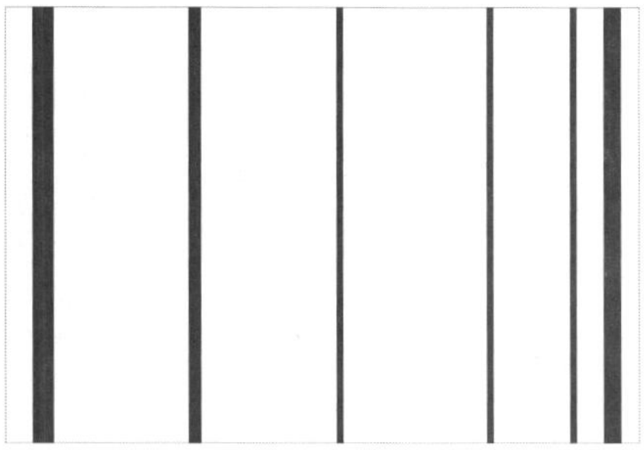
(c)

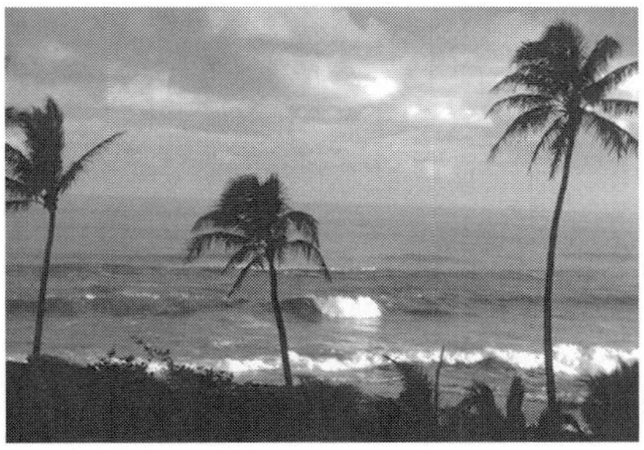
Figure 2.20(a)

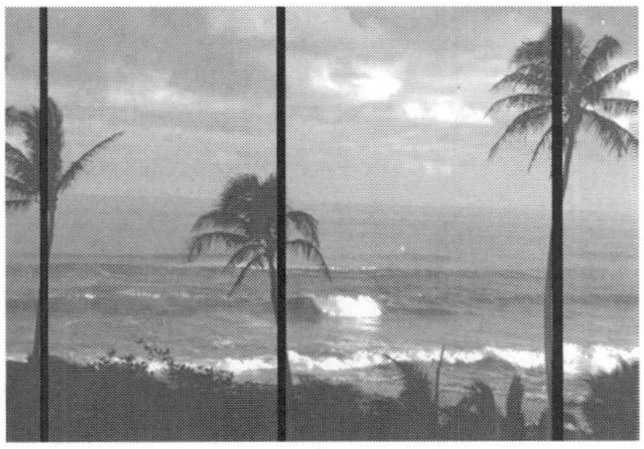
(b)

(c)

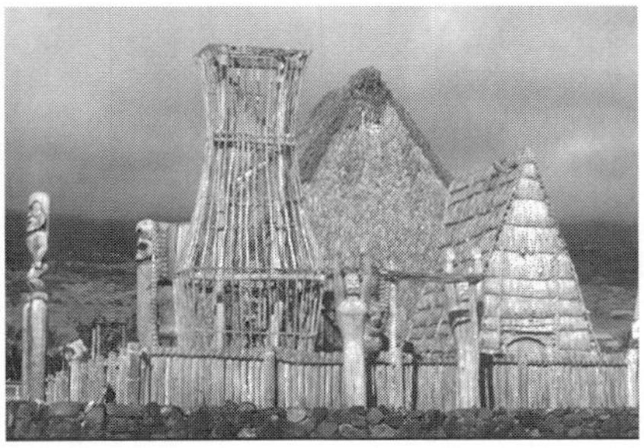
Figure 2.21(a)

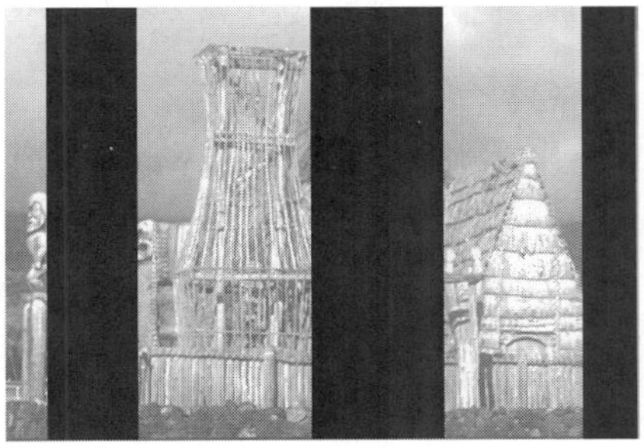
(b)

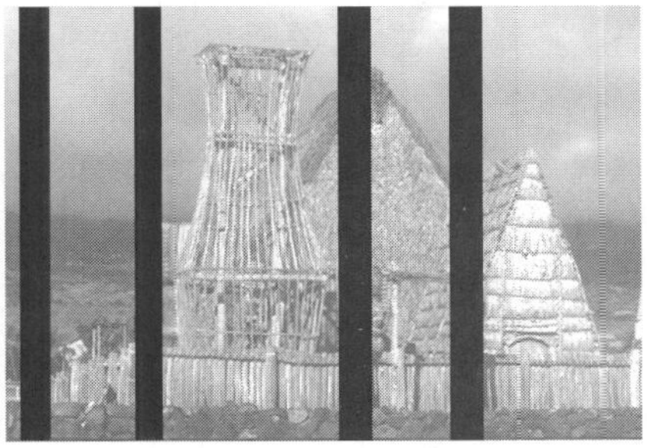
(c)

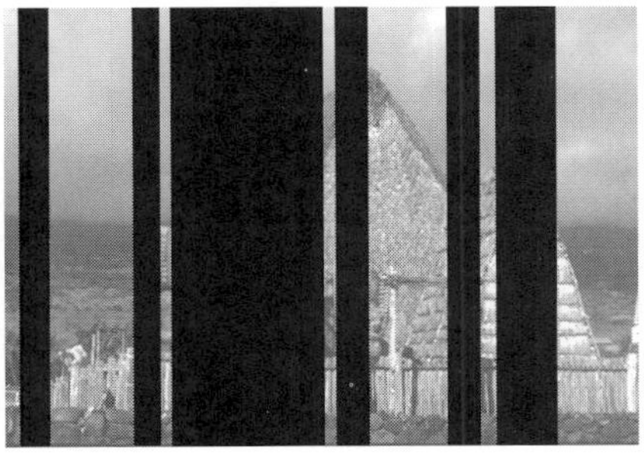
(d)

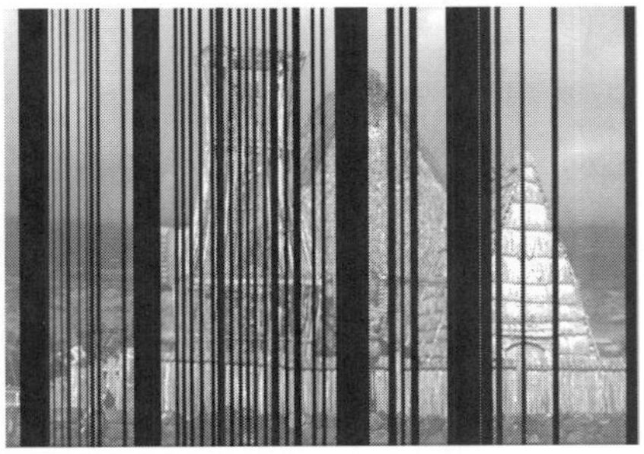
(e)

(f)

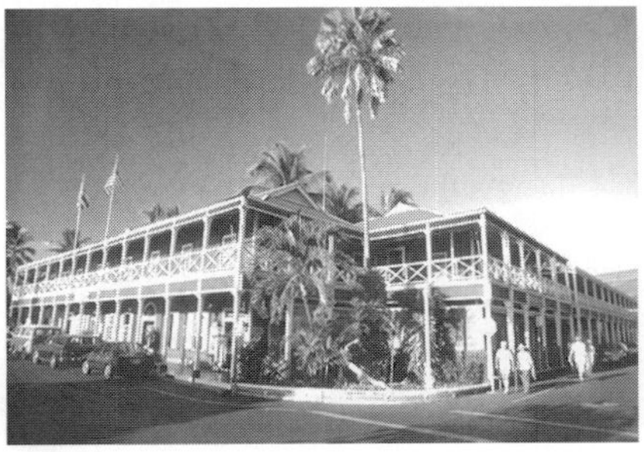
Figure 2.22(a)

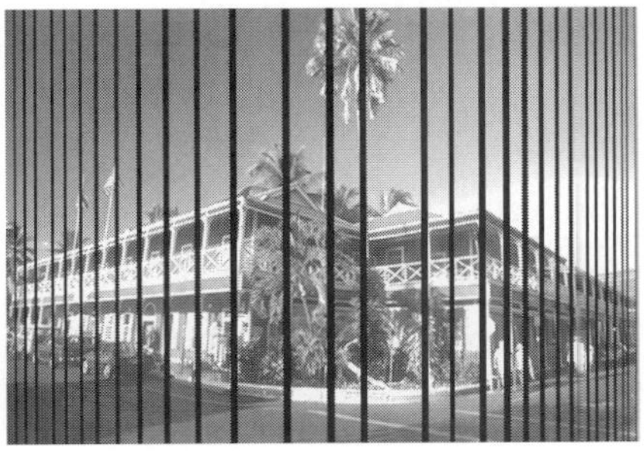
(b)

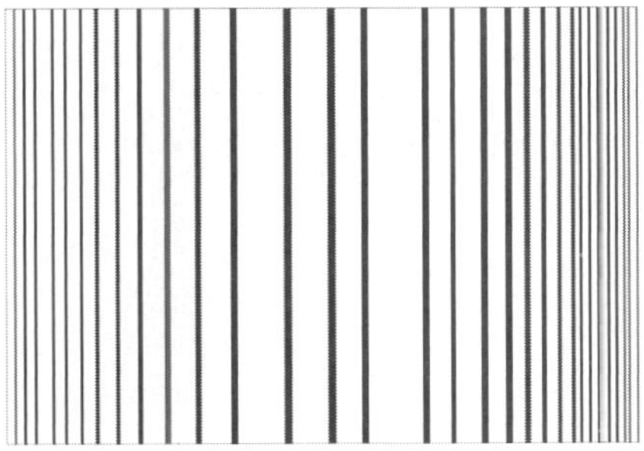
(c)

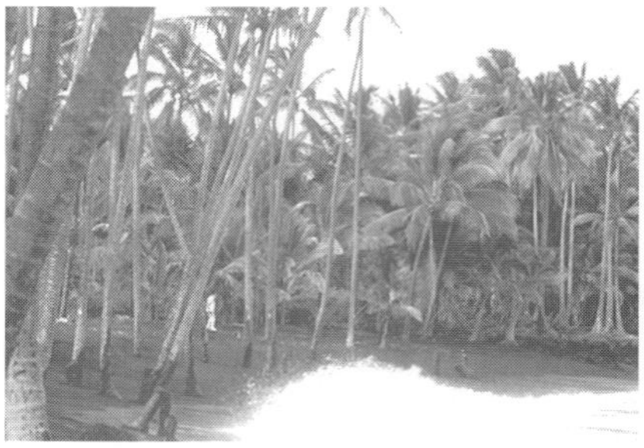

Figure 2.23(a)

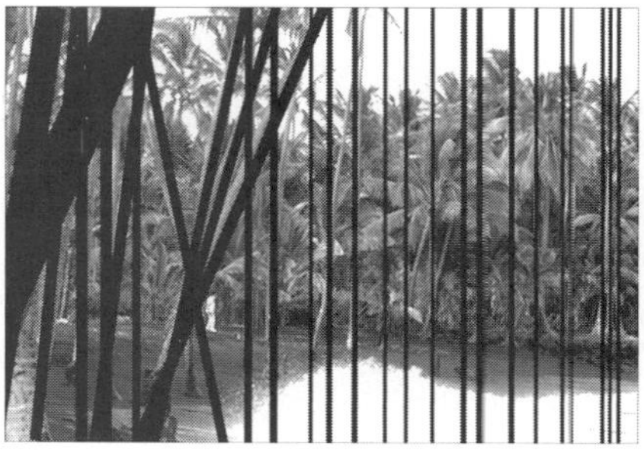

(b)

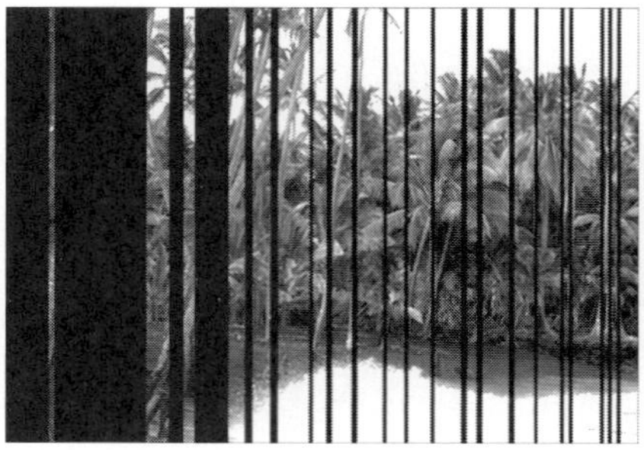

(c)

(d)

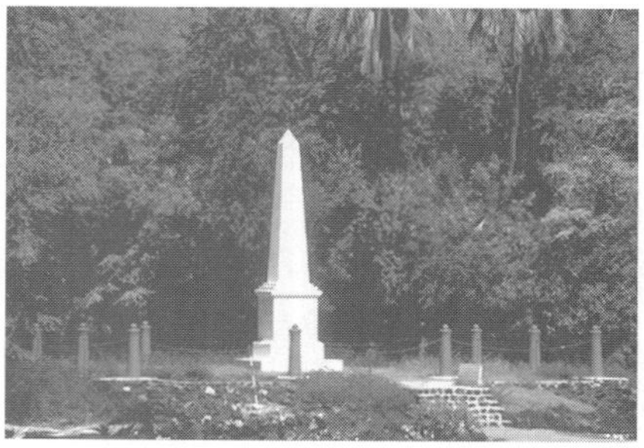

Figure 2.24(a)

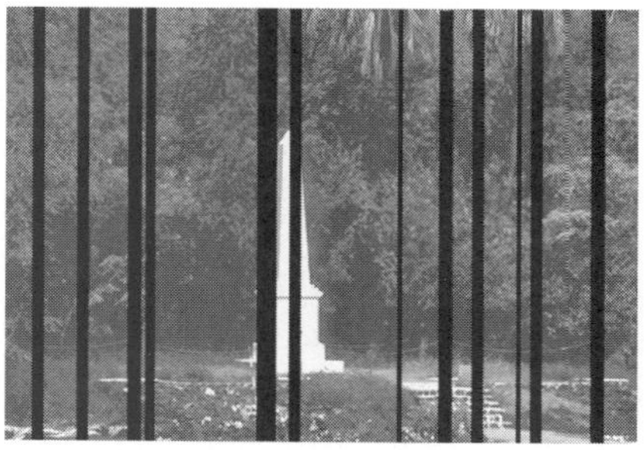

(b)

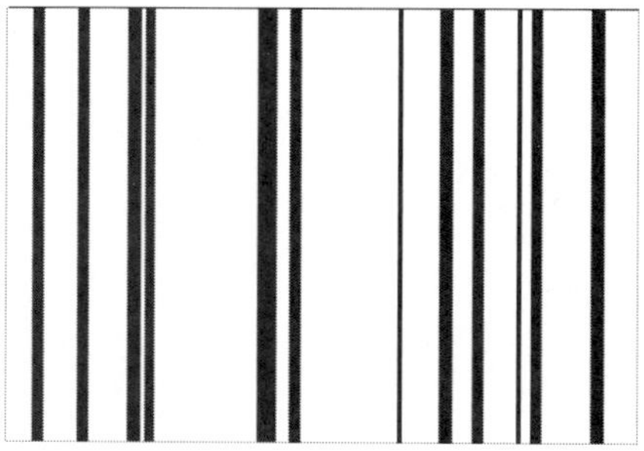

(c)

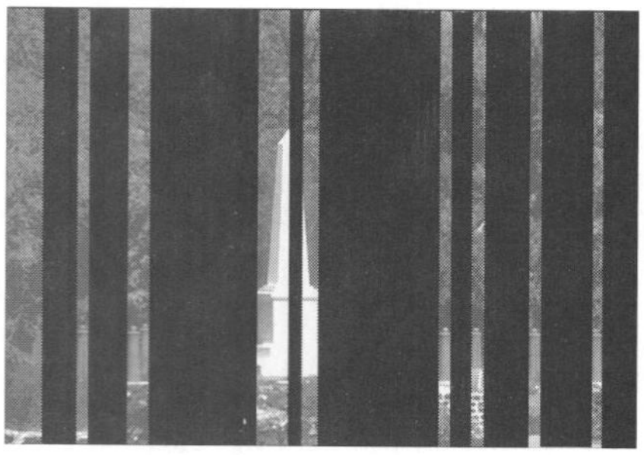

Figure 2.25(a)

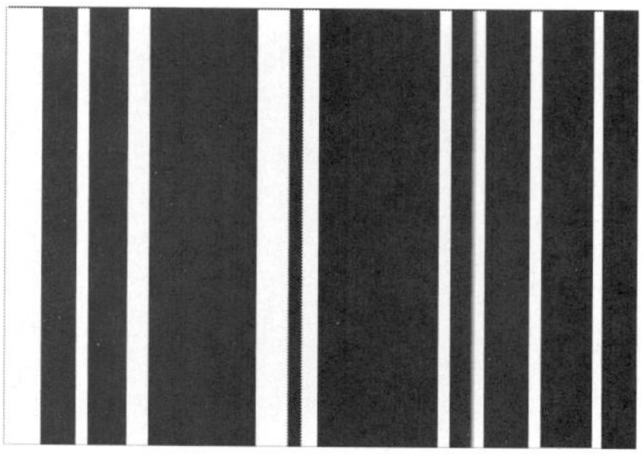

(b)

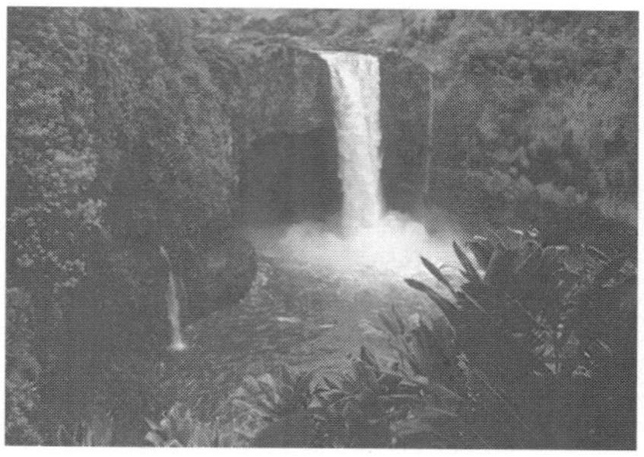

Figure 2.26(a)

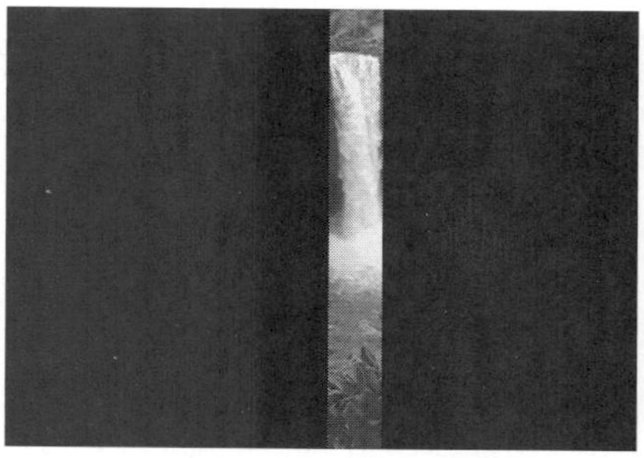

(b)

(c)

Assignment A: THE SEARCH FOR LINE

OBJECTIVES

This assignment is based on the premise that we can draw inspiration from the natural world and learn to communicate with basic design elements. Using one of the most basic elements of design, the line, we will discover the energy and rhythms of the physical world. Rather than exploring the dynamic possiblilites of the diagonal, the goal is to reduce the objects we see to vertical lines of various weight. We will establish a sense of space and movement in the scene with the placement of these lines.

MATERIALS

Electronic: A vector-based drawing program, such as Adobe Illustrator; a source for digital photographic imagery.

Traditional: 3-1/2″ × 5″ pack of unlined index cards; fine-point and broad-tip black magic markers; a ruler if your hand is unsteady.

PROCEDURE

To begin this exercise you will need a source on which you can search for line rhythms. Any subject is fair game, from the interval between cars in the parking lot to the placement of computers in the lab. If you live in a beautiful environment, looking out of the window might be inspirational. For most of us, a collection of photographed images is a better starting place. Depending on your resources, you can scan in your own photographs and slides, or find appropriate imagery on a photo CD.

- Imagine that you are doing this assignment on 3-1/2″ × 5″ index cards.
- Lines must be vertical and parallel when the card is held horizontally.
- Each line must be a solid, single line weight and move from the top to bottom of the page.
- Complete approximately 15 to 20 line rhythm examples, looking for a broad range in subjects as well as a variety of solutions.

In Figures 2.27 and 2.28, an X on a line demonstrates an incorrect and unusable line solution.

DISCUSSION

When you have completed your assignment, look at your samples, and categorize. What are the important issues that enable you to group certain cards together? How will you prioritize which principle is dominant in a particular study?

Figure 2.27

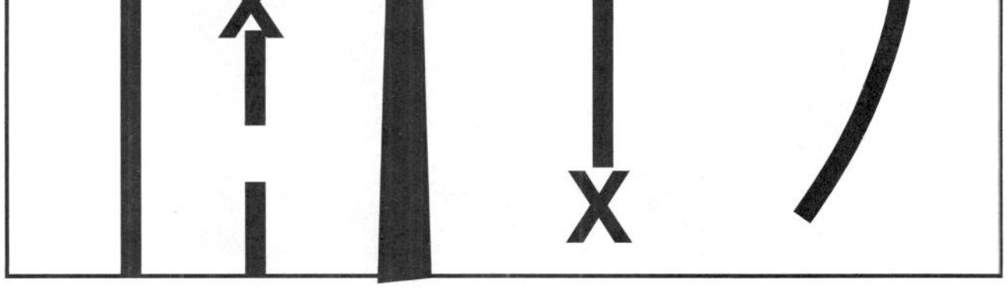

Figure 2.28

Line To Shape To Space: A Matter Of Proportion This single line (Figure 2.29(a)) divides the page in half. Though lightweight, the central placement is quite stable. The line continues to increase in weight, gaining strength and power. How wide can the line get before it stops being line and becomes shape? How much further do we need to go before the shape turns into space?

A Matter of Weight If we look again at a black shape in the middle of the card (Figure 2.30(d)) and shift it to the side, we have a card divided equally into white and black halves. Though physically identical, perceptually are they the same? Is the white in contrast to black in the latter example lighter or heavier, smaller or larger? White becomes lighter, seeming to expand, like a balloon filling with air, while the black, like an iron weight, becomes dense and heavy.

Balance This single line dividing the page in half (Figure 2.31(a)) creates symmetry, two identical shapes on either side balacing, like a seesaw perched on a fulcrum. Adding identical lines, placed in the same location at either end of the card will still create symmetrical balance (Figure 2.31(b)). Shifting the central line even slightly, throws off the balance, ending the symmetry (Figure 2.31(c)). What is not symmetric is asymmetric. How far can we move that line, though still asymmetric, to again find balance (Figure 2.31(e))? And what happens when we remove the single, left-side line. Does the card still balance or is the distribution of weight thrown off?

Formal Rhythm By adding one more set of lines to the first example of symmetric balance and the primary focus can shift to a discussion of rhythm (Rhythm 1a) (Figure 2.32(a)). Whether we change the line interval (Rhythm 1b), increasing the sense of speed, or increase the line weight (Rhythm 1c), adding strength, a formal pattern of repetition is established, moving in a regular rhythm. Both line and interval in each case remain absolutely consistent. When the black and white are the same proportion, which is line and which is interval (Rhythm 1d)?

Does it matter when the weight of each is doubled (Rhythm 1e)? As the black increases, we have a heavier weight line (Rhythm 1f). When the interval then decreases, do we now perceive the white as line and the black as space (Rhythm 1g)? If we reverse the values (Rhythm 1h), is black once again seen as line? Is the question of line or interval a matter of value or proportion?

Value When the black spaces convert to an equal grouping of lightweight parallel lines (new Value), do they maintain their independence or do you see repeating gray columns? If we remove the larger white intervals (new Value1), does the fineness of the rhythm result visually in a gray card?

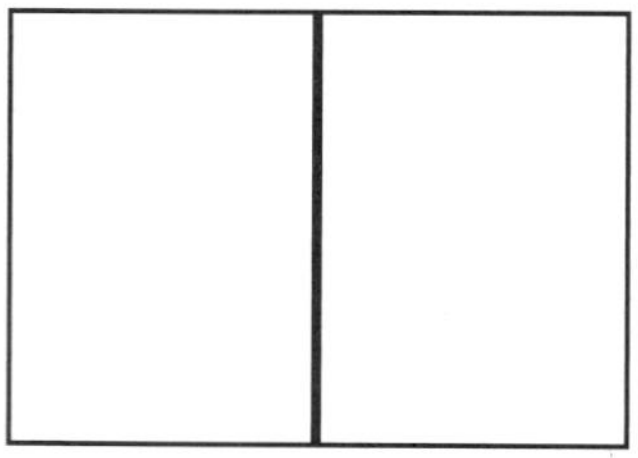

Figure 2.29(a)

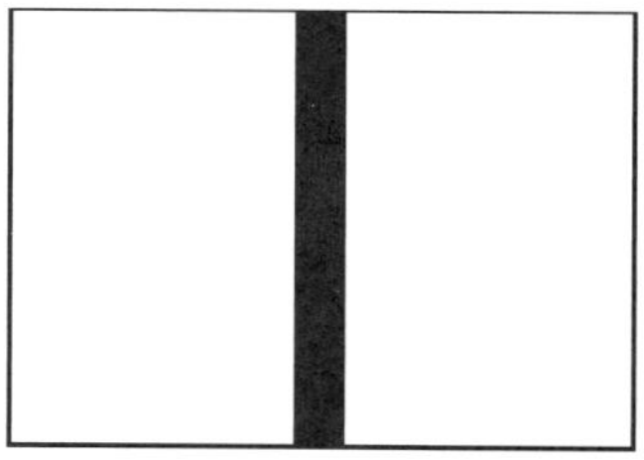

(b)

(c)

(d)

(e)

Figure 2.30(a)

(b)

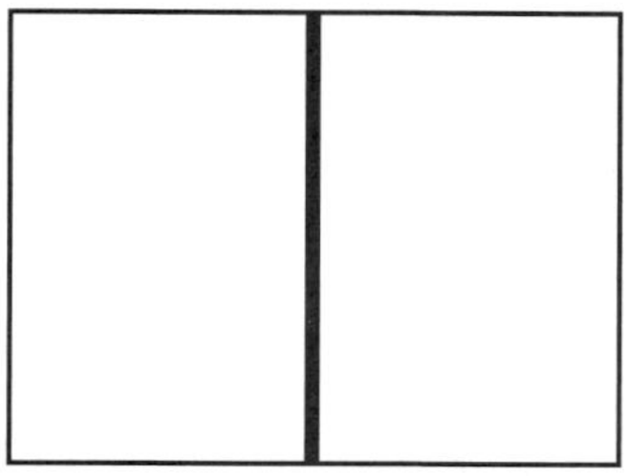

Figure 2.31(a)

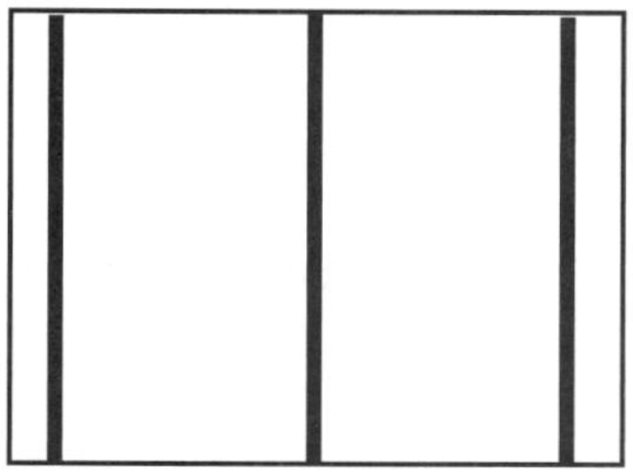

(b)

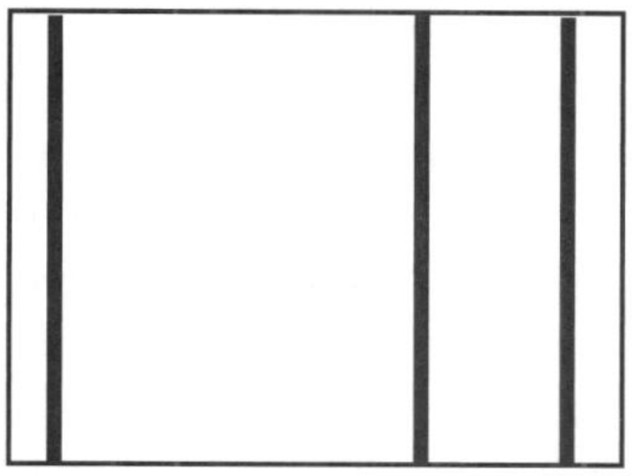

(c)

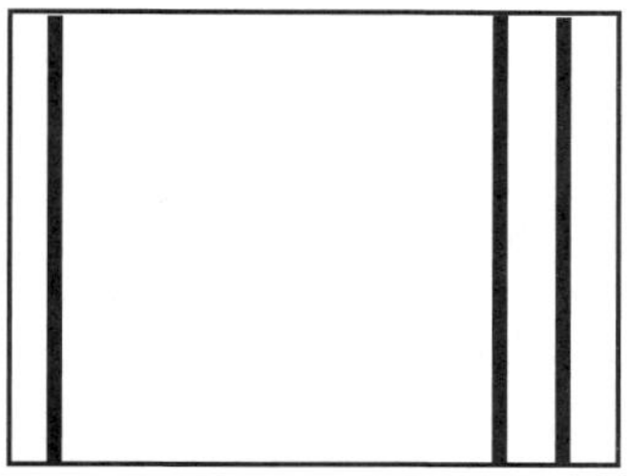

(d)

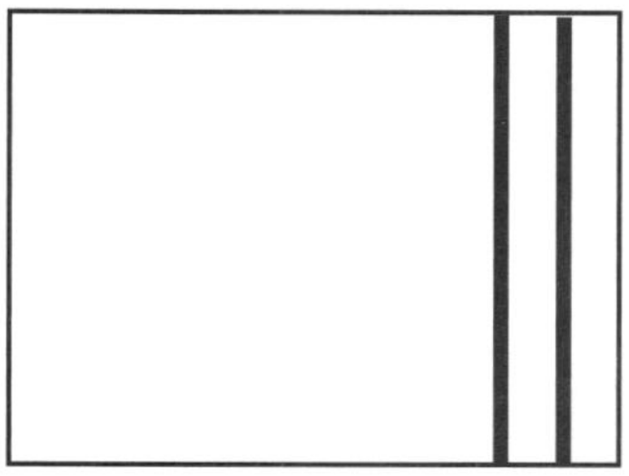

(e)

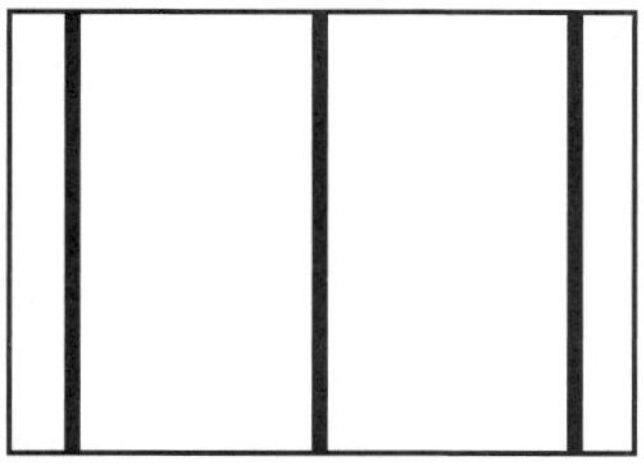

Figure 2.32(a) Rhythm 1

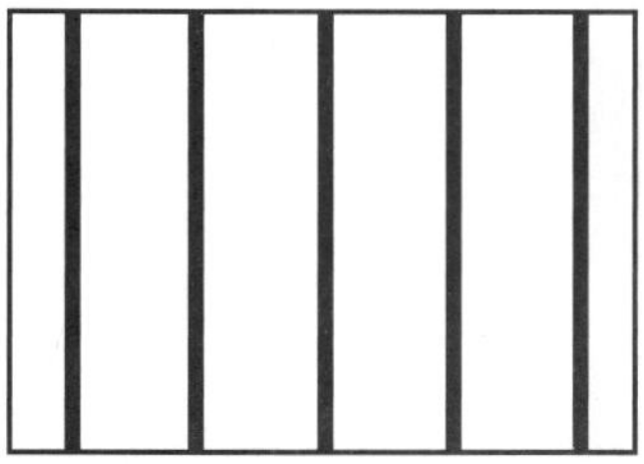

(b) Rhythm 1a

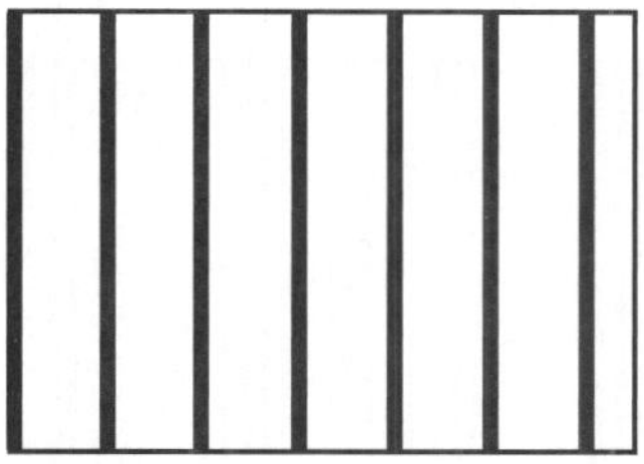

(c) Rhythm 1b

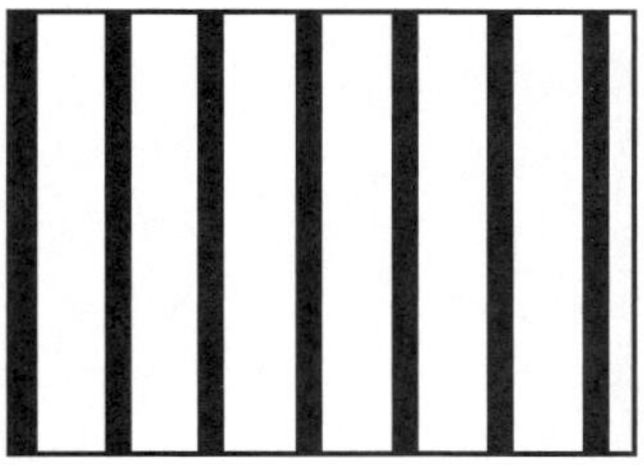

(d) Rhythm 1c

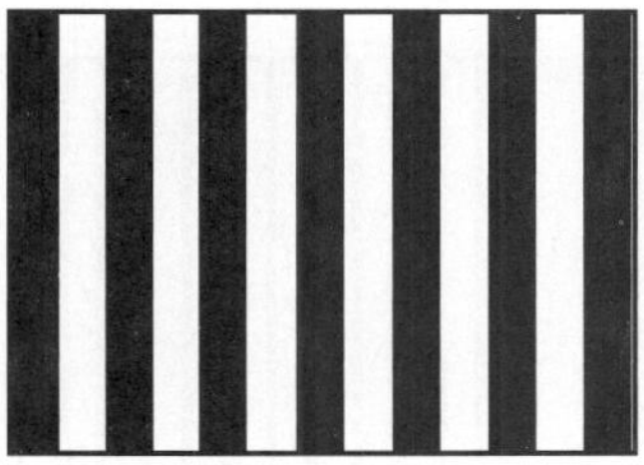

(e) Rhythm 1d

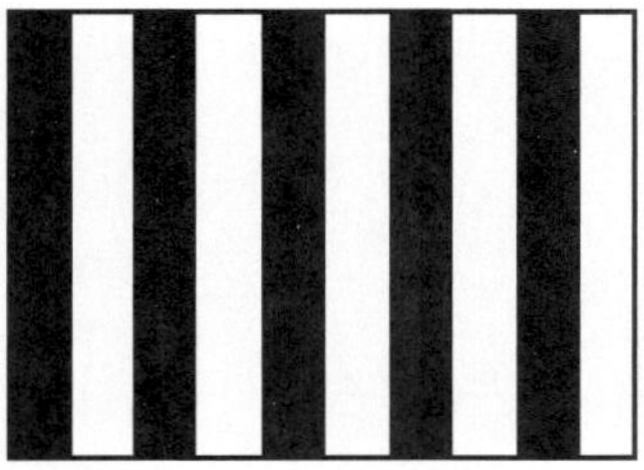

Figure 2.33(a) Rhythm 1e

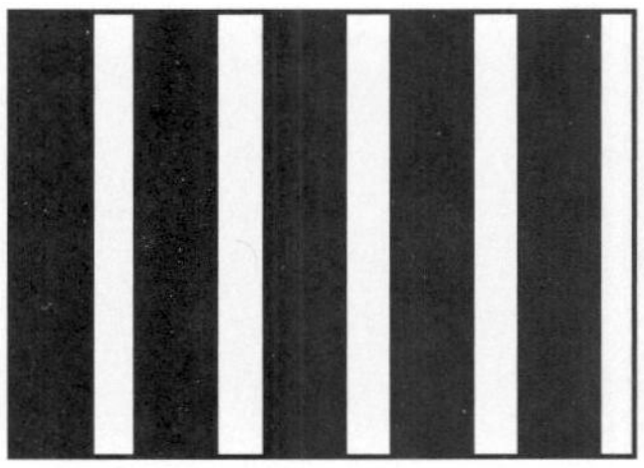

(b) Rhythm 1f

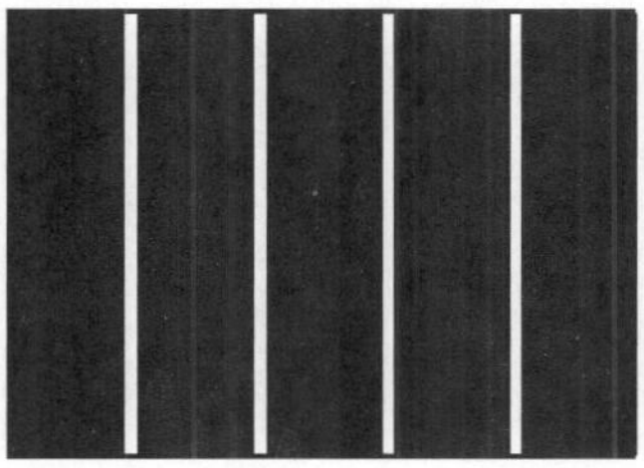

(c) Rhythm 1g

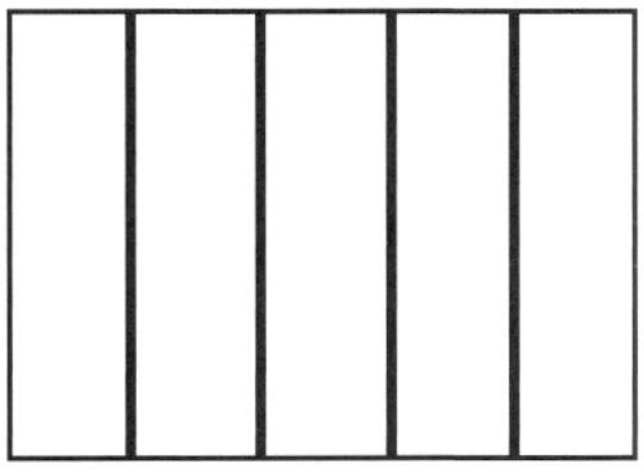

(d) Rhythm 1h

Formal To Regular If we return to our first, formal line rhythm (Regular 2), we recognize the consistency and regularity of the rhythm. Try tapping on the table or clapping the beat—not too exciting. By shifting every other line slightly to the left (Regular 2a), we now have a double beat. Returning to the formal sample, increase the line weight on alternate lines (Regular 2b). The interval is consistent, the 'beat' regular, but with an emphasis. Add another lightweight line consistently to the left of each mediumweight line (Regular 2c), and the rhythm shifts. More importantly, what we recognize as the repeating pattern has altered. Instead of reading [**line** - line - **line**], we tap [line line **line** - line line **line**]. The smaller interval groups the elements into a larger repeating unit separated by the larger interval. In the next example (Regular 2d), we keep the same number and type of lines. A simple shift in the middle line, and our sense of the unit of repetition is altered to [line **line** line - line **line** line]. Whether [line line **line**] or [line **line** line], the fact that a more complex unit repeats consistently leaves us with a regular rhythm. Negative space or interval seems to be the key to the structure of relationships.

To Irregular Changes that are made to any of the elements independently break the pattern and the regularity of the rhythm (Irregular 2). Finally, when we remove all recognition of pattern (Irregular 2b), the rhythm is *irregular,* a random organization of element and interval.

Progression While most rhythms are either regular or irregular, there is an exception. The following example does not create a repeating pattern yet it is hardly a random organization of lines (Progression 1). This systematic change is a *progression.* When you compare the first progression with the second (Progression 2), do you see a change in direction? Do you read the card from left to right, or are you drawn by line weight and value? Does an interval change affect the movement of the progression? The beauty of a progression is that it enables you to provide a sense of direction as well as a movement forward and back in the page. The double progression (Progression 3) curves the page, but is it concave or convex?

Figure 2.34(a) New Value

(b) New Value 1

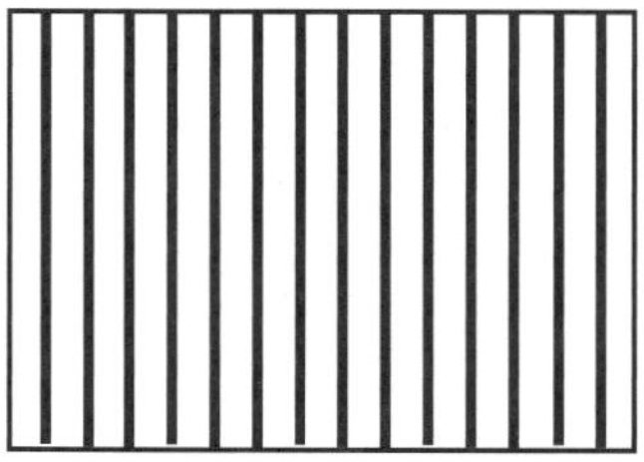

Figure 2.35(a) Regular 2

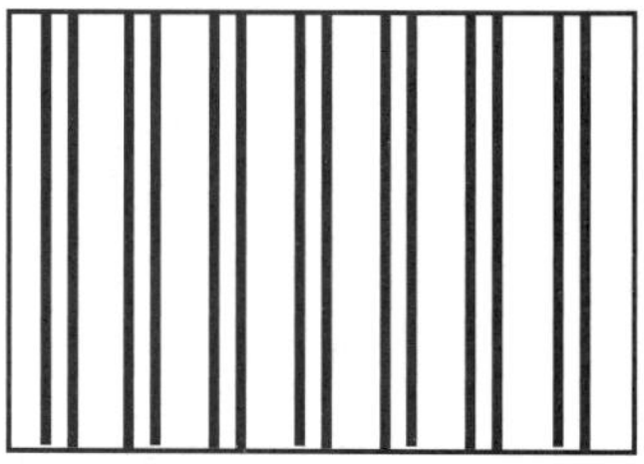

(b) Regular 2a

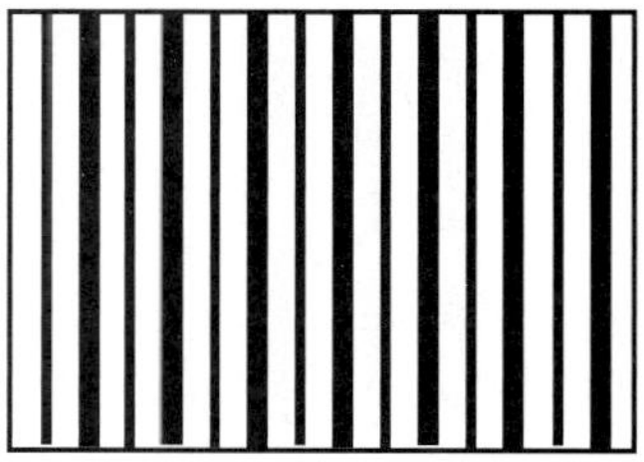

(c) Regular 2b

(d) Regular 2c

(e) Regular 2d

Figure 2.36(a) Irregular 2

(b) Irregular 2b

Figure 2.37(a) Progression 1 **(b) Progression 2** **(c) Progression 3**

ASSIGNMENT B: EMOTIONAL LINE

We have talked previously about the language of non-verbal communication. To communicate we need to express ourselves with appropriate combinations of the elements and principles of design. Through observation we can draw a chair, a desk, something that is tangible, something that can be viewed or touched. But how will you express the way you feel? What does happy look like, or sad?

OBJECTIVES

Using one of the most basic elements of design, the line, we will communicate intangible emotions or states of being. Rather than exploring the dynamic possiblilites of the diagonal, the goal is to communicate with only vertical lines of various weight. Building on the lessons learned through the discussion of line rhythms in Assignment A: *The Search for Line,* you will express both positive and negative feelings at different levels of activity.

MATERIALS

The "stack of index cards" you completed previously for Assignment A: *The Search for Line,* and the discussion section as reference.

Electronic: A vector-based drawing program, such as Adobe Illustrator.

Traditional: 3-1/2″ × 5″ pack of unlined index cards; fine-point and broad-tip black magic markers; a ruler if your hand is unsteady.

PROCEDURE

For this assignment, you need to select ten words that are feelings or states of being, from the following list or words you generate on your own. To explore the range of possiblilities, the list should include a range of words that address contrasts as well as similarities, positive feelings as well as negative, at varying states of energy or intensity. Think about the words and define them, choosing subtle changes rather than redundancies.

Bored	Contented	Happy	Sad	Energetic
Upset	Peaceful	Excited	Nervous	Ecstatic
Angry	Focused	Delighted	Confused	Intense
Isolated	Alone	Joyful	Lonely	Dicouraged
Diffused	Deflated	Drunk	Tired	Concerned
Afraid	Frightened	Enervated	Nauseous	Euphoric
Exhausted	Satisfied	Sated	Miserable	Effervescent

Once again you are going to complete this assignment on a series of "3-1/2″ × 5″ index cards," following the same guidelines as in the previous assignment. Lines must be vertical when the card is held horizontally, parallel, a solid, single line weight, and move from the top to the bottom of the card. Consider all of the points that were discussed concerning the line rhythm examples. Communicate by creating cards that are combinations of the various issues: balance, rhythm, weight, movement, direction, placement, proportion, speed, strength, intensity, space, contrast, and value.

DISCUSSION

Please take a look at the following examples.

The first is an example of **bored.** If you were to tap out the rhythm, this slow, monotonous, formal rhythm would certainly bore me.

Contented, at least for me, holds greater interest yet is not particularly high energy. Therefore, the rhythm is still regular, but with an emphasis.

To be **nervous,** our sense of control and stability is affected. An irregular rhythm of weak lines serves the purpose. When you think about being alone, do you feel positive and relaxed or are you uncomfortable? A single line would certainly represent being one, alone. Increasing the line weight strengthens the power of the individual.

If we move the single line from the center to one side, is the strength of the position reduced? By lowering the stability, have we now made a transition from being alone to feeling lonely?

What happens when we switch sides from left to right? Is one side more or less stable than the other?

Will a switch in value, moving from black on white to white on black, affect our sense of security or isolation?

A black space is very strong graphically. Can we more accurately express a dull feeling of loneliness by creating a spatial plane of gray?

The previous solutions were all simplified to clearly demonstrate a point. Your explorations should utilize the richness of possibilities at your disposal.

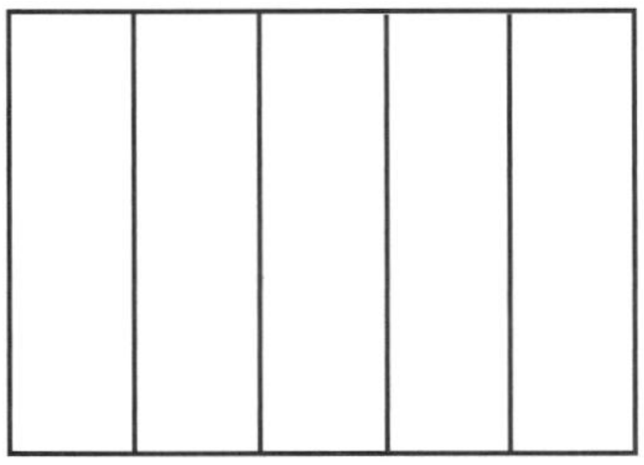

Figure 2.38 Bored

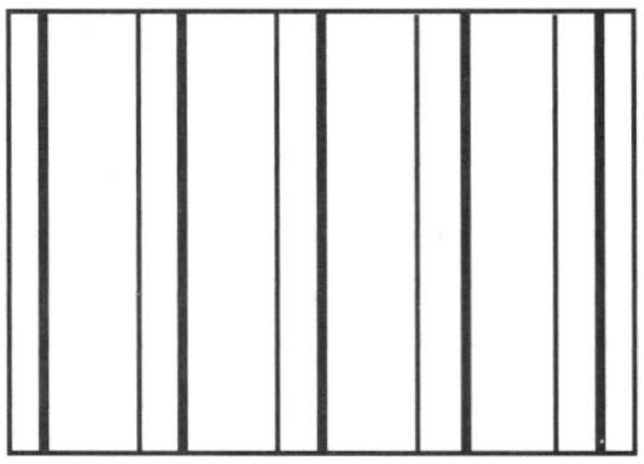

Figure 2.39 Contented

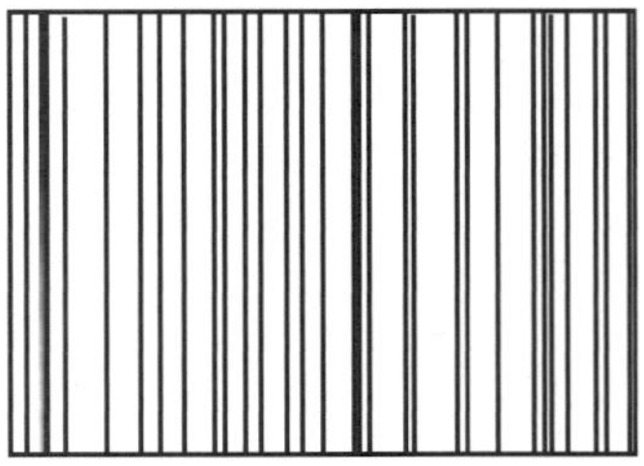

Figure 2.40 Nervous

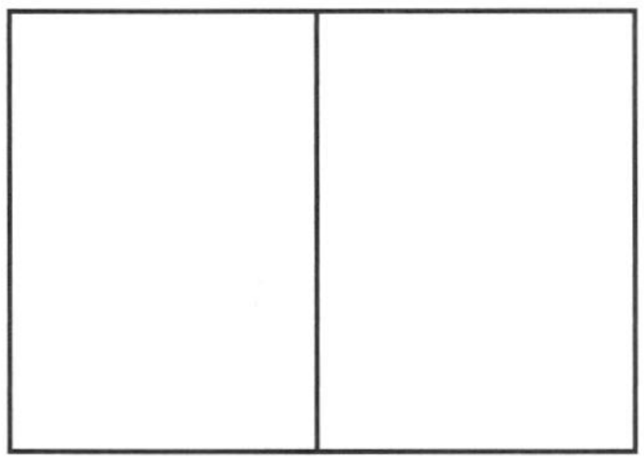

Figure 2.41 Alone 1

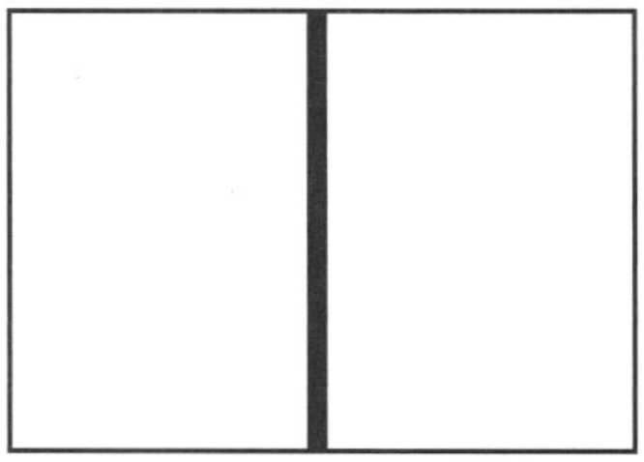

Figure 2.42 Alone 2

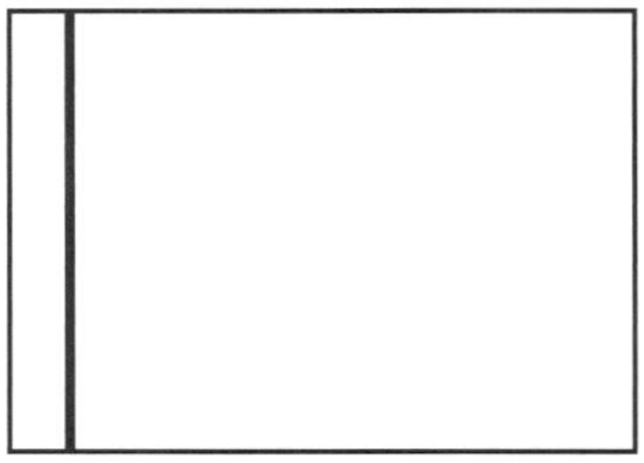

Figure 2.43 Lonely 1

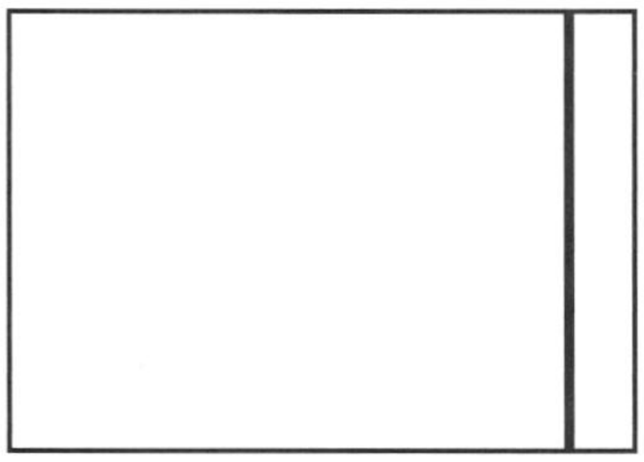

Figure 2.44 Lonely 2

Figure 2.45 Lonely 3

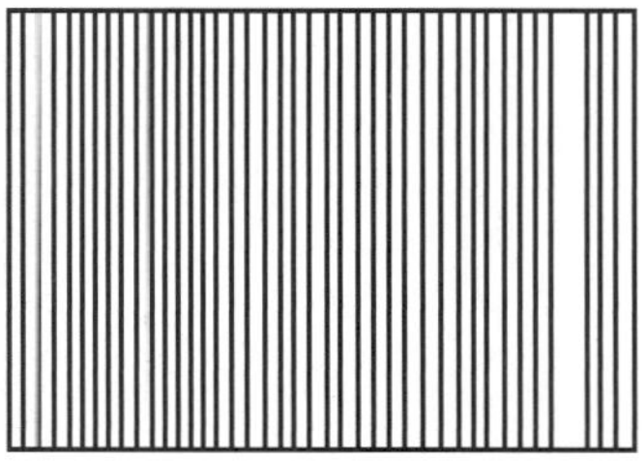

Figure 2.46 Lonely 4

A Student Solution:
Artwork by Clarissa Yang

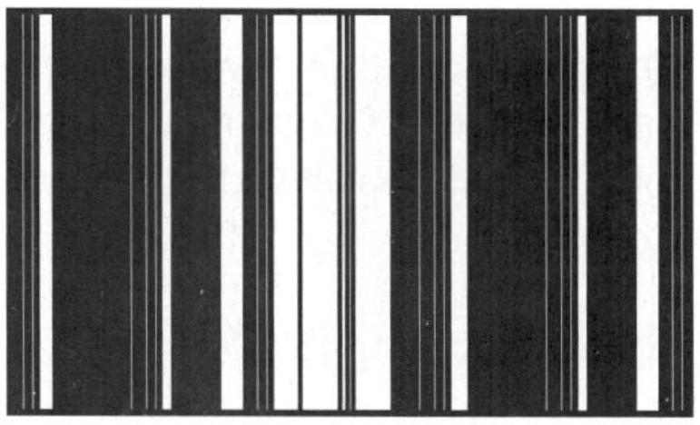

Figure 2.47 Anxious

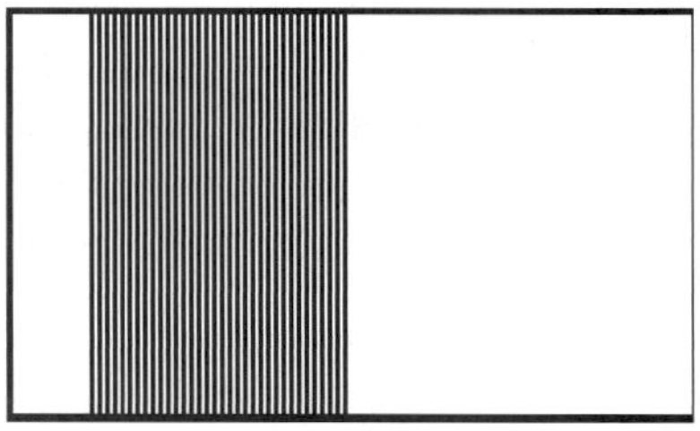

Figure 2.48 Apathetic

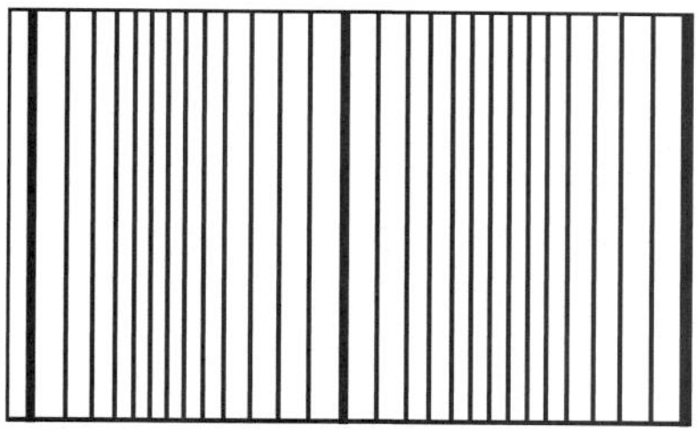

Figure 2.49 Blah

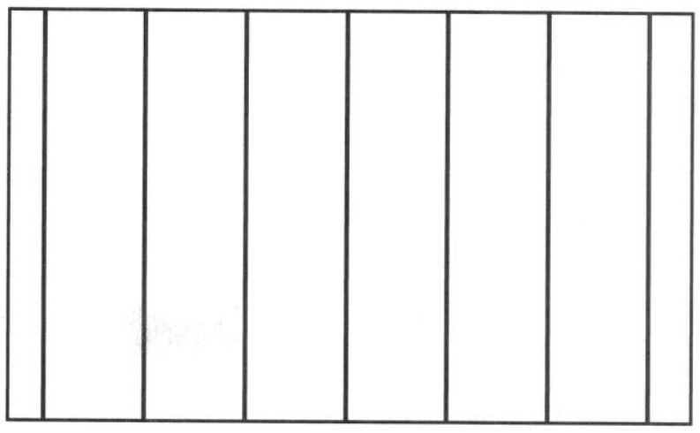

Figure 2.50 Content

Figure 2.51 Eager

Figure 2.52 Ecstatic

Figure 2.53 Excited

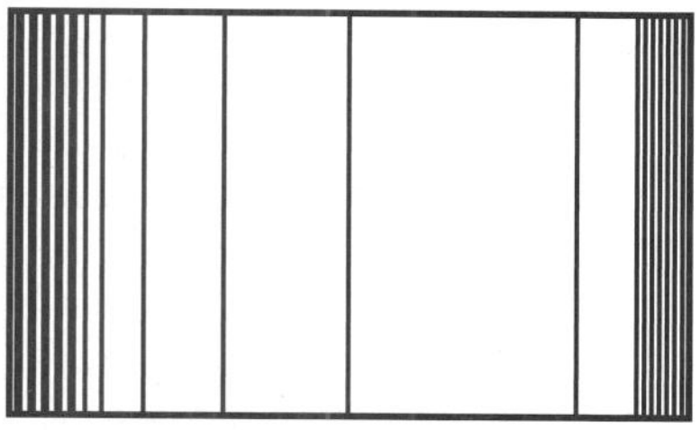

Figure 2.54 Exuberant

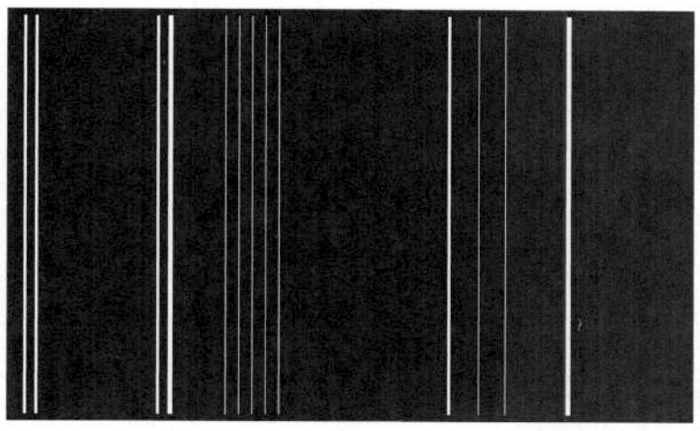

Figure 2.55 Furious

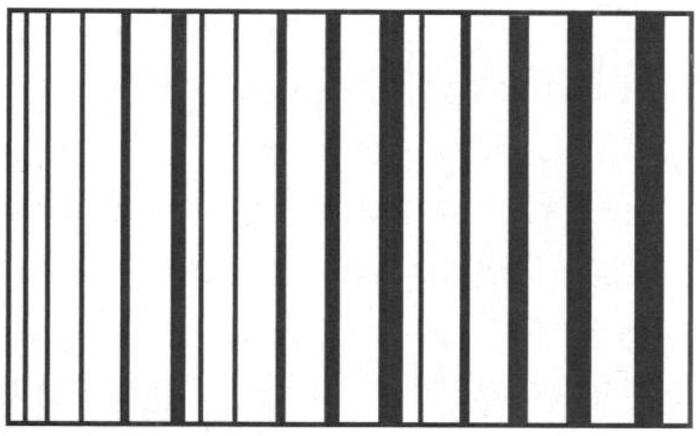

Figure 2.56 Joyful

Figure 2.57 Happy

Figure 2.58 Nervous

Figure 2.59 Numb

Figure 2.60 Sad

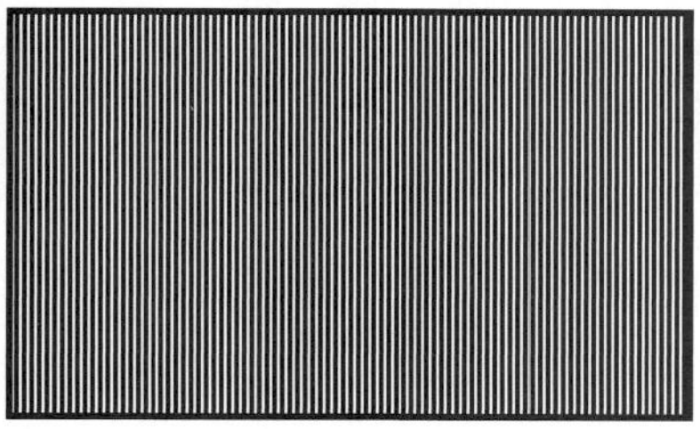

Figure 2.61 Stable

ASSIGNMENT C: LINE RHYTHM TRANSITION

OBJECTIVES

While the previous assignment asked you to apply your understanding of various design principles to express intangible emotions, this next exercise will challenge you to work with your understanding of the physical relationship between elements on cards in search of a cohesive connection.

MATERIALS

The "stack" (electronic or physical) of index cards you completed previously for Assignment A: *The Search for Line* and Assignment B: *Emotional Line.*

Electronic: A vector-based drawing program, such as Adobe Illustrator.

Traditional: 3 1/2″ × 5″ pack of unlined index cards; fine-point and broad-tip black magic markers; a ruler if your hand is unsteady.

PROCEDURE

Select (or create) two line rhythm cards that have the greatest contrast; in value, speed, balance, rhythm. If one is regular the other should be irregular, symmetric/assymetric, black on white/white on black, active/passive.

Consider these two cards as the poles for a transition or metamorphosis, in which you are to find the middle step. If your selections are complex, you may have more than one card between the two ends. When creating the transition, consider different types of movement and which will be the most interesting solution for your choices. Is the movement directional, moving horizontally or vertically, or does it represent the passage of time?

As we move through the progression, examine the relationships to the end card. There are elements that line up, requiring very little movement, while others, as in the first line, need to increase in weight in addition to shifting over. Notice, too, the transitional nature of the rhythm in the middle step, as it incorporates a progression with attributes of the final formal rhythm.

Based on the dynamics of the poles and the type of movement required, your transition might be more effective when arranged vertically rather than horizontally.

Figure 2.62(a) Transition 1a **(b) Transition 1b** **(c) Transition 1c**

(a) **(b)** **(c)** **(d)**
Figure 2.63 Example of Line Rhythm Transition 2

COMPOSITION

A shack built of crate lumber and tarpaper does not appear as elegant a structure as Thomas Jefferson's Monticello. The newspaper pages of your local shopper ad are not as visually appealing as the pages of an upscale mail-order catalog. A preschooler's uncomplicated representation of a person in crayon on construction paper has an ungainly naive quality that is totally different from the conscious intensity of realism and visual drama of a Rembrandt portrait. In all these cases differences in the amount of planning, money, and time spent are reflected. Craftsmanship, materials chosen, and the intended function also dictate the way the finished object looks.

In our experience of life we find everything composed of various subordinate parts and actions. The shack and Monticello, the shopper and the upscale catalog, as well as the child's drawing and Rembrandt's painting, all are composed of numerous parts. The parts of several of these examples were orchestrated with great refinement and intense effort, while little planning or forethought marks others. We make value judgments about these things and set up criteria and define terms to describe these judgments. This is composition analysis. How and why does something work visually as a satisfying unit? What do the individual elements contribute to the whole effect? Why are some combinations more effective than others? What principles or rules apply? Such considerations can make one painting a world-famous museum piece and another a junk shop artifact.

Figures 2.64 and 2.65 categorize the simple ***elements*** and some of the complex ***principles*** of design that are referred to in this book.

We did an in-depth investigation of one of these elements of composition (line) in the previous section. Now we need to reference and address all the pertinent compositional elements and principles used in the construction of a specific two-dimensional picture plane. The two problems that follow will help us to better comprehend the holistic integration of these compositional parts.

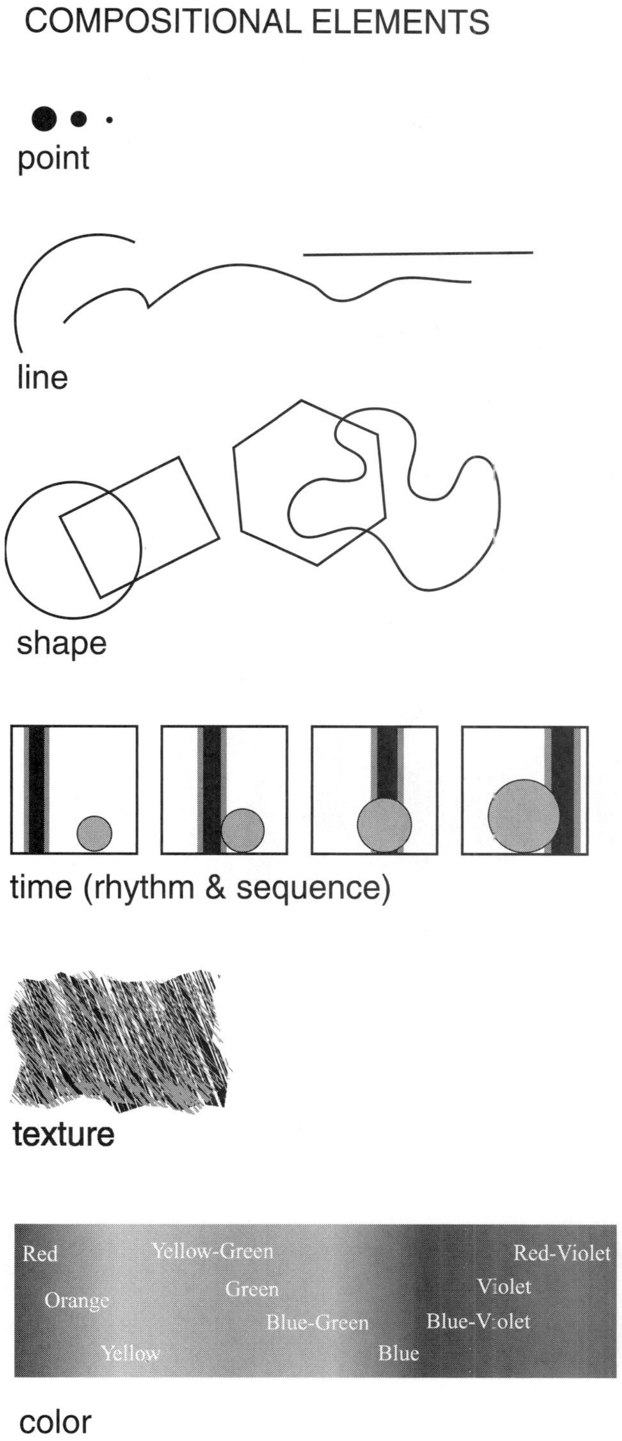

Figure 2.64 Compositional Elements

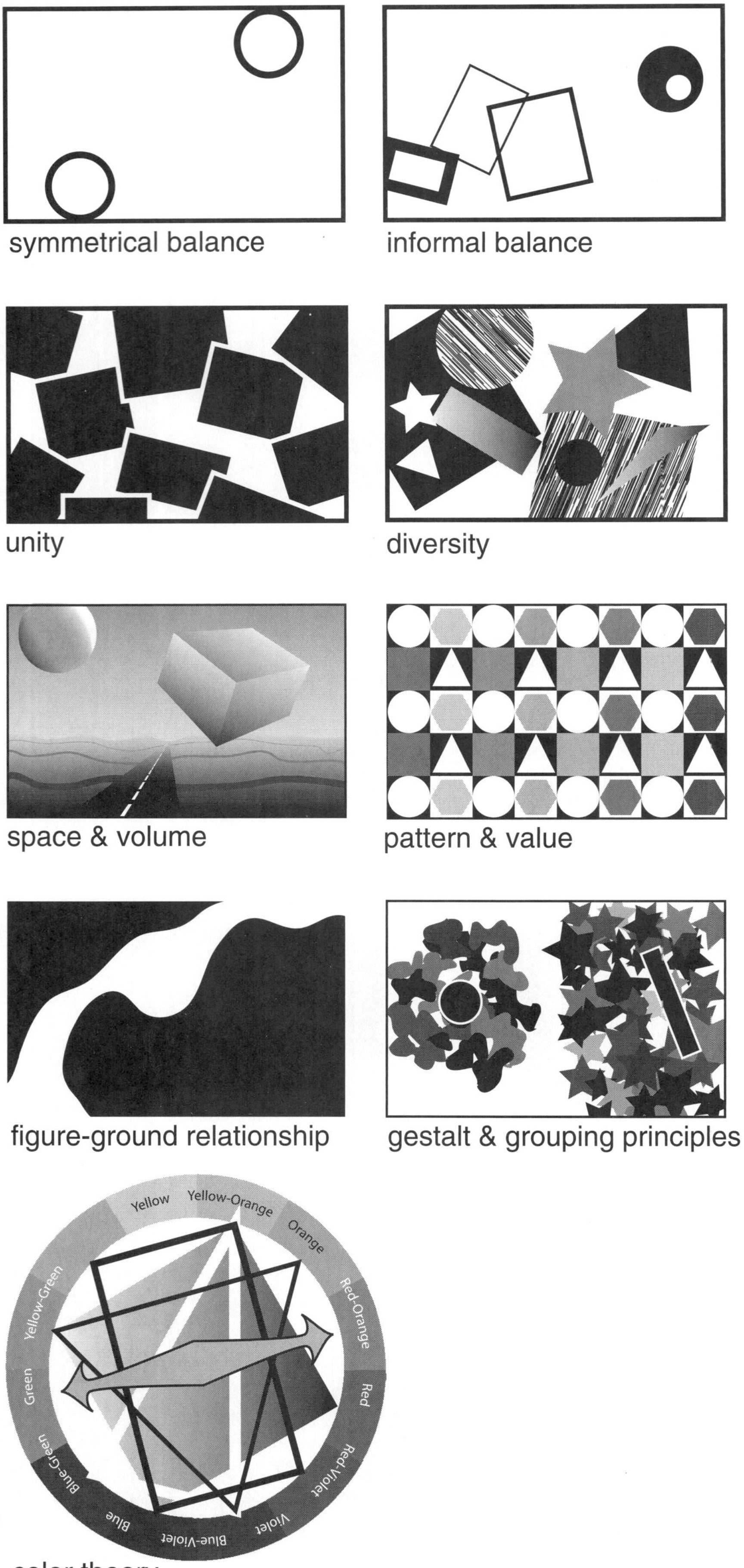

Figure 2.65 Compositional Principles

Assignment A: LANDSCAPE ANALYSIS

The landscape analysis you are about to do will lead eventually to the completion of the Landscape Abstraction assignment. Both are a natural extension of the section in Chapter 1, *To See,* where a visual vocabulary was introduced in the examination of a landscape.

OBJECTIVES

You are going on a journey, to examine the design or ***structure*** of a photographic image. The goal is to discover the ***representational, conceptual,*** and ***abstract*** qualities in a landscape photograph. Through approximately 20 steps, you will clarify the image, reducing the color, texture, and form of the natural environment to a basic expression of shape, balance, movement, and direction. Ultimately, you will synthesize these explorations into a final, abstract, graphic solution.

MATERIALS

Electronic: A suitable landscape, a computer, printer, raster, and vector-based drawing program, such as Adobe Photoshop / Adobe Illustrator.

Traditional: A suitable landscape, additional materials needed for the assignment "by hand": Tracing paper, a fine-point black marker or technical pen. To complete the abstraction you will need illustration or bristol board, black ink and/or technical pen.

PROCEDURE

Whether you are doing the assignment "by hand" or on the computer, you will need to find an appropriate landscape. There should be clear and identifiable information in the foreground, middle ground, and background. Though lovely, a distant seascape with little if any form will not work for this assignment. It is actually easier to simplify from an image that is too complex than to struggle with insufficient information to discover. Notice the amount of detail information in all spatial planes—foreground, middle ground, and background—of this image. (Figure 2.66)

Once your image is selected, prepare a stack of tracing paper by cutting the sheets to cover your photograph. You can leave a border beyond the image area to assemble and attach the tracings. One at a time, lay a tracing paper on top of the image to capture one aspect of the image with your fine-point marker or other drawing tool. Consider the entire image with each tracing, investigating a different concept or element of design.

You will use one photographic image for the entire assignment. There is not, however, only one exact set of considerations that will describe all photographs. There are some basic or general explorations that everyone will work through while other "tracings" will become evident as you delve further into a particular image.

Electronic: **Open** the selected landscape in a raster application such as Adobe Photoshop. Make all size and resolution adjustments to the photograph at this point. To simulate the tracing paper effect, adjusting the brightness should lighten the computer landscapes. The translucent overlay softens the color and contrast, making the drawn elements dominant. Do a **Save As,** to retain the consistency of the base before beginning the series of tracings. (Figure 2.67)

Unless you are working in an application that contains both raster and vector capabilities, you will need to work back and forth between different software applications to complete the series, using whichever environment is more appropriate to complete a solution. For example, if you are painting in a space, or tracing around the organic edge of an element, you will want to be in a raster program. When developing a geometric solution, a vector program is more appropriate.

In a raster program such as Adobe Photoshop, the photograph will open as the background layer. You should always make a Copy of the background to allow for mistakes and corrections. Each study should be developed on a **New Layer** with a clear and fresh examination of the background photograph. If you are working in a program that does not give you the option of layers, do a **Save As** after each exploration, then re-**Open** the adjusted background file. Whether you are creating a series of layers or saving a series of files, each completed "drawing", should be given a name to identify the concept explored. Each study

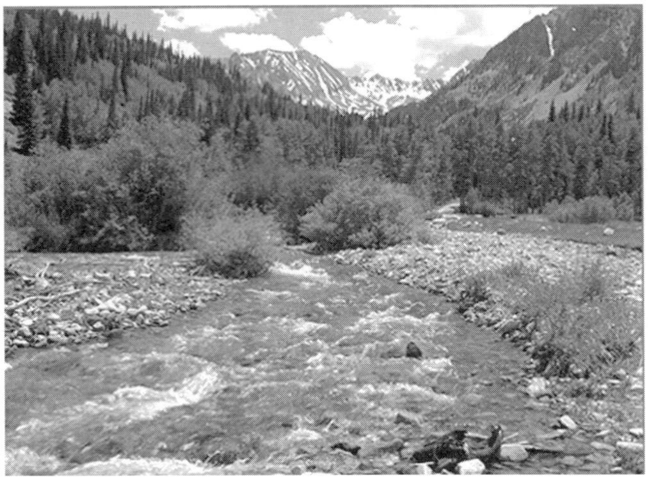

Figure 2.66 Mountain

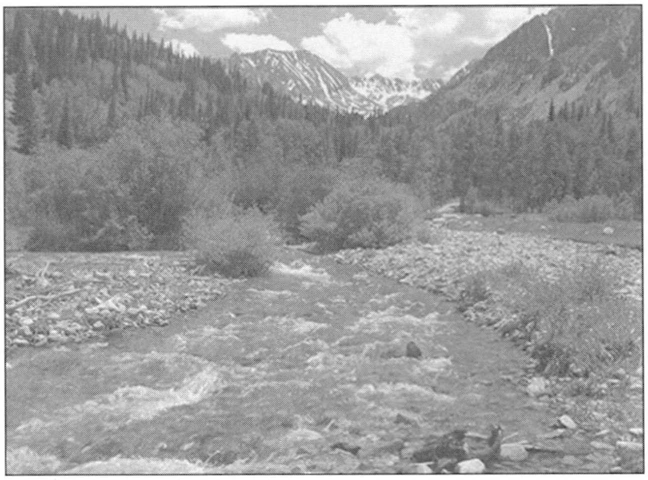

Figure 2.67 Tracing

or "drawing" should be printed independently, without the background photograph, as a tracing or overlay.

First, complete a thorough *contour* of the image, discovering all of the subtle characteristics by drawing an outline around large and small shapes, differentiating changes in texture and value. (Figure 2.68) Through contrasts in color, texture, or character, major forms are distinguished and identified as shapes. (Figure 2.69) Isolate areas that visually unify because of color, texture, placement, and so forth, dividing the page spatially into planes. (Figure 2.70)

Reduce the image down to major divisions of space based on distinctions of form. (Figure 2.71) We can reduce the division of space one step further, to a basic foreground, middleground, and background, using a simplified line rather than the exact contour of form. (Figure 2.72)

To help clarify the planes with value, create a shape (using the pen tool) over the lines you have drawn, and **Fill** one of the planes with black. The middle ground would probably be the most logical choice. (Figure 2.73) As mentioned previously in the lesson, we can look for the smallest element, or point, in the image. Isolate the conceptual points at intersections of two lines, which draw our eye to these spots. (Figure 2.74) Also identify point as form—those objects small enough to be read as point.

Trace the conceptual line formed when we follow the path of the points. (Figure 2.75) Look for point as texture, creating a plane without outline. (Figure 2.76) Having already visualized conceptual lines, mark those forms that can be read as line. (Figure 2.77)

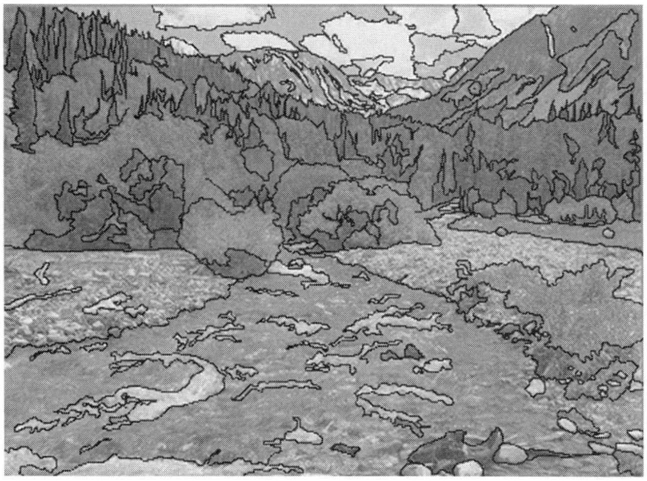

Figure 2.68 Contour

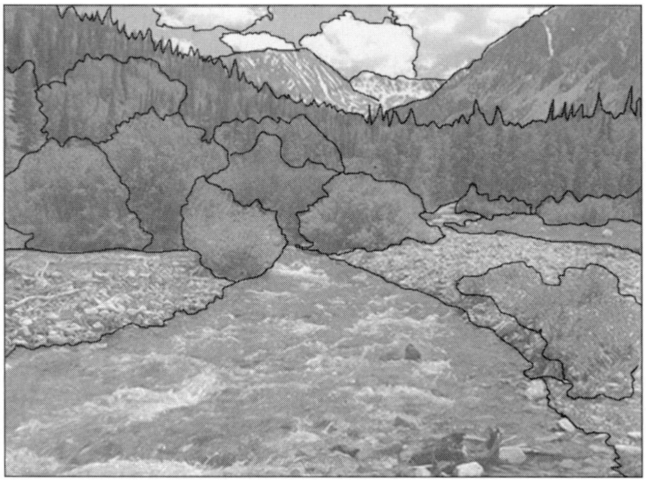

Figure 2.69 Major Shapes

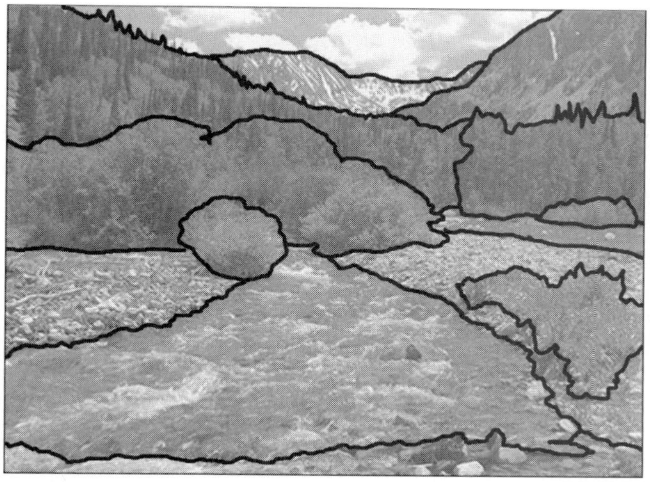

Figure 2.70 Major Planes

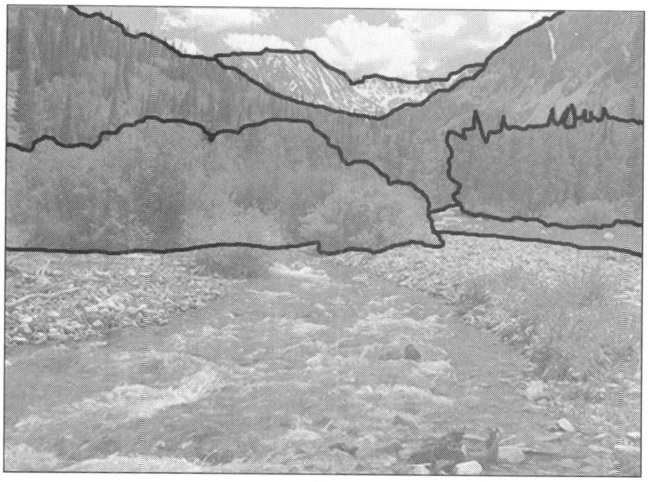

Figure 2.71 Divisions of Space

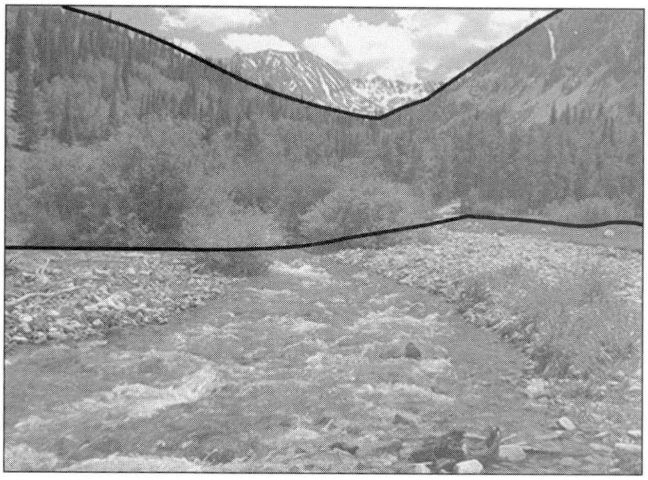

Figure 2.72 Simplified Space

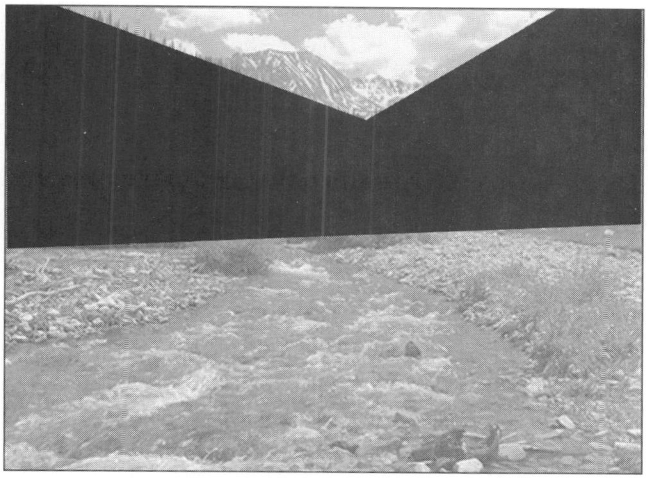

Figure 2.73 Black Plane

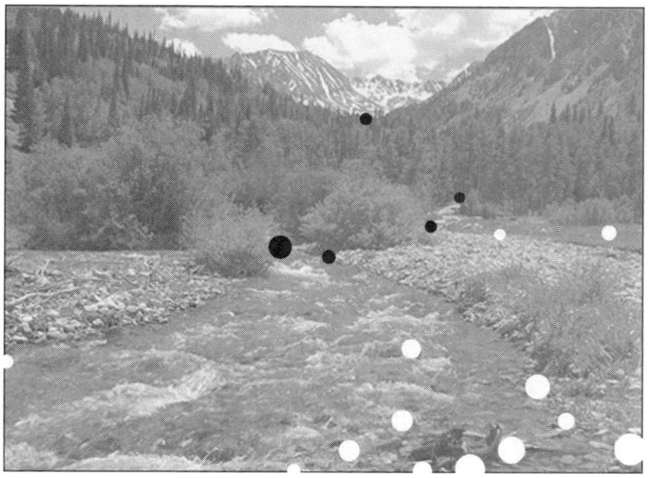

Figure 2.74 Point

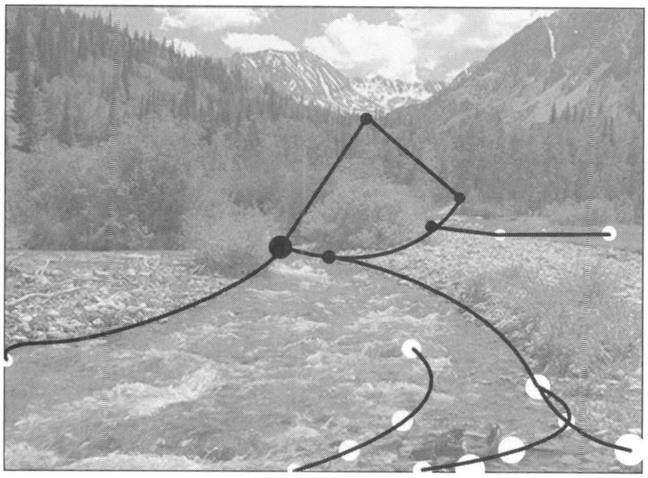

Figure 2.75 Concept/Line

Next, trace line as texture or detail. Notice in this image the curved, fluid quality of the detail. (Figure 2.78) Curved line is a natural lead-in to recognizing form as circular shape. (Figure 2.79)

Another avenue to follow is the directional forces at work in the image. If we utilize the changes in direction, we can use lines creating planes to record those contrasts (Figure 2.79). Continue the search for undiscovered information in your landscape, moving beyond the obvious to a discovery of those aspects particular to your chosen image.

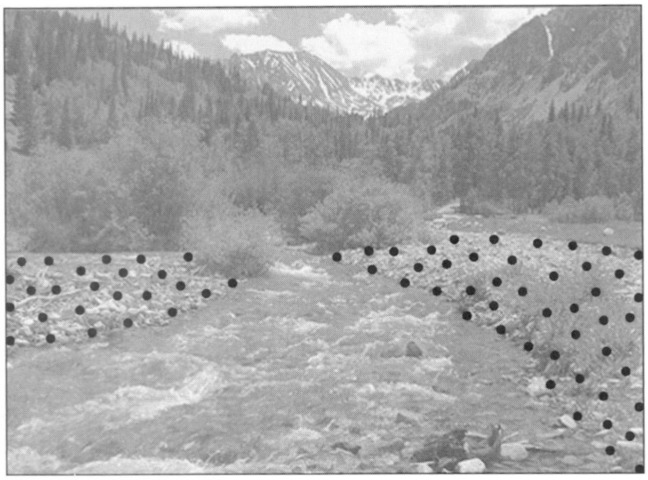

Figure 2.76 Texture/Point

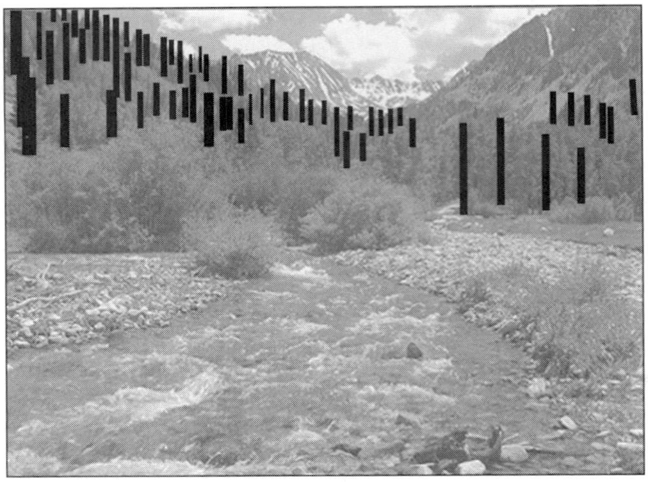

Figure 2.77 Vert Line

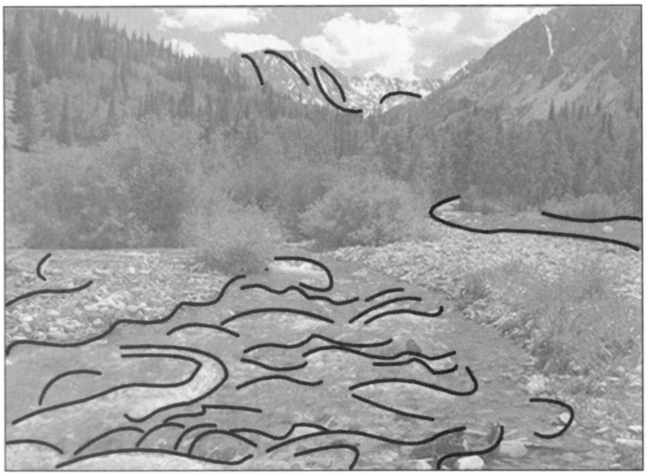

Figure 2.78 Texture/Line

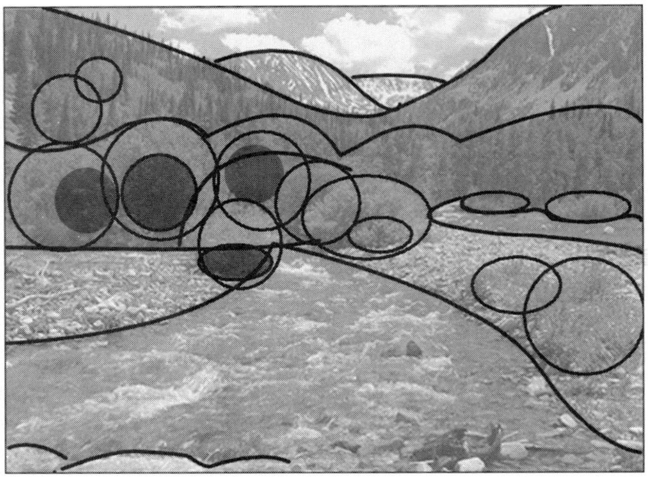

Figure 2.79 Curved Line

Assignment B: LANDSCAPE ABSTRACTION

When you have completed your search for the visual, conceptual, and dynamic aspects of the image, review what you have discovered. Select aspects of different "tracings," that best represent the character of the image. Create a synthesis of that information, reducing it to the simplest visually graphic form that continues to express the visual and conceptual essence of the composition. The solution can be completed on the computer in basic black-and-white elements. If the tracings were done by hand, the abstraction can be completed, at the same scale, on illustration board with ink.

Following are two different student solutions to both the landscape analysis and the synthesis of that discovery into a final landscape abstraction. One solution is entirely electronic (Figures 2.80-2.88) while the second is completed in traditional processes and materials (Figures 2.89-2.96).

Landscape Analysis and Abstract 1
Electronic Artwork by Amie Ciluffo

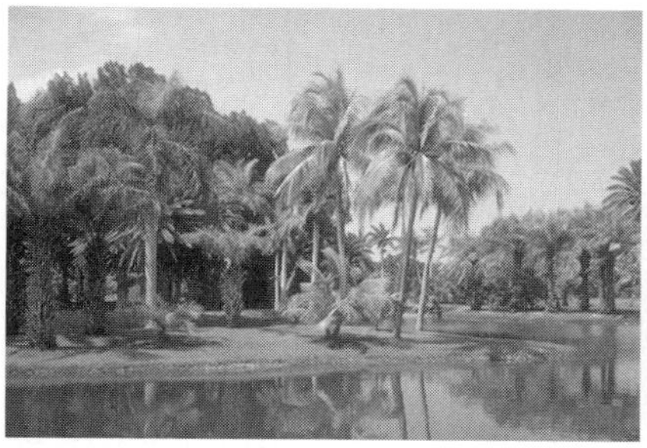
Figure 2.80 Palms

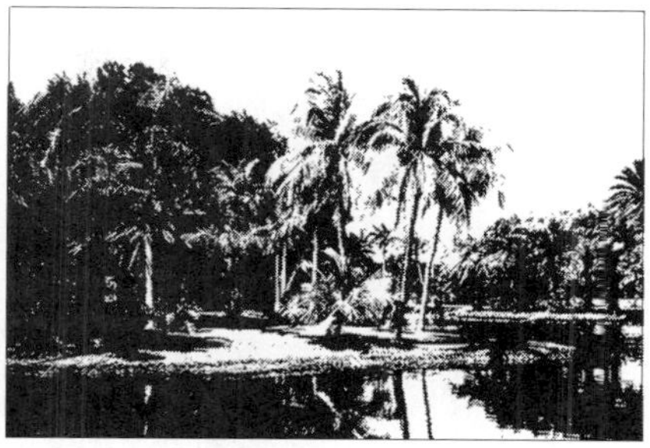
Figure 2.81 High-Contrast

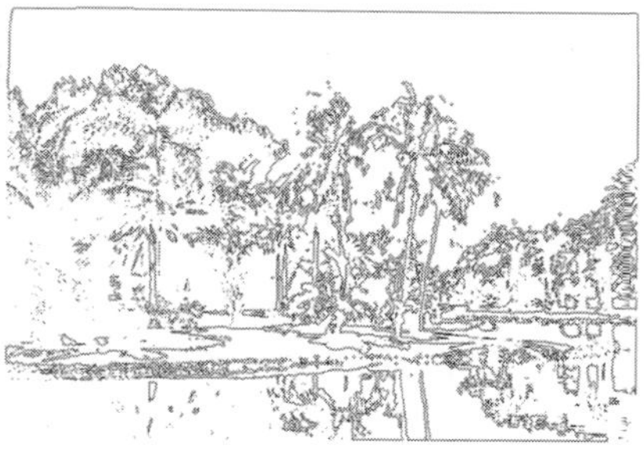
Figure 2.82 Contour

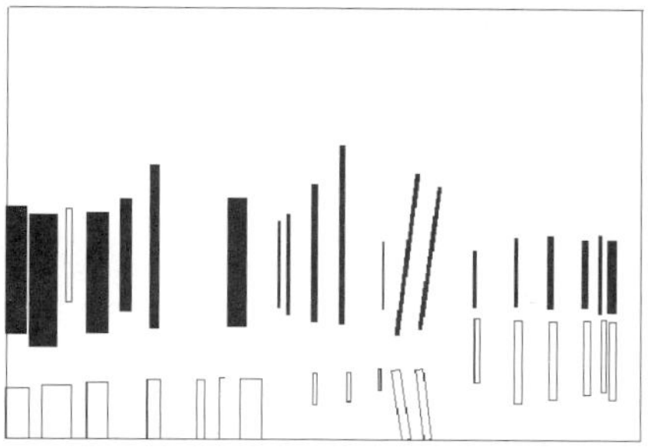
Figure 2.83 Vertical line

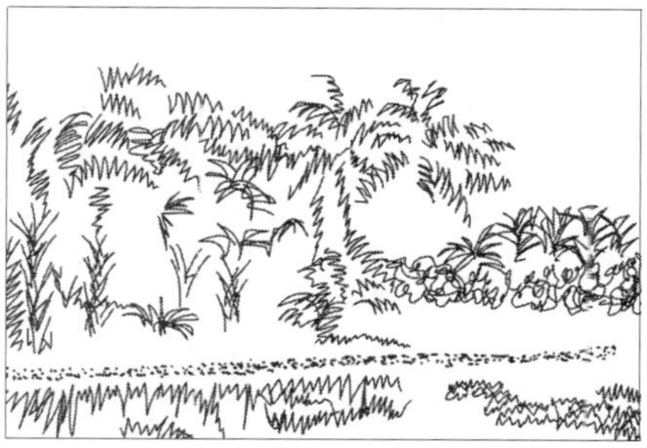
Figure 2.84 Textures

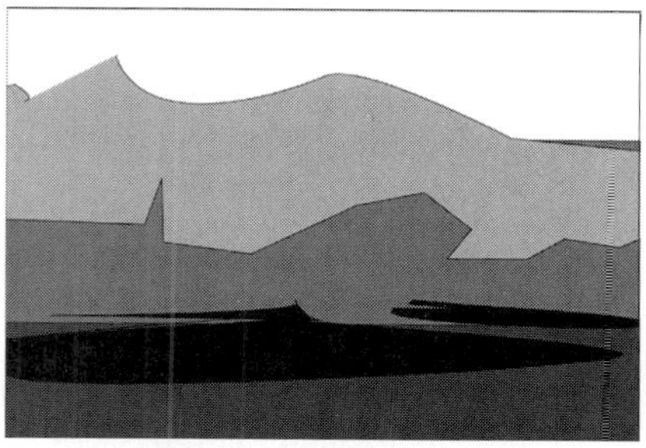
Figure 2.85 Planar Divisions of Space

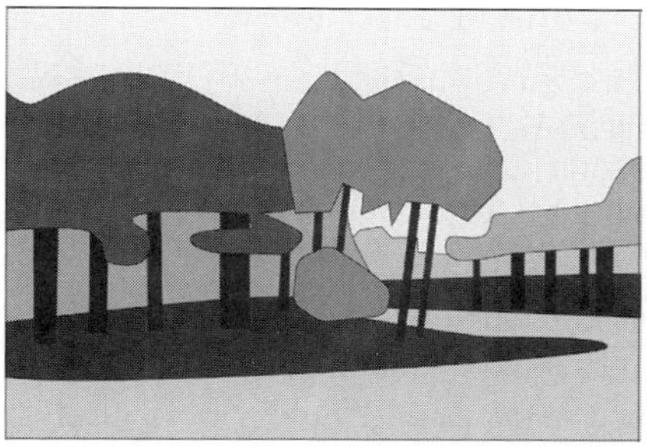
Figure 2.86 Planar Shape

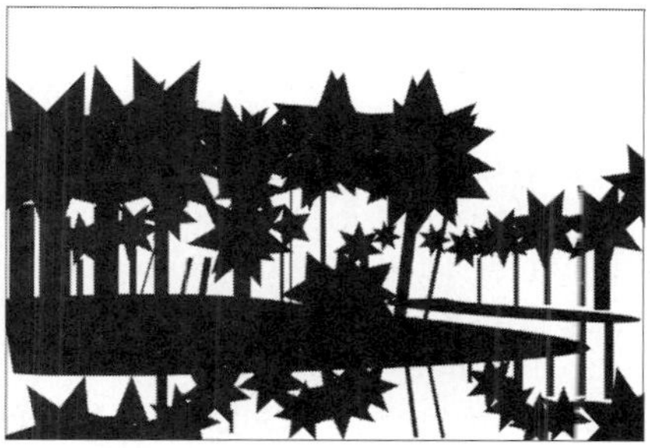
Figure 2.87 Stars

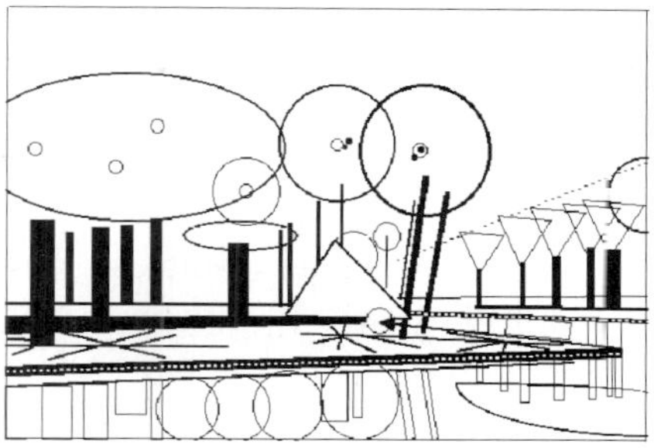
Figure 2.88 Abstraction

Landscape Analysis and Abstraction 2
Traditional Artwork by James Perkins

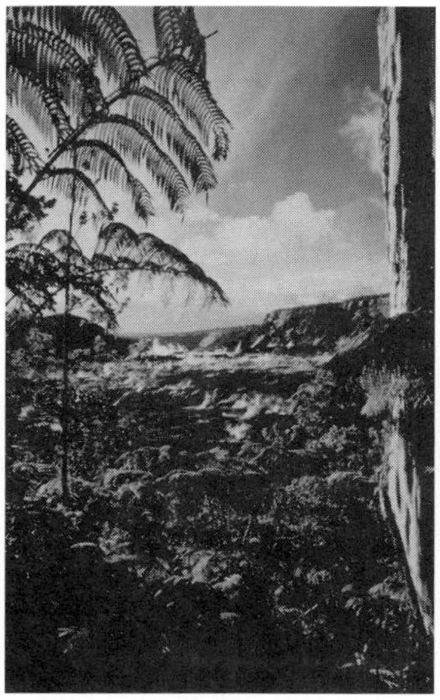
Figure 2.89 Island

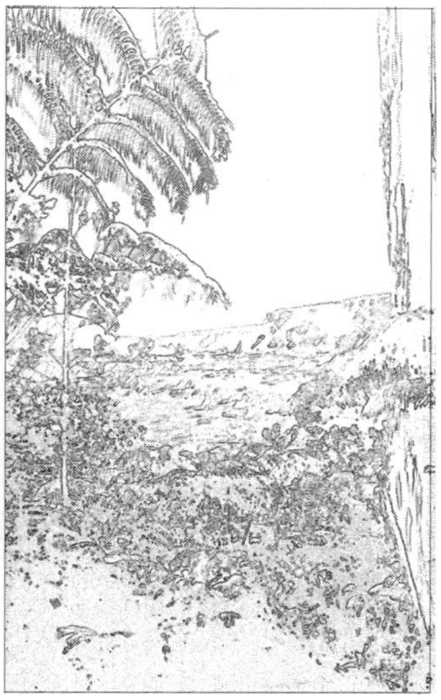
Figure 2.90 Contour

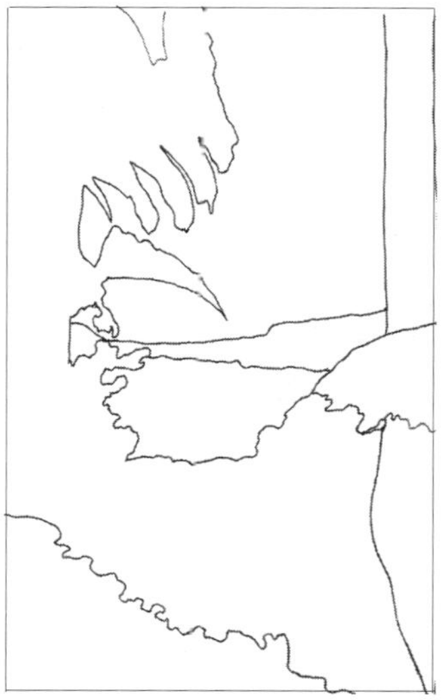
Figure 2.91 Contour Planes

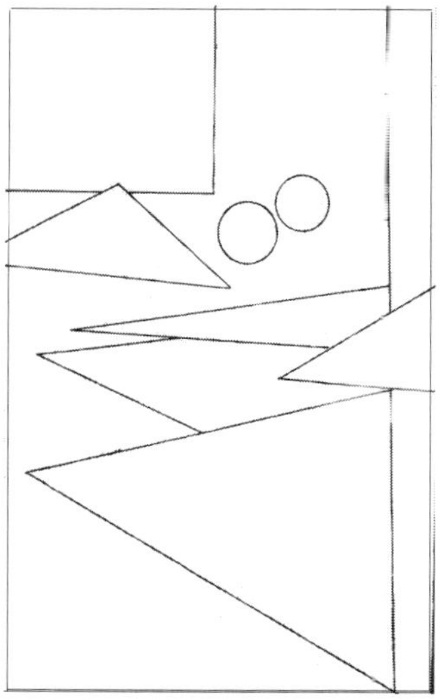
Figure 2.92 Geometric Planes

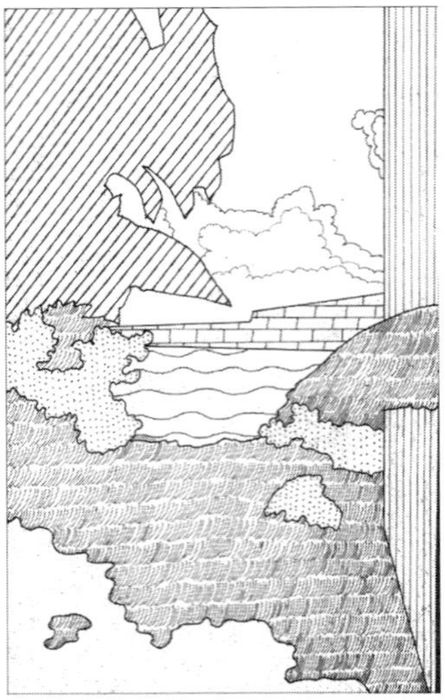

Figure 2.93 Texture

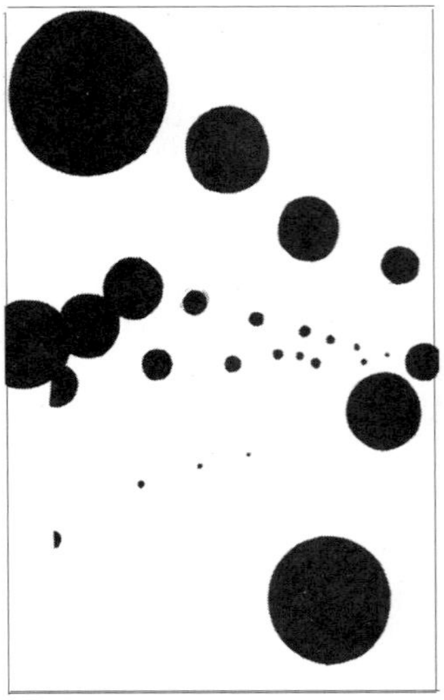

Figure 2.94 Circular Elements

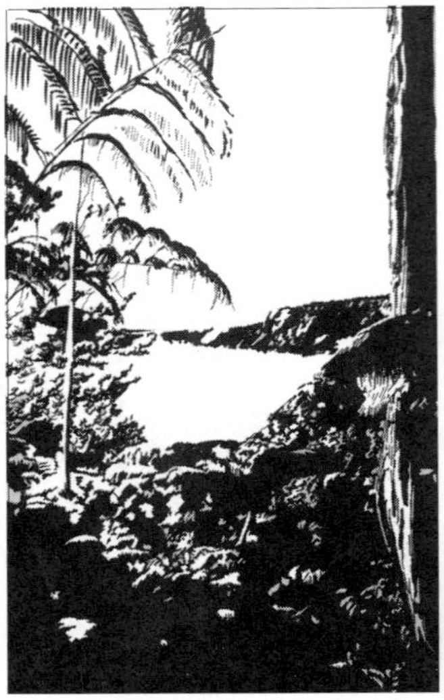

Figure 2.95 High-Contrast

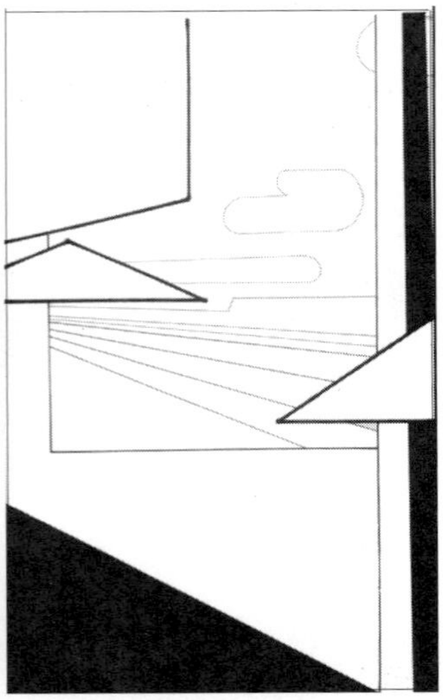

Figure 2.96 Abstraction

GROUPING PRINCIPLES

As we interact visually with the world around us, we are attracted by those forms and images that allow us to easily process and comprehend information. Specifically, we are drawn to visual forms and fields in which the relationship between parts is organized and recognizable. These visual compulsions, called ***grouping principles,*** function to establish basic organizational relationships between the ***elements*** of a ***composition.***

Forms within a two-dimensional field may be related in a variety of ways through the use of grouping principles. ***Proximity*** or relative nearness establishes physical connection between neighboring forms (Figure 2.97). The grouping principles of ***similarity*** and ***repetition*** establish familial bonds between elements with like physical characteristics (Figures 2.98 and 2.99). ***Closure*** connects elements that are seen as portions of a greater whole (Figure 2.100). ***Continuation*** aligns contours, establishing relationships between separate elements that fall along continuous visual paths (Figure 2.101).

In many visual images, several grouping principles operate simultaneously within the same design. Both the brain and the eye constantly attempt to organize the visual world using any of the grouping principles available. Psychologically and visually, we are drawn to images that intrigue us and can be logically decoded. Organization facilitates a desire to explore a visual field, which in turn aids mental recognition and comprehension.

In the previous investigations, Landscape Analysis and Abstraction we concentrated on compositional relationships that are inherent in preexisting photographic images. In the next problem we are addressing organizational strategies that may be used in the construction of two-dimensional designs.

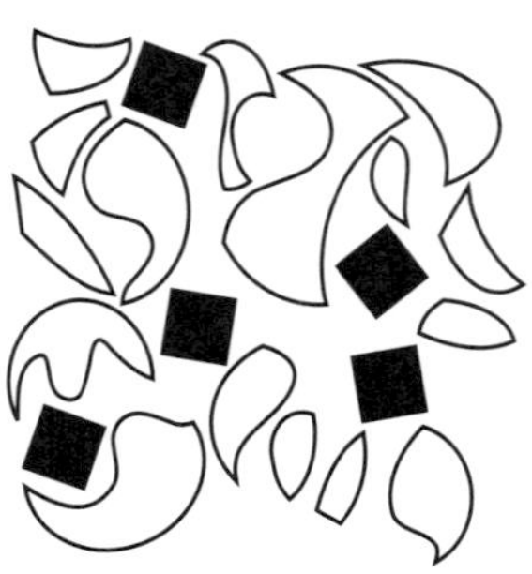

Figure 2.97

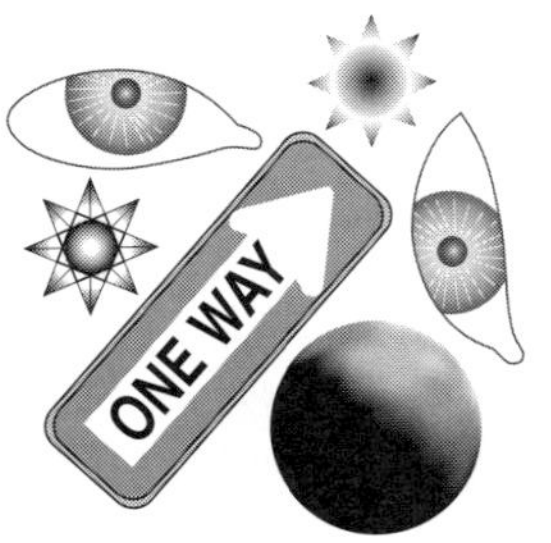

Figure 2.98

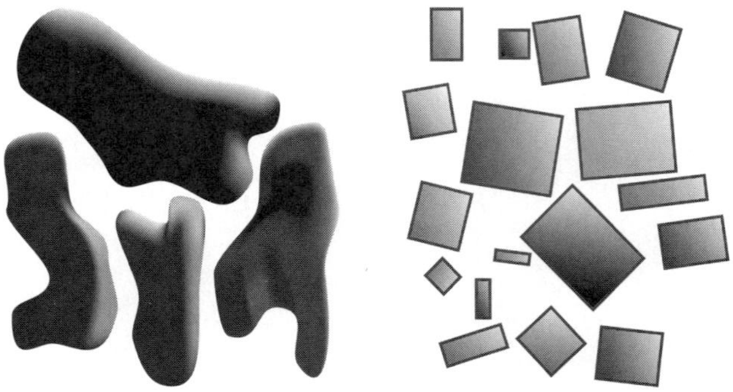

Figure 2.99

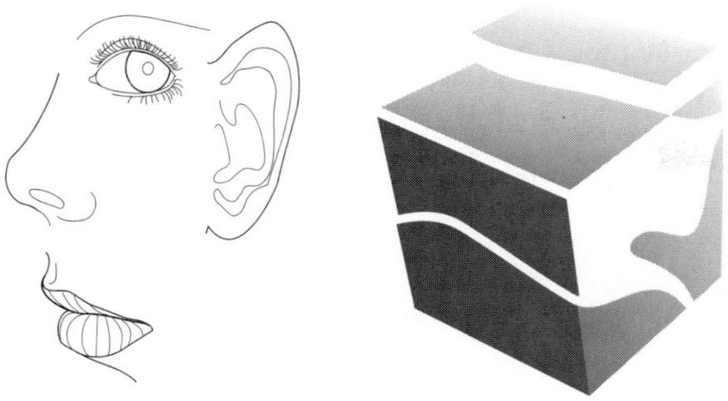

Figure 2.100

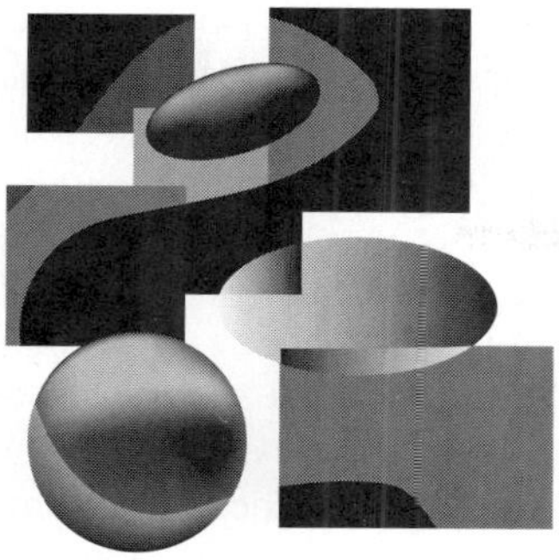

Figure 2.101

A MATTER OF CONTRASTS

Composition is a fundamental design activity that determines the arrangement and organization of ***elements, forms,*** and ***spaces*** within a two-dimensional image. Emerging as a function of personal preference and operative intent, composition depends on the relationship between forms within an image. These relationships cannot, however, independently organize and unify a visual image. Unified designs also depend on the relationships between forms and the two-dimensional containers they inhabit. Our ability to interpret elements as either ***positive, filled space*** or ***negative, unfilled space*** depends on their relationship to the ***format.*** These form-to-format relationships create focal points and may elude to subject within a design. Our ability to see, understand, and interpret a visual image depends on the multiplicity of relationships that emerge from the compositional process.

OBJECTIVES

This problem involves the creation of a series of three designs that use ***shape*** to experiment with positive and negative space. We will experiment with the process of abstracting shapes from actual three-dimensional objects with a flat bed scanner. In addition, grouping principles will be used to create relationships between forms and thereby organize a composition.

MATERIALS

Electronic: Two small objects of relatively flat depth; a computer; a raster-based drawing program such as Adobe Photoshop; flat bed scanner; laser printer; mounting board; rubber cement; pen or utility knife

Traditional: Photographs; tracing paper; black paper; graphite pencils; x-acto knife; scissors; bristol board

PROCEDURE

Electronic

Creating the Shapes

Choose two small objects whose contours suggest a sense of opposition in terms of shape. For example, you may choose an organic form (a leaf) and a geometric form (a hex bolt), or pair a representational form (a pair of pliers) with a non-objective form (a blob of chewing gum), and so on (Figures 2.102 and 2.103). Make your selections based on visual preference and the knowledge that they will be utilized within a 6″ × 6″ format.

When selecting your forms you must also consider the means by which they will be abstracted. The flatbed scanners, like copy machines, have a limited depth of field. This means that objects that are too thick will have edges that are fuzzy, (for example the hosta flower in Figure 2.102) because the scanner cannot "read" edges too far away from its surface. Your objects need to have a limited depth.

Scan each of your objects separately into the computer. If your forms can scratch, or are sticky or crumbly, be sure to protect the surface of the scanner by using a sheet of acetate under the objects. **Transform** your acquired forms into relatively high-contrast shapes. **Open** the scanned forms in a raster program and utilize the **Adjust** functions to reduce them to high contrast (predominantly black) shapes on a white ground (Figure 2.104). You do not need to eliminate all details from the surface to the forms. **Invert** one of your shapes so that it appears as a white shape on a black ground (Figure 2.105) and **Save** it to your disk.

Creating the Designs Using a raster-based graphics program, create a series of three designs that have a visual connection when aligned horizontally or vertically. Begin by creating a 6″ × 6″ document within the graphics program. This will be a black-and-white series, so the **Mode** should be set on **Grayscale.**

The First Design

Select, Copy, and **Paste** the scanned shape that is not inverted into the new format. Use **Edit** functions to create a composition by pasting and moving this shape repeatedly within the picture plane. Additional manipulations can be applied by transforming the shape (rotating, flipping, changing scale, or changing proportions) as you compose. Forms may appear whole or they can be cropped by the edge of the format. Utilize grouping principles to create strong relationships between elements (Figure 2.106). The goal of this first study is to create a design with a great amount of positive and minimal negative space.

Incorporate an *anomaly* within the design with your inverted white shape. This relatively small second shape will appear as a negative shape, with no actual contour line. The anomaly will "punch out" a portion of your positive shape(s) and appear as a white

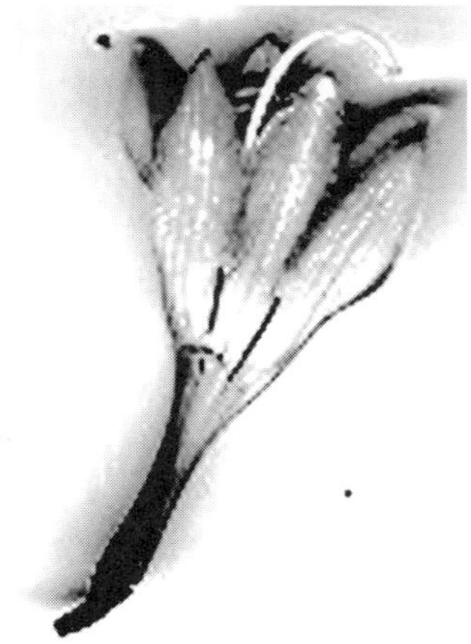

Figure 2.102

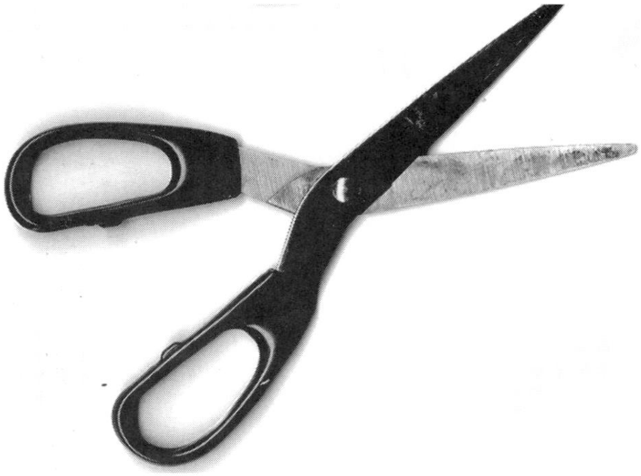

Figure 2.103

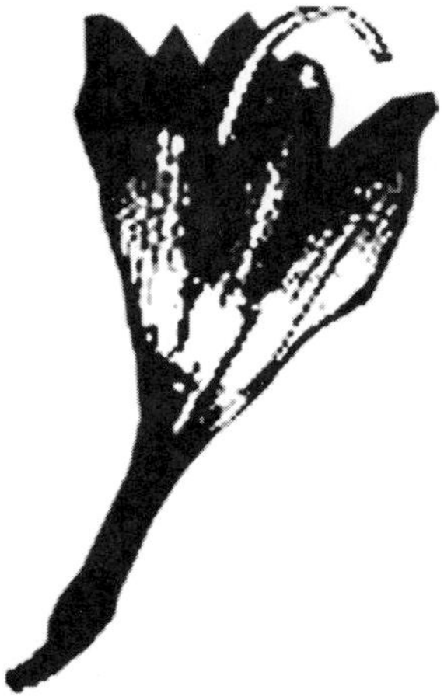

Figure 2.104

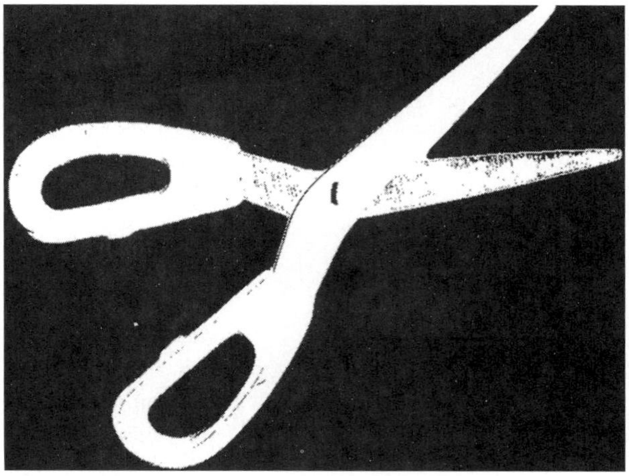

Figure 2.105

negative space. You may use any number of these shapes as long as positive space remains predominant. As with the positive, the inverted shapes may also be flipped or rotated through the use of the **Transform** functions (Figure 2.107).

Transforming the Perception of Space—The Second Design

Using the first design as a base, create a second, in which you increase the negative space to the point where positive and negative space appear equivalent. Make a **Copy** of your first design, adding more of the white shapes that functioned as anomalies. Increase the amount of negative space until it equals that of positive space. This is called a **figure–ground reversal.** If you are successful, you should not be able to tell if the design is black on a white ground or white on a black ground (Figure 2.108).

Changing the border around the composition to either black or white will quickly demonstrate your success. This can be quickly accomplished on the computer by changing the screen color on the bottom of the **Tools** palette. As with the first design, carefully consider the use of grouping principles and balance to create a unified composition.

Inverting the Values—The Third Design

In the third design you will continue to decrease the positive space and increase the negative space until it becomes dominant. As before, make a **Copy** of your previous design and add white shapes until the negative space is dominant (Figure 2.109).

Once you have completed the series, **Print** a copy of each of your designs.

Traditional: This project may be done as a ***collage*** problem without the computer. The original shapes may be attained from magazines or other photographs through the use of tracing paper. The contours may be transferred directly to black paper through use of the graphite transfer method. This involves applying graphite to the back of the tracing paper drawings, placing these drawings graphite side down on the black paper, and retracing the original shapes. These transferred shapes are then cut out and used as collage elements. The same conceptual and formal parameters apply to the problem.

PRESENTATION

Cut out your designs and mount them on a single black or white board, leaving margins and borders that best suit the relationship of the images, to create a progression (Figures 2.110, 2.111, and 2.112).

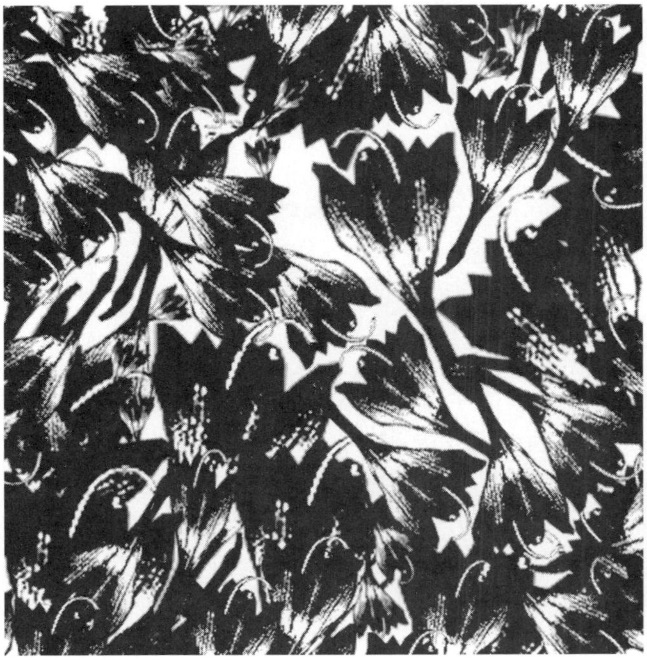

Figure 2.106

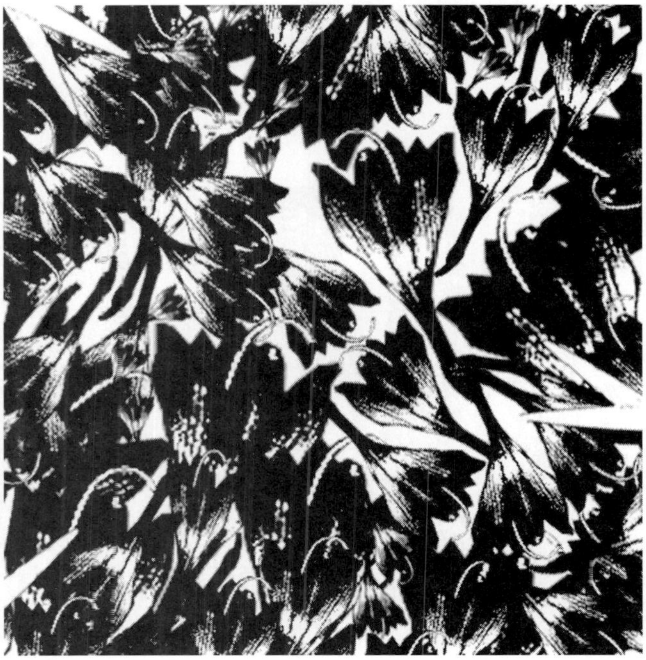

Figure 2.107

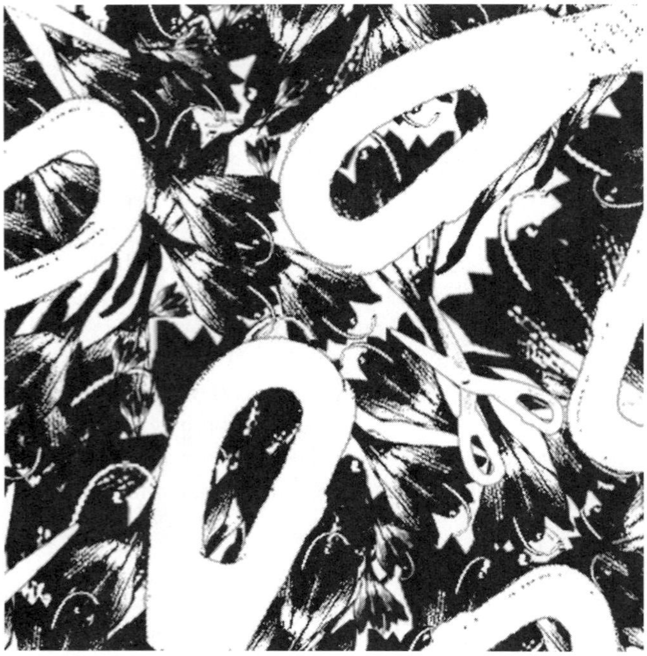

Figure 2.108

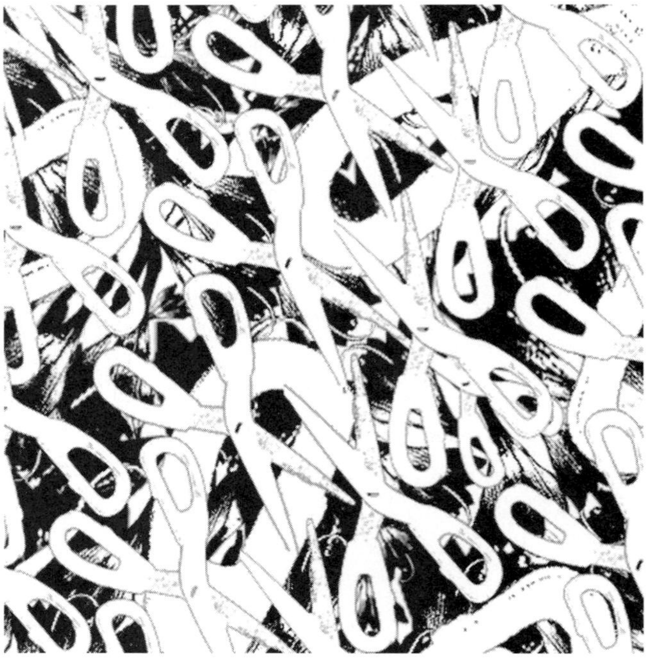

Figure 2.109

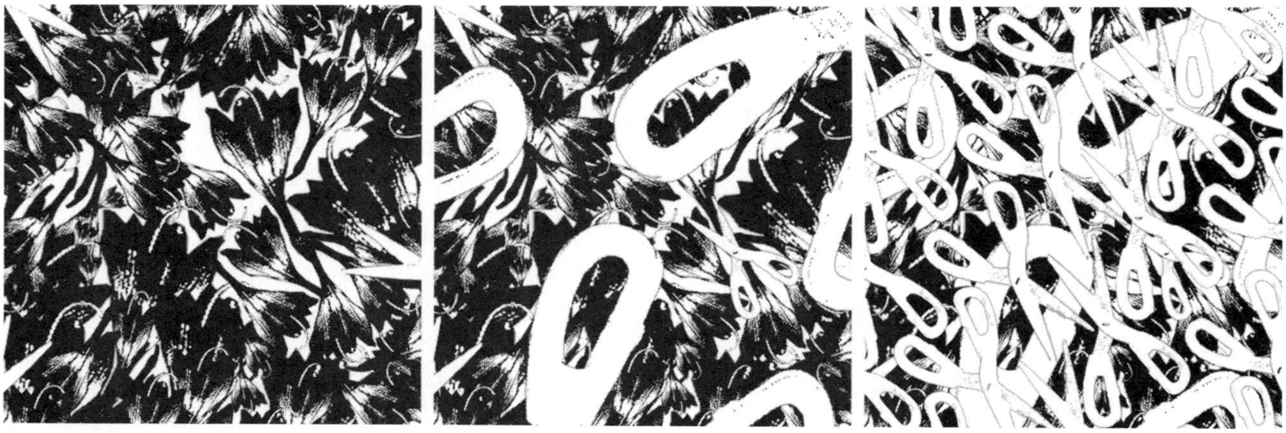

Figure 2.110(a) **(b)** **(c)**

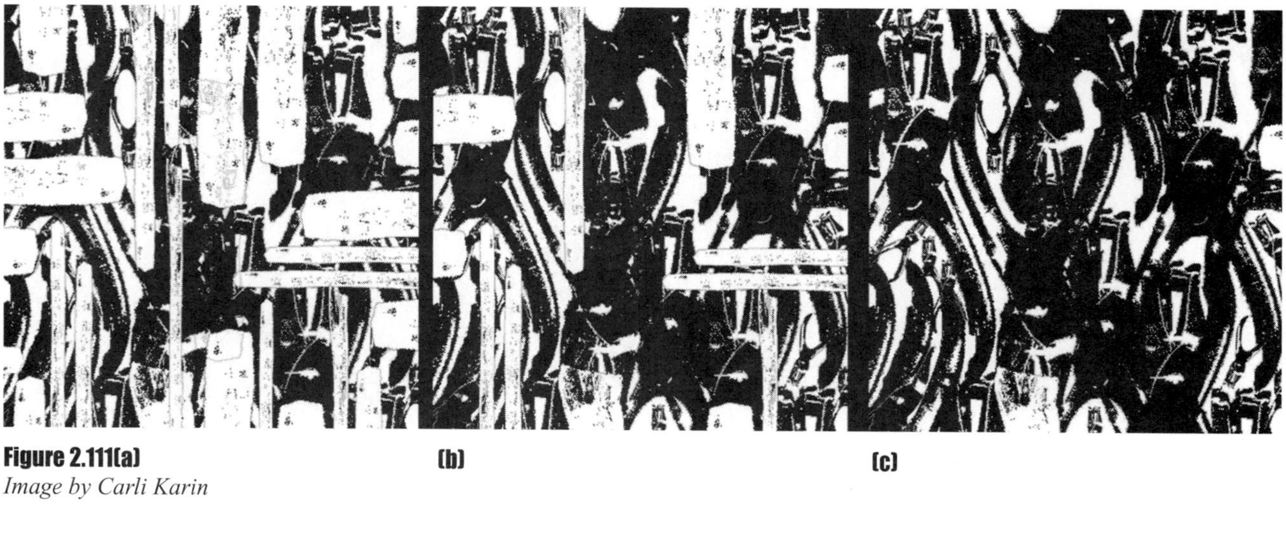

Figure 2.111(a) **(b)** **(c)**

Image by Carli Karin

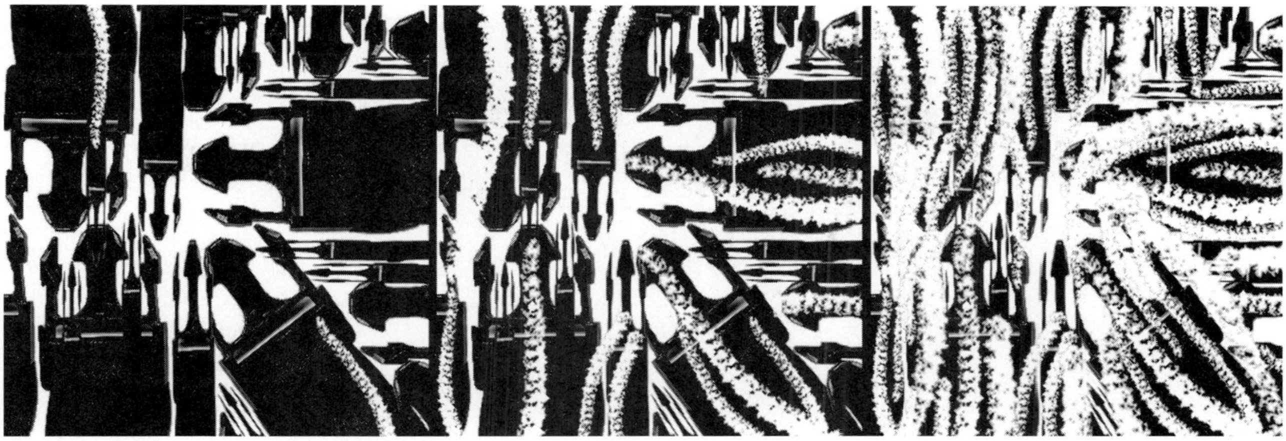

Figure 2.112(a) **(b)** **(c)**
Image by Jennifer Wilson

DISCUSSION

This problem allows for the exploration of shape as it emerges from our surrounding environments. Once abstracted onto the picture plane, the interaction of shapes provides numerous compositional issues for discussion. Critique may include consideration of the function of anomaly, especially in the first design, as a means of enhancing unity within the series through the use of repetition. The second design provides an opportunity for visual problem solving that may be achieved in a variety of ways. A figure-ground reversal can occur when positive and negative spaces are equally divided within the design or along the edges of the design. This visual split may also be achieved through the use of gestalt, where the sense of identity of one or both shapes increases their emphasis and power within a composition regardless of their relative quantity within the overall image. Finally, the third design provides an opportunity to discuss the challenge of composing with a vast amount of white space and very little black form.

CHAPTER 3

SEEING AND PERCEIVING: COGNITION

UNDERSTANDING SHAPE

Shape is a basic two-dimensional ***element*** of design that is identified by its contour edge and sense of position on the picture plane. Defined by ***line, value, texture,*** or ***color, shapes*** may emerge from our environment, our language, or our imaginations.

Shape Analysis and Application Shape is enclosed two-dimensional space. While form has three dimensions, measured by length, width, and depth, a shape is flat, with no depth. A shape can be positive or negative and need not be object specific. Shapes that emerge from our environments may have real or suggested visual connections. ***Representational shapes,*** such as maple leaves or silhouetted figures, have a sense of identity that we can readily name. Gestalt is an exciting possibility we will explore later in this chapter, but object recognition is not essential to determining shape. A group of elements, through their relationship to each other and their surrounding by greater negative space, may be viewed as a shape.

Determining Shape Type Shapes can be classified by their character and the description of their edge.

Geometric shapes, (Figure 3.1) considered most basic, are shapes that are mathematically deduced. Whether created by combinations of straight lines or curved, geometry and simplicity are the connections.

Stylized shapes emerge from the abstraction of forms that we find in our visual world. Mickey Mouse's hands are an example of shapes that emerge from this process.

Invented shapes are those that emerge from our imaginations. These shapes do not directly reference anything in our visual or verbal environments, but their creation is dependent on our history with, and experience in, both.

Shapes surrounded by all straight lines, with no mathematical guidance can be called ***rectilinear,*** while ***curvilinear*** shapes combine both curved and straight elements (Figure 3.2).

All of the preceding shapes can be classified as ***inorganic,*** or not organic. With the exception of geometric shapes, they can be somewhat irregular, exhibiting no formal control, and can appear quite random yet mechanical.

Certain shapes, such as kidney beans or other amoebic shapes, reference their sources in nature. These are ***organic shapes,*** which may also have a strong sense of identity, or may embody curvilinear aspects of natural forms that draw intimate connections. An organic shape is one that appears to have "life," being bound by free curves.

Regardless of their sources, the identity of shapes can profoundly affect our interactions with any given image. ***Simple shapes*** possess uncomplicated contours and are quickly "read" and visually understood. ***Complex shapes*** have characteristically complicated contours that require more time to comprehend, both visually and conceptually. Our ability to read and comprehend shapes is influenced by both our history and experiences with visual forms and by our actual visual interaction with these elements.

Understanding Shape Dynamics—Finding the Axis With the exception of an uninterrupted circle, shapes have a sense of direction, balance, stability, and position. We can determine these attributes by finding the axis of a shape. Think of a globe that spins on its axis (Figure 3.4), or the skeleton that supports dynamic movement of a form.

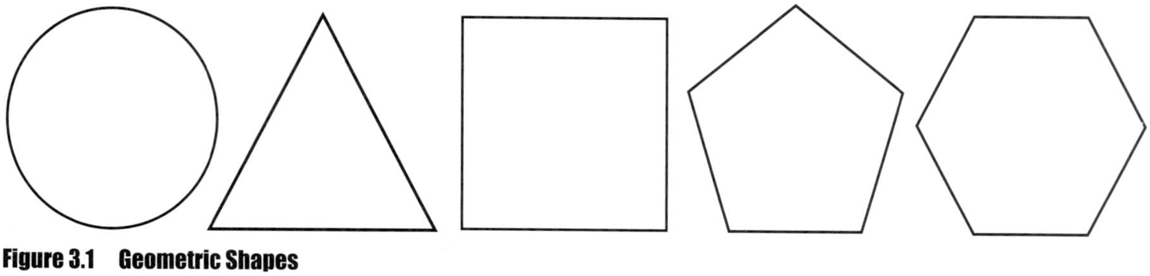

Figure 3.1 Geometric Shapes

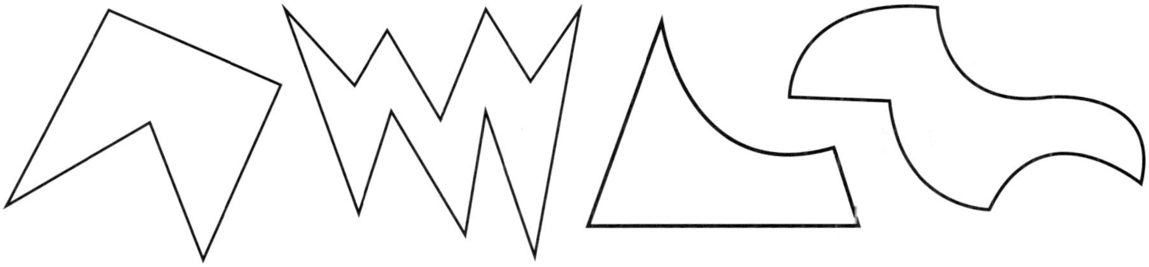

Figure 3.2 Shape Type

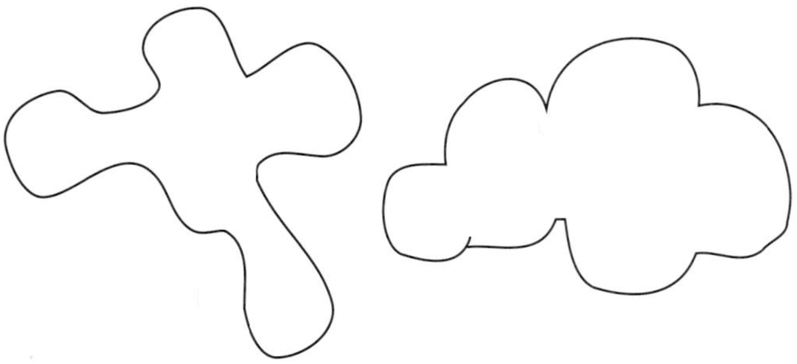

Figure 3.3 Shape Type

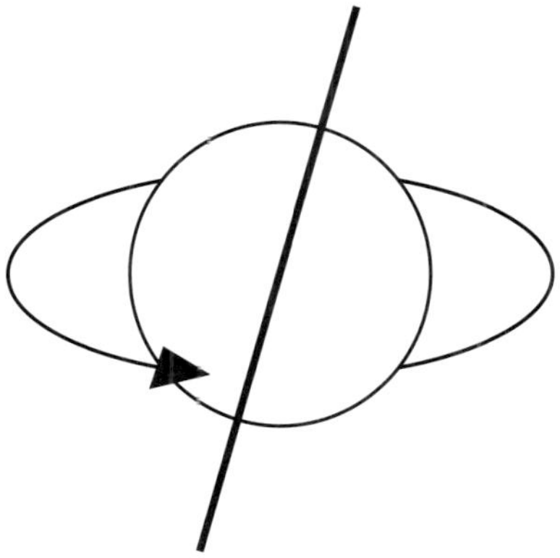

Figure 3.4 Axis

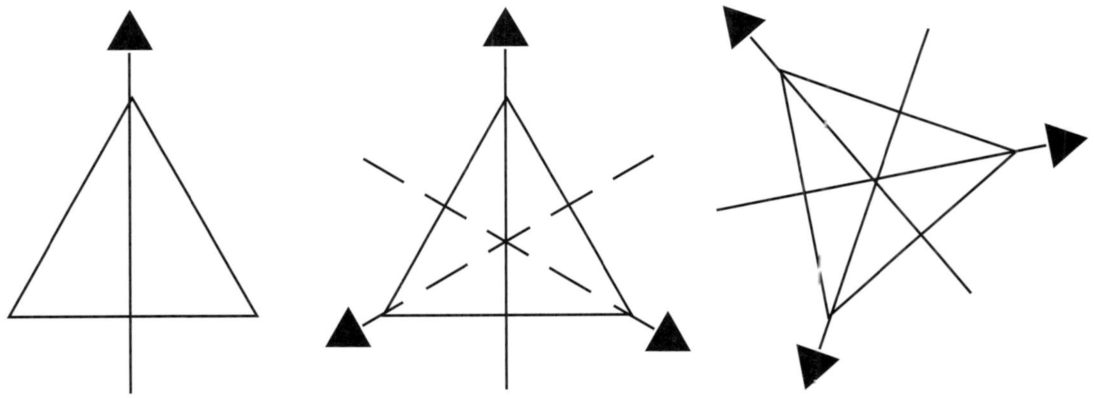

Figure 3.5 Axis

An equilateral triangle with a base parallel to the picture plane is very stable, with a clear choice for axis. As the triangle rotates in space, dominant direction is selective (Figure 3.5).

Triangles, other than equilateral are more singular in the direction they display (Figure 3.6).

When dealing with shapes having a concave indentation or contained negative space, close the distance between the endpoints. This will help you see the actual space needed or displaced by the object. It is then easier to find the dominant axis of the shape. (Figure 3.7)

Shape Interactions The process of relating any two preexisting shapes may result in the alteration or even transformation of their forms. ***Overlapping*** (Figure 3.8) and ***penetration*** (Figure 3.9) crop and subdivide whole shapes. ***Abutment*** (Figure 3.10) and ***union*** (Figure 3.11) transform original contours and merge shapes to create new forms. ***Subtraction*** (Figure 3.12) modifies shape by using a second figure as a cookie cutter of sorts, eliminating parts of the first. ***Intersection*** (Figure 3.13) deals with the creation of new shapes by focusing only on those pieces that overlap when two shapes merge. A relationship may exist between shapes that are ***detached*** (Figure 3.14) or separated spatially, but the manipulation of the sense of ***mutual tension*** (Figure 3.15) between them can considerably enhance the sense of connection. This may be accomplished by pointing two shapes at each other or ***interlocking*** (Figure 3.16) portions of their forms.

Within this process of shape discovery and exploration, some of the most compelling interactions occur between those shapes that we recognize. These are the representational shapes that move beyond mere categorization, having an identity that we can actually name.

Emerging from a myriad of sources and occurring in infinite variations, shape is one of the most divergent of the basic elements. Shapes function to contain and define much of the formal visual information that is transcribed on a

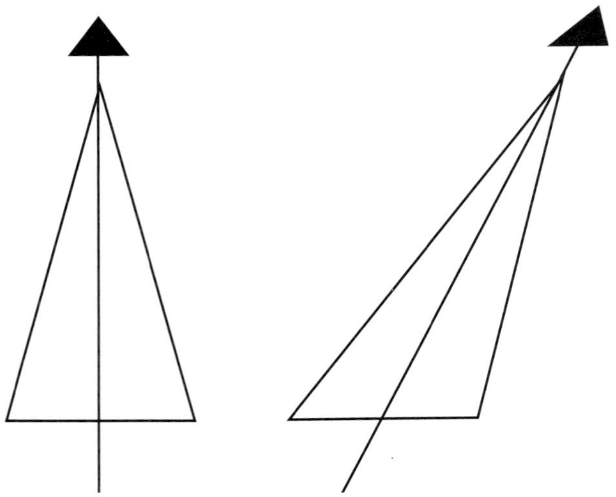

Figure 3.6

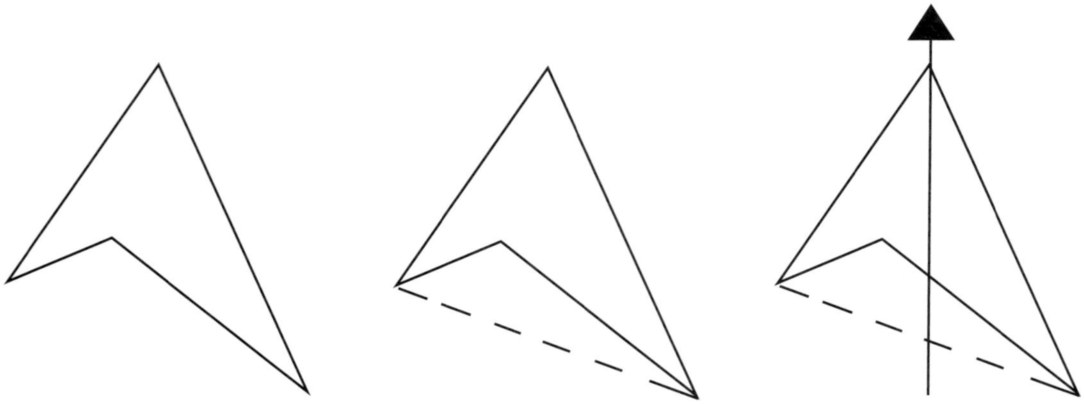

Figure 3.7 Axis

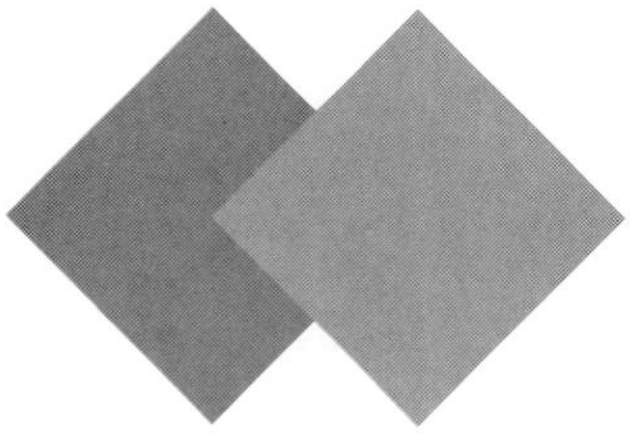

Figure 3.8 Overlap

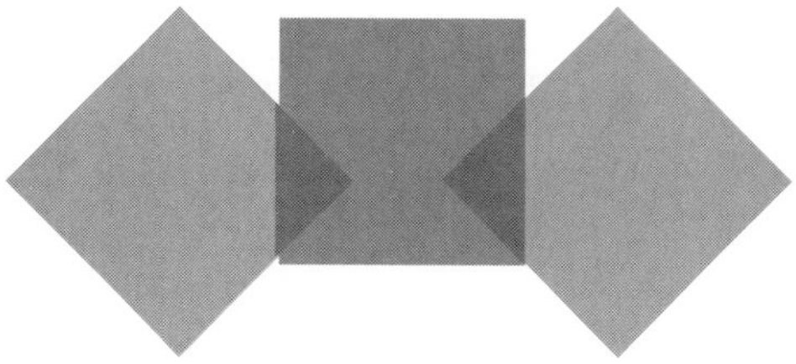

Figure 3.9 Penetration

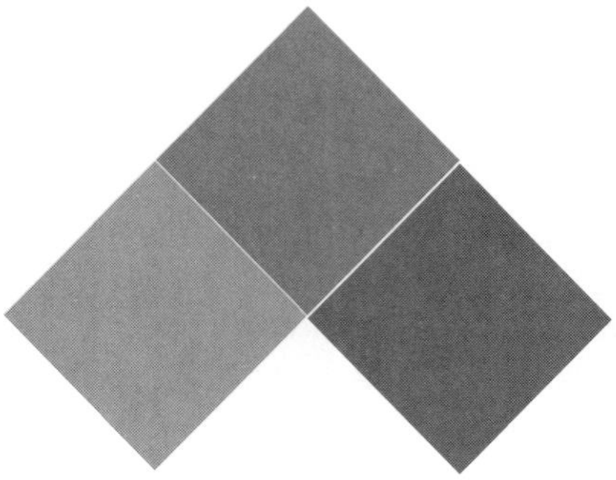

Figure 3.10 Abutment

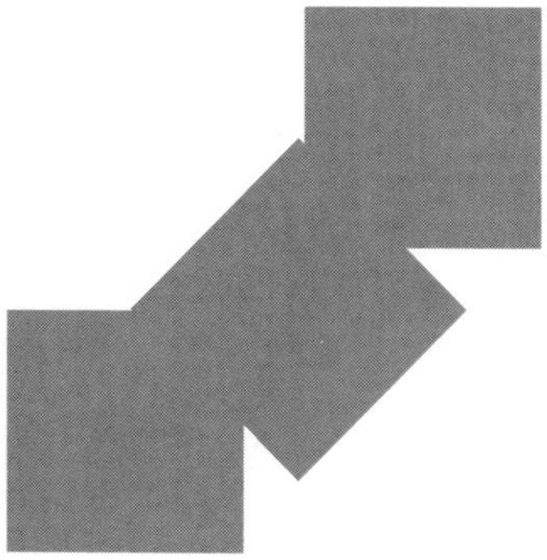

Figure 3.11 Union

two-dimensional surface. Their identities, activities, and interactions also circumscribe the events that occur within the visual arena of the picture plane. Perhaps most compellingly, shapes are defined and transformed by the perceptual and conceptual interplay of both vision and experience that defines our interaction with two-dimensional imagery.

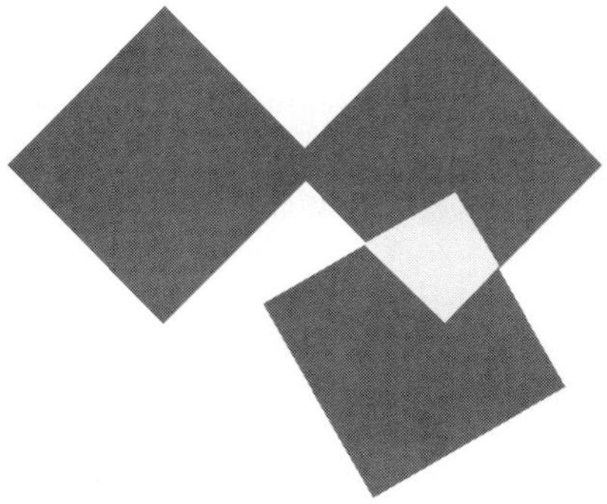

Figure 3.12 Subtraction

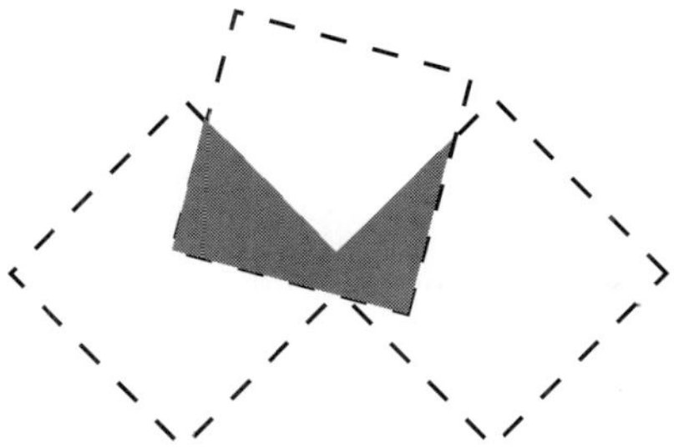

Figure 3.13 Intersection

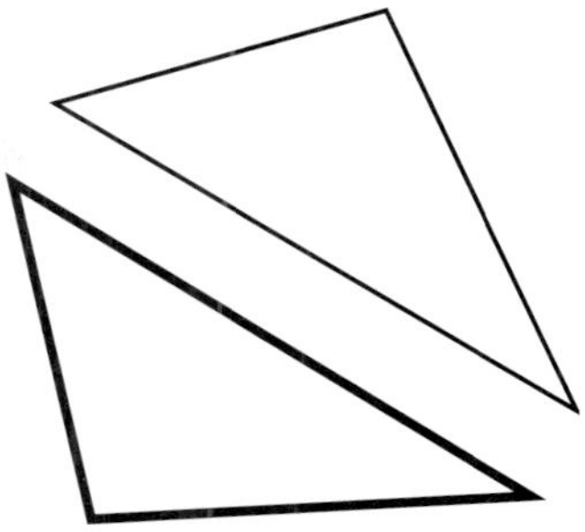

Figure 3.14 Detached

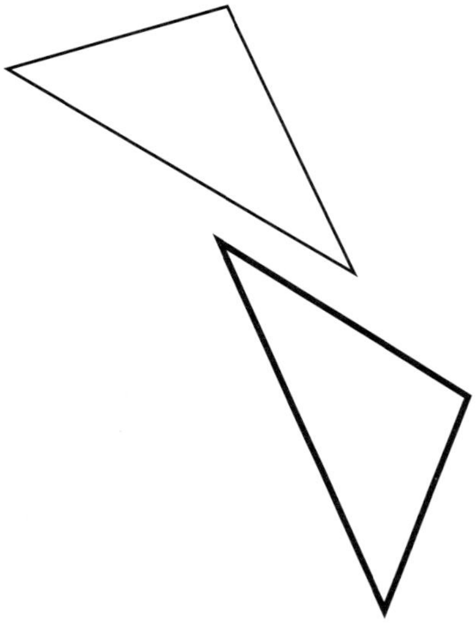

Figure 3.15 Mutual Tension

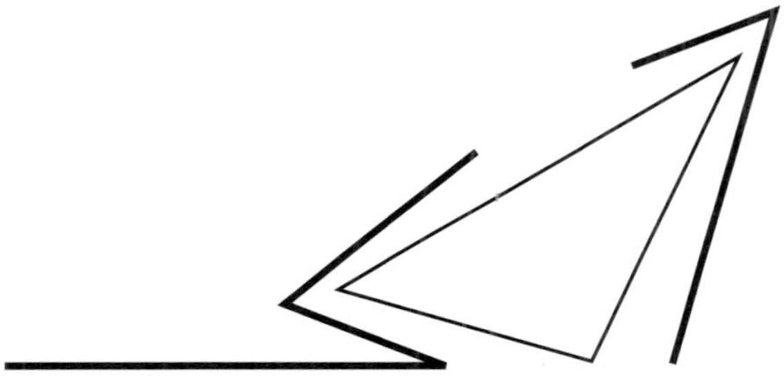

Figure 3.16 Interlocking

A COMPOSITION OF COMPOUND SHAPES

INTRODUCTION

As we move through the basic elements of design the next important step to work through is the discovery of shape. We must understand the attributes of shapes in order to generate them and use them as effective communication. Individual shapes can be rich in the quality of an edge and the simplicity of the gestalt. Understanding the dynamics of a shape can be critical to its expression and the successful placement of that element in a composition.

This project involves the organization of nine compound shapes in a square, creating a strong composition and successful image. The nine compound shapes are created by superimposing selected organic and inorganic shapes in combinations based on shape type and orientation of axis.

OBJECTIVES

Through this assignment, you will be able to recognize and isolate interesting shapes, identify the shape type, and determine the axis to understand shape dynamics. The development of nine, energetic, compound shapes based on dynamic forces is the crux of this project. The relationships established by their placement are essential to the creation of an interactive and balanced composition. Maintaining shape clarity is required as the elements are organized and integrated with a surface development. The surface development should consider the interaction of elements with the structure that supports the composition. A well-crafted, cohesive, and dynamic image is the expected outcome.

MATERIALS

This exercise can be completed by hand or with the computer.

Electronic: A raster-based application such as Adobe Photoshop; digital images. If you have a scanner, scan images from printed matter. If not, CDs with various types of imagery serve as electronic magazines. A digital camera will allow you to capture objects against a white background, making it much easier to cut and paste.

Traditional: Magazines; tracing paper; pencils; 15″ x 15″ illustration board; black match paper with an x-acto knife and scissors, or black ink with a brush.

PROCEDURE

The first step is to identify and isolate at least twenty different shapes in your traditional or electronic magazines or other photo resources at your disposal. Trace the outline of the shape, looking for the qualities of the edge. Remember, a shape may have contained or internal negative space as you describe detail information. Another consideration is that the shapes you discover may not be a single object, but the outline surrounding a collection of elements that merge together for visual interest. Classify each of your shapes, placing them in either the organic or inorganic category, and then determine the dominant axis.

After shape discovery, identification, classification, and axis determination, select two organic and two inorganic shapes. Recognizable shapes with a thematic relationship will open the possibility for an underlying concept in the final project. Once you have selected your four shapes, you need to ensure that they are of equivalent mass and scale to be used effectively in the assignment.

Scaling Shapes to Adjust Size If one of your shapes needs to be larger or smaller, you can accomplish this in a number of ways. If working traditionally, you can "grid-off" the shape to be altered. By marking key points of the shape and transforming them to a second grid that is larger or smaller but proportionate, you can recreate the shape at the appropriate size (Figure 3.17). If you have access to a copier, you can also enlarge or reduce the shape more quickly, especially if it is a complex shape with great detail.

Electronically, most software lets you scale an object. Whether you have captured your images from Photo CD, created them with a digital camera, or used a scanner, you are probably working in a raster-based program such as Adobe Photoshop. If that is the case, select the shape; then scroll down the **Image** menu to **Image Size.** Constrain the width and height, then alter one of the settings to keep the shape in proportion. Remember to keep a consistent resolution among all of your shapes.

Equivalent Mass Shapes of great contrast, such as this ring and the pencil, would not be compatible when superimposed, with one clearly overpowering the other for visual dominance (Figure 3.18).

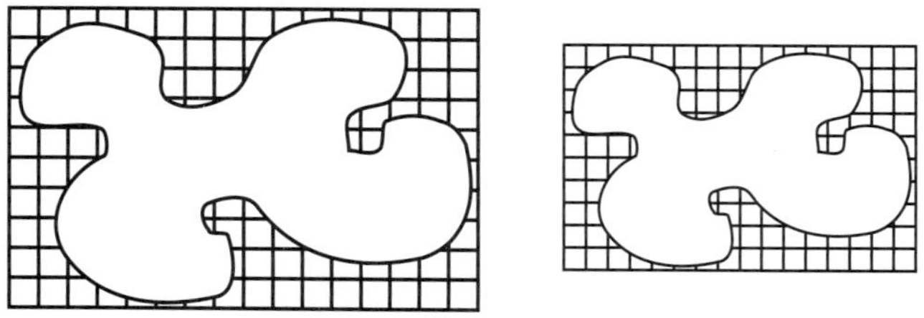

Figure 3.17(a) Scale **(b)**

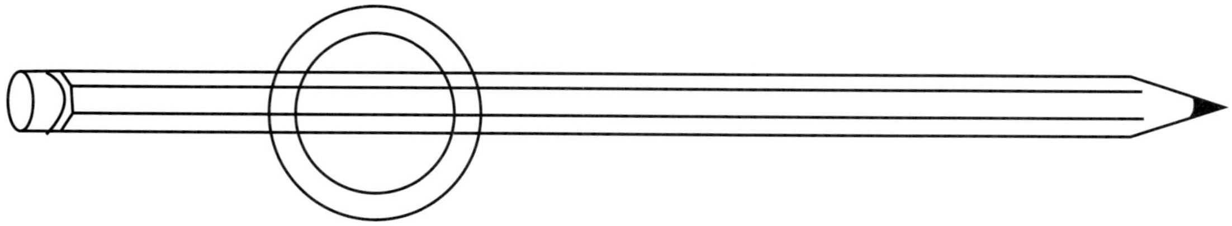

Figure 3.18 Mass

If we create a frame of reference and scale the ring to the appropriate size, we find that trying to apply the pencil to the same frame is inappropriate. The ring would now clearly overpower the pencil (Figure 3.19). Try instead to imagine how a linear object might be divided to fit within that frame of reference (Figure 3.20) Reassemble the image, keeping the newly scaled size. We now have a linear pencil and a circular ring that are more balanced in their visual weight and in the attention they demand (Figure 3.21). This is an example of extreme contrast. Generally, shape choices are more equivalent in mass and may need a less extreme adjustment in size.

Creating Compound Shapes Using your selection of organic and inorganic shapes, comparable in mass and with their axes determined, it is time to create the nine compound shapes that will be the basis of your composition.

Select the two organic shapes, and superimpose them with their axes parallel (Figure 3.22(b)), perpendicular (Figure 3.22(c)), and on the diagonal (Figure 3.22(d)).

Now select the two inorganic shapes, and superimpose them with their axes parallel (Figure 3.23(b)), pependicular (Figure 3.23(c)), and on the diagonal (Figure 3.23(d)).

Finally, select one of the organic shapes and one of the inorganic shapes, and superimpose them with their axes parallel (Figure 3.24(b)), perpendicular (Figure 3.24(c)), and on the diagonal (Figure 3.24(d)). Be consistent and use the same organic and inorganic shapes for the sequence.

Notice that the axes do not have to fall right on top of each other and do not need to be centered. You are trying to find the most interesting relationship, observing negative space and contained negative shape. Shapes may be negative, positive, or a combination.

You now have a total of nine compound shapes that form relationships based on classification and axis orientation.

Composition Organize the shapes within a square format to create a dynamic, balanced, interactive composition of nine independent shapes. Consider not only the relation of the elements to each other, but their relationship to the page. If the nine shapes lose their identity when overlapped or cropped to fit all nine on the page, you should scale the compound shapes down in size. By contrast, shapes too small to collectively command the space may be scaled up in size, or you can creatively reduce the negative space to accommodate them.

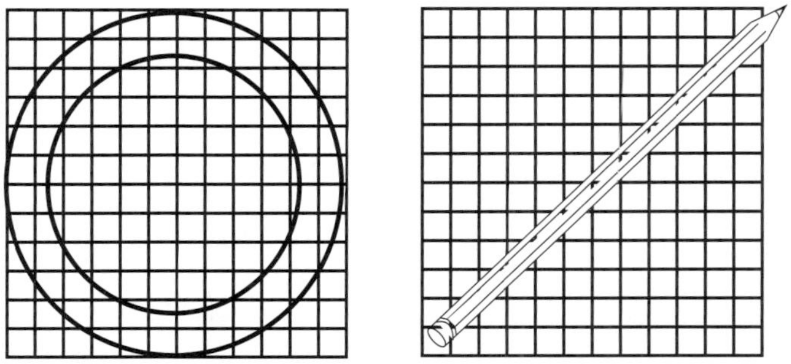

Figure 3.19 Mass

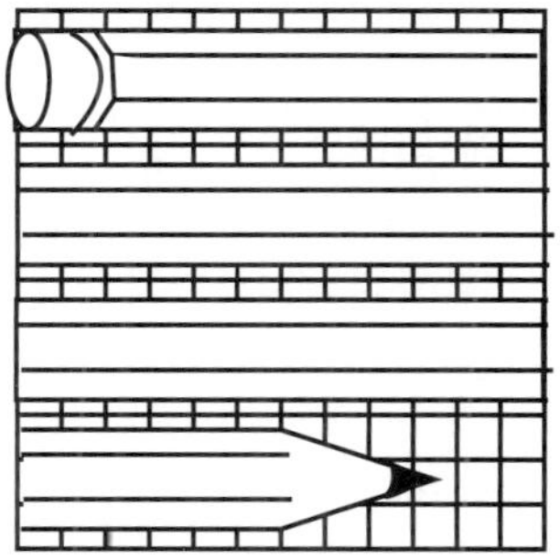

Figure 3.20 Mass

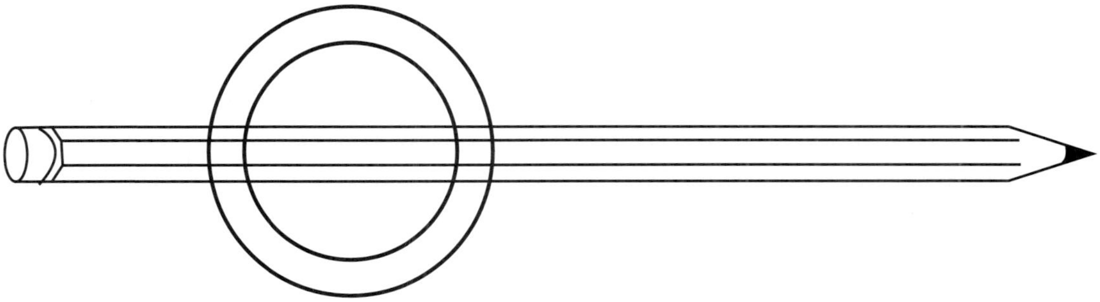

Figure 3.21 Mass

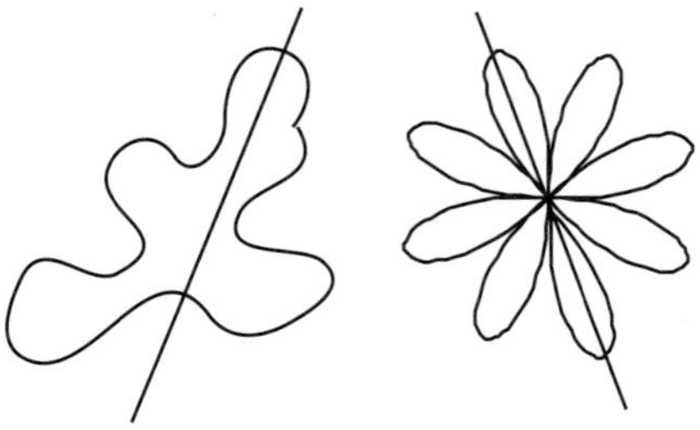

Figure 3.22(a) Organic

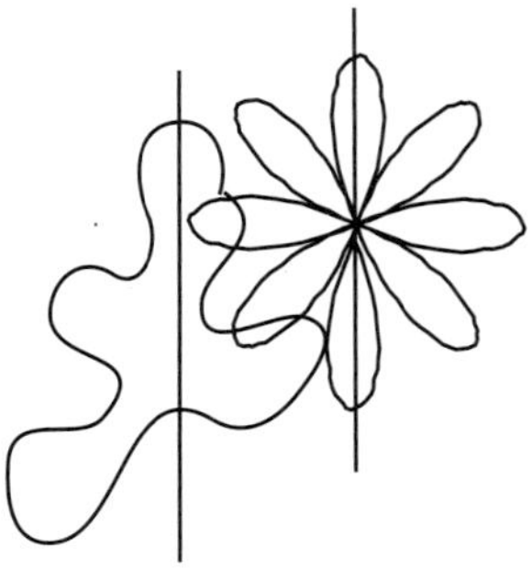

(b) Organic

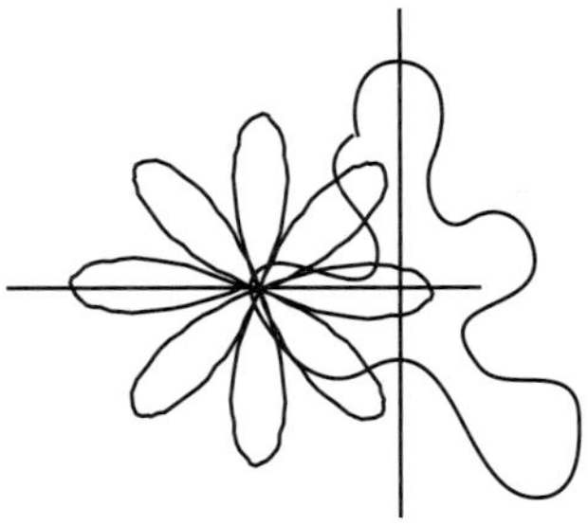

(c)

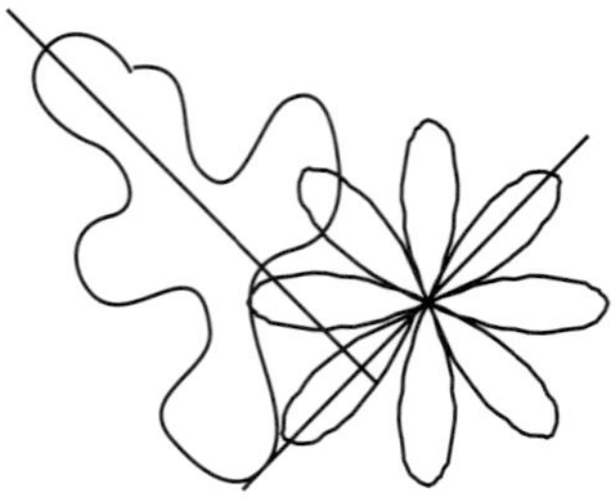

(d)

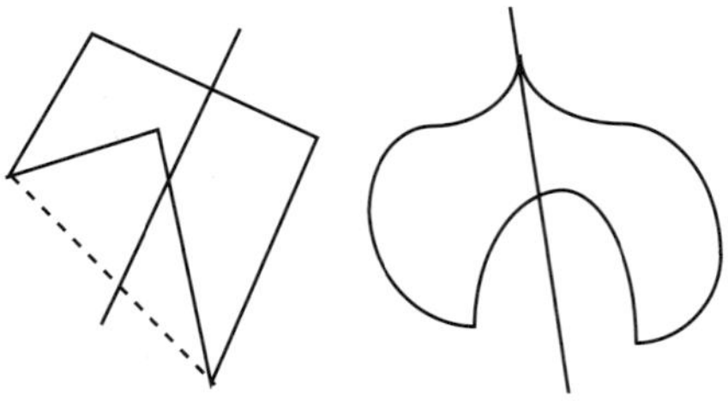

Figure 3.23(a) Inorganic

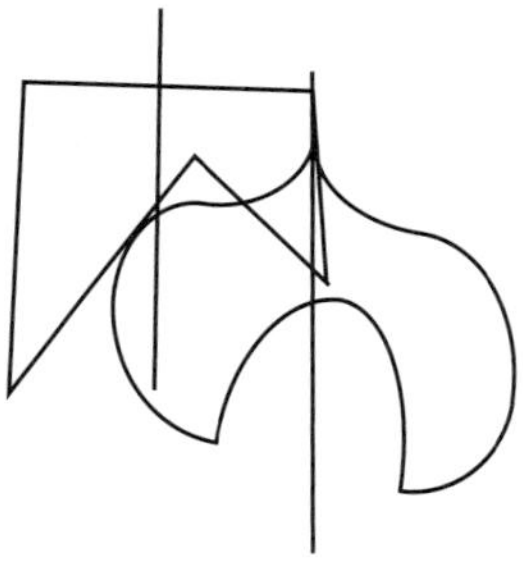

(b)

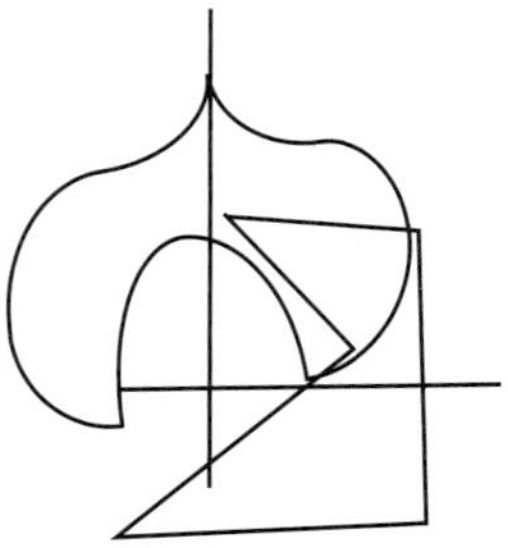

(c)

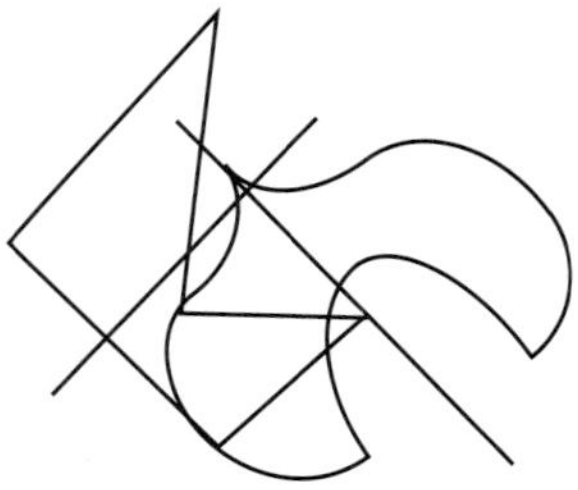

(d)

The structure may be formal, informal, or semi-formal. You can use primary and secondary structures to guide placement. The structure may be visible, invisible, active, or inactive. The structure in this first composition is implied by the corner elements that help form a conceptual border. (Figure 3.25) Selecting the conceptual border and inverting the selection **(Image, Adjust and Invert)** helps to emphasize the structure by making it visible. (Figure 3.26) The grid in this example (Figure 3.27) is made visible by the figure/ground change on alternating blocks, creating a checkerboard. With the visibility comes the recognition that the grid is semi-active, with some elements contained by the frame and others overlapping their boundaries. Secondary and arbitrary structures can also be imposed on the surface to help with the ultimate design. (Figure 3.28)

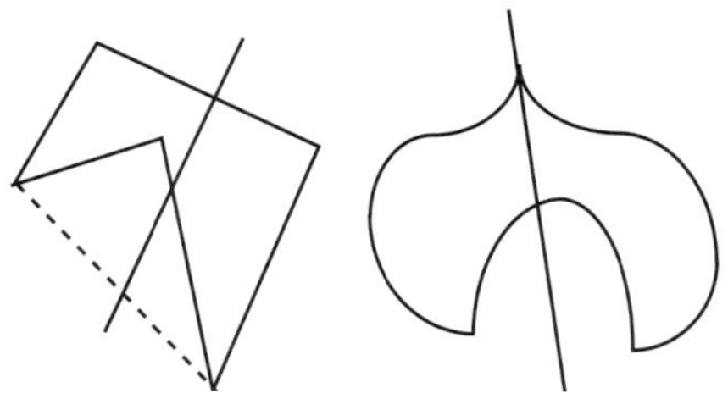

Figure 3.24(a) Combo

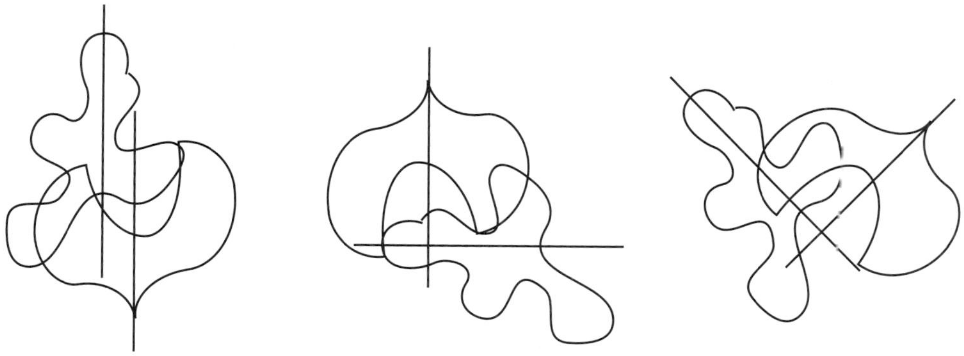

(b) **(c)** **(d)**

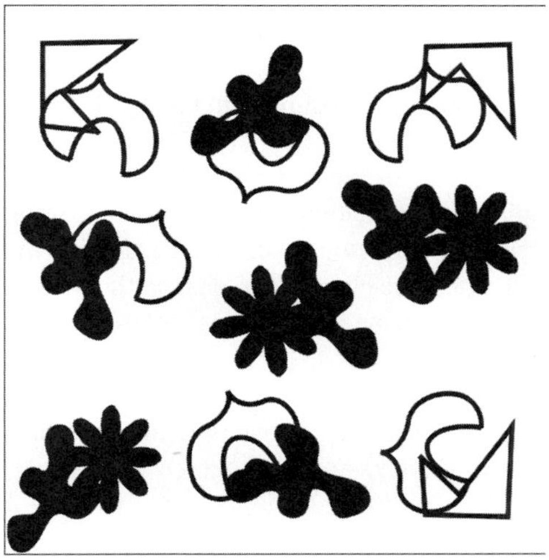

Figure 3.25 Composition

Figure 3.26 Invert

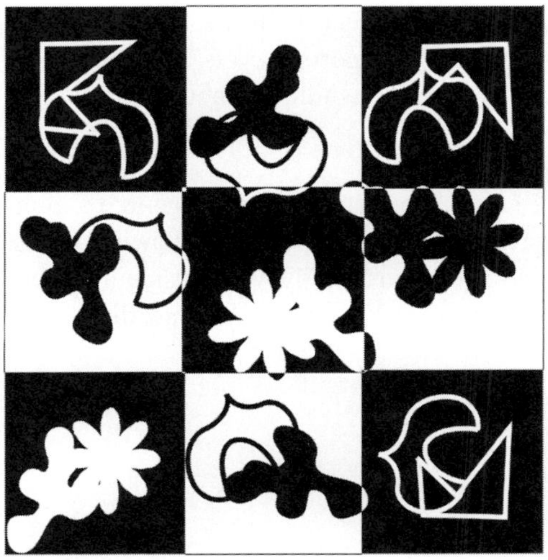

Figure 3.27

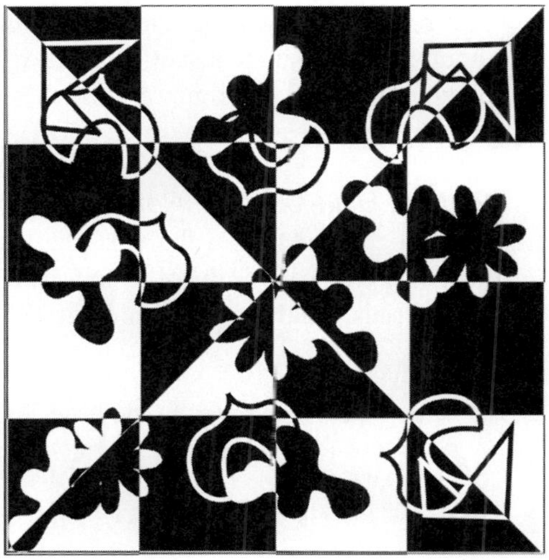

Figure 3.28

A MATTER OF PERCEPTION

Mankind has been using symbols to represent aspects of the environment from the time of our cave-dwelling ancestors. With simple tools and natural materials, the most recent hunt was conveyed through drawings on the cave wall. Cave paintings served to record the experience and provide a way in which early man could communicate and share his history. Though reduced to simple lines and shapes, the figures were recognizable and the narrative of the experience was understood through a set of symbols placed in a particular context.

OBJECTIVES

In this project you will develop a series of 'plates' or pages based on a photographic image. The first goal will be to understand how to effectively simplify an image, creating a visual symbol while retaining recognition and comprehension of the image. Through analysis you will also learn to recognize what is key to that perception, understanding what is essential versus extraneous information. Is context important to perception? Can we reorganize the elements of a composition successfully? Finally, you will examine the fine line between creating an ordered composition and an organization that falls into chaos.

The first plate will be a translation of the photograph from continuous tone to high contrast, creating a graphic representation of the image that can be reduced to shapes of black and white and still communicate effectively. On examination of the high-contrast representation, we will analyze the solution, searching for an understanding of what is necessary for that comprehension to take place. The goal is to identify the smallest denominator that allows closure and therefore perception to take place. For example, if I draw a circle, we recognize that circle. How much of that circle can be removed while still allowing recognition as a circle? (Figure 3.29)

In reverse, what minimum must be removed to prevent closure from taking place and prevent recognition of the image on the part of the viewer?

Another objective is to understand the importance of the context in which elements are placed. Returning to the high-contrast graphic representation, identify the interesting shapes defined in the original context that promote perception of the image. Divide the graphic representation into these shapes and reorganize the elements to change their original context. Using the same group of shapes within the same size frame of reference, create two original designs, one to reflect order and the other chaos.

MATERIALS

Electronic: An appropriate, digital, photographic image; a raster-based software program such as Adobe Photoshop; an output device or printer.

Traditional: An appropriate, photographic image; access to a copier; tracing paper; pencils; illustration board; black ink with brush and technical pen.

PROCEDURE

Select a photographic image to use as a source for this assignment. The image should appear relatively close to the viewer, with clear and specific objects in the negative space. Although this assignment can be done with a close-up of a portrait, you will find that a photograph of an environment, whether interior or exterior, with or without a figure, will be more manageable.

Plate A: High-Contrast Representation To turn a continuous-tone image into a high-contrast representation, the first step is to develop an intricate contour drawing of the image. If the image is in color, convert it to grayscale electronically. When using traditional materials, create a grayscale image with a photocopier. You can either draw directly on

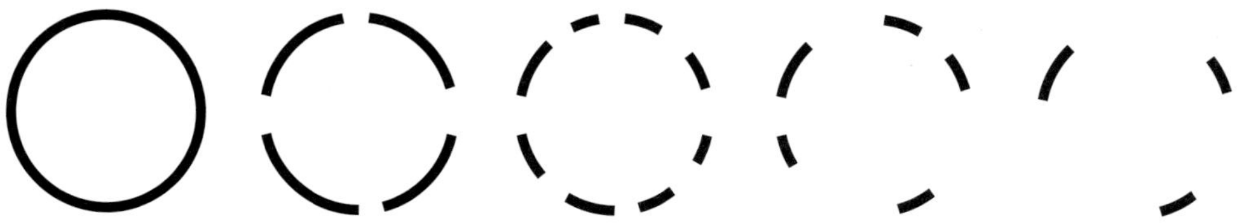

Figure 3.29

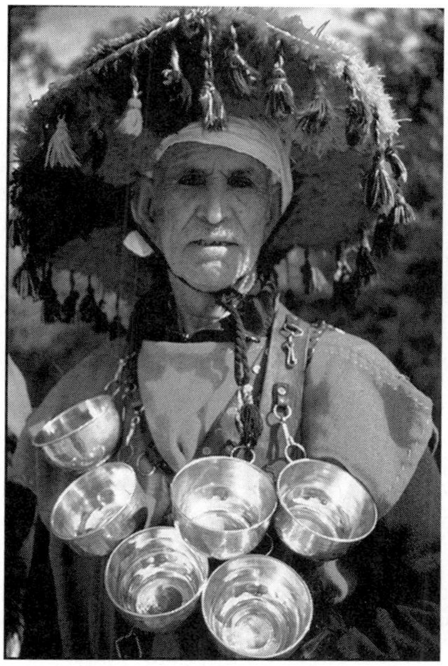

Figure 3.30

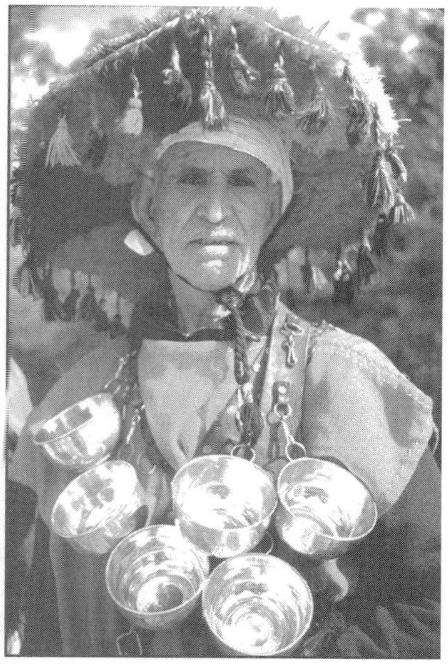

Figure 3.31

the copy, or on a sheet of tracing paper placed on top of the image (see *Landscape Analysis* in Chapter 2 to reference electronic tracing paper). (Figure 3.31)

Using a pencil, either graphite or electronic (or the paintbrush tool with a small brush size), identify and trace around changes in value and differences in texture, making the contour complex. It is easier to have many lines available for use if needed rather than too few. You should always make several copies of the contour study.

Electronic Contour

Open the photographic image in a raster program such as Adobe Photoshop. Pull down the **Image** menu to **Image Size.** Adjust to approximately a 6″ x 8″ image size and **Constrain Proportions.** (When you set either the width or height the other dimension will automatically change accordingly.) **Resample Image.** When this is selected, you can change the image size and select the resolution independently. Use the lowest resolution that will still ensure a continuous tone on your printer. Pull down the **Image** menu to **Mode** and select **Grayscale.** Discard the color information? [YES]. This will also reduce the file size. (RGB=3x image size). **Save As.** Again, pull down **Image** menu to **Adjust the Brightness/ Contrast.** Move the controls to increase the clarity of distinct values in the image until you are happy with the results. **Save As.** If you are working in a raster program, you should now begin the contour on a new layer. Go to the menu **Window** and scroll down to **Show Layer,** selecting **New Layer** (Figure 3.32). When you are finished with the tracing, you can "delete the background" by hiding or turning off the background layer (which is the photographic image). This will give you a clear view of your contour study (Figure 3.33). If Layers are not available, complete the contour with the photographic image present. **Save As, *Contour.*** You can then go to the **Image** menu to **Adjust the Levels,** or use any brightness/contrast controls to visually remove the continuous tone image. **Save.**

Add a Border

Once the image is in contour line with all value removed, you will need to add a border to contain the shapes and complete the edge. Go to the **Tool** menu and select **Marquee tool** or **Edit menu** and **Select All.** You can now go to the **Edit menu,** scrolling down to **Stroke** and then **Dialogue Box.** The following settings will stroke the edge of the marquee with the foreground color. **Save.**

Width [1]pixel

Location [center]

Opacity [100%]

Mode [normal] [OK]

You are now ready to fill the contoured shapes with black. Make sure black is selected as the foreground color. Pull down the **Tool** menu and select **Fill Tool** (spilling paint can). Place the **Fill Tool** in the area to be filled and click. Experiment with filling in the contour lines selectively to reduce the composition to black and white shapes. Gray might appear to exist through the description of textures in the image or by defining fine detail, not through shading. Continue filling shapes until you see the image represented graphically, as a black-and-white composition (Figure 3.34). It is helpful to keep a version of the grayscale open to maintain your perspective of the image. If you are successful, the image will still communicate clearly in this simplified state.

'Auto' Electronic High-Contrast

Re-open the photographic image (see Figure 3.30). Return to the **Image** menu, scrolling down to **Mode** to select **Grayscale.** Next, pull down the **Image** menu to **Adjust the Threshold.** Check the preview to monitor your adjustments. Slide the triangle Δ control to manipulate the contrast. If it loses too much detail when reduced to black and white, return to the continuous tone image (in Grayscale mode). Return again to the **Image** menu to select **Mode,** and **Adjust,** scrolling to **Posterize.** You can set the number of value levels to discern more subtle, yet distinct levels of value. You can then repeat the previous instructions to control the **Threshold** or **Brightness/Contrast.** Move the Δ slide on the brightness and contrast rules to adjust the value. This is a "quick and dirty" solution for those in a hurry, it will not provide either the subtleties or the clearly defined shapes you will need later in the project.

To develop a more sophisticated, "instant" high-contrast solution, try using **Levels** and/or **Curves** found under the **Image** menu for greater control and subtlety of the value range. After manipulating the value, work back into the solution by adding lines for greater refinement. Overfill residual graytones to reduce the image to the extreme black and white of a successful, high-contrast representation. (Figures 3.35(a)(b)(c))

Traditional

Once the blacks are determined in the tracings, transfer to illustration board and complete the plate in ink. (HINT: One way to transfer an image is to turn the tracing over and cover the back with graphite by rubbing the surface with pencil lead. Place the tracing paper on

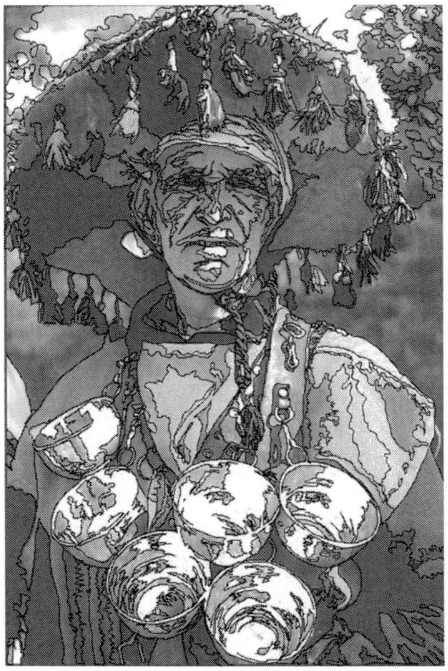

Figure 3.32

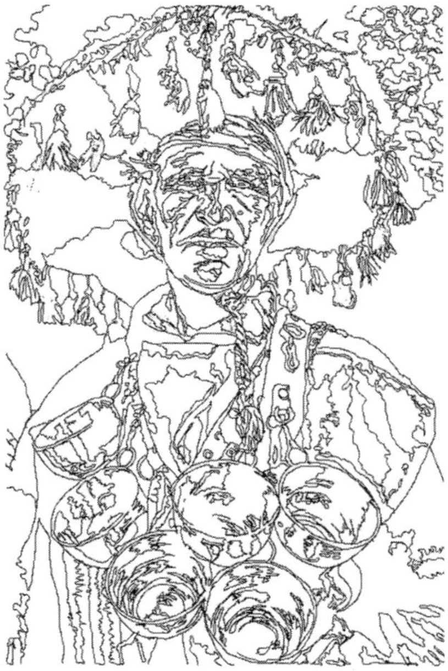

Figure 3.33

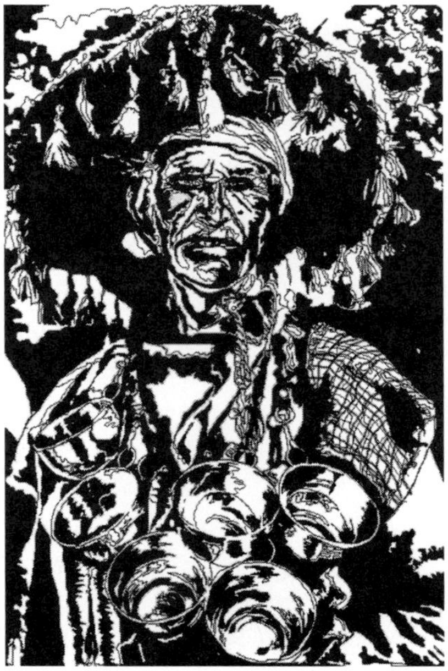

Figure 3.34

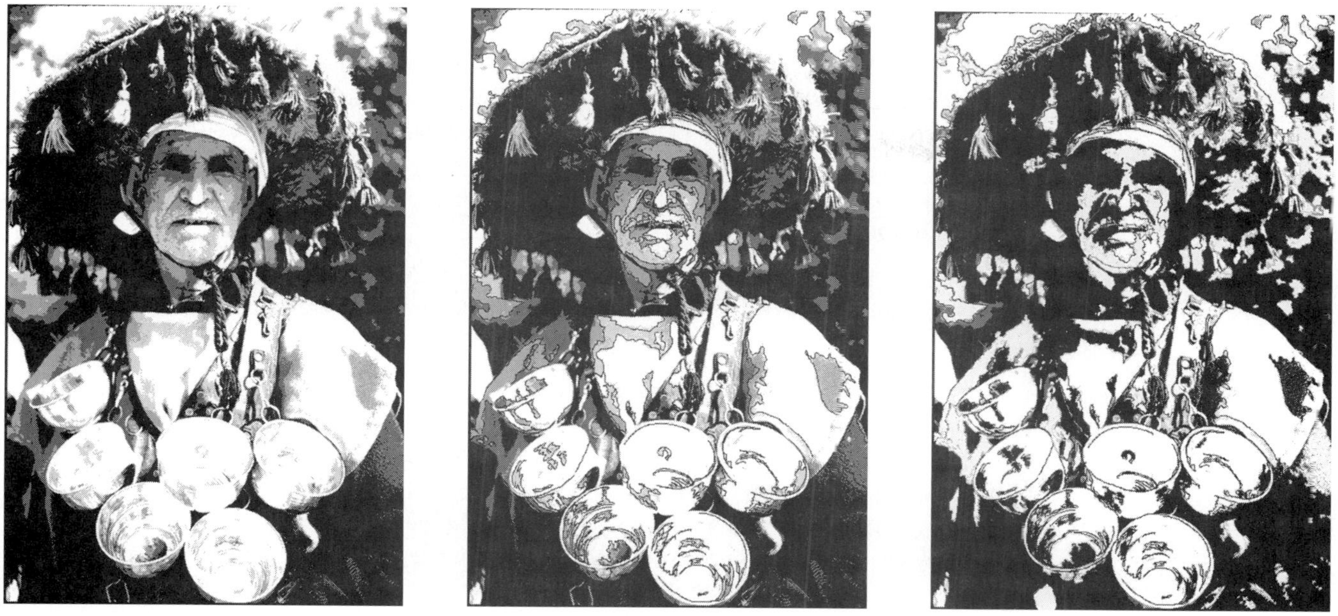

Figure 3.35(a) **(b)** **(c)**

top of the illustration board, right-side up. Draw over your lines and they will be transferred to the board underneath.)

Plate B: Anti-Closure How much information is really necessary for us to communicate visually? A truly elegant visual solution is often quite minimal, as in the previous example of the disappearing circle. As you examine the completed first plate, analyze the visual information to discover what is essential to our recognition of the subject. How little do you need to remove to prevent that recognition, or prevent closure from taking place? You can "erase" either the black or white elements, or parts of elements to complete the assignment.

Our understanding of the human face and form is so intrinsic that it is often a good place to concentrate the alterations that will prevent perception. How much of the face must be filled in before the viewer can no longer focus on what the image is really about? Does it matter that we can see the cups in the foreground if the rest of the image does not make sense? What else in the deconstruction of the image will prevent our putting a figure in perspective? (Figures 3.36(a)(b)(c))

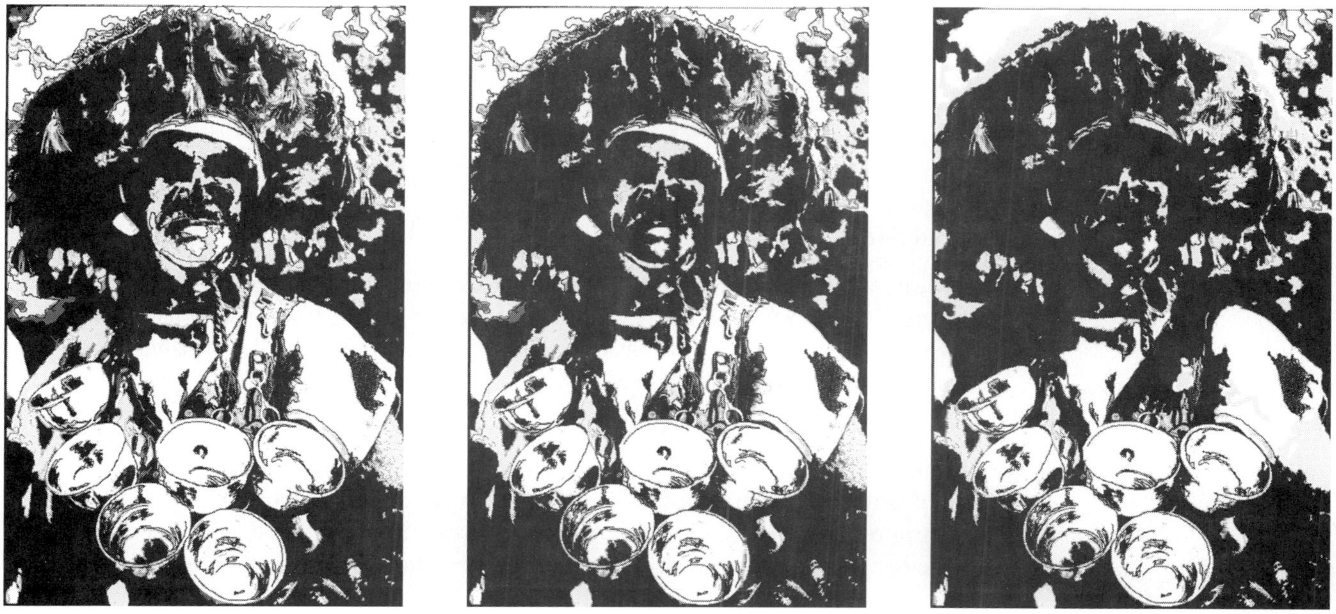

Figure 3.36(a) **(b)** **(c)**

Electronic

Save As, *Anti-Closure.* Go to the **Tool** menu and scroll down to **Eraser** to remove black elements from the image. Use the **Fill** (spilling paint can) to erase an occasional white space by adding black, or **Paintbrush,** with either black or white as the foreground color.

Traditional

Transfer the original contour to a second piece of illustration board. After analyzing Plate A, complete Plate B in ink, with the changes you think will prevent closure.

Plate C: Abstract Composition Another aspect critical to perception is the context in which elements are placed. Just as we need to hear a word used in a sentence to understand the correct meaning, a simplified element can be used to represent many different things. Return to Plate A, the high-contrast representation. Divide the image into the many interesting shapes that exist in the composition. Shapes need not be tied to recognizable objects. They can be black from the positive elements, white from the negative space, or a combination of black and white if what you select can be seen as a defined shape in the high-contrast composition. If you choose, you can fill in shapes to make them all black or outlined in white to improve your final composition. You should not be arbitrary in your selections or randomly cut through shapes or cut apart shapes. Once you have all of your shapes defined, organize them successfully in a new context on a fresh page that has the same dimensions as the first two plates.

Electronic

Re-open Plate A and **Save As,** *Abstract Composition.* Pull down the **Window** menu to **Show Layers.** When you open the **Layers** box, the high-contrast image will be on the background layer, which is often locked. Scroll down and select **Duplicate Layer.** This will give you the same image, but allow you to select actual pixel data. You can use the **Lasso** under the **Tool** menu or any of the selection tools you are comfortable with to "cut-out" and isolate interesting shapes. When you select a shape and the selection is active, make sure you are in the correct layer, in this case the copy of the background. While a shape is selected, copy or cut the shape. Return to the layer menu and scroll to **New Layer,** then paste the selection. To ensure that you have done this correctly, turn off the image layers to see the shape on a white page. Repeat this procedure until you have captured all of the interesting shapes you discover in the original composition. With each shape on a different layer, you can go to the **Edit** menu and scroll down to **Transform** to rotate the shape and use the **Move Tool** to change the placement, creating an interesting and dynamic composition. Remember to **Save As** this page when you are finished, as *Abstract Composition.* (Figure 3.37)

Traditional

Clearly, you should not physically cut apart your completed Plate A. You can either make several copies to work with, or continue to use the tracing paper technique, transferring your shape choices to a new piece of illustration board. As with the previous plates, this study should be completed in ink.

Plate D: Chaos When we create a composition, are we giving order to a page? At what point is the composition no longer ordered, but out of control, chaotic? When do we lose control of our composition? Is it possible to create chaos within the confines of a page? Whether you choose to work electronically or traditionally, use the shapes already created and repeat the steps you went through to complete Plate C, as you attempt to answer the chaos question. **Save As,** *Chaos.* (Figure 3.38)

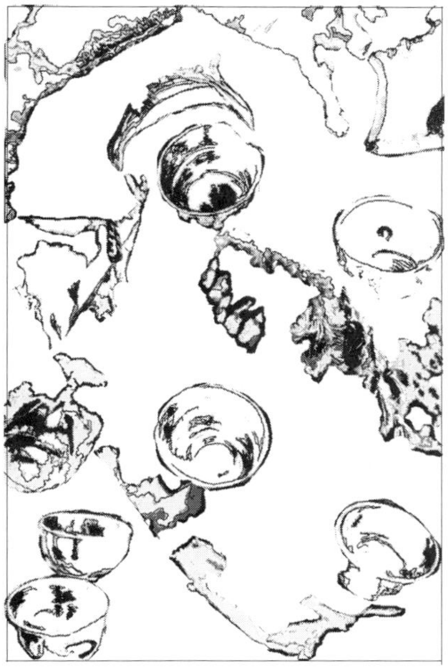

Figure 3.37

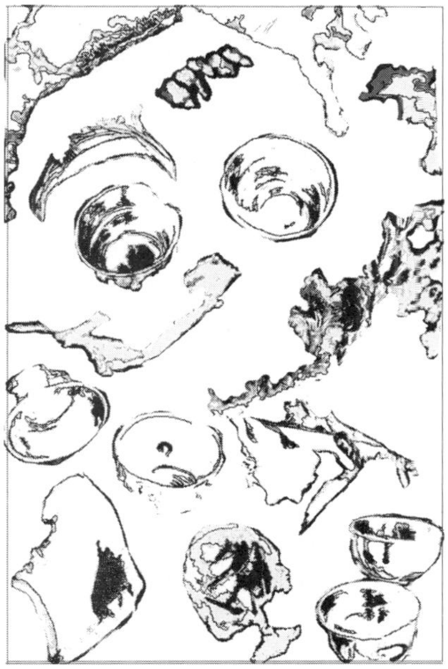

Figure 3.38

TRADITIONAL STUDENT EXAMPLE
Artwork by James Perkins

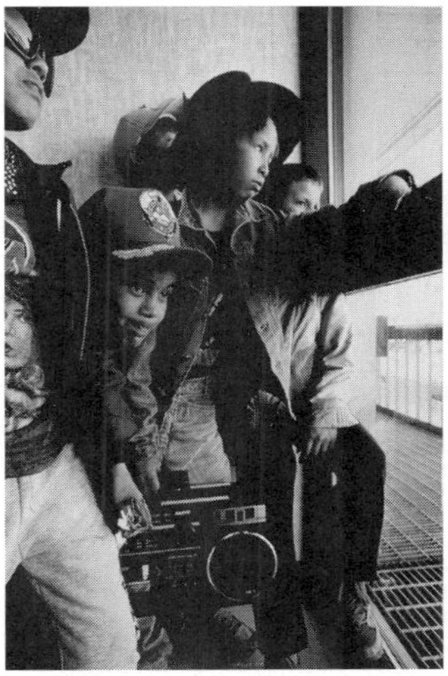

Figure 3.39(a)
The Continuous Tone Image

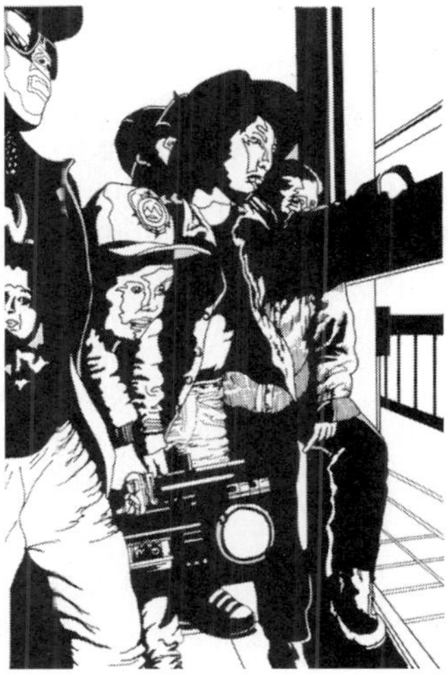

(b)
High-Contrast Representation

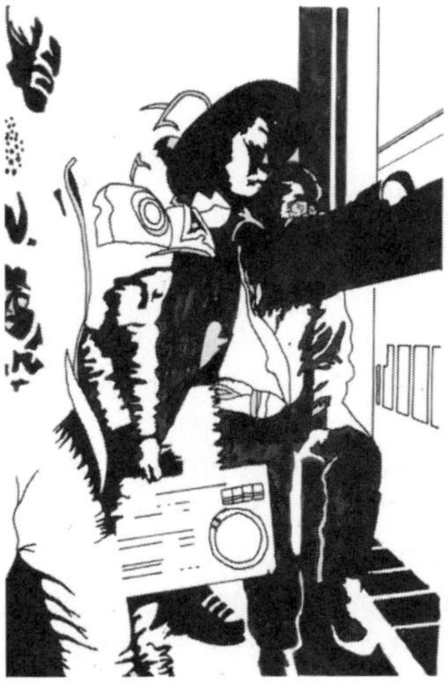

(c) Anti-Closure

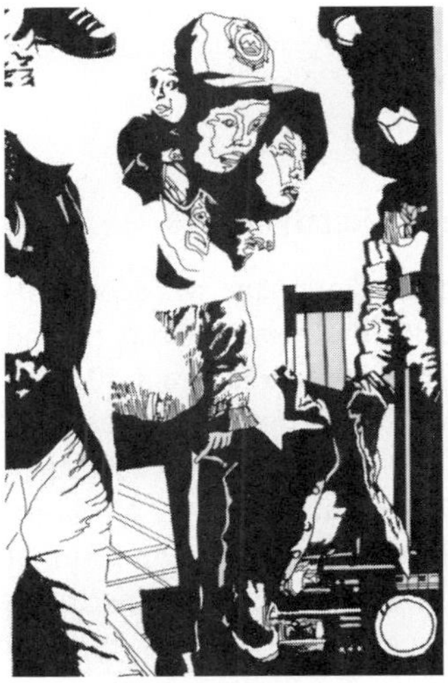

(d) Abstract Composition

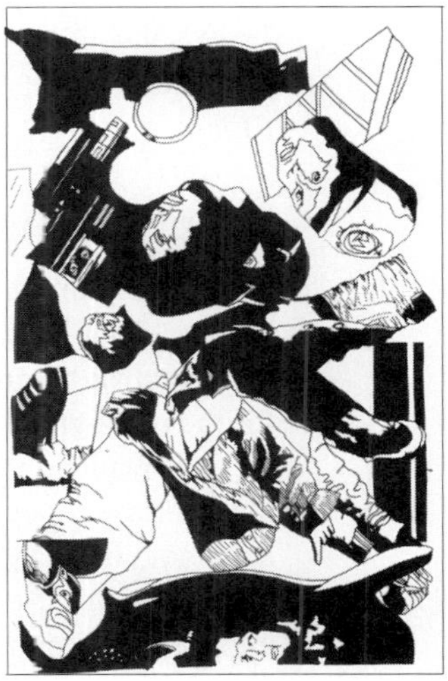

(e) Chaos

GESTALT

Some of the ***shapes*** and ***forms*** that we use in two-dimensional design have a sense of visual identity that is recognizable. These forms conjure conceptual, psychological, and visual associations that allow us to identify them by name. The study of this perceptual process began in the early 1900s. Psychologists working in Germany began to explore the organizational strategies utilized by the eye to interact with form. They found the senses to be intelligent and able to organize information before it is actually processed by the brain. Psychologists also studied and documented the profound impact that culture, education, and learning environments have on the perception of visual elements. These explorations were categorized under the term ***Gestalt,*** roughly translated to mean "form" or "thing." Their findings encompassed ideas of configuration, structure, and wholeness.

Additionally, Gestalt psychologists established the importance of *context* in the determination of visual perception—that is, within any given field of reference, forms interact and the interaction alters our comprehension. Gestalt theories established our predisposition to view images as complete entities rather than the sum of individual parts. Our understanding of figure and ground and pattern emerges from larger contextual relationships we see. Isomorphic correspondence, which is the perception of symbolic form, emerges from the context of education and experience. Other contextual issues of viewing distance, scale, orientation, and relative contrast also serve to alter and transform our visual understanding.

The following project involves the creation of a series of designs that explore the impact of recognizable, gestalt images on a composition through the use of ***shape integration*** and ***cropping.***

FIGURE AND GROUND: THE MANIFESTATIONS OF GESTALT

The use of gestalt forms can facilitate the creation of images that are both visually and conceptually intriguing. As with all elements, their ultimate impact depends on their interrelationships and compositional context. By altering gestalt shapes through ***orientation, overlapping, cropping,*** and ***deletion,*** one can also redefine the identity of the original image. Within the whole composition, activity and balance may be manipulated through the use of these redefined forms.

OBJECTIVES

We will explore the nature of gestalt forms and the limits of their manipulation. In addition, students will explore the relationship of ***positive*** and ***negative space,*** the processes of overlapping, cropping, and deletion, and the dynamics of ***grouping principles*** within a design. These designs will be created using a raster-based program or traditional collage techniques.

MATERIALS

Electronic: Digital camera; a computer; a raster program such as Adobe Photoshop; laser printer; mounting board; rubber cement; pen or utility knife

Traditional: Photographs; tracing paper; black paper; graphite pencils; x-acto knife, scissors and bristol board

PROCEDURE

Electronic

Experimenting with Shape Relationships

Create a digital photograph of an image whose identity is apparent from its contour or silhouette. This form must be whole and uncropped and may be a figure, animal, or object that is active in terms of its contour (Figure 3.40). Place your form on a light background for the photograph, so that the contour may be easily read.

Download the image onto a computer and **Open** it up into the raster program. Alter the contrast if necessary to create a strong, black, graphic form on a white ground. You need not eliminate all of the value within the form, but you should have a relatively low-contrast image. **Select** your form, **Copy** and **Paste** to create ten separate examples of shape integration. This process creates new forms by combining two or more of the original

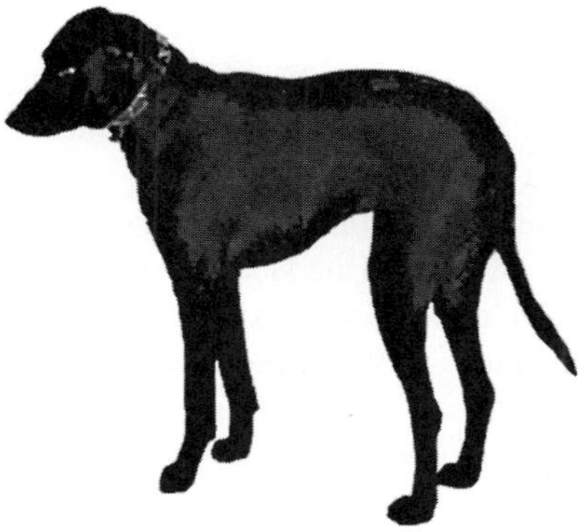

Figure 3.40

shapes. As you work, consider that your shapes may relate in any number of ways; **detachment, abutting, overlapping, intersection, union, subtraction, penetration,** or **interlocking.** These forms may appear as solid black shapes or as white shapes with black contour lines. Shapes may also appear to be solid or transparent. One shape may be used to crop another, leaving only part of the original form remaining. In addition to the **Copy** and **Paste** functions, you may change the image by rotating and/or flipping it, using **Transform** options. Filters that find contours can create white shapes with black outlines. Any residual gray within the white forms can be removed with the **Eraser** or **Pencil Tool.** (See Figure 3.41)

The composite shapes that you are creating may retain their identity or create new shapes whose identity is strongly differentiated from the originals. You will need to create at least three samples in which the sense of gestalt is retained within the composite shapes.

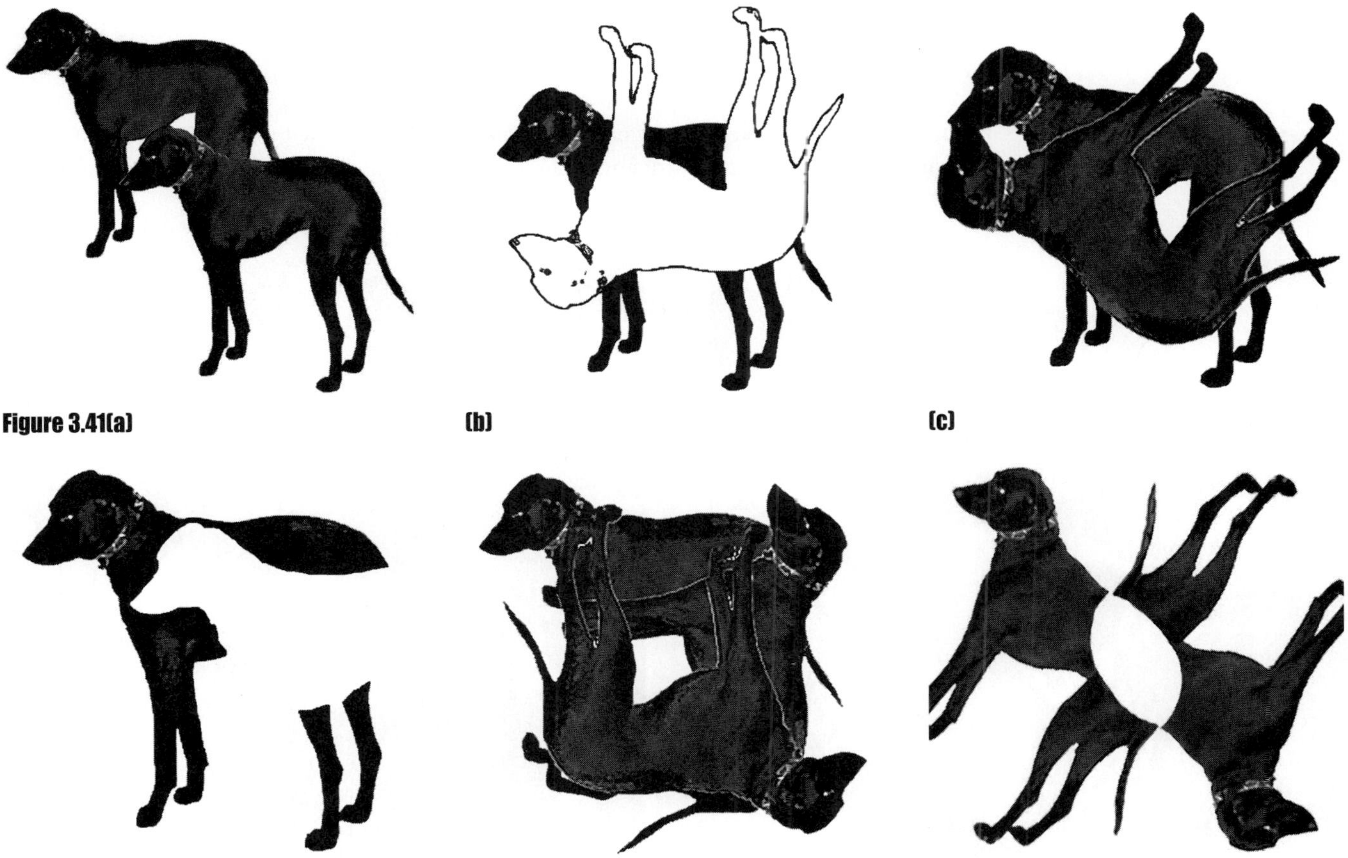

Figure 3.41(a) **(b)** **(c)**

(d) **(e)** **(f)**

The First Design: Exploiting the Gestalt

Using your ten (or more) composite shapes as a reference, choose those in which the identity and sense of gestalt is retained. The total number of shapes used is optional. The **Canvas Size** (the format size) is 8″ x 8″.

As you are developing the ***composition,*** shapes must interact with the format and may be cropped by it. Composite shapes may relate in the same ways that your original shapes related, and all of your composite shapes may be flipped, rotated, or altered in scale. Consider that the amount of ***positive and negative space*** within the design and along the edges of the format can greatly affect the reading of both shapes and spaces within the design. As with any visual image, grouping principles and ***balance*** are the primary means of achieving ***unity*** within this composition. The final design should use a variety of dynamic shapes that relate, together creating strong positive and negative spaces within a balanced composition (Figure 3.42). Once your design is completed, **Print** out your solution.

The Second Design: Losing the Gestalt

Utilizing your ten (or more) composite shapes as references, choose those in which the identity and sense of gestalt is lost or masked through their integration. You will need to have at least three possible combinations from your original ten composites for this design. The total number of shapes used is optional. The **Canvas Size** (the format size) will be 8″ x 8″. The same compositional issues considered in the first design should be used in the creation of this design.

Although many of the shapes within this design will not have a sense of recognizable identity, the design as a whole may allow for the creation of identity through the use of ***interval*** and the orientation of non-gestalt forms. These new "gestalts" may be created by increasing the ***proximity*** of shapes or abutting them, and by focusing on the shapes of the negative space that may be created by this new alignment. The final design should use a variety of dynamic shapes that relate in order to create strong positive and negative spaces within a balanced composition (Figure 3.43). Once your design is completed, **Print** out your solution.

Traditional This project may be done as a ***collage*** problem without the computer. Gestalt shapes may be attained by tracing images found in preexisting photographs. Overlapping

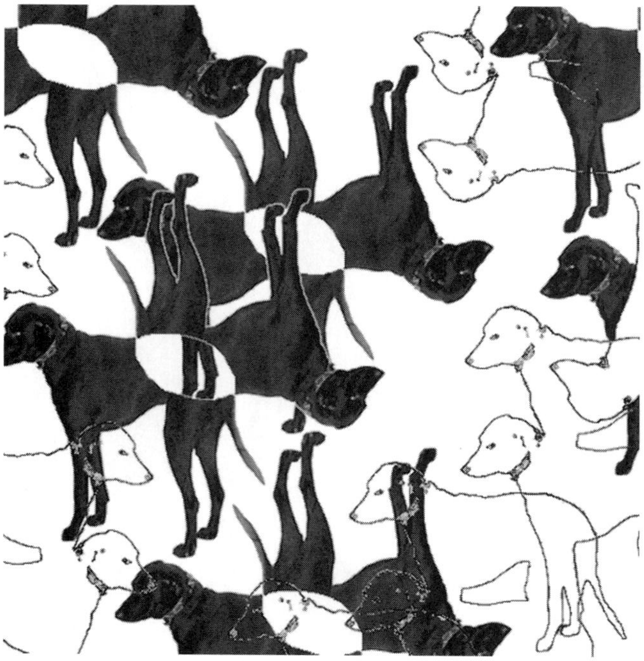

Figure 3.42

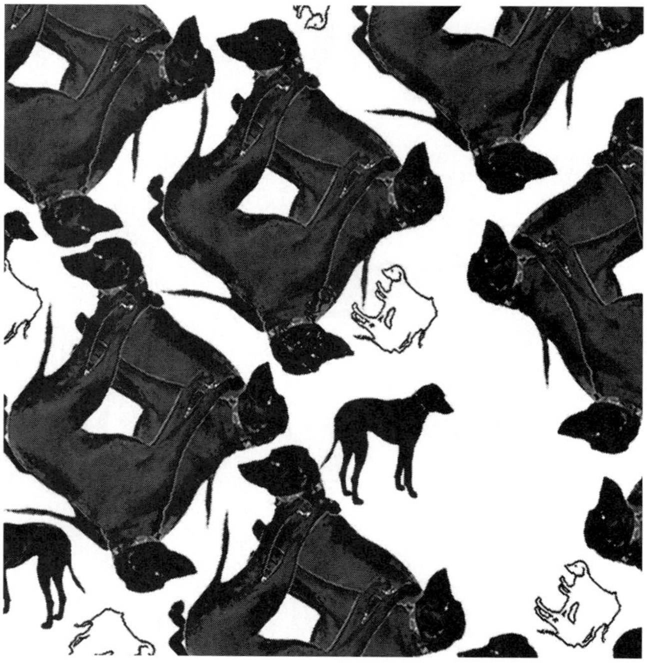

Figure 3.43

the original tracings and creating new tracings of the resulting shape relationships then creates composite shapes. These composite shapes may then be transferred directly to black match paper by a graphite transfer method, cut out, and utilized as collage elements. The same conceptual, formal, and technical parameters apply to the problem.

PRESENTATION

Cut out your designs and mount them on Bristol board with appropriate borders. If you are using rubber cement, be aware that any excess that moves onto the surface of the computer print will take ink with it as it is removed. The scan of the original shape and the ten composite shape examples should be included in the final presentation.

DISCUSSION

The composite shapes and designs generated for this project often reveal the strong subjective connections that individuals have to certain visual forms. The abstraction of three-dimensional form to two-dimensional shape in the form of a silhouette can present an interesting perceptual challenge that can profoundly affect the success of the completed designs. Critique should include a discussion of the effect that orientation plays in the legibility and power of gestalt forms within compositions, the effects of cropping to modify or destroy the power of a gestalt, and the effect of scale reduction on the impact of these forms within the overall design. Other issues that may emerge within the dialogue include the presence of gestalts within gestalts that retain their power even when cropped from the whole (heads, hands, and feet are examples) and the use of closure to create gestalts from nonobjective shapes that are aligned in particular configurations.

LETTERFORMS, NUMBERS, AND SYMBOLS

During the Modernist era, designers developed new forms of ***typography***. The development of "Stencil" type by Joseph Albers at the Bauhaus (Figure 3.44) is a good example of this as is Bauhaus type (Figure 3.45).

During this period, simple geometry was used to create a dynamic type and background juxtaposition. Eventually corporate firms used these graphic type designers to create logos and symbols. This new period of corporate "mark making" was a return to the ancestral concepts of ***pictographs*** and ***ideograms*** (Figure 3.46 and Figure 3.47).

With the advent of computers, digital ***type*** has replaced conventional typesetting. While some forms of digital type push typography to the limits of legibility, others maintain the beauty of traditional letterforms.

The shape and meaning of traditional letterforms has become significant subject matter for artists. For example, Kurt Schwitters used letterforms as collage elements, while Paul Klee played with letterforms and symbols as shapes delicately balanced within a composition as seen in a variation of his work (Figure 3.48).

Innovative forms of type emerged during different design movements. High-contrast letterforms were used by the Dadaists to create attention and communicate a message. Curvilinear, natural forms created a distinctive type style employed during the Art Nouveau period. In contrast, Art Deco designer A.M.Cassandre used a barely legible typeface called Bifur, which used simple geometric letterforms that replaced portions of letters in shaded silhouette (Figure 3.49). This stylistic trait required the viewer to complete the typeface by means of closure.

STENCIL

Figure 3.44
Stencil Style

Bauhaus

Figure 3.45
Bauhaus Style

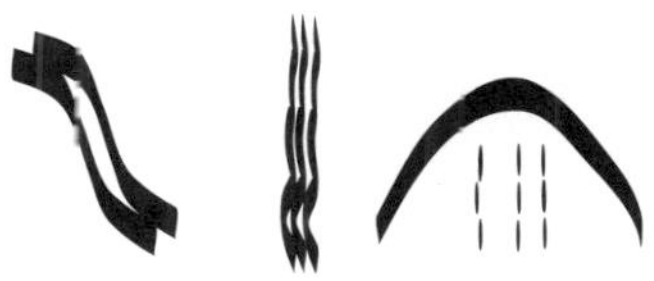

Figure 3.46 Water and rain

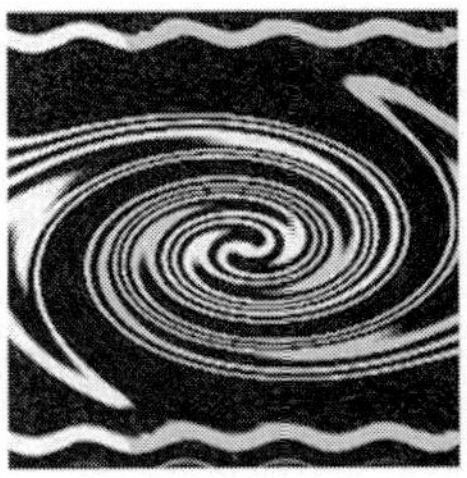

Figure 3.47 Logo

Contemporary letterforms have evolved from the original marks and drawings of our ancestors. Some cultures use language symbols that have pictographic forms of representation, such as Egyptian hieroglyphics (Figure 3.50 and Figure 3.51).

In conclusion, letters, like signs, are forever etched in our memory, yet they can be altered to create unusual forms and shapes that still convey meaning.

OBJECTIVES

This project involves the use of letterforms, signs, and symbols as basic shapes to explore structure, gestalt, and figure-ground reversal. The recognition of a letter is linked to the shapes of its negative spaces. The morphology of letters is revealed through the correct proportion of "black and white" between figure and ground. Letters can be altered to a new form without completely nullifying their legibility by applying *gestalt* principles. The overall goal is to create a four-part unified composition that has balance, harmony, simplicity, and complexity.

MATERIALS

Electronic: A vector-based program such as Adobe Illustrator; printer

Traditional: Gouache; pencil; ruler; brush; illustration board

PROCEDURE

Electronic Open a vector program and use **Grids** and **Rulers** to create four square boxes. Arrange all four boxes in a square configuration with a 1″ space between each module (Figure 3.52). Use the **Type Tool** to create letter and number forms. Fill each box with invented letterforms, numbers, and symbols that maintain consistency in terms of style. To create your own drawn symbol, use the **Pen Tool** and draw your symbols. Manipulate, distort, change the scale, and invert the invented letterforms, numbers, and symbols (Figure 3.53). The quantity of elements can be varied so that boxes change from simple to complex while maintaining figure–ground reversal. Consider the use of compositional structures that are referenced by the letterforms you are using. Take these elements to the edge of legibility while maintaining similar shape relationships to achieve unity (Figure 3.54 and Figure 3.55).

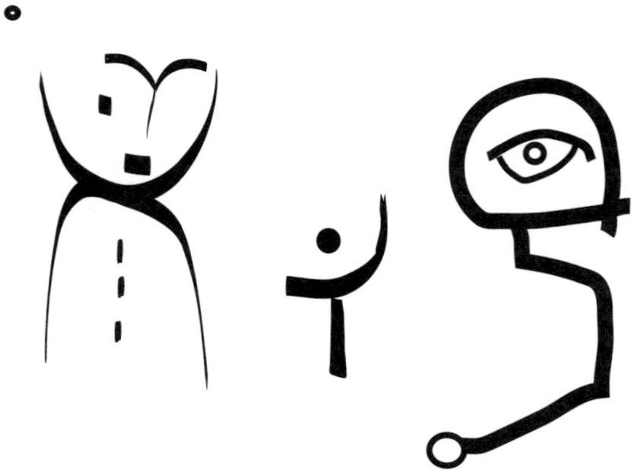

Figure 3.48 Paul Klee drawing variation

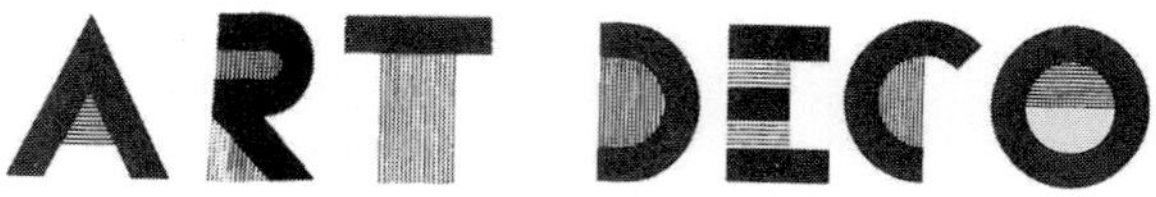

Figure 3.49 Art Deco Style

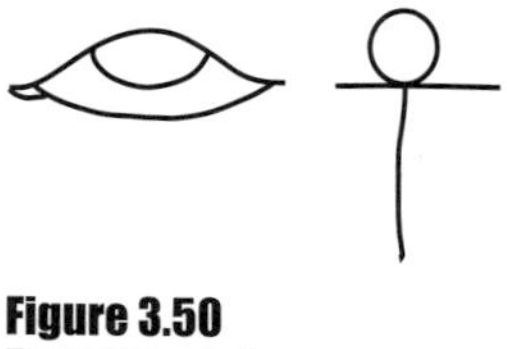

Figure 3.50 Egyptian pictograms

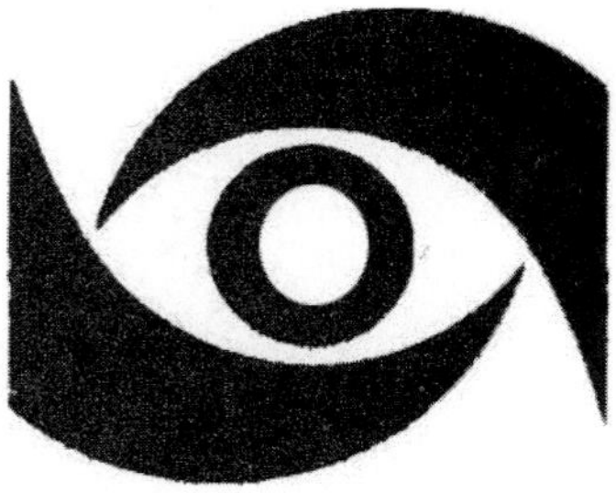

Figure 3.51 Logo

Traditional Sketch preliminary layouts in a sketchbook and draw the final design freehand with pencil on illustration board. Carefully consider the same conceptual and formal parameters for this project as stated in the objectives and electronic procedure. Paint the drawn letterforms, numbers, and symbols using black, white and gray gouache. (Figure 3.56 and Figure 3.57)

ALTERNATIVES AND VARIATIONS

Create a letterform collage. In the paint and draw layer of a computer program create a variety of letter and number forms. You may also utilize pattern backgrounds and gradients. Print out positive and negative images for collage material. Take the letterforms and combine them with found materials and create a balanced relational composition. (Figure 3.58)

DISCUSSION

How is there consistency in typeface from one square to another? How effective is the overall movement and figure–ground reversal? Comment on rhythmical repeats, scale, structure, and simplicity to complexity of the solutions. What grouping principles are utilized to achieve unity? How does the design and meaning of the letterforms, numbers, and/or symbols impact the overall composition? How does graphic or historical style of type impact the overall design?

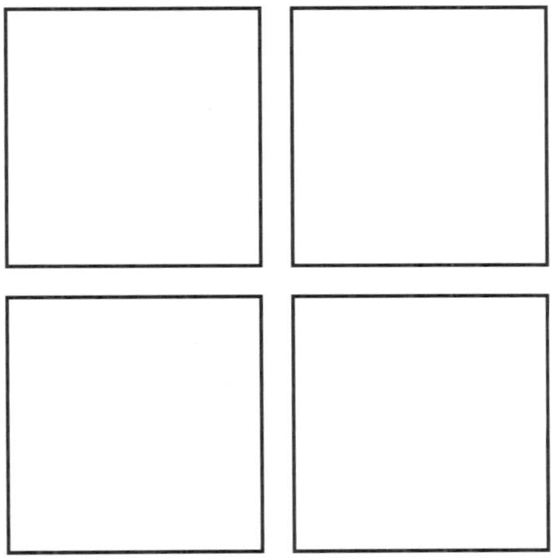

Figure 3.52 Four-part grid

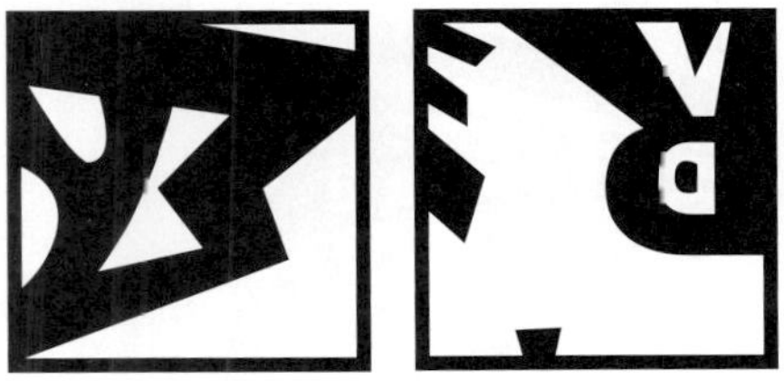

Figure 3.53(a) (b)
Images by Michelle Chasse

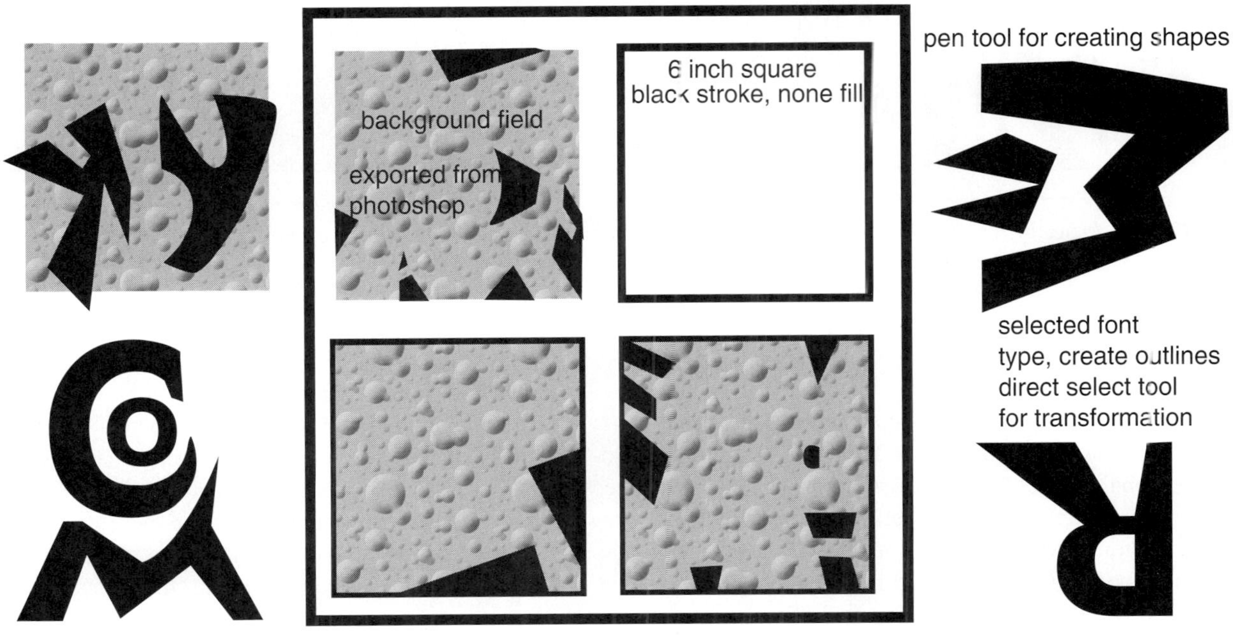

Figure 3.54 *Images by Michelle Chasse*

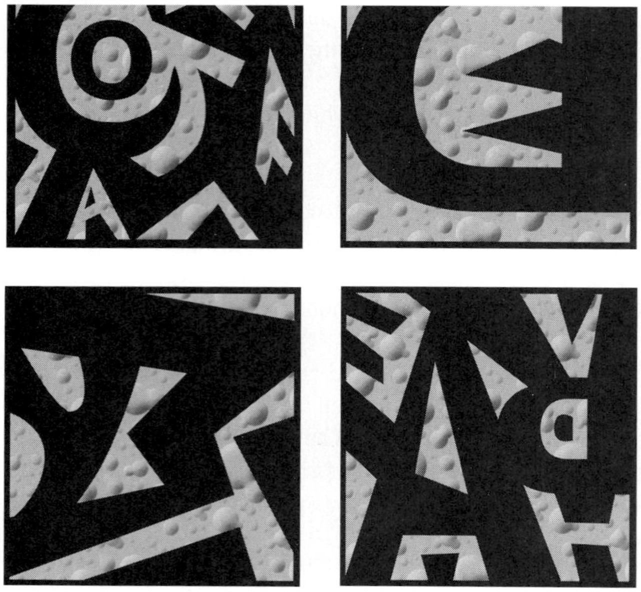

Figure 3.55 *Images by Michelle Chasse*

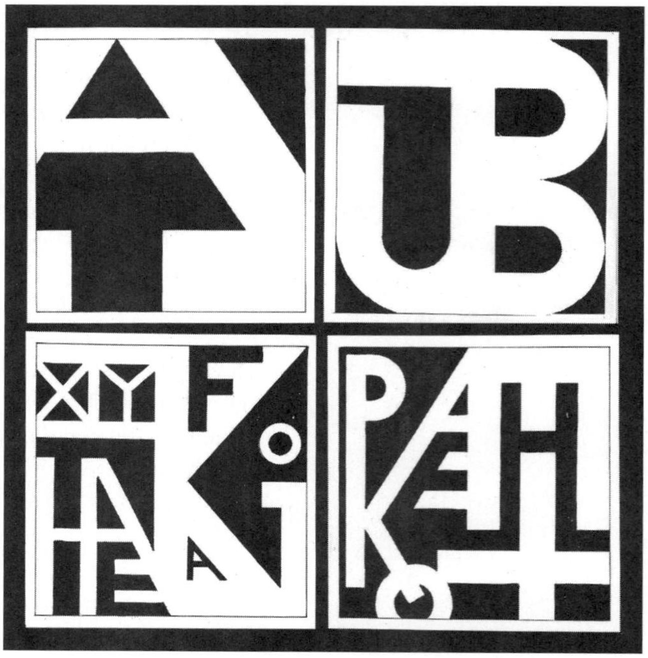

Figure 3.56 *Image by Steven Wetherby*

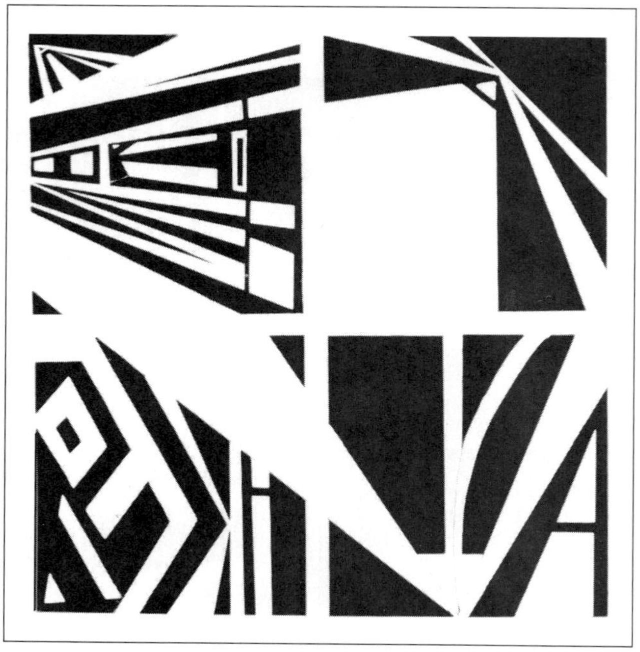

Figure 3.57 *Image by Eric Scafetta*

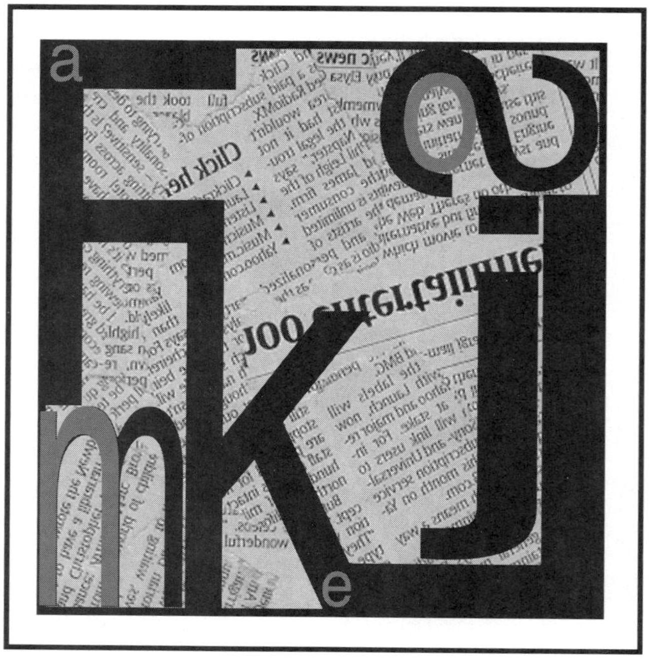

Figure 3.58 *Image by Nicole Cornett*

BALANCE

Balance is a design ***principle*** concerned with the equating of visual forces, emphasis, or happenings within a two-dimensional image. Our understanding of pictorial balance almost always refers to the equating of forces across a bilateral division of the picture plane. Within a unified image, balance is often intuitively perceived. Analytically it may be achieved in a variety of ways (Figure 3.59).

Symmetry refers to the exact reflection of elements across a central, most-often vertical, axis (Figure 3.60). The organizational strategies involved in achieving symmetrical balance are more objective and easily achieved. Textiles and artifacts of many traditional cultures have utilized symmetrical balance as a means of diminishing the impact of personal decision making and therein the hand of the artist on the work, allowing the spiritual and ritualistic intent to dominate. In general, we as humans tend to find

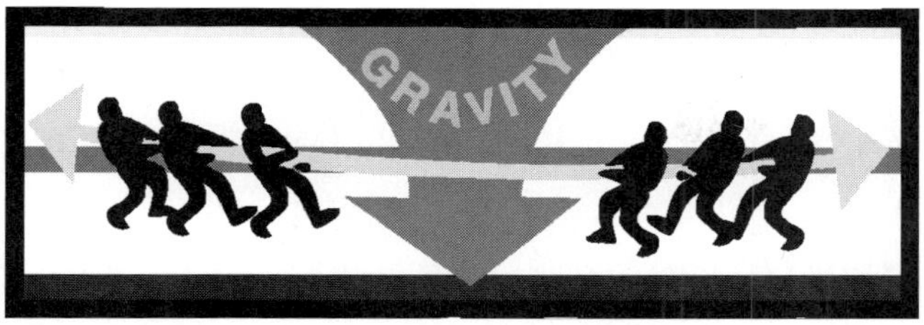

Figure 3.59

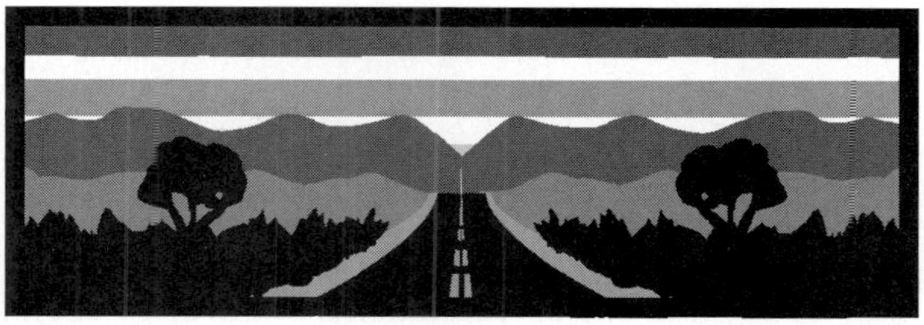

Figure 3.60

symmetry profoundly compelling because of the bilateral symmetry of our own bodies. The exact equating of forms and actions imbues symmetrical compositions with an overall sense of stability and calm.

Derivations of traditional bilateral symmetry establish different types of movement within rigidly balanced images. ***Translational symmetry*** utilizes the same modules repeated along a specific directional path (Figure 3.61). ***Patterns*** that adorn elongated borders such as the edges of awnings are an example. ***Radial symmetry*** utilizes the same visual ***elements*** mirrored or repeated around a central point (Figure 3.62).

Elements that are arranged to create equal emphasis over an entire format can result in the creation of ***crystallographic balance*** (Figure 3.63).

Similar arrangements where elements are equally distributed but result in compositions that lack contrast or emphasis result in the creation of ***neutral balance*** (Figure 3.64). Some ***compositions*** retain a strong sense of symmetry without adhering to bilateral equivalence. These designs are balanced with ***approximate*** or ***implied symmetry,*** using slight visual differences between areas of the composition that may not be immediately or initially perceived (Figure 3.65). Approximate symmetry serves to elevate the level of activity within an otherwise stable organization.

Many of the images that we are exposed to on a daily basis are organized to achieve balance in a way that does not involve the exact repetition of forms. These two-dimensional images are balanced ***asymmetrically,*** utilizing dissimilar forms or elements that have similar visual weight or eye attraction (Figure 3.66). Color, high-contrast, visual texture, and complex shape are examples of elements that hold stronger visual attraction. Because of their emphasis within an image they may be used in smaller proportions to their related opposites of modulated value, low contrast, smooth surface, and simple shape.

The most frequently used method of achieving asymmetrical balance is through the presence of equal amounts of weight on both sides of the composition. One large circle can be balanced by a number of smaller circles because their visual weights are equivalent. Balance may also be achieved between elements of differing weights by adjusting their positions within the composition. A large element can achieve balance in a composition with a much smaller element if the larger shape is moved toward the center or fulcrum of the

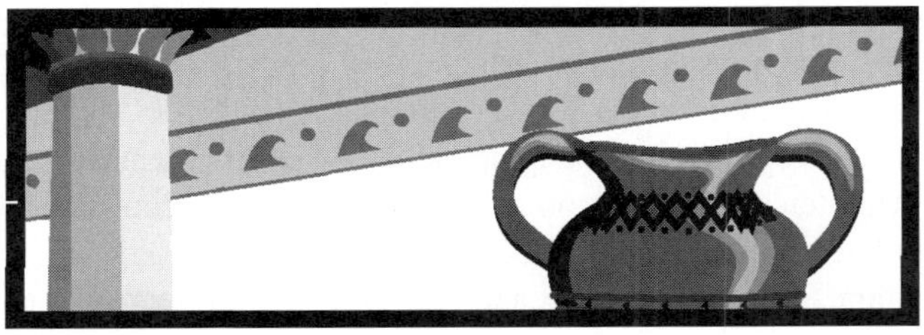

Figure 3.61

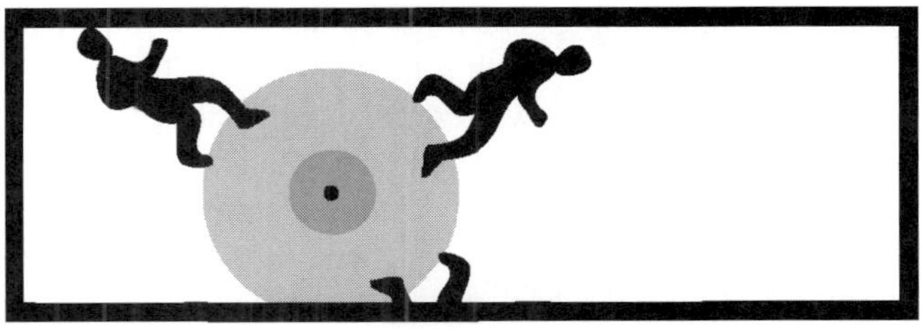

Figure 3.62

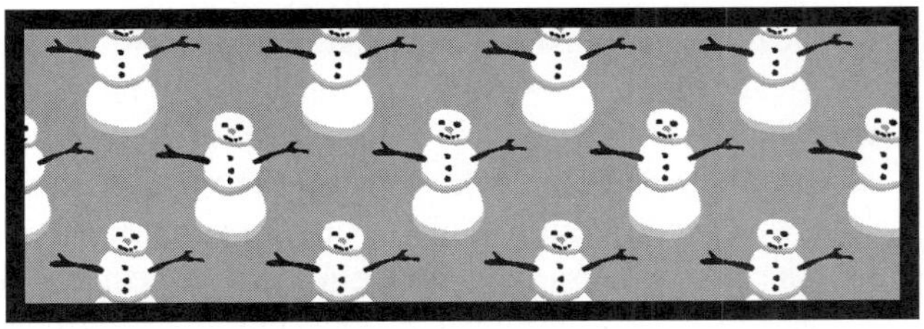

Figure 3.63

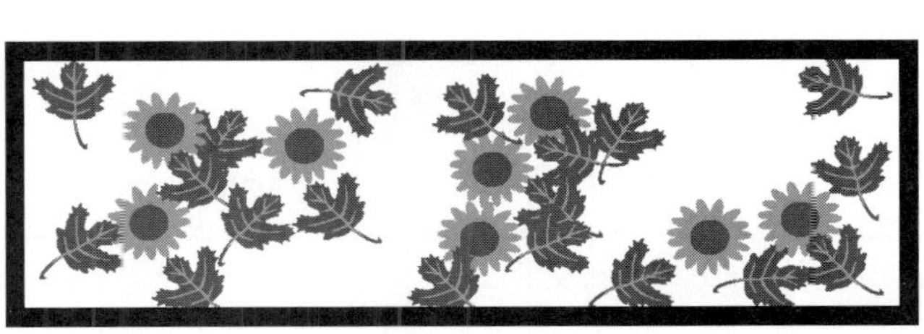

Figure 3.64

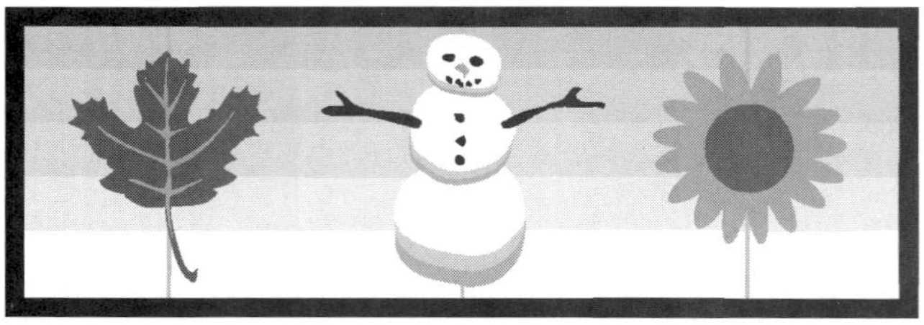

Figure 3.65

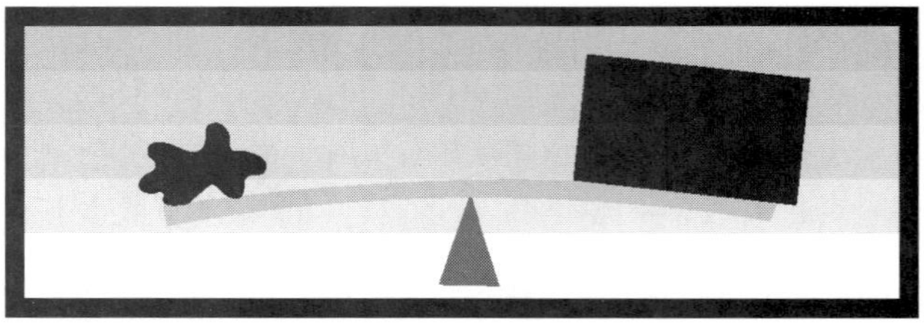

Figure 3.66

composition. The large ***shape*** may move toward the edge of the format and still retain a sense of balance if it points to the smaller form. The dynamics involved in achieving asymmetrical balance are subjective and more difficult to achieve, giving these designs a much greater sense of activity and connection to the individual artist.

Our physical, conceptual, and psychological connections to a sense of balance within our everyday lives invests the visual application of this principle with a deeper significance. Balance becomes a goal, often intuitively, in the construction of strong, unified compositions that we perceive of as good, well done, and logical.

SPACE—A SENSE OF SPACE/A SENSE OF PLACE

In the ***two-dimensional*** world, our perception of space relies on our frame of reference, the ***picture plane.*** The boundaries that confine the space of the picture plane (the edges of this page, for example) create a spatial construct that allows for endless combinations of visual forces. The relationship of these forces to each other and to the ground on which they exist provides for the myriad of interactions that we understand as visual information. These spatial dynamics are further complicated by our own perceptions of space, perceptions that begin with birth and continue to become more sophisticated as we weave our way through the ***three-dimensional*** environment in which we live.

The transference of our experiential sense of space from the three-dimensional environment to the two-dimensional one carries with it the remnants of those interactions. We rely on what we know and that which is familiar, to help us decipher the visual images that we read on the two-dimensional plane. Our understanding of ***scale*** relationships helps us to understand what is near or far. Our sense of space is heightened when we encounter parallel lines that converge in the distance. The sense of place that allows us to feel in control of the world around us is anchored by the sensory input that constantly monitors the environment for changes that could easily throw things off kilter. Visual "cues" that help us navigate through our everyday goings-on also help us unlock the mysteries of the flat picture plane.

Flat and Illusory Space Basic pictorial elements such as line and shape, and the factors that describe them such as texture, value, and color, are the dominant players in this spatial field. They coexist in various combinations that are dictated by the visual principles of unity, harmony, variety, emphasis, balance, and scale or proportion.

Flat space is presented on the picture plane as having only two dimensions–height and width. Within this limited field, artists and designers manipulate ***figure*** and ***ground*** to create dynamic images that transcend simple configurations. The concept of figure/ground is essential to the understanding of how we see an object on a page. By regarding the figure as a shape that exists on the background, or ground, we begin to clarify the parameters that signify the image field. Equal divisions of figure/ground can create a fluctuating effect that energizes an image and creates a synergistic whole. The foreground and background allow for the viewer to imagine the picture plane as a window through which the events in the image take place. As forms overlap in this perceived space, and those forms change size in relationship to their distance from the viewer, the picture plane transforms from the flat page to an illusionistic world that parallels optical experiences.

The creation of illusionistic space is a complex endeavor. Spatial cues such as ***atmospheric perspective, transparency,*** and ***amplified perspective*** create illusion by reinforcing familiar spatial dynamics. In Western culture, the image field has been traditionally viewed as if through a windowpane. This strategy of imitating on a two-dimensional surface the way in which objects in space are perceived by the viewer includes linear perspective. Other cultures have presented space on the picture plane in ways that coincide with their own traditions and beliefs. In Eastern cultures, ***isometric perspective*** (parallel lines do not converge) and ***vertical location*** (bottom portion of the image is perceived as near and top portion as farther away) represent other strategies that are used to explain space on the flat plane.

Additionally, changing value and color characteristics heighten the perception of depth on the two-dimensional plane. Atmospheric perspective describes the transition of color from more distinct and saturated in the foreground toward a more neutral and/or bluish hue in the background. Also evident is the change from clearly defined edges to less distinct contours. Through the push and pull of ***value*** and ***saturation,*** with lighter and less saturated color that recedes and bolder, more intense color that jumps forward, the image field can vibrate with interactions that can make flat space come alive.

The following problems focus on the ways in which the illusion of space can be explored on the two-dimensional plane. The first problem studies the effects of shape manipulation and placement and their relationship to spatial relationships, and the second one focuses on the ways that the inclusion of pattern can flatten an illusionistic image.

PLANES IN SPACE

In previous discussions, we examined the differences between two-dimensional and three-dimensional design. Three-dimensional objects are tangible and therefore more accessible when measuring their success as designed objects. With two-dimensional composition, we must develop an innate understanding and vocabulary to reach our design goals. The flatness of a two-dimensional plane forces us to establish the illusion of depth or space in the composition or two-dimensional images we create.

There are a number of criteria or principles we can use to encourage this illusion.

1. Size: On a comparative basis, larger items will appear closer to the viewer (Figure 3.67).
2. Overlap: An opaque element that appears to overlap, or sit in front of another, appears closer to the viewer. When the element is transparent, it is difficult to determine proximity based on this principle alone (Figure 3.68).
3. Placement: Elements placed toward the bottom of a two-dimensional surface will appear closer to the viewer, as the bottom edge of your windshield captures the part of the landscape closer to you in the car (Figure 3.69(a)).

The first figure (Figure 3.69(a)) clearly shows the large circle on the bottom closer to the viewer. Are the receding circles deeper in space or smaller? By comparing identical circles in the next example (Figure 3.69(b)), the lower circle is definitely closer. Is the left circle farther away, but larger if compared on the same plane?

4. Color: Continuing with the landscape viewed through a windshield, colors are generally stronger and brighter closer to the viewer. The hills usually soften their tone as they fade into the distance. (Figure 3.70)
5. Detail: Proximity provides the opportunity for greater clarity and detail. The bark on a tree is quite visible when it is near. The stand of trees in the distance fade into a blur of value. (Figure 3.71)
6. Perspective: This is a drawing system used to create the illusion of three-dimensional space on a two-dimensional surface. However, perspective systems will not be used in this assignment.

OBJECTIVES

In this exercise you will learn to establish the illusion of depth or space in a two-dimensional composition through the development, placement, and enhancement of planar objects or shapes. Using the first three principles of spatial development—size, overlap,

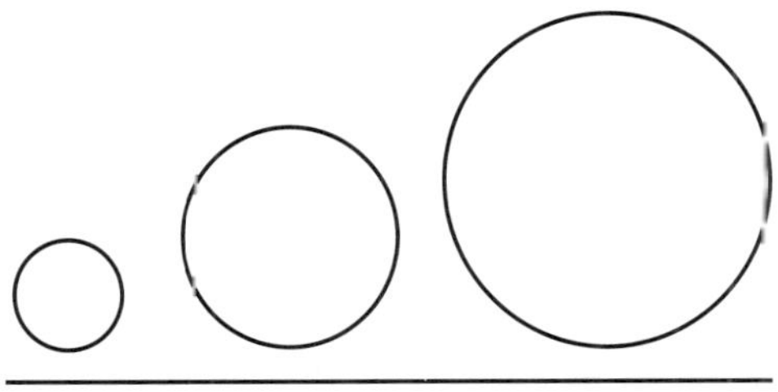

Figure 3.67

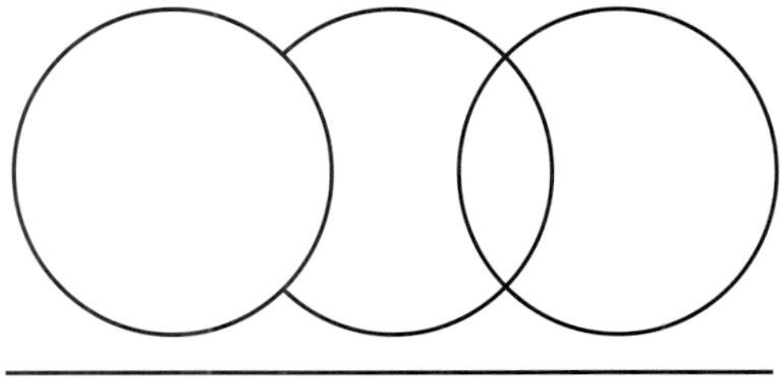

Figure 3.68

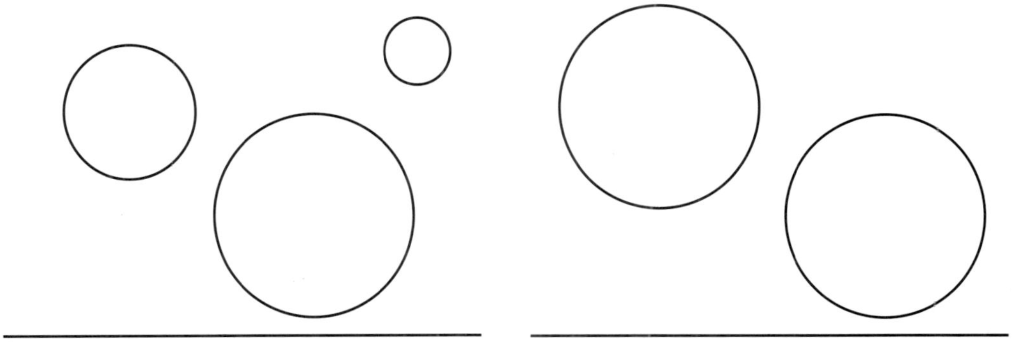

Figure 3.69(a) **(b)**

Figure 3.70

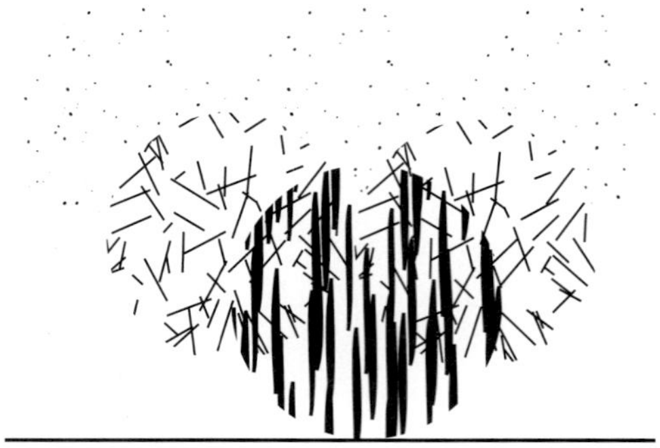

Figure 3.71

and placement— you will create an interesting and dynamic composition that challenges the two-dimensional plane.

MATERIALS

Electronic: Raster- and vector-based software (Adobe Photoshop and Adobe Illustrator); a printer; an input device such as a scanner or digital camera, or photo CDs for a source of digital photographic information

Traditional: A 15″ x 20″ piece of bristol or illustration board; black ink with a ruling pen, technical pen and/or brush, or a disposable technical pen, like a "Penstix" that contains ink (no solvent-based markers that bleed); at least five planar objects

WHAT IS A PLANAR OBJECT AND WHY DO YOU NEED THEM?

A shape is a two-dimensional element, while an object is a three-dimensional form. This project requires tracing around the edge of objects to create an outline. A plane, for an object, is relatively flat, making planar objects flat objects and therefore more conducive to being traced or outlined. If you place your open hand on the page to trace around, you create a reasonable representation of your hand. But what happens when you try to outline your fist? (Figure 3.72)

PROCEDURE

A minimum of five planar objects will be used in developing the composition. If you are working traditionally, the objects should be selected with a range of sizes to help establish distance. Each object may be repeated as the composition warrants. If you are working electronically there are a variety of means at your disposal to develop shapes that can be cut out or traced. In addition, you have the luxury of scaling the same element to achieve contrasts in size and therefore the illusion of distance you want to achieve.

The inclusion of a border is a requirement in this assignment, but the definition of an acceptable border is left up to you as the designer. Varying the line weight of objects to support their location in space can enhance their outlines.

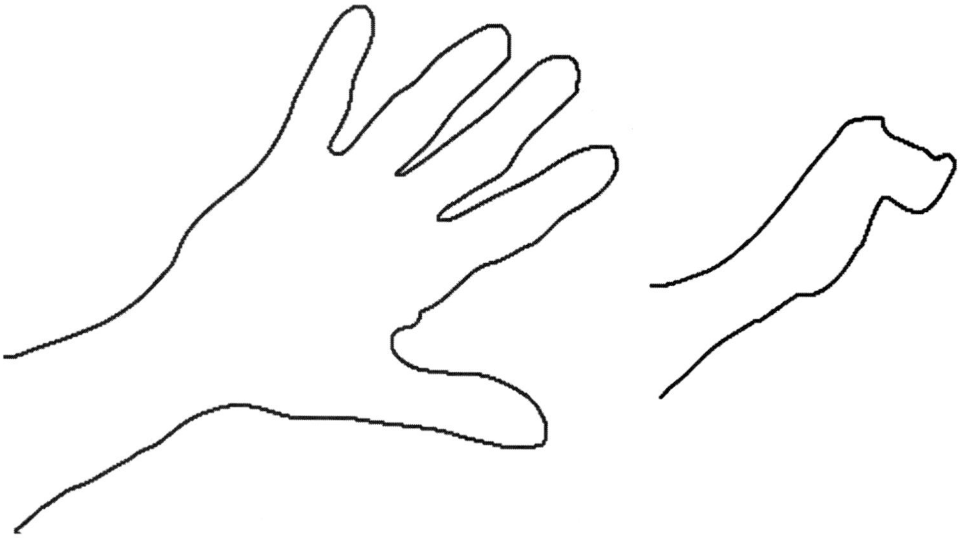

Figure 3.72 Hands

The project can be worked in either a vector- or raster-based program. If you are working in a vector program such as Adobe Illustrator, open the program to a new page. The first step is to create a border to set the *frame of reference.* You can use the **Rectangle Tool,** setting the **Stroke** to black and the **Fill** to transparent. Place the cursor in a top corner, hold the mouse button down, and drag. As your composition develops, you may find that the border needs to be altered to become a more integral part of the design. The beauty of a vector program is that changes can be made easily when an object is selected. Place the select arrow on the outline, click and hold the mouse down, then drag the object to a new location. When you touch an anchor point with the select arrow, it changes to a double-headed arrow. Holding the mouse button down at this point will allow you to push and pull the shape as needed to change size. As you manipulate the border, changing size, placement, and line weight, watch the effect such changes have on the composition.

The shapes you use can be as easily maneuvered. You have the option of generating interesting shapes in the vector drawing program, then **Copying, Pasting,** and **Scaling** the elements as needed to organize an exciting composition.

A visible border can be generated by the alignment of shapes or implied by their careful placement to allow closure to occur. The border can be active and contain the elements it surrounds or inactive as shapes pass over, under, and sometimes through the edge.

Once the basic composition is established, return to the individual elements and verify their location in space by altering the line weights accordingly. Consider the location of the border as well, determining whether the plane is in the foreground, middle ground, or background.

If you are working with traditional materials, complete the project with ink on board, following the same guidelines as with the electronic solution.

DISCUSSION

The first two examples that follow were completed by students using traditional materials and processes. Notice the recognizable planar objects that form the composition. What is your relationship as viewer to the two surfaces? When you compare the two studies to a similar view in the real world, what do you imagine? In the first study (Figure 3.73), I see a horizontal plane, like a desktop, on which elements are placed. I am looking down so that my gaze is vertical and perpendicular to the horizontal plane.

The second traditional example (Figure 3.74) is a perpendicular picture plane, with a horizontal line of sight. The elements spill out of the tunnel with a few flying closer to the viewer.

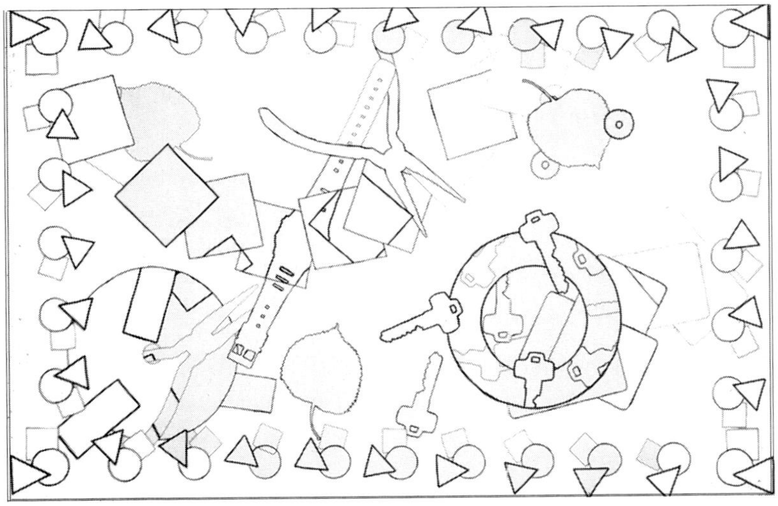

Figure 3.73 *Image by Michael Battle*

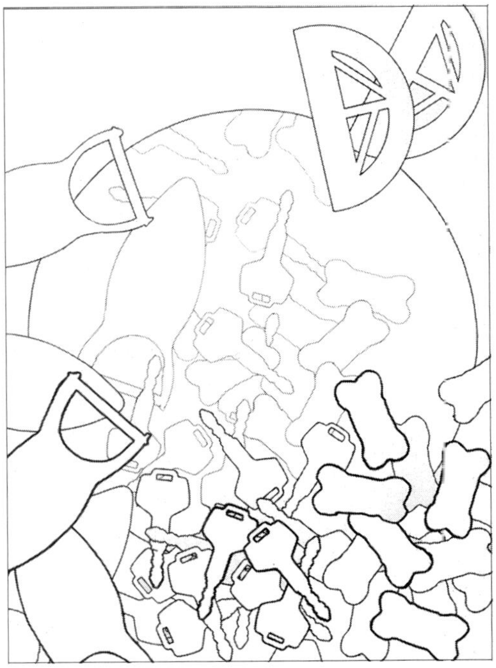

Figure 3.74 *Image by James Perkins*

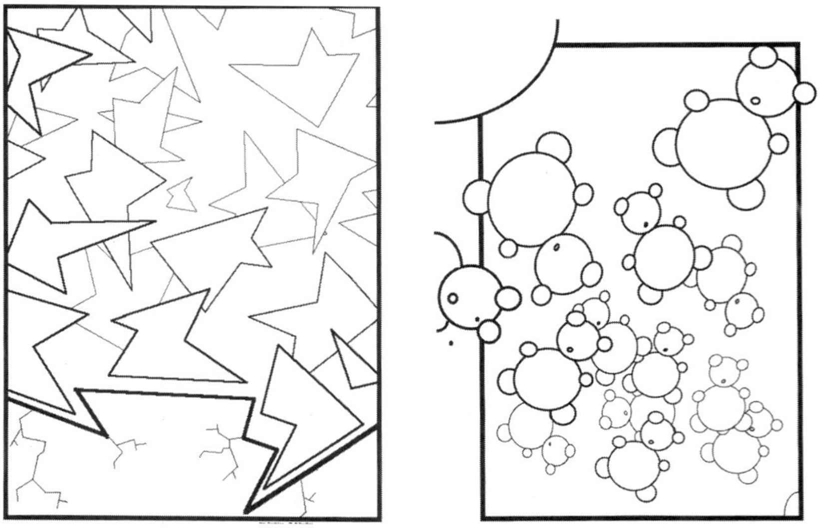

Figure 3.75(a) (b)

The last two examples compare electronic solutions. The study on the left (Figure 3.75(a)) was completed in a raster-based program. The one on the right is a vector solution (Figure 3.75(b)). Do you recognize some of the pros and cons to each system, and how they might affect the approach to design you would take?

FLAT AND ILLUSORY SPACE

Used by contemporary artists, surface ***textures*** and ***patterns*** can be manipulated to control spatial suggestions. ***Flat space*** can be arrived at through the repetition of pattern ***motifs,*** or by bold flat shapes that demand attention. As we have mentioned, the ***illusion of space*** on a flat plane is created through the control of devices such as ***linear perspective, scale, value*** and ***color transitions,*** and ***atmospheric perspective,*** to name a few. The elimination of any of these spatial cues is important if the representation of ***three-dimensional space*** is **not** desired. Decorative relationships permit a freer interpretation of object shapes and encourage variations that contribute to the organic unity of the pictorial elements.

OBJECTIVES

Students are asked to transform a photographic image that represents the illusion of real space into an image that depicts flat space. The strategy of replacing basic shapes in the photograph with decorative patterning eliminates spatial cues and results in an abstract, flat design. The exploration of pattern and value is an important aspect of the problem. Students make decisions about the placement of "value shapes" (areas of pattern that have differing scale and value relationships) as they work toward a resolution of their design. The final image will include well-balanced value and pattern relationships, variety of pattern motifs, and be able to stand on its own as a solid, cohesive design.

MATERIALS

Electronic: Magazine image of an interior of a room or an architectural space; tracing paper; pencils, fine-tip black marker; graphics program such as Adobe Photoshop; flatbed scanner and scanning software; good-quality printer; patterns scanned from a variety of sources: magazine depictions, patterns from artwork, created by hand, and patterns created on the computer; rubber cement; illustration board.

Traditional: Magazine image of an interior of a room or an architectural space; tracing paper; pencils; india ink; ink pen; good-quality black markers, fine tip and extra fine tip; illustration board

PROCEDURE

Electronic Choose a FULL-PAGE photograph from a magazine, depicting an interior of a room or an architectural space. Choose a few photos to begin with so that you can decide on the best one. Using tracing paper and pencil, trace the major shape divisions in the image. Go over the pencil tracing with a good-quality fine-point black marker. **Scan** this tracing into the computer as a Grayscale image at 200 dpi. **Crop** right to the edges of the tracing. Make sure all the lines go right off the edge. **Save** the scan with a descriptive title. **Open** this image in a program such as Adobe Photoshop and clean up the image so that it is only black lines on a white background (the tracing paper may scan as a light gray). To do this you can use the **Brightness and Contrast** adjustment up to a point. If you increase the contrast too much you will degrade the lines in the image. To get a bright white background use a **Selection** option like **Color Range** and with a tool like the **Magic Wand, Select** the background and **Delete** using the delete key. Continue until you have a clean white background and black lines that do not have any breaks in them (Figure 3.76). Save this file with a new name.

You will now have to begin to create or develop patterns that will be used to fill in the shapes that you have defined in the image. You can do this a number of ways. If you have some magazines or books that have pattern samples or distinctive patterns in imagery, you can Scan those as long as the scale works. You can look at artwork and use patterns that you scan from them (i.e., Gustav Klimt). Only Scan the pattern area; don't include parts of the image that you will not use. Save these pattern samples as separate files on your disk (make sure you are always working with identical resolutions so you are not surprised at the size of your pattern when it is brought into the image file). You can also open a program such as Adobe Photoshop and create your own patterns. Just create a New File, and draw or paint a repeat motif into a small format (20 x 20), and Save to disk. You can use the Custom Shape Tool to repeat the shapes that are stored there as well.

You will need to be concerned with the distribution of pattern in regard to value. Distribute small patterns over the picture plane within the spaces defined. Intersperse them with larger, bolder patterns. Fill a small shape with a large pattern, or a large area with a small pattern. The representation of value in pattern structures relies on an understanding of how repeated forms are perceived on the picture plane. Small linear motifs repeated close together can present a gray value, whereas large dark motifs repeated next to each other will read as a bold, dark value. Is the overall tone of the pattern dark, light, or does it seem to have a gray tone to it? You should have examples of all of these.

To begin to fill the shapes with pattern, you must first add patterns to the ones that are already saved in the graphics program. One way to do this is to **open** each pattern file separately and then go to **Edit** and **Define Pattern.** This will open up a pattern title window. If you don't want to change the name of the pattern, select okay. This pattern will now be included in the pattern choices when you select **Fill** and **Custom Pattern.** The drop down box will show all the patterns that you have included in this manner. They can then be used to fill the shapes in your image.

Open your line-tracing file. Use the **Magic Wand** to select each area shape in your image. After you have selected one go to **Edit** and **Fill.** Choose **Custom Pattern,** then **Select** the pattern you would like to use to fill the shape, and say **Okay.** Proceed to fill the shapes in your image with various patterns. You may use a pattern more than once. Again, pay attention to the ways that the patterns can be used to ultimately balance the image with areas of pattern value.

The final image will be a flat, abstract image that will be a stark contrast to the original photo, which depicted the illusion of space on the two-dimensional plane. The final solution should appear clearly organized with a well thought-out distribution of value shapes, and a variety of creative patterning evident. The image, although abstract, should be able to hold its own from a formal standpoint (Figure 3.77).

Print out your file on photo quality or glossy computer paper. Trim and mount with rubber cement to illustration board. The size of the image will be the size of the original tracing.

Traditional: Begin with a photograph of an architectural space or room interior. Trace as previously described, and transfer tracing to illustration board. Fill each shape with a pattern using black markers or ink pens and india ink. Consider pattern character and value. As in the electronic version, emphasis will be placed on flattening the image along with

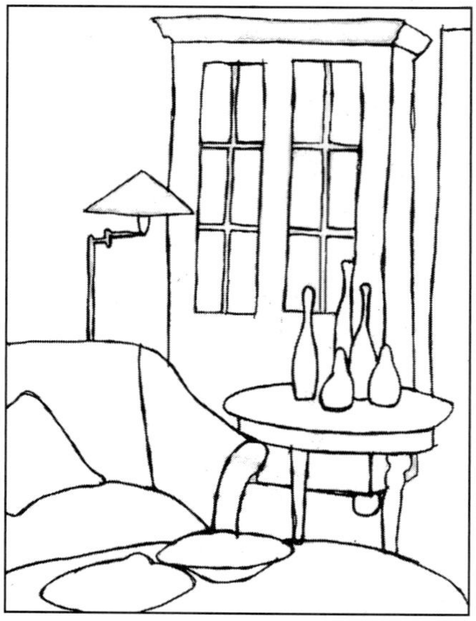

Figure 3.76

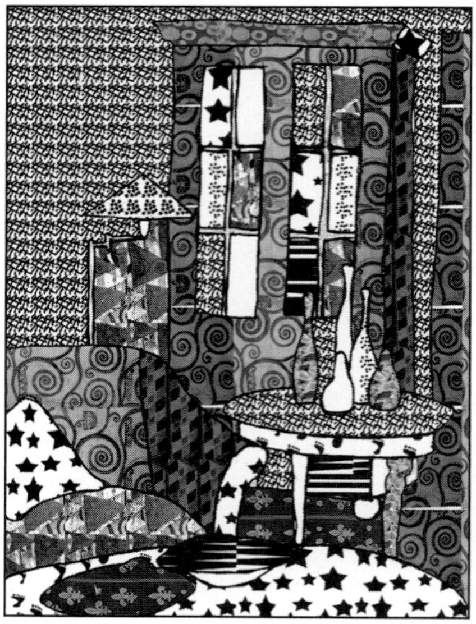

Figure 3.77

creating a new, flat, abstract design that holds together because of the successful arrangement of pattern/values.

DISCUSSION

What clues can be identified in the original magazine image that describe the three-dimensional space? How was that space eliminated in your design? What qualities in the final abstract image can be read as good composition/design?

CHAPTER 4

THE DYNAMICS OF STRUCTURE

STRUCTURES

Basic ***structures*** abound in the natural world. Crystals are beautiful examples of formal chemical structure. The organization of silicon and oxygen atoms produce the familiar quartz crystal. The tasty structure halite is arrived at by combining two very dangerous elements—sodium and chlorine—to make what we call table salt. Structure literally makes these two poisons palatable.

When you pick up a ladybug or click beetle and gently press it between your fingertips, you meet the resistance of its exoskeleton. Stepping on a large insect such as a June bug or cockroach produces an unpleasant crunching sound. This exoskeleton is the reverse of our own human skeletal structure. An X-ray of your body shows how it is organized around your bones. Your hard supporting structure is internal whereas the insect relies on external "bone" to support itself. These are both examples of organic informal structure.

In our daily lives we define, regulate, organize, and utilize various structures, both real and imaginary. For an example of real structure, drive through a new housing subdivision observing the construction of homes in various states of completion. In the early stages of building the most basic elements of structure can be seen. The footing of concrete is placed below the frost line and then cement block or poured concrete walls are put on top of that. Soon to follow are floor joists to support flooring and the stud walls, which in turn support the ceiling joists, which in turn support the roof rafters.

Mathematics is an exemplary "imaginary" or "virtual" structure counterpoint to the real physical structures we build. You use a ruler (math device) to measure the lumber that you cut while following the architect's plans (math device) as you build the house. Numbers and letters can stand in for cerebral/imaginary plans applied to the actual: $2 + 2 = 4$ or $ax^2 + by^2 = c$.

In art, a wide variety of formal and informal structures have been used to organize the visual field. The most formal structure originates in the field of textiles. Dividing a format with regularly spaced horizontal and vertical lines can form a grid of repeated modules.

From the Renaissance through the 17th century, rectangles were divided mathematically in several ways. One grid structure was a simple proportion of 2:3 or 3:5 (see Figure 4.1). Various mathematical schemes have been worked out to make these formal rectangular grids appear more informal. For instance, a square unit can be extended by the square root of two, the square root of three, or the square root of five (see Figure 4.2).

The ***Golden Section*** was invented by the Greeks and appropriated by many Renaissance artists to create a compositional structure that was both dynamic and harmonious (at least that was the theory!). To construct a Golden Section rectangle, start with a square. Find the middle point of its base and extend an arc from the top corner of the square with a compass point at the one half point on the baseline. Bring the arc down to level with the baseline. Add this new area to the original square and you'll have a Golden Section Rectangle (see Figure 4.3).

The careful preliminary planning of mathematical structure schemes tends to result in formal art or art of tightly designed appearance. We usually see the evidence of this approach most often in architecture and commercial graphic design for print and the World Wide Web. Many examples of the deliberate rejection of these structural rules occur in 19th- and 20th-century art. Artwork that is aimed at your

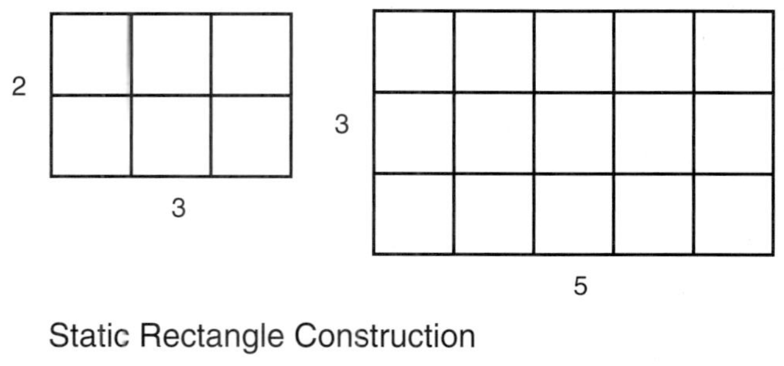

Figure 4.1

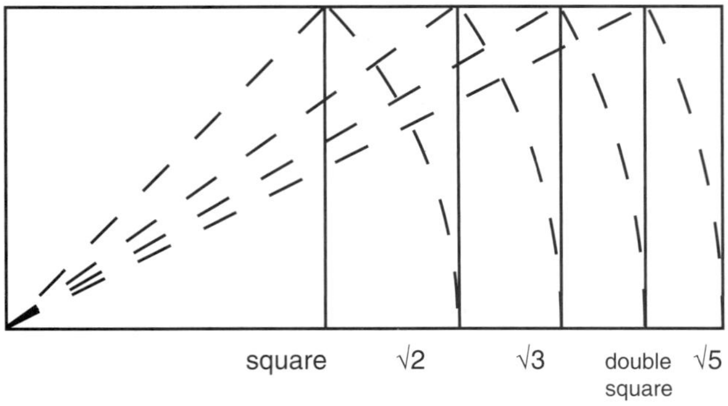

Dynamic "Irrational" Rectangle Construction

Figure 4.2

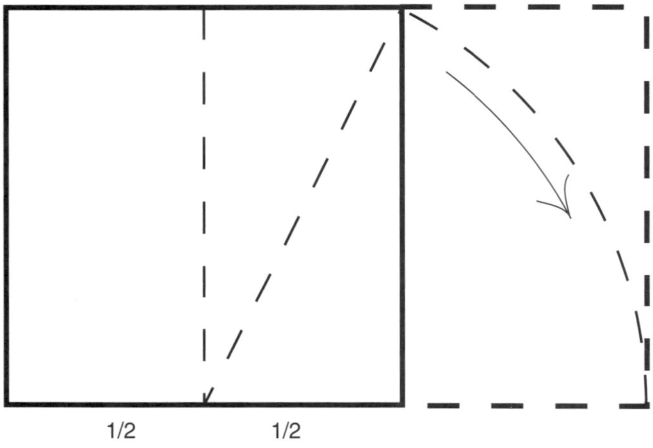

Golden Section Construction

Figure 4.3

emotional fiber rather than intellectual being often ignores structural conventions. The Romantic paintings of Delecroix often negate the academic structure taught by the French Academy of his day. Most artists who were called Expressionists at the beginning of the 20th century, and the more recent Neo Expressionists, ignored careful preliminary structural planning to enhance the immediacy of emotional intent.

In Chapter 2 and Chapter 3 (Seeing and Perceiving), we concentrated on compositional elements and principles. In Chapter 4 we are addressing issues of surface quality and structural systems. For this first section in Chapter 4 we have selected four problems that specifically address the structural unit, working within particular constraints.

STICKS—LINE IN NATURE

The outdoor environment offers many opportunities to observe design as a natural occurrence. Line is represented in nature in a multitude of ways . . . paths in the woods, footsteps in the snow, rivers, waterfalls, rain. The branches of trees follow a pattern that is reminiscent of the branching of arteries or the branching of rivers. Natural structures present us with fundamental strategies for organization.

A mirroring structure allows us to study the effects of ***randomness*** as well as controlled arrangements. This elemental organization can be seen as a very direct and expedient way to ensure ***unity*** and ***balance*** in a design.

OBJECTIVES

Natural stick forms are used to imply line in this design. The random fall of the sticks and the ordered and logical ***repetitions*** of the chosen segment come together to create a module that can be repeated within the confines of a four-part grid structure. The effects of ***randomness*** and ***order*** in a design will be studied to enable the manipulation of space or interval to create movement in the image. The project will utilize grid and mirroring structures to create a symmetrical design, and will explore the design potential of positive and negative space.

MATERIALS

Electronic: Sticks; computer; scanner; graphics program (i.e. Adobe Photoshop); storage disk for images; printer paper

Traditional: Pencils; black marker (medium thickness); sketchbook (9″ x 12″); brushes; india ink or black acrylic; ruler; rubber cement; tracing paper

PROCEDURE

Take ten sticks that have been chosen for the character of their edge as well as their straightness. Hold them vertically in your hand with the bottom of the bunch touching the tabletop or scanner. Let them fall randomly (like pick-up sticks). Try dropping them a few times until you find the most interesting patterns in the crisscrossing of the sticks. Decide if you want to eliminate any of the sticks (you must have at least five sticks left). Study the patterns that the sticks create as you look at both the linear quality of the sticks and the rhythm of the negative space.

Electronic Using the scanner software, set resolution to 200 dpi, **Scan** in grayscale, crop out a 4″ x 4″ square, and **Save** to disk (Figure 4.4).

To make a more graphic representation of the stick scan, open up an image manipulation program such as Adobe Photoshop and use **Tools, Selections,** and **Masks** to move it toward a ***high contrast*** black-and-white image. Try the following technique to do that.

In the **Tools** palette select the **Magic Wand** and set **Tolerance** to about 50. **Select** the background of the stick scan. Hold down the shift key while clicking, to **Select** all the white areas that you can without including any of the sticks themselves. Now switch to **Mask Mode** and, using white as a foreground color, choose a small brush and remove the mask from the areas that you want as your selection. You can add and subtract from the mask by changing from white to black on the color picker. Return to **Standard Mode** and **Fill** the selection with white. **Inverse** the selection and **Fill** that with black. You should now have a good representation of your stick scan in black and white (Figure 4.5). When working with a high-contrast image, another way to select areas of same or similar value is to go to the **Select Similar** command found in the **Select** menu.

To repeat this module in the design, use the **Edit** functions of your application program and follow the following steps:

Create a new file with a canvas size that is 8″ × 8″, which will be divided into 4 quadrants (each 4″ × 4″). This is the format for your design. Go to the **Edit** menu and select **Save As. Save** this file titled as *Sticks One.* **Open** your sticks scan and **Select All** and go to **Edit** and **Copy.** Once the stick scan is copied onto the clipboard (which is the computer's short-term memory), go to the **Edit** menu and **Paste** it into the top left-hand quadrant of the *Sticks One* window.

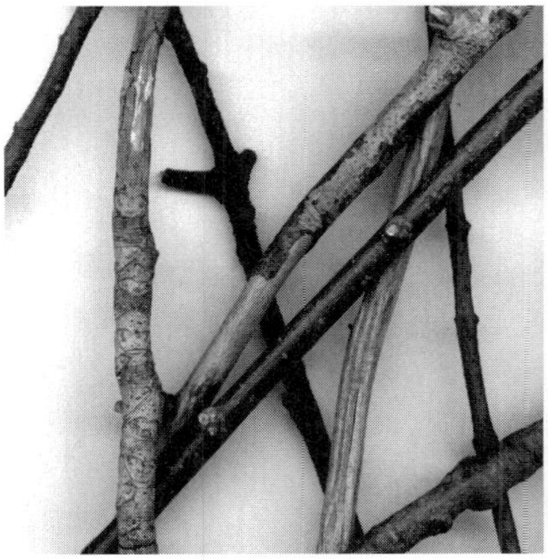

Figure 4.4

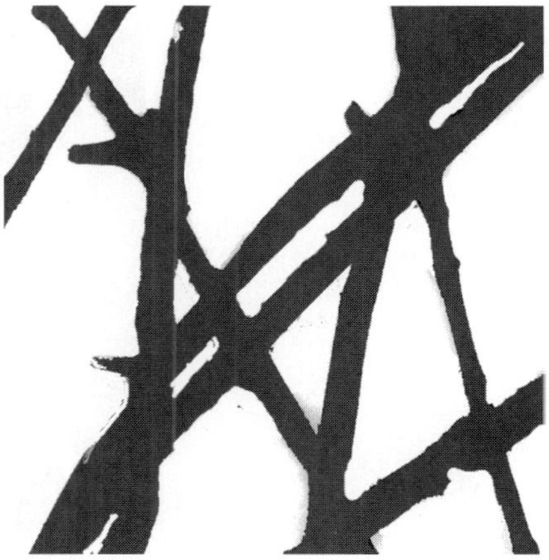

Figure 4.5

Now that the stick scan is on the clipboard you can go to the **Edit** menu and **Paste** the scan into the upper right-hand quadrant. Go to the **Edit** and **Transform** command to **Flip** this horizontally to create a mirror of the first quadrant. For the third quadrant (directly below the second), and the fourth quadrant, mirror what is directly above them by continuing to use the **Paste** and **Edit** and **Transform** functions.

At this point you will need to **Flatten** your image. In most graphic programs the **Paste** function will bring the imagery in as a new layer every time you select the **Edit** and **Paste** commands. In order for you to complete the project, **Flatten** the image by going to the Layer menu and selecting **Flatten Layer.**

For the final presentation **Select** your whole image by going to the **Select** command and **Select All. Invert** your image by going to a command like **Image** and **Adjust** and **Invert** to get the effect of white lines on a black background (Figure 4.6).

Once you have completed the requirements of the assignment, **Save** these changes and **Print** out your image on good-quality paper. Trim off borders and, using rubber cement, mount on illustration board with a two-inch border all around.

Traditional As in the electronic version, use the fallen sticks as your subject and create a black-and-white design that chooses an area within the sticks that has interesting compositional elements. In a sketchbook draw that design within the confines of a 6″ square, using the technique of a simple contour line drawing. Be faithful to the particular "line" of the individual sticks and allow for the unique character of the edge information. Do a number of drawings based on stick designs that are created by newly dropped sticks.

Choose the design that you feel is the most interesting. Trace it onto a 6″ × 6″ piece of tracing paper. Transfer (trace with pencil on back of traced image) and repeat this design onto a piece of bristol or illustration board. The board should be 14″ ×14″ to allow for a 1″ border. The board will have four quadrants with the design flipped and rotated clockwise in the same manner as presented in the preceding electronic version. Paint in either the negative or positive areas with black gouache, being careful to keep the paint flat and opaque.

DISCUSSION

What relationship do randomness and order have as design concepts, and what relationship do they have to natural structures? In what ways have the choices of cropping and contrast adjustments (electronic) or the drawing of the sticks (traditional) influenced the total design? How have the individual sticks and the character of their shapes played an important role in the effect of the whole design? Discuss the organizing potential of grid structures

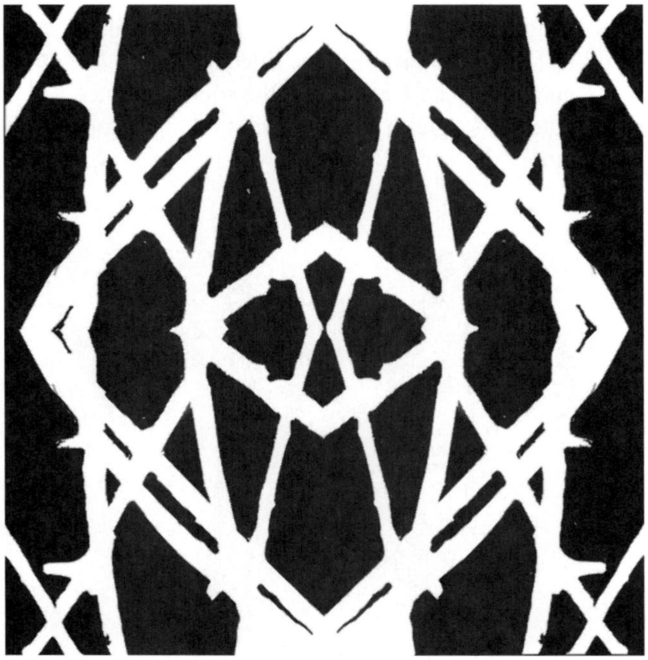

Figure 4.6

and mirroring arrangements, and the effects of ***radial balance*** and ***symmetrical balance*** on the final design.

LINEAR KALEIDOSCOPE COMPOSITION

Kaleidoscopes have been popular since the 1800s as forms of wondrous visual entertainment. Commonly known as "a great philosophical toy," kaleidoscopes have been seen as an instrument for viewing beautiful forms of ever-changing colors, shapes, and patterns. Kaleidoscope designs utilize mathematical precision, ***mirror symmetry,*** and have perfectly balanced ***radial*** form. (Figure 4.7)

Snowflakes, flowers, shells (Figure 4.8), and crystals are some examples of kaleidoscope images found in nature. Folk designs, psychedelic posters, and religious mandalas are cultural examples of kaleidoscope design. Today, creative computer plug-ins and filters can generate dazzling visual effects that mimic the kaleidoscope.

OBJECTIVES

The objective of this project is to utilize ***radial structure*** with recurring reflection around a central point in a circular format. A linear motif will be designed, processed, and repeated to create a kaleidoscope structure.

Facets will be used as basic linear design units, repeated, flipped, inverted, and joined with a mirror image to create a larger unit of repetition. Each new reflected unit will continue to repeat until the process completes a circle.

MATERIALS

Electronic: A vector program such as Adobe Illustrator; mounting board; glue and protractor

Traditional: Mounting board; two mirrors, each 5″ x 10″; protractor; rulers; glue and utility knife; pen and ink; brush; copier; light table or window

PROCEDURE

Electronic This project can be done on the computer using a vector program such as Illustrator or by hand using traditional materials. Steps to execute the project are included in the diagram of the Linear Kaleidoscope Composition. (Figure 4.9)

First we choose a set number of facets that correspond to specific angles to create a ***radial structure.*** Then the angle is determined. The angle choices are as follows: 45 degrees = 8 facets, 36 degrees = 10 facets, 30 degrees = 12 facets, 25.7 degrees = 14 facets, 22.5 degrees = 16 facets.

Create a linear design to suggest space, value, and/or movement inside a triangular module. The module is then reflected to create a mirror image. Both facets are joined and repeated around a central axis to complete a circle. The number of repeats equals the chosen angle divided by 360 degrees. Methods of transformation in a vector program include a **Reflect Tool,** which creates a mirror image of an object across a designated axis, and a **Rotate Tool,** which rotates an object around a designated point at a chosen angle of rotation.

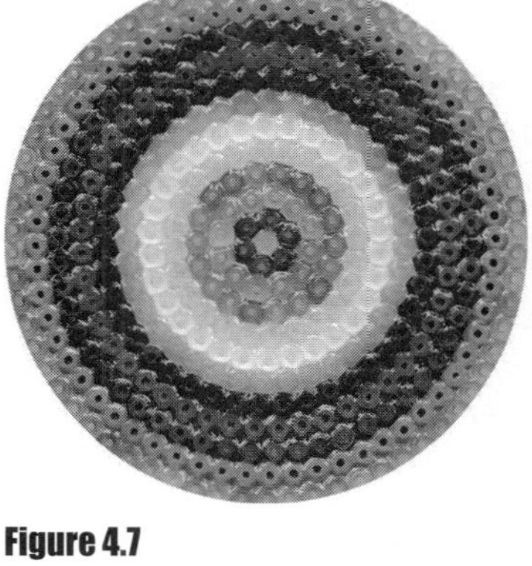

Figure 4.7

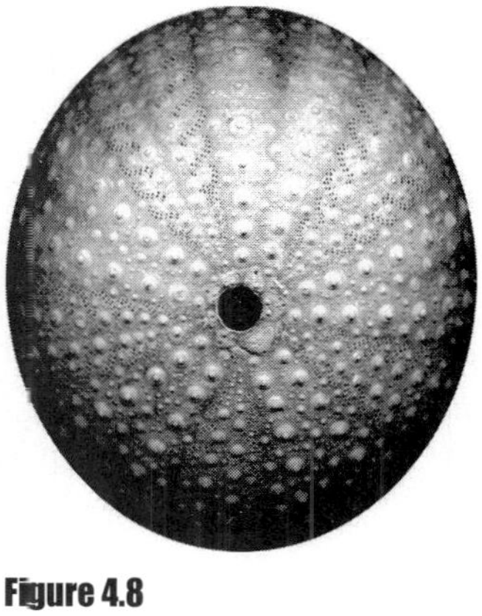

Figure 4.8

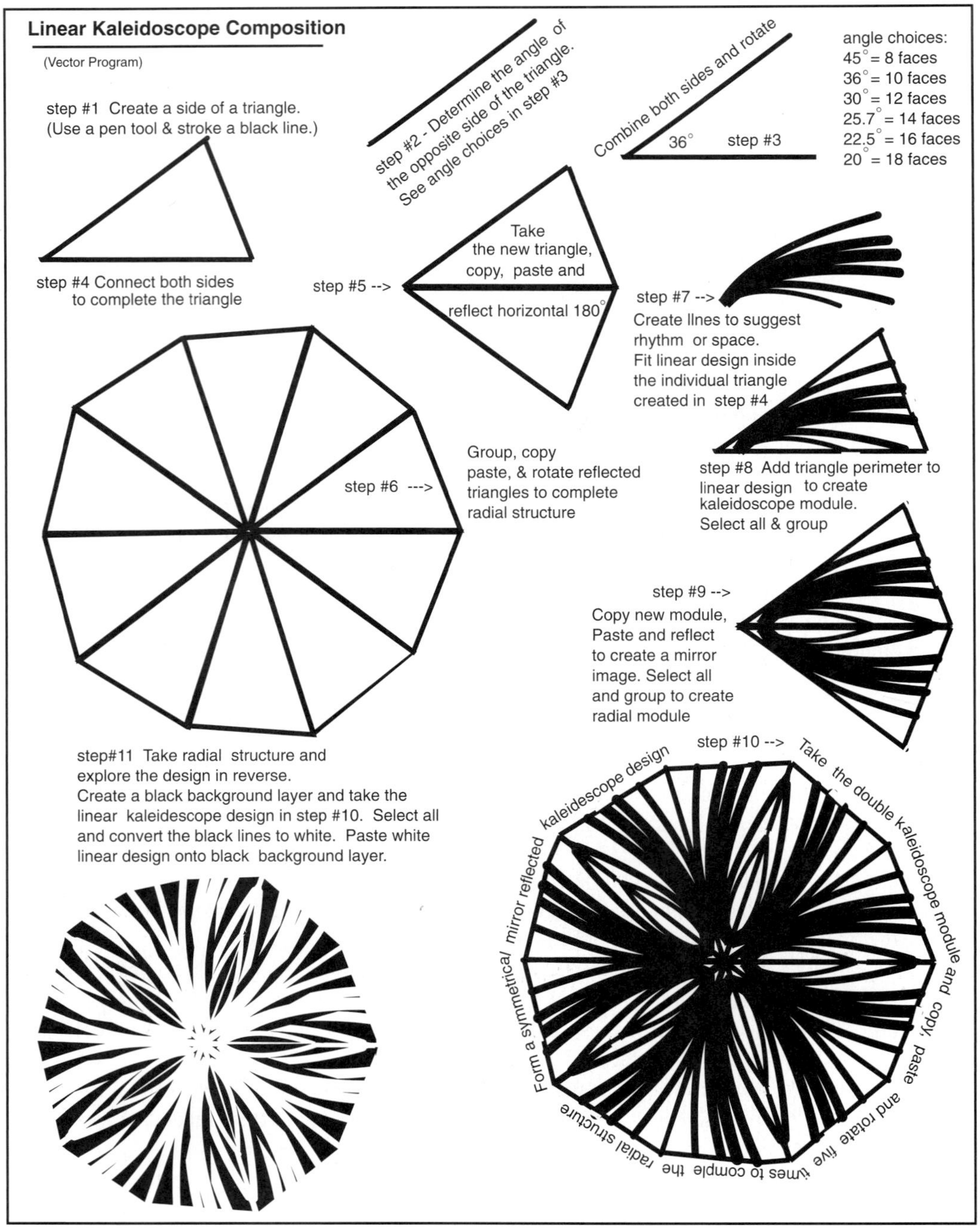

Figure 4.9

Print out your final circular design. If you want to print out a large-scale image, you can increase image size and print out your final design in tiles.

Traditional Create a linear design motif by hand using pen and ink and/or brush. This linear motif should have varying widths of straight, curved, and/or organic lines, and varying line intervals to create the illusion of depth. Carefully consider the same conceptual and formal parameters for this project as stated in the objectives and electronic procedure.

Electronic and Traditional This project can marry the two procedures. Mirrors, the original device used to fracture form and duplicate the image, may be employed here for exciting visual solutions.

First create a dynamic line composition. Hold two mirrors joined at one edge to form an angle on top of your line composition, using a protractor. Choose one of the following angles to be successful: 45°, 36°, 30°, 27.5°, 22.5° or 20°.

Experiment with the angles to find a dynamic radial design. Concentrate on linear elements that work from a complex center outward toward simplicity. When you find a design that works, isolate that triangle. **Print** the triangular motif out as a positive and then **Print** another as an **Inverse** with a **Flip Horizontal** so that you are creating a mirror reflection as seen in Figure 4.10, Figure 4.11 and Figure 4.12. If you chose to complete this design by traditional materials, use a light table and flip your image. Redraw the same design. You can then use a copier and print out duplicates. Print out the appropriate number of prints, depending on the angle of your radial module. (Divide this angle into 360 degrees to determine the number of facets that you will need for your design.) Keep an even number of facets so that the final kaleidoscope design works exactly. For example, a

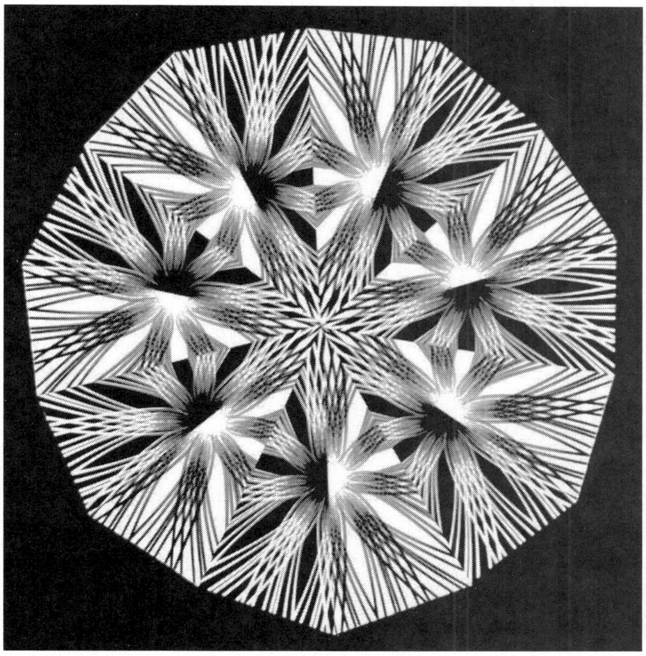

Figure 4.10 *Image by David Fernandez*

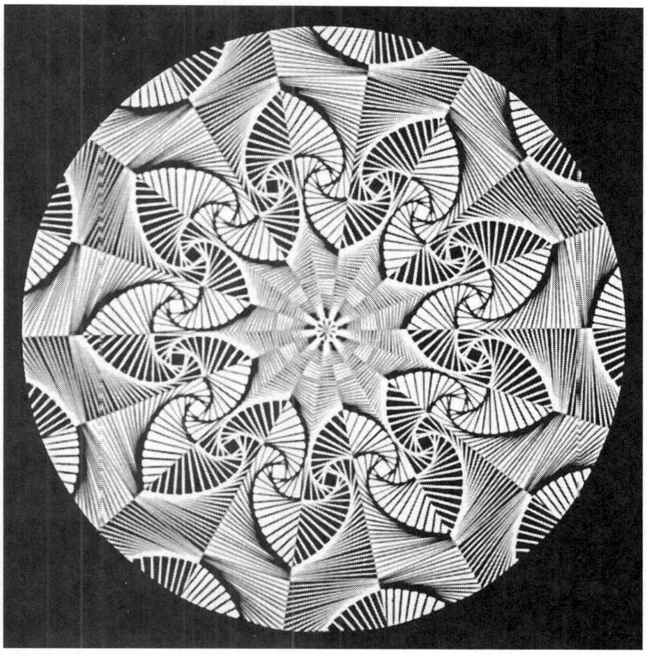

Figure 4.11 *Image by Poe-Wen Liu*

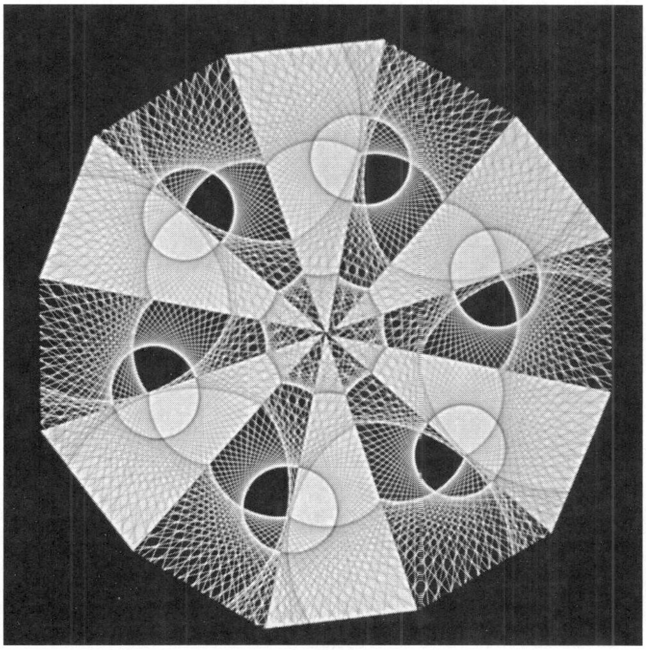

Figure 4.12 *Image by Johnathan Wetjen*

30-degree triangular module would require 5 positives and 5 negative (reflections). With precise measuring, cutting, and pasting onto a crescent board you will create a dynamic radial structure. Examine the movement further by spinning the composition.

ALTERNATIVES AND VARIATIONS

Explore further radial structures by moving your central radial point off center. Multiple points can also be designed into an all-over radial structure. Color and shape variations could create radial structures with formal explorations of color temperature and shape contrast. By utilizing such programs as Photoshop, radial structure can be further explored utilizing photographic imagery that is repeated and reflected around a central radial point.

DISCUSSION

How do line, shape, reversal, scale, and value contrast impact the concentric radial structure? How does radial fractal design serve a purpose for designers, artists, and architects? Explain how the idea of the spiritual in art relates to kaleidoscope design. How do radial fractal designs mimic nature? What is the relationship of the grouping principles and gestalt to kaleidoscope compositions? What cultures emphasize radial structures and patterns? How did the design of the kaleidoscope composition change by spinning it around?

SIX FORMATS

The perimeters within which an event can occur give a structured look and feel to the multiple internal possibilities that happen. If the same event is played out in differing formats, the structure of the perimeters will alter the configuration of the internal elements but not the total effect of the event. A good example of this is a theater production of a Shakespearean play. Many different sizes and shapes of stages have been used to produce the Bard's plays through the centuries. Although the stage, props, and actors change, the original intended "event" does not.

Most of the two-dimensional art of the western world utilizes a rectangular format because our architecture is based on that system. Occasionally other shapes are used, such as the semi-circle or triangle. More common are combinations, such as the semi-circle joined to the top of a rectangle to echo the shape of an arched window or doorway.

Formats are often grouped together functionally. European Church altarpieces are good examples of this. The physical way they are hinged together dictates the multiple grouping. This physical construction was then appropriated for symbolic purpose. Hence we have ***triptychs*** (3 formats/panels) and ***diptychs*** (2 formats/panels).

Today most of our two-dimensional art is still rectangularly formatted. This is a continuing homage to the architecture and machinery of western culture.

OBJECTIVES

This project allows you to study the structural relationship of the format to the overall design, arrangement of geometric shapes for optimum design, and the visual expression of a verbal concept.

MATERIALS

Electronic: a vector-based drawing program such as Adobe Illustrator; computer; laser printer; single-weight white illustration board; rubber cement; utility knife.

Traditional: a compass; technical pens; India ink; ruling pen point for compass; brushes; ruler; triangles, French curves, T square; high-quality single-weight illustration board.

PROCEDURE

In this investigation we will use the same design or design concept in six formats. Construct the formats as in the example (Figure 4.13). Use at least three circles, three squares/rectangles, and three triangles in each format to express the concept of either alienation or concord. Organic shapes and lines may also be used in conjunction with the geometric shapes. Each format must be the same design concept but shrunk or expanded to the format constraint. Whatever modification is necessary should maintain "good" design in each format. Construct the shapes as hollow forms initially and then fill them later or fill the background as needed later. Design the square format first and base the others on that design.

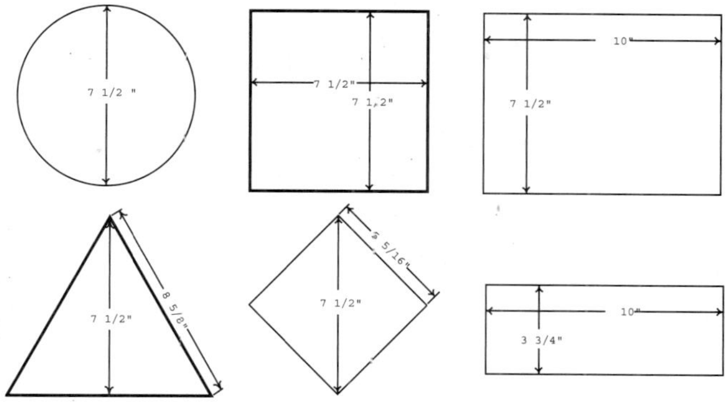

Figure 4.13

Electronic If your program has a layers feature, isolate the border of the format in its own locked layer. Use the solid **Black Selection Arrow** to select whole objects. Use the hollow **White Selection Arrow** to select the outside edge paths of shapes so you can modify the shapes manually by pulling and pushing the points on these paths.

Use the **Scissors** or **Slice** or **Knife Tools** to cut the paths that extend beyond the formats. **Select** the cut-off pieces and **Clear** them. Use the **Pen Tool** to redraw the cut sides of shapes (if necessary), following the format edges. In Adobe Illustrator open line paths can be joined by **Selecting** the two ends of the lines with the hollow white arrow and then using the **Join** command in the menu side bar under **Path** in the **Object** menu.

Make use of the **Rotational Tool,** the **Scaling Tool,** the **Mirror Tool,** the **Gradient Fill,** and the **Gradient Mesh** as available in your program. Please note: The computer function of compression and/or stretching a selected area will not give proper results unless used very sensitively. Also avoid the "equilateral triangle trap" and the "parallel and perpendicular trap" that the computer offers as its #1 technical solution.

Print out each format as it is designed so that the next format made can be compared to it. Use the "dry into dry" rubber cement method to glue the pieces to the illustration board or use a drymount press. See Figures 4.14, 4.15, and 4.16.

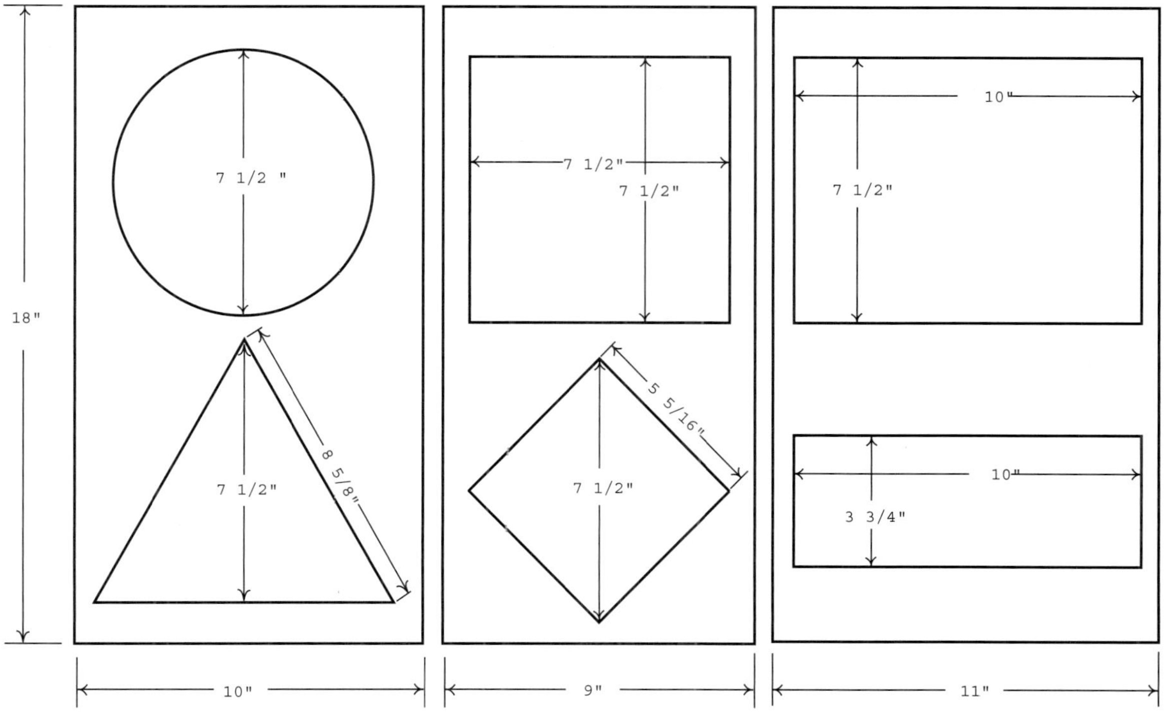

Figure 4.14

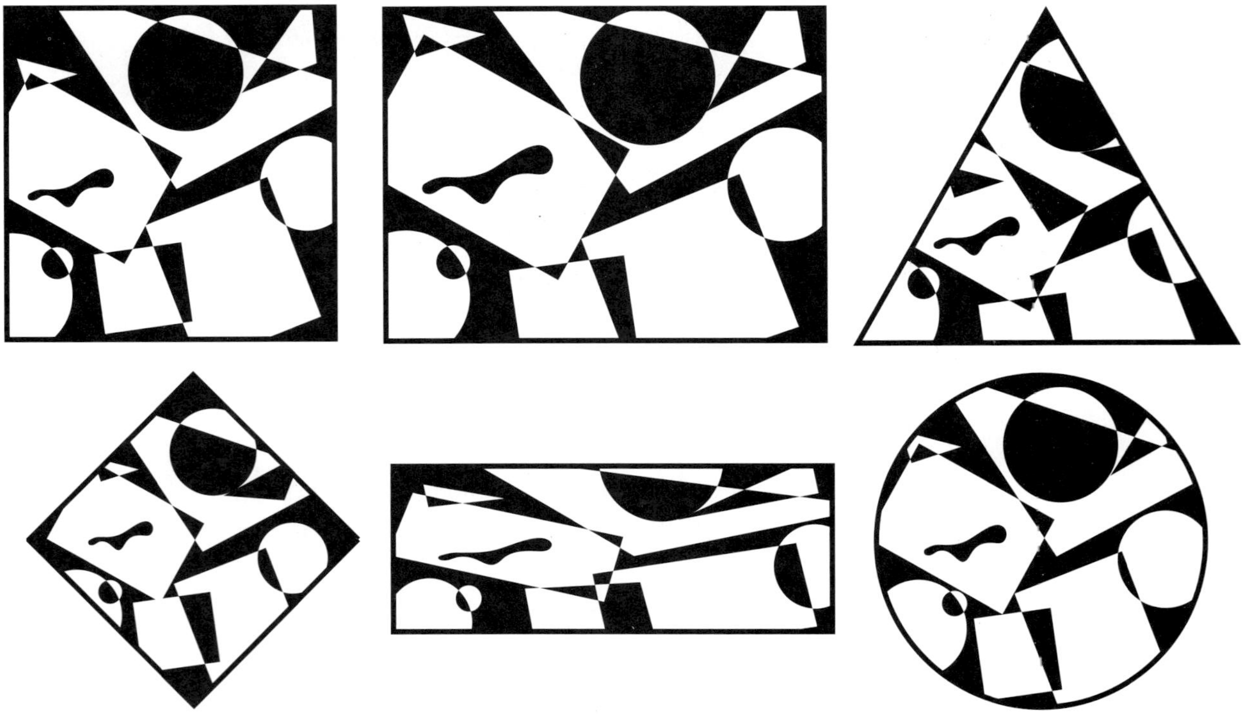

Figure 4.15

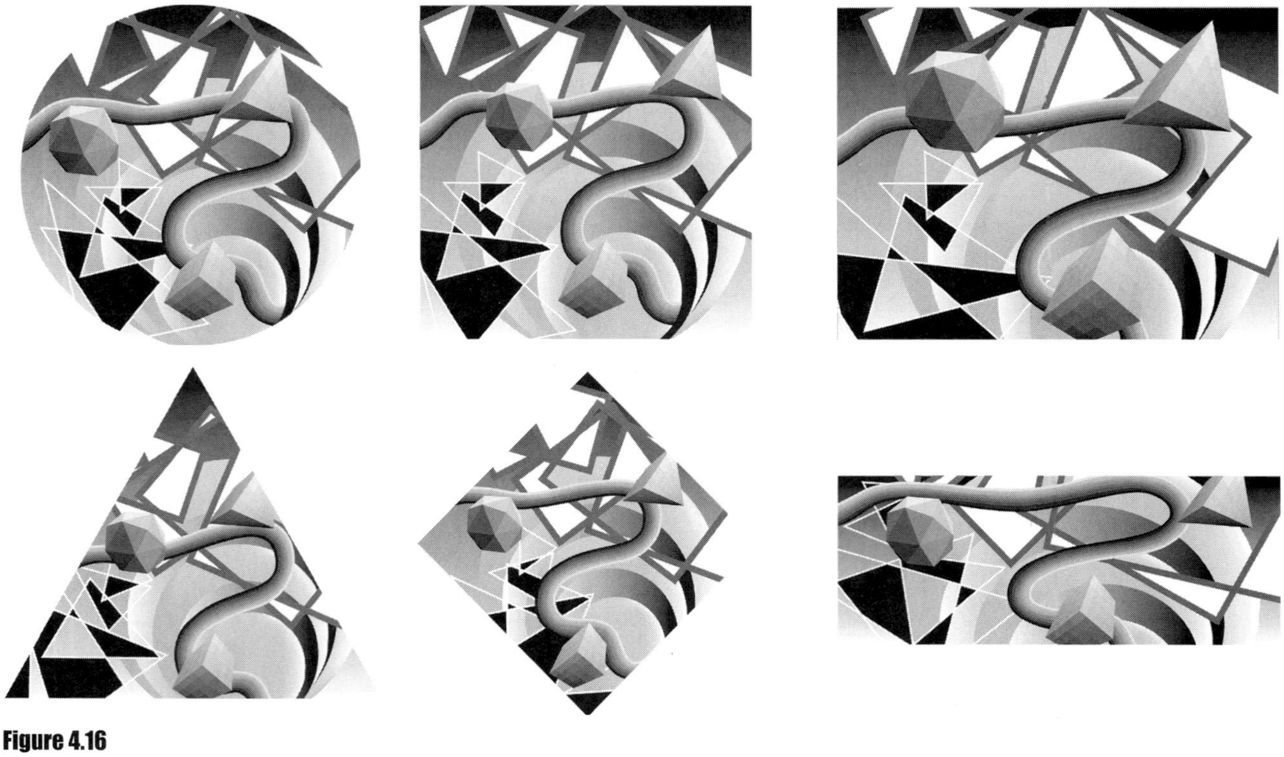

Figure 4.16

Traditional To do this project with traditional media you need to layout all formats in pencil on high-quality white illustration board as in Figure 4.14. Start with the square format and draw the design in light pencil line. All shapes and lines must be drawn with a ruler, compass, or French curve. Do not make this design too complex because the inking process requires a good deal of time.

Interpolate the first design into each of the remaining five formats. After this is satisfactorily done, begin the inking process. Use ruling pens or technical pens held against a ruler to draw all straight-line segments. Circles need to be drawn with the ruling pen point or technical pen in a holder attached to the compass. Organic curves can be achieved by holding the ruling pen or technical pen against the edge of a French curve for each segment of the curve. Fill in between the lines with brush and ink for solid black-filled shapes.

DISCUSSION

Other formats could be used to research the limits at which it is no longer feasible to maintain the integrity of your original design. For instance, is it possible to use an acute or oblique triangle or a very narrow rectangle? How does working in traditional media versus working on a computer affect possible outcomes?

FACE FIELD MOSAIC STRUCTURE

While the origin of ***mosaics*** is lost in the remote past, these structures have been used throughout our history for representational and decorative purpose. Examples of pattern mosaics are common at archeological digs simply because floors survive and the simplest way to permanently decorate a floor is with a repeat pattern in stone or fired clay.

In more recent history, the window openings in churches, mosques, and synagogues have often been designed as translucent tile space. This makes for a spiritually rich medley of mosaic pictures or symbols of pure contemplative decoration. Tile mosaics are also frequently found on the floors of ornate public buildings and corporate headquarters. A number of artist/photographers have investigated a free-form version of mosaic tiling. Taking twenty to thirty photographs of a scene or subject from slightly differing vantage points, they later reconstruct its image by assembling all the photos into one large mosaic.

OBJECTIVES

Through this project you will study distortion, mosaic structure systems, and cubic spatial illusion vs. flat decorative surfaces.

MATERIALS

Electronic: A raster software program such as Adobe Photoshop that can show a ruler and grid and contains a transformation menu that includes perspective, skew, flip, invert, and distort; digital camera or scanner and quality photograph of your face; printer; illustration board; rubber cement; straight edge; knife and pencil.

Traditional: Pencil; ink; technical pen; ruler; high-quality white illustration board; knife; erasers; high-contrast photograph or an actual still life object.

PROCEDURE

Electronic Generate a series of individual “mosaic tiles” on the computer by distorting a photograph of yourself. These “mosaic tiles” must all be proportionally related equilateral triangles and parallelograms. Your finished artwork will be built from these individual pieces to make a large mosaic.

Use a digital camera to take a close-up photo of your face or use a scanner to capture a traditional photograph of your face. Bring this image into a raster software program such as Adobe Photoshop. If necessary, convert the **Mode** of the photograph to **Grayscale.** Turn on the **Grid** and **Rulers.** With the **Selection Box Tool** capture an exact 4″ × 3-1/2″ rectangle of your face that includes the eyes, nose, and mouth. **Copy** this selection. **Open** a **New** page with the page set to approximately 14″ square. This will provide you with extra work area. Turn on the **Grid** and **Rulers** again and if available, the **Snap To Grid** feature. **Paste** the selection on this new page **Select** several other sections of your portrait that are precisely 4″ × 3-1/2″ and **Paste** them on this new open page without overlaps. Include both vertical and horizontal orientations. In addition, use the **Flip Horizontal, Flip Vertical,** and the **Invert** features on several of the portrait selections. **Save** this page as “clip art.”

Bring up a **new** page. Adjust the page size to 3.5″ × 4″ or 4″ × 3.5″ depending on the orientation of the portrait you plan to paste into it. Turn on the **Ruler, Grid** and **Snap To Grid** functions. Make sure that the lefthand corner of this small page is set at the 0″ × 0″ point. Bring the “clip art” page forward. **Select** and **Copy** one of the portraits oriented like the small page you just made. Now bring the small page forward again and **Paste** the portrait into the page. While the selection is still active, use the **Perspective** or **Distort** feature

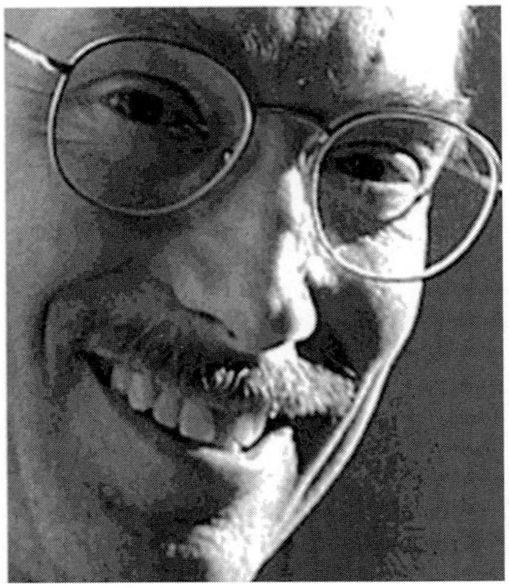

Figure 4.17

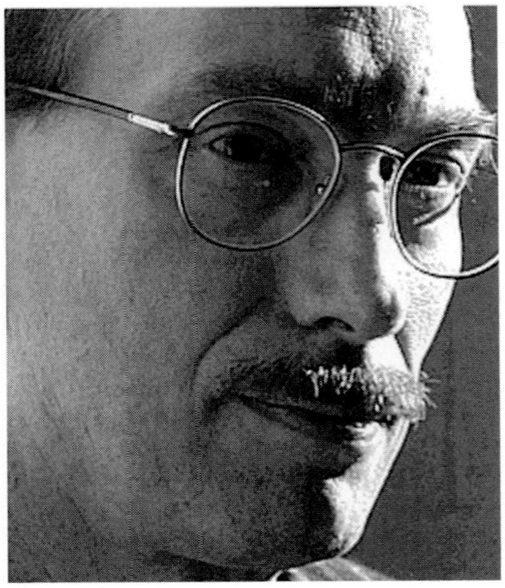

Figure 4.18

to force the corners of the rectangle to the middle (2″) point on one of the long sides of the rectangle. You will now have an exact equilateral triangle. Create at least five different triangle variations from your "clip art" page. Save these but do not print yet.

Create a number of parallelogram variations of your face as well. Set up a new page as you did for the triangles, but change the size to 3.5″ × 6″. Check the orientation to make sure that it matches up with whatever "clip art" portrait you are selecting. After pasting the "clip art" into this page, move it so that it is bound by a format edge on three sides. Use the **Skew** feature to force the corners of the rectangle to the 2″ and 6″ points along one of the long sides of the original rectangle. **Save** these but don't print them yet.

At this point you should consolidate as many triangles and parallelograms as you can get per page without overlap. Use a **line tool** to enclose any triangle or parallelogram that "bleeds" into the negative space.

After you are done manipulating all of the triangles and parallelograms, make a **New** page and set its size as large as your printer will allow. **Save** it as "art page." If the printout size will be small (8-1/2″ by 11″) set the "art page" pixel per inch resolution approximately twice as high as that of the pages that the parallelograms and triangles are stored on. This will force the parallelograms and triangles to shrink in size without losing detail when you **Paste** them into this new page. If you have a printer that can print out large sheets, do not increase the pixel per inch resolution of the "art page" as much. With the "art page" open and the storage pages of parallelograms and triangles open, use the **Move Tool** to drag selected parallelograms and triangles on to the "art page" to build the mosaic.

The mosaic can form any shape desired but all edges of the triangles and parallelograms must be joined to a neighbor except at the edges of the design. Holes may appear in

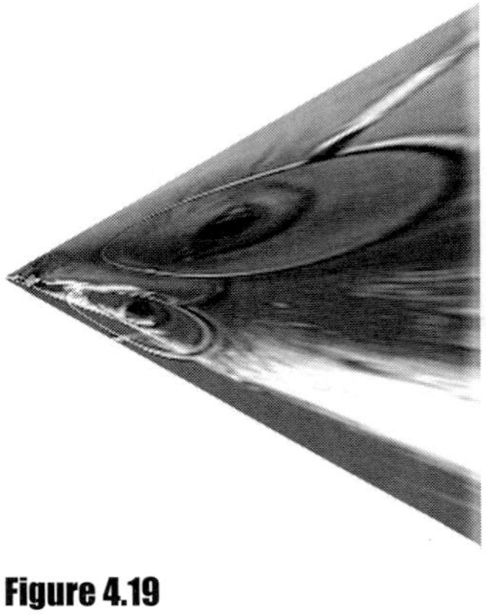

Figure 4.19

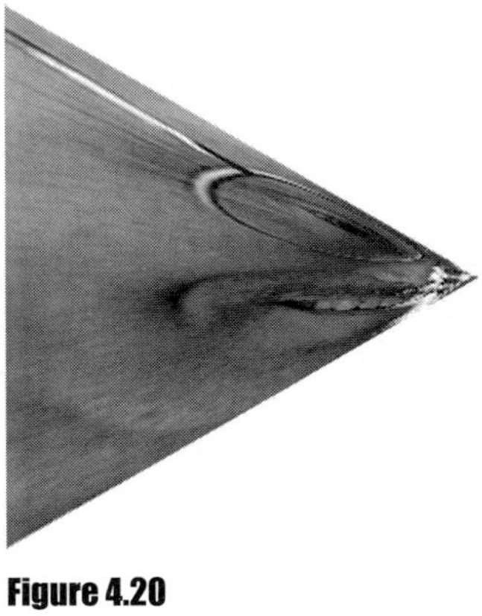

Figure 4.20

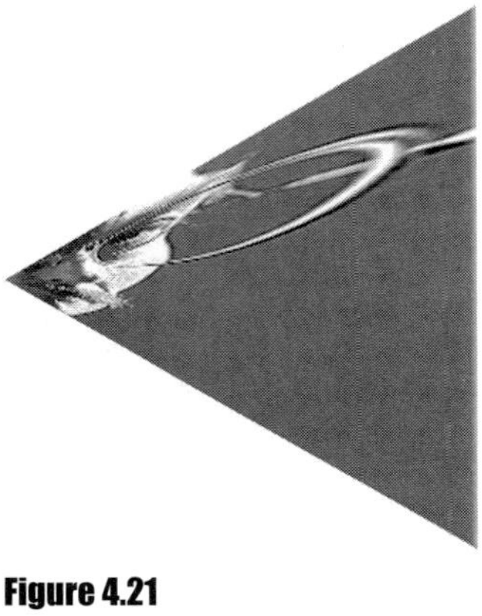

Figure 4.21

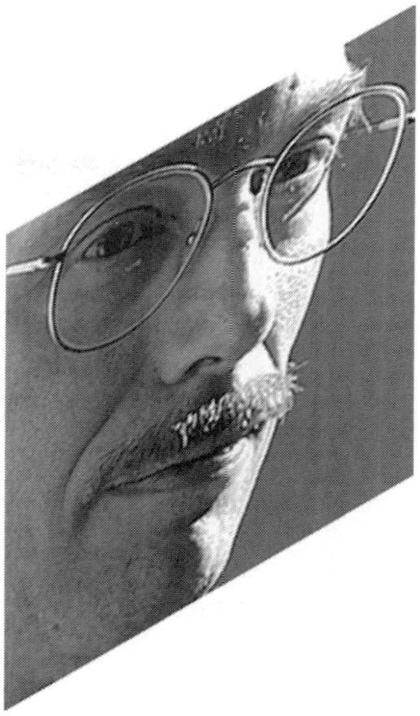

Figure 4.22

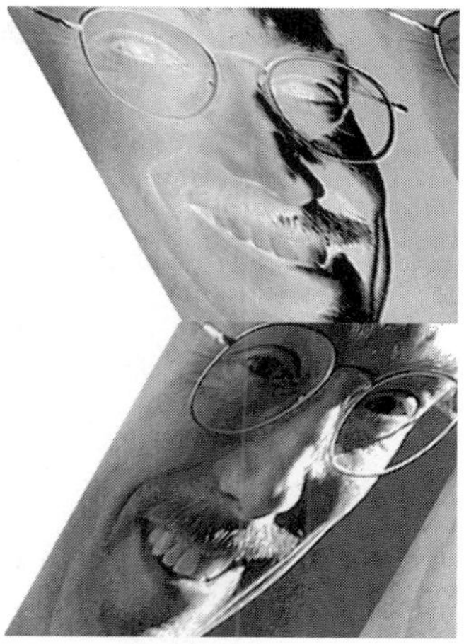

Figure 4.23

central parts of the design as well. **Print** and fasten the finished design to illustration board with rubber cement or spray mount. Use the dry-into-dry method with the rubber cement. Cut the card to shape after all assembly is complete. Leave a quarter inch border around the design.

Traditional The traditional approach will be more successful using a high-contrast, rather than a continuous-tone, image. The simplified shapes can be more easily interpolated to conform and adjust to the angle formats. Another way to maximize success is to use rectangular formats. Start with a fairly large piece of illustration board, about

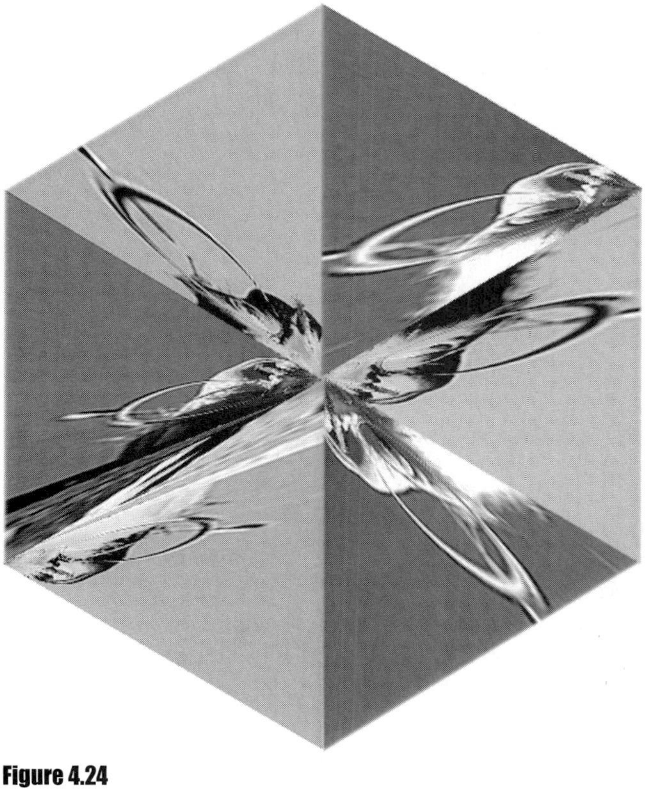

Figure 4.24

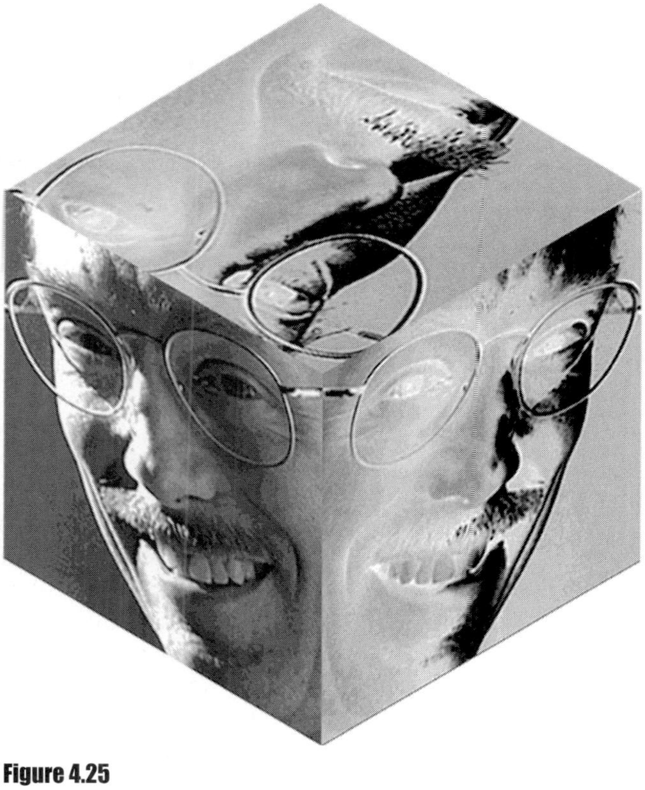

Figure 4.25

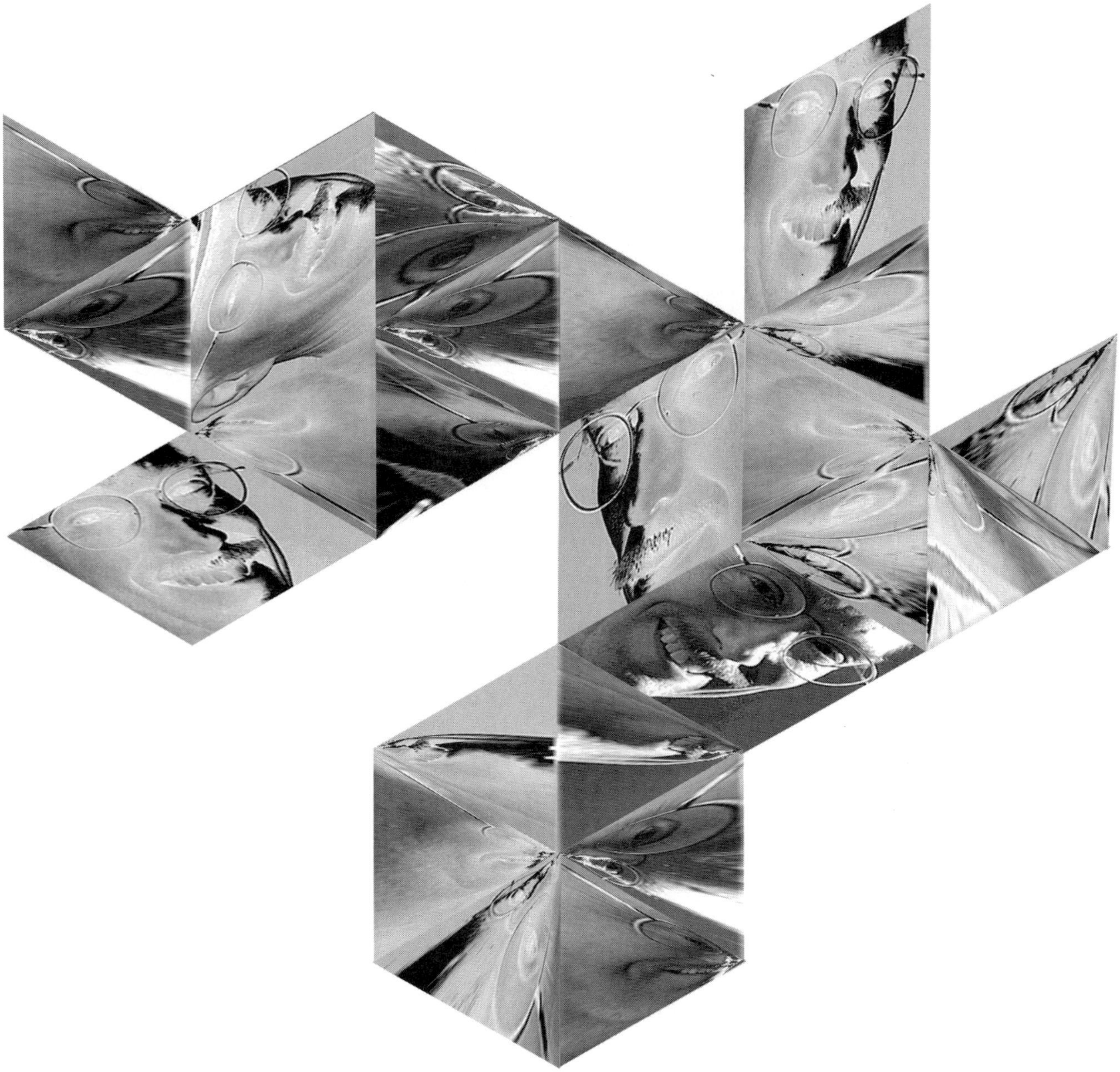

Figure 4.26

15″ × 20″. Consider using one of the structural schemes described in the introduction to structures (Figures 4.1, 4.2, 4.3) for dividing rectangles. As you divide the format into eight to twelve various rectangles, keep in mind that no two rectangles should be the same size dimensions and they all need to abut rather than overlap. Careful division of the space will yield a structure that is integrated, fluid, and balanced.

ALTERNATIVES

Consider using other geometric shapes to form the mosaic grid—rectangular, right triangles, or perhaps hexagons. Consider differing subject matter or thematic subjects. Consider a mosaic that minimizes distortion. What kind of color effects might be achieved by using differing sets of harmonious or dissident or analogous colors?

To add color to the triangles and parallelograms, it is most helpful to have a program that allows you to apply a dither pattern to the artwork. In Photoshop, go to **Image** and down to **Mode** and pick **Bitmap.** Then **Flatten Layers.** The dialogue box for bitmap will come up on the screen. Leave the output as it is and use the **Diffusion Dither** method. **Select** all of each bitmap page and copy to new pages. When the new page dialog box appears, change the **Mode** setting to **Grayscale** and the **Resolution** to about 100. **Paste** the selections into these new pages. Go to **Image** and change the **Mode** to **RGB color.** Do not flatten the image. **Save** these pages with new names.

With the artwork on the screen, go to **View** and **Zoom** in once or twice. Use the **Magic Wand** selection tool to **Select** a black area, The magic wand options should be set at a **Tolerance** of 10 and the **Anti-Aliased** should *not* be checked on. Anything selected in Photoshop can be painted or manipulated while unselected areas are closed or masked. With the selection active, go to **Select** in the menu bar and go down to **Similar.** Now select any paint tool to fill the selected area. Use the **Inverse** command in the **Select** menu to toggle the mask between what was originally black and the white background. Do not deselect until all color effects are completed.

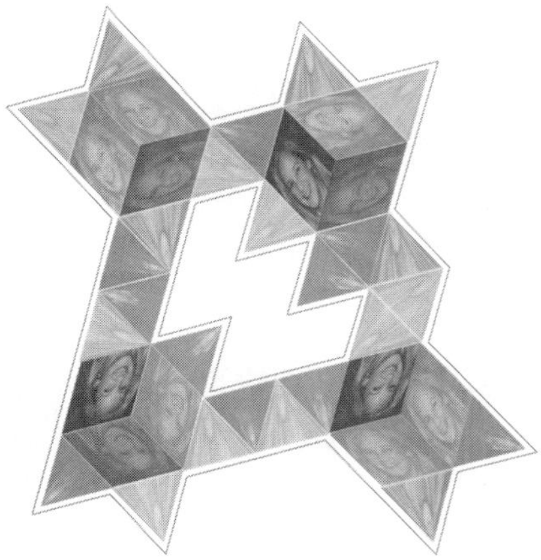

Figure 4.27 *Image by Hillary Banas*

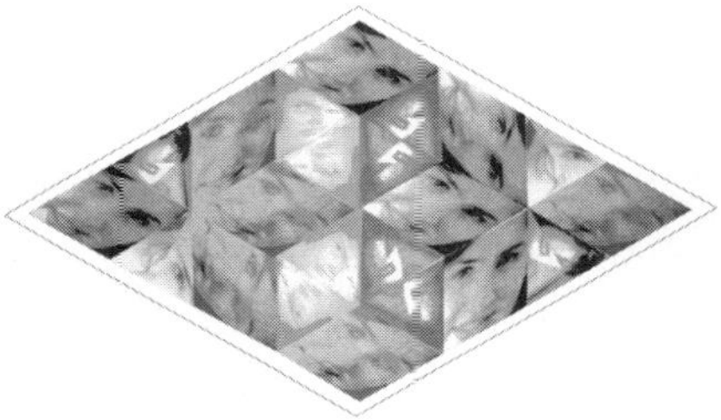

Figure 4.28 *Image by Jessica Lahita*

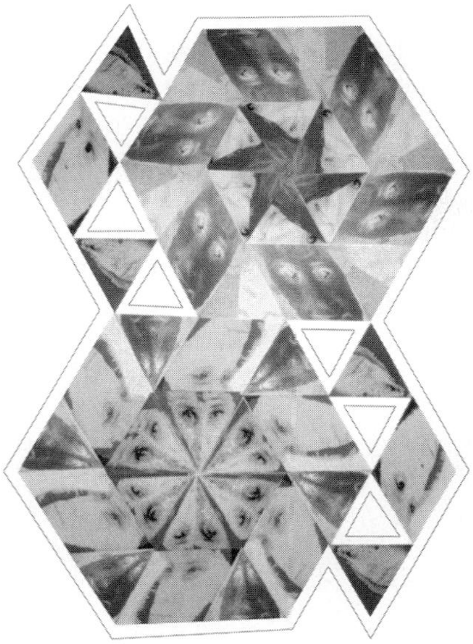

Figure 4.29 *Image by Nichole Frenyea*

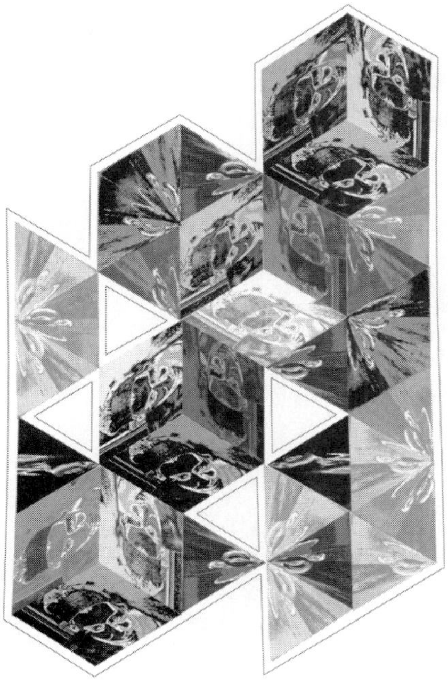

Figure 4.30 *Image by Salvatore Zimmerman*

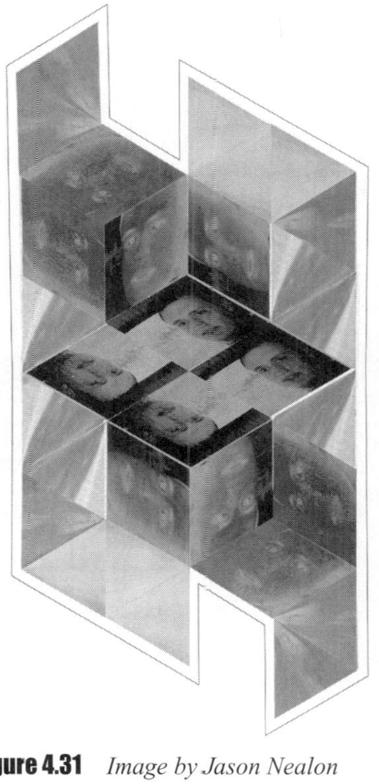

Figure 4.31 *Image by Jason Nealon*

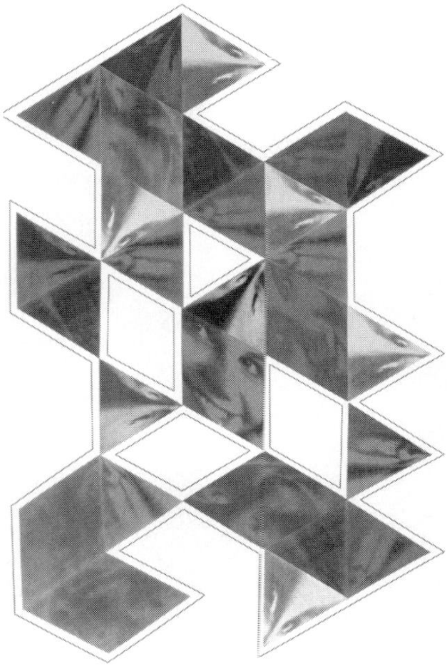

Figure 4.32 *Image by Liz Diller*

PATTERN

Repetition brings comfort and stability to our lives. Actions and events of our lives that are repeated or duplicated in some regular fashion form ***patterns.*** You enjoy the same-size bowl of your favorite cereal every morning. Every Tuesday evening you watch the same detective show right after the network news. You generally go to the neighborhood supermarket every Thursday evening to purchase your weekly groceries. When you are upset about something, you eat more of your favorite "sinful" chocolate bars. Our habits define a large part of our personality and can be studied as psychological patterns.

In the visual arts, our comprehension of any piece of artwork depends on our ability to understand its visual structure and the relationships between its ***forms*** (parts). When this structure is systematized and the individual parts of a composition are relationally repeated, our visual perception is reinforced and comprehension is simplified. Pattern exemplifies this formal iteration.

The human roots of pattern making lie within our ancestral invention of pre-writing symbols and, perhaps even more importantly, the invention of weaving. It was this very ancient invention that brought regular patterns into human artwork. Weaving by its nature produces patterns, and as the craft evolved more variations developed. These patterns were interpreted in ceramics and on flat surfaces for decoration. Culturally, various populations favor pattern to enhance political and religious objects. The repetitive structure of pattern does remove some personal decision making from the artistic process, but this sacrifice is for a "higher" purpose. Pattern is intended to visually engage the viewer into transcendence from ordinary reality to a higher spiritual power plane. Considering this rich heritage, it is no wonder that archaeologists have filled our museums with pattern decorated objects.

The basic visual component of pattern is ***motif.*** This is usually relatively small in scale and may be representational, abstract, or non-objective. See Figures 4.33 through 4.42 for an example of one motif cycled through several pattern schemes. The use of content-based motifs offers the possibility of introducing thematic or conceptual issues to the artwork. Visual pattern making today is generally for decorative effect rather than overt symbol meaning. One of the

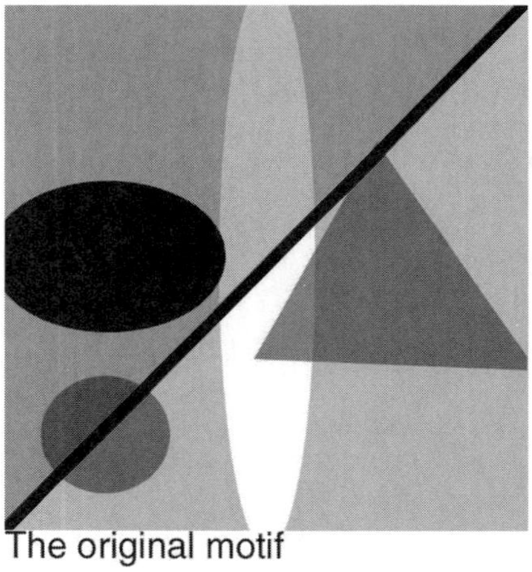

Figure 4.33

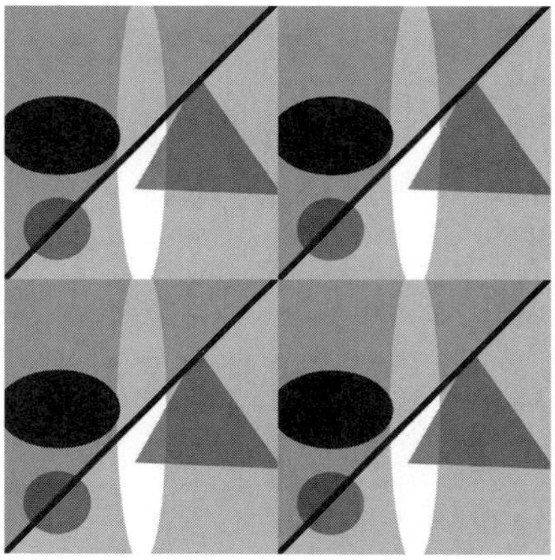

Figure 4.34

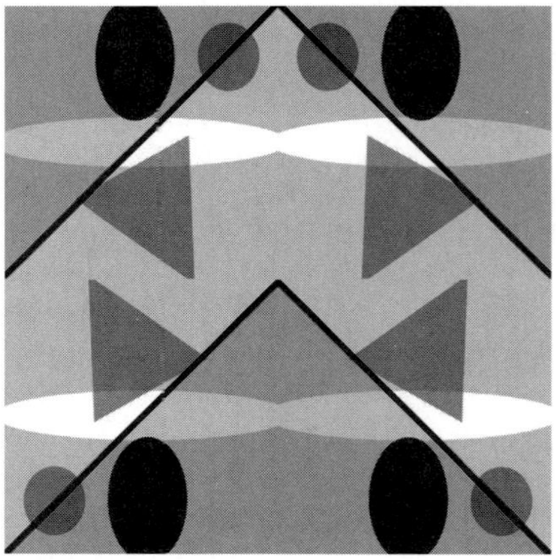

Figure 4.35

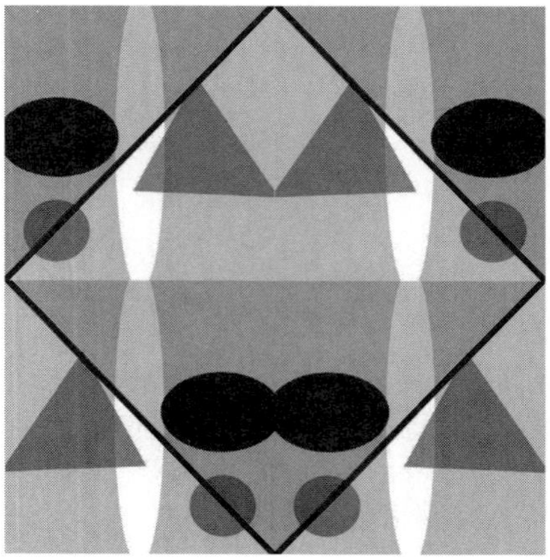

Figure 4.36

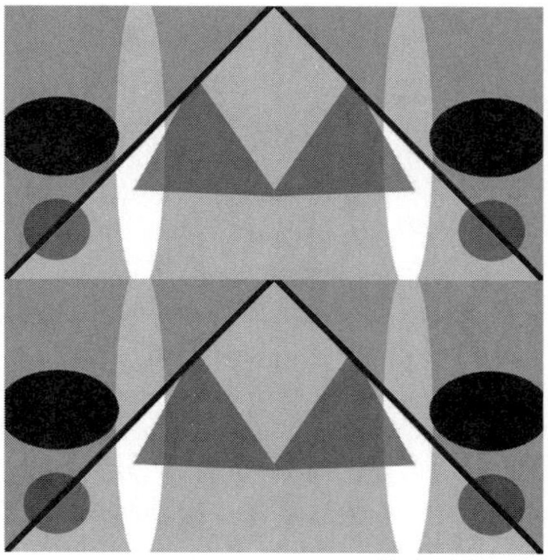

Figure 4.37

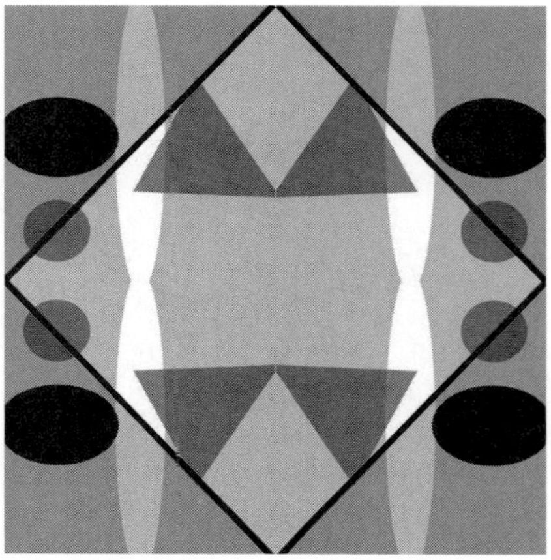

Figure 4.38

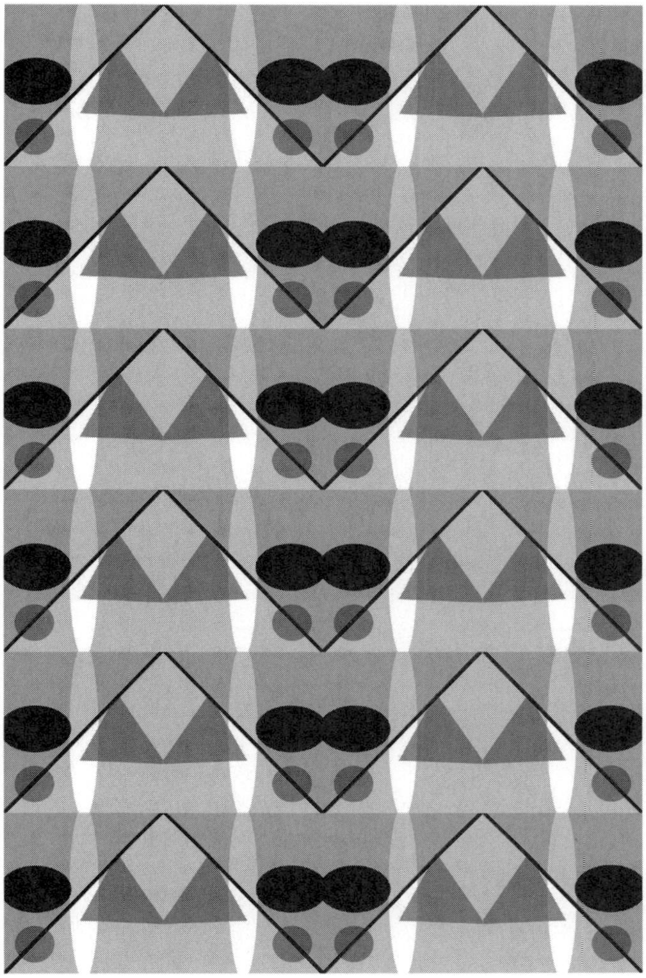

Figure 4.39

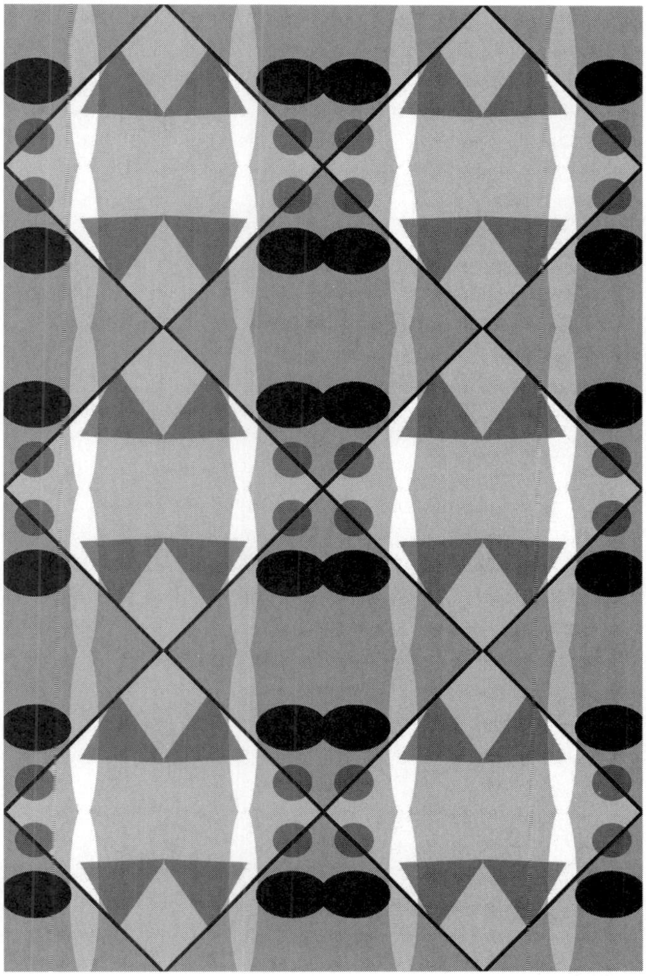

Figure 4.40

best examples is wallpaper, where we find the repetition of motifs within systematic structures.

A motif that simply repeats in lockstep order within the grid is referred to as a ***block repeat pattern*** (Figure 4.43). A ***drop repeat*** or ***slip reflection pattern*** (Figure 4.44) occurs when a unit of the grid partially slides down vertically as its motifs move across horizontally.

Another common arrangement is to move every other row of the grid one-half motif down, creating a ***drop-middle*** or ***slip-middle pattern*** (Figure 4.45). Other effects can be achieved by rotation or flipping one or more motifs. Pattern motifs that arrange themselves systematically around a central point are referred to as ***concentric patterns*** (Figure 4.46).

In the "fine arts," a variant with much more expressive possibilities is referred to as ***random pattern*** or irregular random pattern. This is similar to what you see when looking at the fallen leaves on a forest floor. Imagine many different leaves, tumbled at angles and overlapped, varying in size and type. This riot of shapes pushes the envelope of pattern definition as far as it can go without entering pure textural chaos.

Many of the design problems in this book secondarily deal with pattern while pursuing other primary design considerations. For this section we have selected five problems that center specifically on the issue of pattern formation and manipulation. Each approaches pattern from a different perspective of technique and visual utilization.

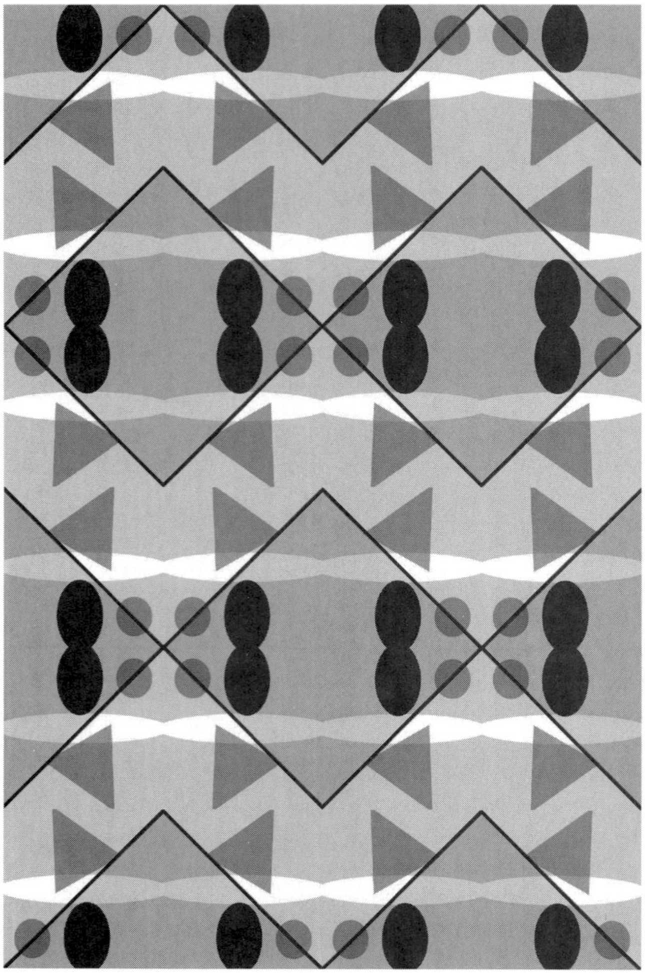

Figure 4.41

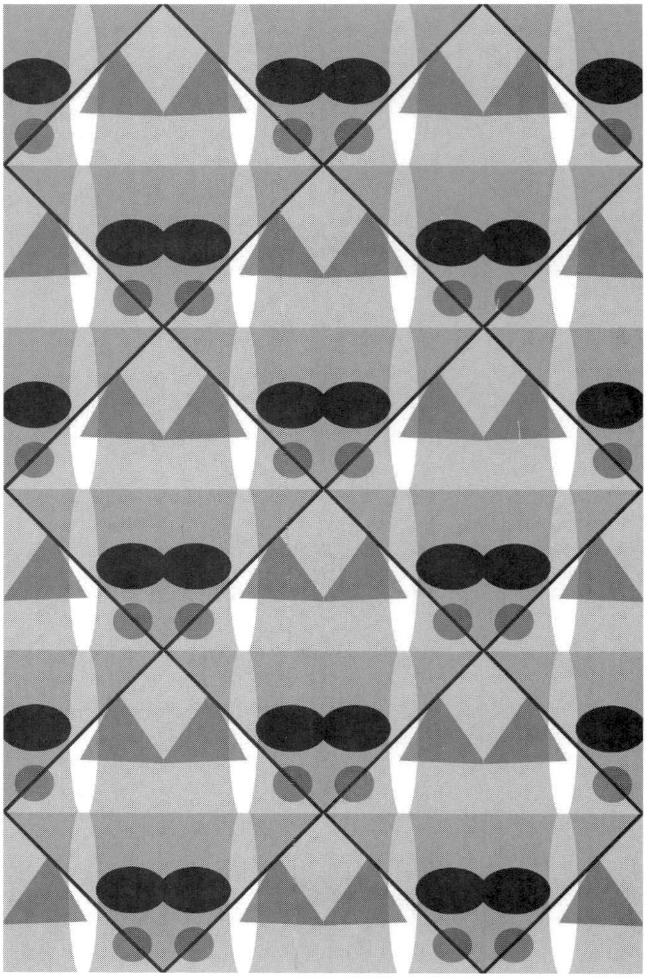

Figure 4.42

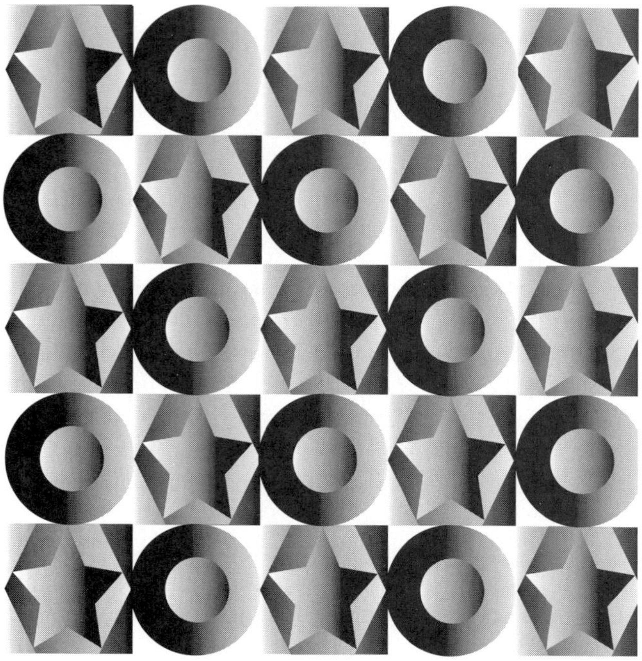

Block Repeat Pattern

Figure 4.43

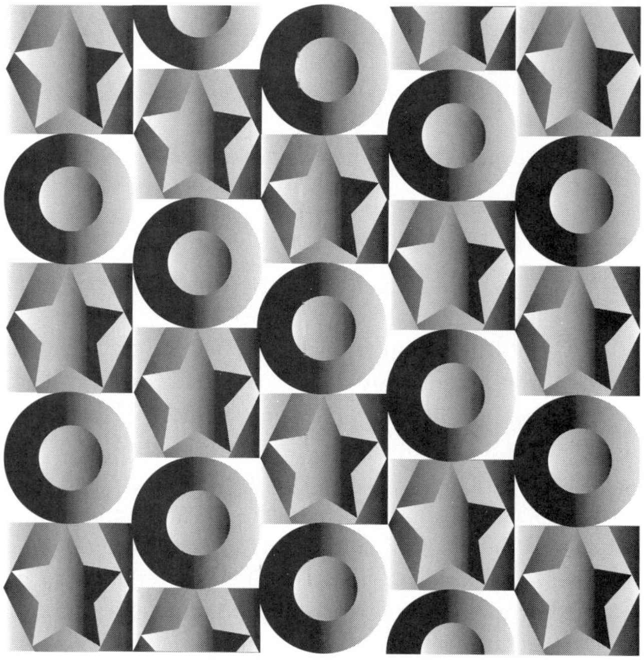

Drop Repeat or Slip Reflection Pattern

Figure 4.44

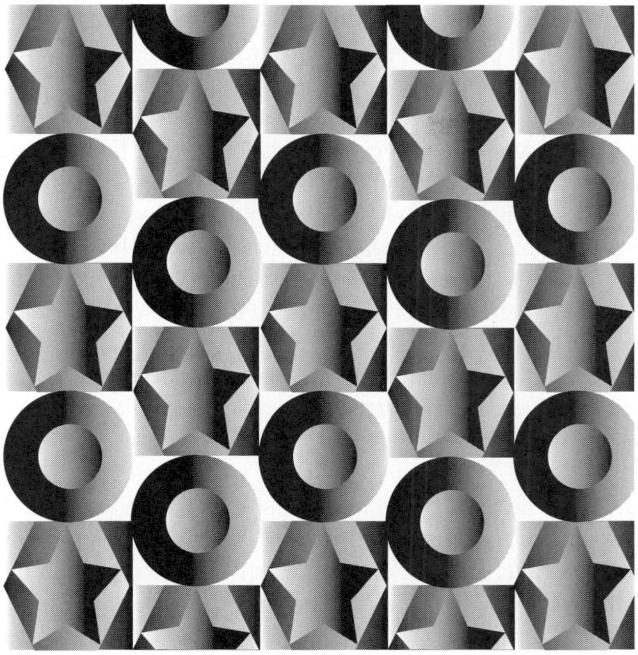

Drop Middle or Slip Middle Pattern

Figure 4.45

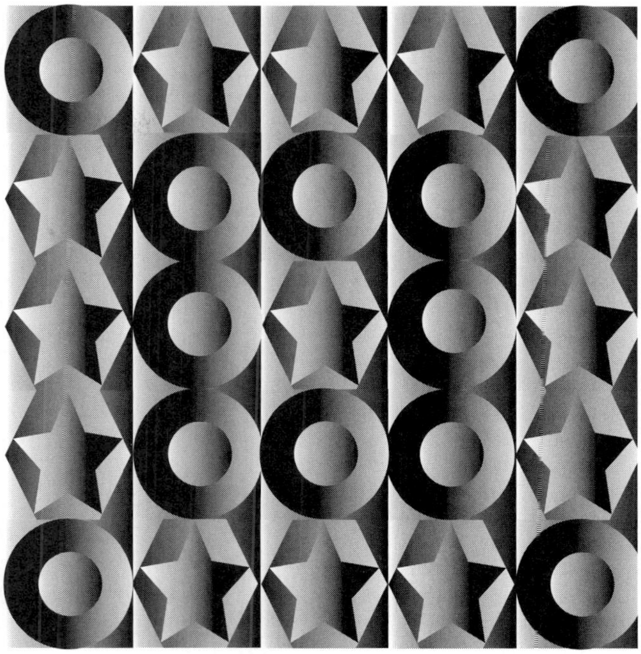

Concentric Pattern

Figure 4.46

MOTIF TO PATTERN: CIRCLE, SQUARE, TRIANGLE

The repetition of shapes usually conveys an immediate sense of ***harmony.*** It is easy to understand why a design composed of forms that are of similar or identical shapes in a repeat pattern can unify a design. Designs based on repetition structures or variations of those structures (subdividing and repeating elements of a repeat design) will tend to be perceived as carefully organized and very controlled.

OBJECTIVES

This assignment will help you become comfortable working back and forth between ***vector-*** and ***raster-based*** programs. At the same time, you will be working with ***geometric shapes*** to develop compound shapes. Organized effectively in a ***frame of reference,*** the combined geometric shapes become a ***unit of repetition.*** Placed in a ***formal*** grid structure, the unit is repeated in a variety of ways as an introduction to ***pattern*** development. The surface or "color" changes explored in "Part 2: Color Change Experiments" will open up a range of image solutions. Maintaining an understanding of pattern versus composition will be emphasized and the infinite visual possibilities from a single, basic source will be explored.

While this exercise can be completed with traditional materials, the computer affords greater opportunity for experimentation in less production time, while also learning how to work electronically

MATERIALS

Electronic: A raster program, such as Adobe Photoshop; a vector program such as Adobe Illustrator; a printer or output device.

Traditional: Bristol or illustration board; pencils; ruler; template with 1″ geometric shapes; black art paper with a utility knife and adhesive or black ink with brushes and pens.

PROCEDURE

Drawing a Grid The first step in developing the circle, square, triangle project is to develop a 2″ square grid. When you open a drawing program, like Adobe Illustrator, you will see a page designated. Turn on the ruler option to see where on the page you will be working. In Illustrator, go to **View** menu and **Show Rulers.** In the upper left corner of the screen is a square with a crosshair. If you put the cursor on the crosshair and pull over to the edge of the "page," you will set the zero point at the upper left page corner. For this project, set the zero point at the margin corner. Under the **View** menu scroll to **Show Grid.** In the dialogue box, select **Snap to Grid.** When you begin drawing your grid, lines will be forced straight to the grid line. Select the **Pen Tool** from the **Tool** menu. Click on the (1″,0) point, then on the 1″ mark on the bottom margin. If you hold down the shift key before the second click, you will have a straight line. The line will be a blue "drafting" line. For the line to be visible, make sure the stroke is black and the line weight is 1 pt. by checking the **Show Stroke** window. Once you have drawn your first line and it is still selected, **Copy** the selection and **Paste** to "draw" the remaining lines. Use the select arrow to move the lines into place or, when a line is selected, use the keyboard arrow keys to move an element. When you have drawn all of the vertical lines, repeat the process for the horizontal lines of the grid. **Save As,** *Grid.* (Figure 4.47)

Creating Geometric Shapes With the **Show Grid** function still turned on, a one-inch grid fills the entire work area. Using the shape tools, create a 1″ circle, 1″ square, and 1″ triangle in the workspace outside the page. Holding down the shift key when you use the **Ellipse** and **Rectangle Tools** will give you a perfect circle and square. To create the triangle, use the **Pen Tool** and click on appropriate points on the grid guide to create an ***equilateral*** triangle. (Figure 4.48)

Developing Compound Shapes Using the selection tool, move the three shapes into one of the 2″ squares of the grid to make a composition. Each shape must touch at least one other shape, and the combined shape must touch all four sides of the grid. Select each of the three shapes and **Copy** and **Paste** them into one of the other 2″ squares of the grid. Deselect the shapes and move them around in the 2″ square individually to create another composition. Remember, shapes can be rotated to make them more dynamic by going to the **Object** menu and scrolling down to **Transform,** then **Rotate** setting the **Angle** to **[45]°.** Repeat this process until you have completed at least ten experiments. **Save As,** *Compound Shapes.* (Figure 4.49)

Pick the compound shape composition that you find the most interesting. Hold down the shift key and click on all three shapes to select them. Go to the **Object** menu and **Group,** to make them selectable as one shape. **Copy** the selected shape to save it to the clipboard.

Part 1: Pattern Generation You are now ready to begin a series of pattern generation experiments. From the **File** menu, **Open** *Grid* then **Paste.** The compound shape you selected and copied will appear on the page. Move it to the top, left 2″ square of the grid. Continue pasting until you have filled each 2″ square of the page with the compound shape. **Save As,** *Formal Repetition.* (Figure 4.50)

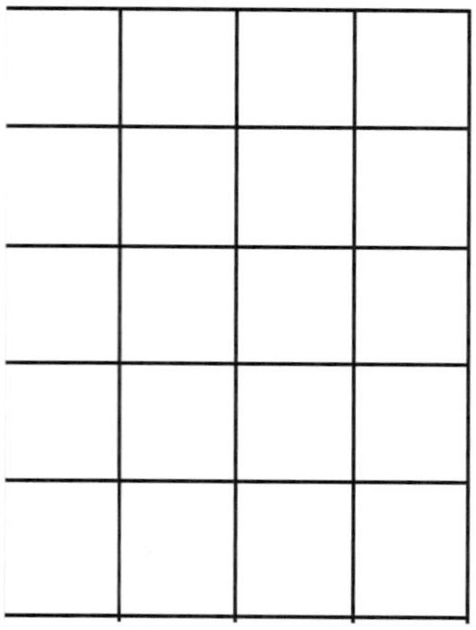

Figure 4.47

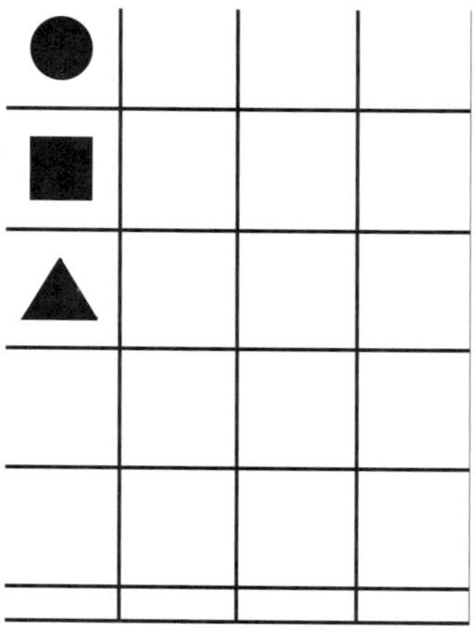

Figure 4.48

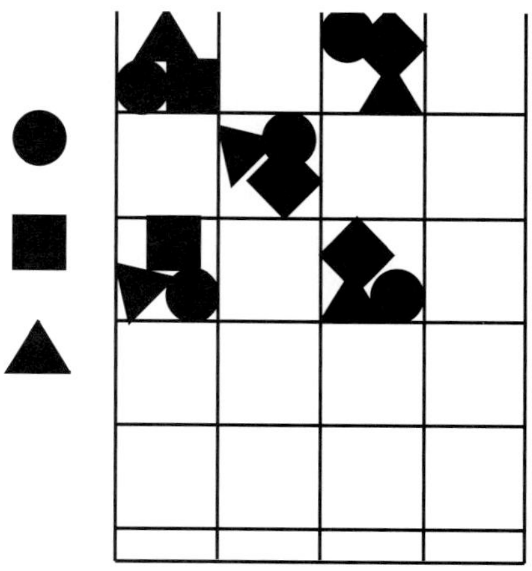

Figure 4.49

You will continue with pattern generation experiments. You can either repeat the process, re-opening the *Grid,* or make a copy of the file and modify the *Formal Repetition.*

To begin the process, re-open *Grid.* When you **Paste,** the compound shape you selected and copied will appear on the page. Move it to the top, left 2″ square of the grid. **Paste** again and move this shape to the second box in the top row. While the object is selected, scroll to **Transform,** then **Reflect,** picking **Axis [Vertical].** The shape appears to be a reflection of itself over the vertical line. **Paste** again, moving the shape to the second box down on the left. **Transform** this shape by selecting **Reflect,** this time with the **Axis [Horizontal].** The shape appears to be a reflection of itself over the horizontal line. **Paste** again, moving this shape to the second box down and the second box over. This time you will **Reflect** the **Axis** both vertically and horizontally. The shape appears to be a reflection of itself over both the vertical and horizontal lines of the grid. Continue this way until the entire page is filled. Another option is to select all four squares, copy and paste them as a group into the next block of four. **Save As.** *Mirrored Image.* (Figure 4.51)

Re-open the *Grid* and **Paste.** The compound shape you selected and copied will appear on the page. Move it to the top, left 2″ square of the grid. **Paste** again and move this shape to the second box in the top row. This time, instead of transforming with reflect, **Rotate** the shape with the **Angle** set to **[270°].** This rotates the object a quarter turn to the right, the direction you are going. Instead of pasting the original object, select the quarter-turned version, and **Copy. Paste** and place this shape in the next box to the right, performing the same **Rotate Angle [270°].** Continue on this way until you complete the page with a quarter-turn rotation, changing the Angle [X°] you used by the direction you are moving. **Save As,** *1/4 Turn* (Figure 4.52).

Repeat the process one more time to create an experimental pattern, using combinations of formal repetitions, reflections, or rotations to create a new, original pattern. Remember that the finished surface must still be a pattern. **Save As,** *Experimental.*

Part 2: Color Change Experiments After you have completed all four movement studies, you will begin to experiment with "color" changes. The final assignment will include

1. Black on white
2. White on black
3. A figure/ground change based on the 2″ grid
4. An experimental coloring system.

There are four pattern studies and four color system choices. You will use each set of four one time only, mixing and matching patterns and color systems. Determine which color system should be applied to a particular pattern study to create the most interesting overall result. For the sake of demonstration, I will use the formal repetition for all four color changes.

To perform some of the color changes, we need to convert the files from vector to raster (Illustrator to Photoshop). Go to the **File** menu and **Save a Copy.** Return to **File** to **Export** as **TIFF.**

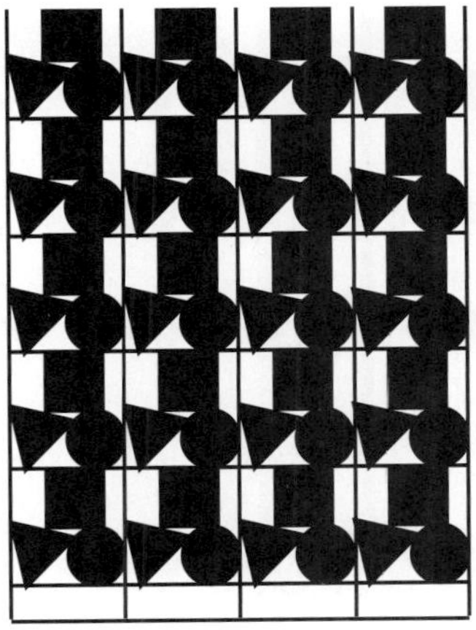

Figure 4.50

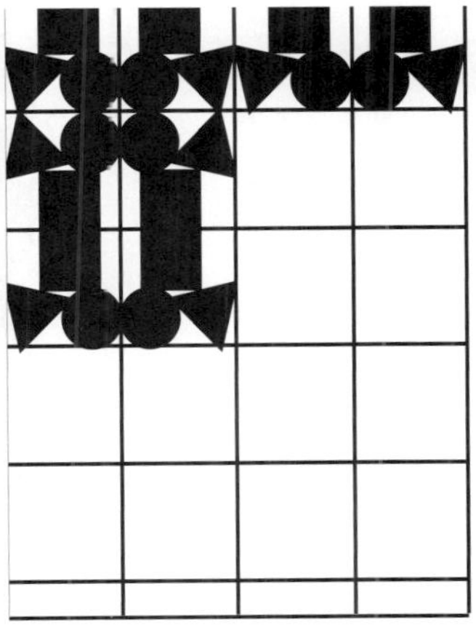

Figure 4.51

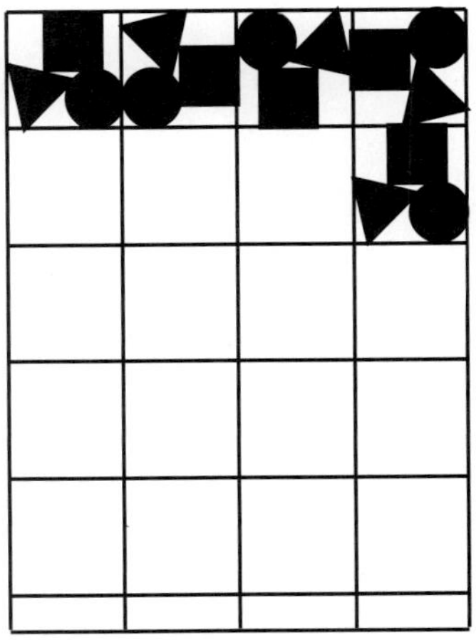

Figure 4.52

Open the exported pattern in Photoshop. You are now ready to make color alterations. To create a white on black solution, go to the **Edit** menu and **Select All.** Next, scroll down the **Image** menu to **Adjust** and **Invert.** What was black (the figure) is white, what was white (the ground) is black (Figure 4.53).

For the Figure/Ground change solution, you will select alternate grid boxes and then invert. To ensure that your selection of the grid makes a perfect square each time, double click on the select box or **Window** menu and **Show Navigator.** When you go to **Option,** select **Marquee Options** and **Style.** For **[Constrained Aspect Ration],** choose **Width: [2]** and **Height: [2].** Select alternate boxes, creating a checkerboard (Figure 4.54).

For the experimental coloring system, you are free to explore. You might choose to continue inverting random line rhythms (Figure 4.55). You might also want to explore unfilled shapes or the effect of a heavier grid line, or no visible grid. To accomplish the last three explorations, you will need to return to the vector study, where it is easier to make these changes, then return the pattern to Photoshop for coloring, repeating the **Export** process. (Figure 4.56)

Traditional To complete this assignment with traditional materials, you will follow the same steps and concepts outlined in the electronic procedure. What changes is the way in which you cut, paste, fill, and repeat and the way in which you create the grid.

With a ruler, you can measure off and create the one-inch circle, square, and triangle, or trace the three shapes from a template. Mark off a series of two-inch squares on a piece of bristol board to create your compound shape experiments. When you find the one that is most interesting, the compound shape cut out of bristol will serve as a traceable template for your pattern experiments.

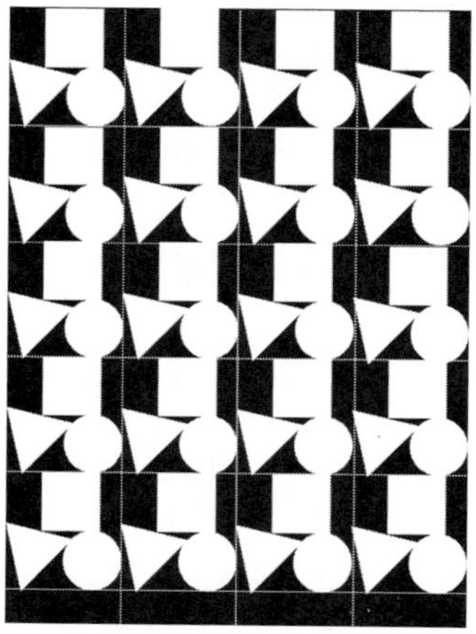

Figure 4.53

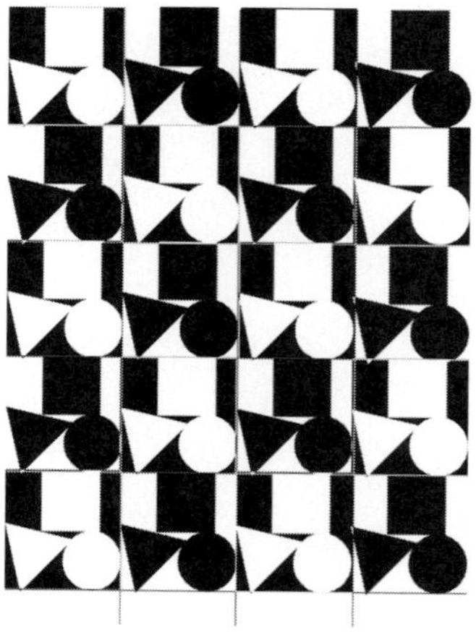

Figure 4.54

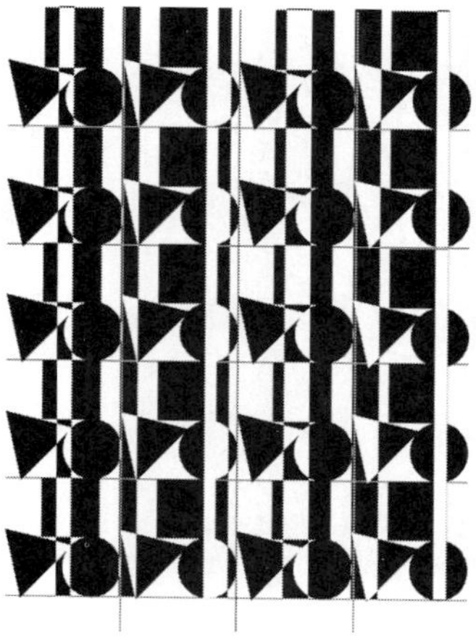

Figure 4.55

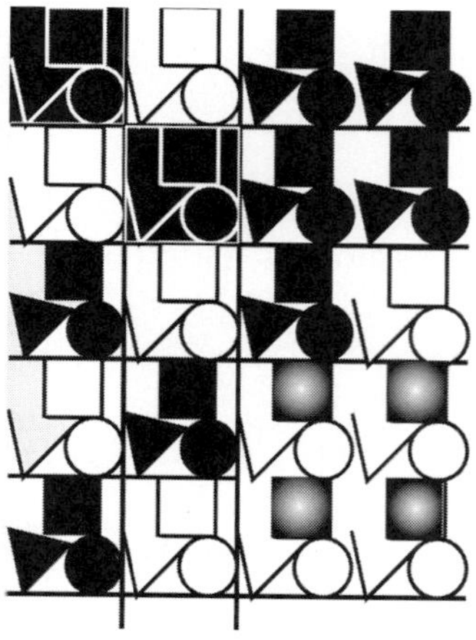

Figure 4.56

Any stable surface, whether bristol or illustration board, will serve as a support for your pattern studies. A 15″ × 20″ piece of illustration board will work well for all four studies. You can either cut the board into four 7-1/2″ × 10″ pieces, or leave it whole, dividing it visually. In either case, using a pencil, mark off the surface with a two-inch grid.

Place the compound shape template in each box of the grid and trace, filling each of the four "pages" with the four patterns. If you are using ink to complete the assignment, you can paint directly onto the illustration board at this time. Remember the four "color" studies, and paint the positive and negative shapes accordingly.

To complete the "color" with cut black paper, there is an additional approach you should consider. Pre-determine which pattern will be black on white, inverted, or a figure/ground change. Cut a piece of black paper to the size of the finished study and mark off a two-inch grid. Trace the template onto the black paper. When you cut out the compound shapes from the black paper, they can be glued to the illustration board for the black on white solution. The remaining negative space left on the black paper can be adhered whole to a different section of illustration board, completing the inverted study. This approach is also quite effective for the figure/ground change.

Student work by Amie Clluffo

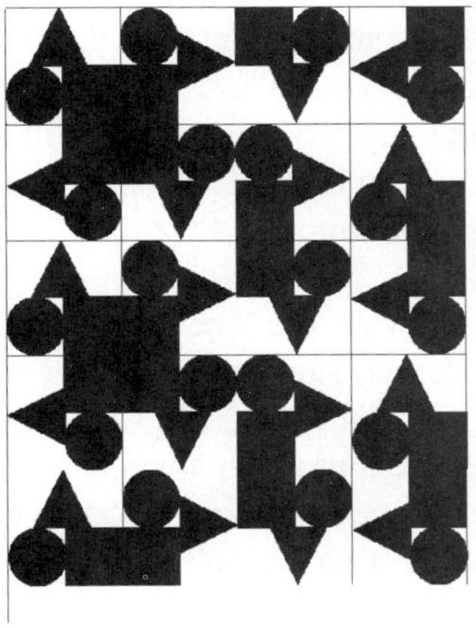

Figure 4.57 Quarter-turn with black figures on white ground

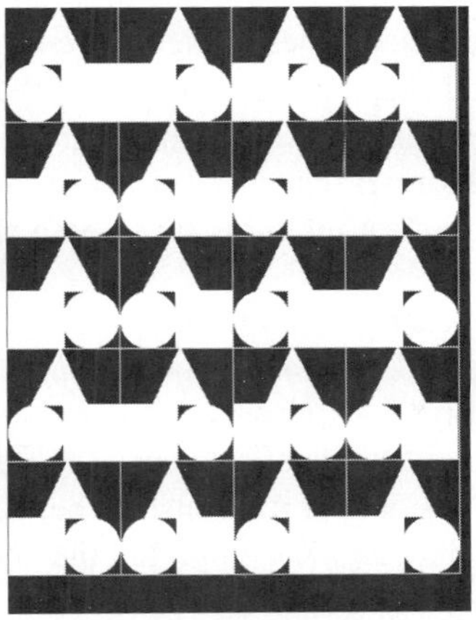

Figure 4.58 Experimental pattern with inverted color

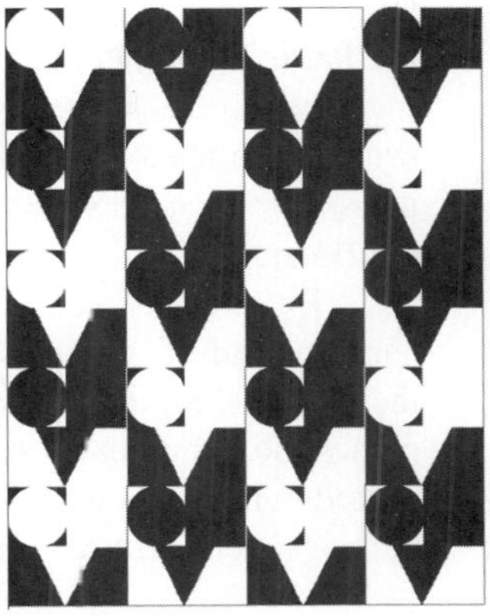

Figure 4.59 Formal repetition with figure/ground change

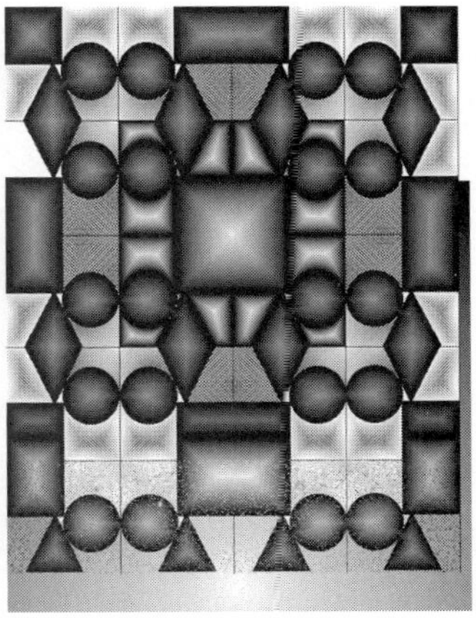

Figure 4.60 Mirror image with experimental color

MOTIF TO STRUCTURED COMPOSITION

The repetition of shapes can convey an immediate sense of harmony. It is easy to understand why forms that are of similar or identical shapes can unify a design. Designs based on repetition structures, or variations of those structures (subdividing and repeating elements of a repeat design), will tend to be perceived as carefully organized and very controlled.

OBJECTIVES

The overall goals of this project explore the creation of a dynamic design through the organization of the unit into a ***grid structure.*** Different than the basic repeat-motif designs that we explored earlier, where pattern development is emphasized, the motif (unit) will be repeated, but will be subjected to manipulation not only of shape, but of variations to the grid. The design will be constructed with a focus on maintaining order through structure, and will consider the compositional elements of ***balance*** and ***symmetry*** integral to the exploration. Spatial illusion, evident through overlapping and structural connections, will be identified as the design process unfolds.

DEVELOPMENT OF THE MOTIF

The objective of this aspect of the project is to create a shape ***(motif)*** that is unique in character by exploring the process of developing shapes through reference, transformation, and materials exploration. The individual elements or repeated motifs within a grid structure can be referred to as units. A unit is considered to be a ***motif*** that is confined by the boundaries of a designated contour such as a square, and both positive and negative qualities of the shape are considered important.

A unit can be created in a variety of ways. It can be hand drawn or ***organic, irregular,*** or ***geometric,*** or even accidental. Shapes can be derived from the environment, and can then be manipulated and transformed into units.

MATERIALS

Electronic: Sketchbook; scanner; disks for storage; a raster-based software program such as Adobe Photoshop; good-quality ink jet printer

Traditional: Sketchbook; pencils; black markers; black gouache; brushes; scissors; rubber cement; black paper; rulers; french curves; flexible curves; bristol board; illustration board.

PROCEDURE

Electronic Using a graphics program that allows you to draw freehand as well as use tools to create shapes, create a minimum of 24 shapes. Open a **New** file (the file window should be 8″ wide and 12″ high), go to **Image** and **Mode** and **Select Grayscale.** Then, using the **Grid** and **Guide** options in the menu, set up a grid structure of about 24 or so 2″ squares (4 units across and 6 units down). Use the **Snap to Grid** function so that each shape works within the specific confines of the square. In each square, using tools such as the **Paint Brush, Pencil,** and shape creation tools like the circle, square, etc., experiment with the various ways of creating a shape. Work right to the edges of the square. **Fill** a square with black (use the **Paint-Bucket** Tool with the foreground color set as black) and then subtract areas with the **Selection Tools** (the **Lasso** and **Rectangular Marquee**) and the **Delete** key.

Be aware of your environment; use it as a source for new shapes. Feel free to use parts instead of wholes. Consider ***animate*** and ***inanimate*** forms; study the ***contours*** of their shapes. Simplify. Modify. Look closely at the shapes you are making. If a shape becomes too complicated it may lose its effectiveness and become a problem when it is repeated in the grid design. Consider the relationships between shape and space; bleeding to the edge; centered; off centered; etc. Keep in mind the negative space as well as the positive space. You can also work in a sketchbook with black marker or black paper and then **Scan** the shapes at a resolution of 300. Keep all units 2″ × 2″ whether they are created on the computer or in a sketchbook.

Choose a few of your most interesting shapes. Refine them, making changes when necessary to produce an exciting shape. Finally, choose the most successful solution and present it in its positive and negative form (Figures 4.61 and 4.62) by printing them out as a 4″ x 4″ squares (enlarging to 200 percent).

UNIT IN A REPETITION GRID

In this part of the assignment a basic grid (equally spaced horizontal and vertical lines) will also be elaborated on by subdivisions that cross diagonally from corner to corner within the unit.

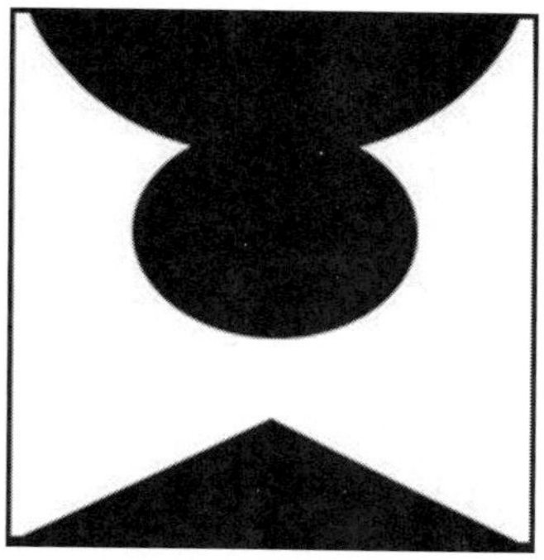

Figure 4.61

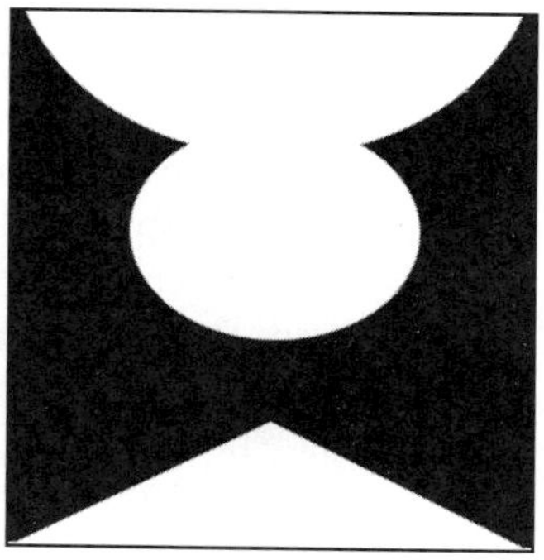

Figure 4.62

PROCEDURE

Electronic Use the motif (unit) that you chose for the solution for the first stage of the assignment. Continue to work in grayscale mode because you don't need the color information. **Open** a **New** File and create a grid that is 6 units by 6 units with each unit 2″ square (12″ × 12″). Set the **Snap To Grid** command under the **View** menu so that the unit can be pasted into and restrained by the grid. Some units may be filled in completely black; some may be left white (or half-diagonally white or black). They can be cut diagonally to reveal only half of the unit. To cut the unit, use the **Polygon Lasso Tool** and the **Delete** key. The unit may be used in its positive or negative form; it may be reversed or turned within the square (the whole square must turn, not just the form in the square). To turn the whole square, **Select** it with the **Rectangle Marquee Tool** and then go to **Edit** and **Transform** and select **Rotate.** Choose the direction you would like to rotate. The unit can also be repeated continuously (Figure 4.63) as in the manner of a repeat pattern.

You may also cut the unit diagonally (Figure 4.64) and experiment with half of the shape in its positive or negative form or try half positive–half negative.

You must be aware of the new shapes that will be created within the grid structure as a whole. If the software program has a **Define Pattern/Fill** option you can fill the whole 12″ × 12″ format with one version of your unit and then **Cut, Transform,** and **Arrange** from there. When you cut and paste, each element will come up on its own layer. You should **Merge Layers** when possible to keep the size of your files manageable. Make a copy of your background layer because some functions will not work on the background layer itself. You can **Copy** and **Paste** four units at a time to work quickly and to create subdivisions within the design.

Utilize the **Cutting, Pasting, Define Pattern,** and **Fill** components of the software program to make experimenting with the rotation and placement of the units easier and faster. You should be able to try out many possibilities. Save each one and then decide which one is your most successful (Figure 4.65).

If you have a large format printer, you can print out the image 12″ × 12″ on good-quality paper and mount on illustration board with a 2″ border all around. If you have to

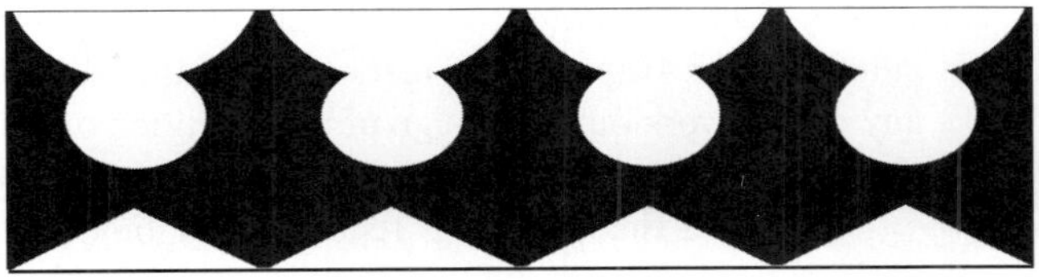

Figure 4.63

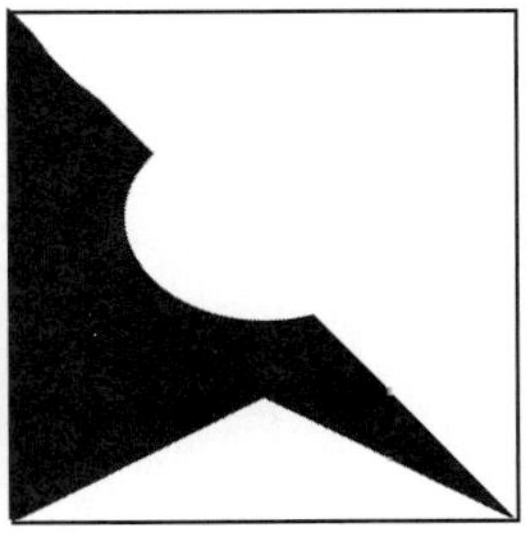

Figure 4.64

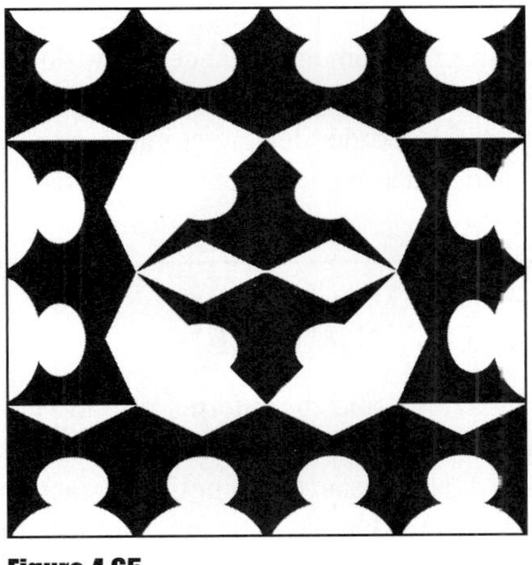

Figure 4.65

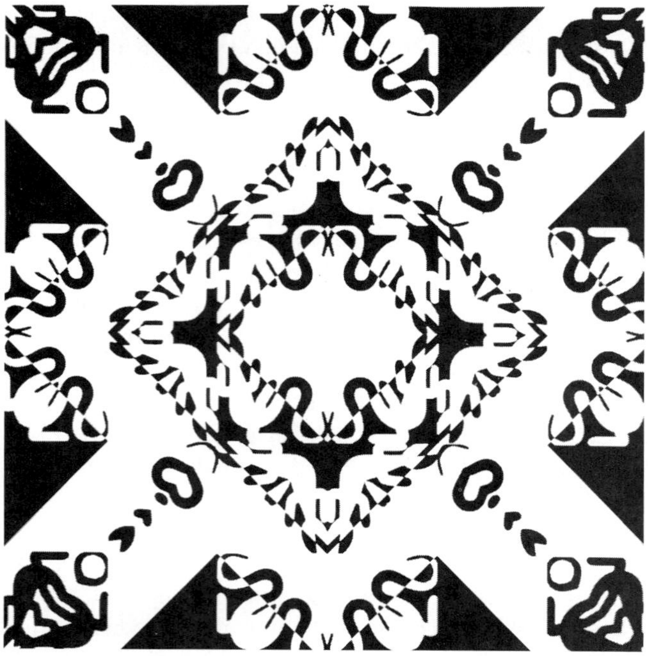

Figure 4.66 *Figure by Dave Scott*

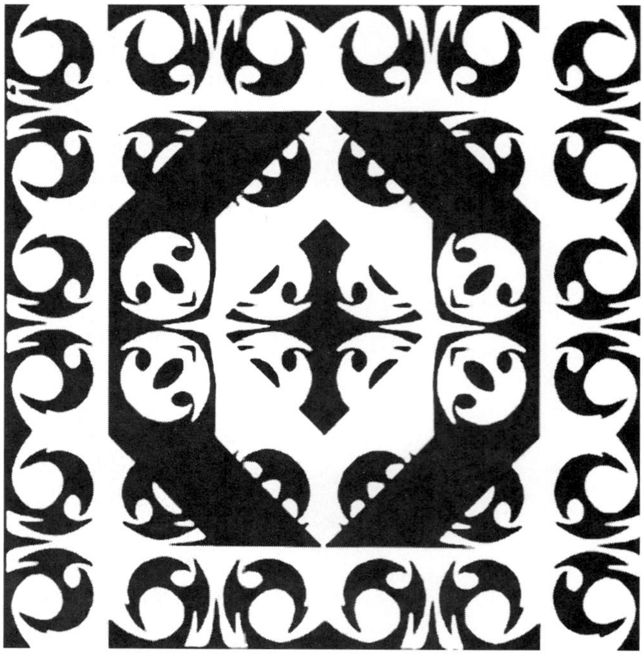

Figure 4.67 *Figure by Mike Salkewicz*

print smaller, scale down the image to the desired size. Here are a couple of student examples (Figures 4.66, 4.67).

Traditional As before, create a minimum of 24 shapes. Using a sketchbook, experiment with material manipulation. Draw, cut, combine pieces of paper. You should experiment with pencils, markers, mechanical tools (scissors, compass, flexible curves) to create shapes. Once you have chosen the shape that you find to be your most creative, present a positive and negative version of your shape with black gouache or black paper on illustration board.

Unit in Grid Structure Make sketches of your unit in a grid structure using proportional cutouts of the shape, or use markers to do quick renderings of placement ideas. Look for any way to work out the design of the repetition of the shape easily—photocopies stencils, etc. Begin to make choices in regard to placement, direction, and position.

Create a final design by repeating, rotating, and mirroring as in electronic procedure until you have a successful design. Transfer the design information to illustration board and paint with black gouache. Make a 3″ border all around.

DISCUSSION

What qualities do the most successful designs have? Cite shape relationship to edge; uniqueness of shape; variety of contour, etc. How does the overall design hold up in terms of creativity; rhythm; movement; balance? How do the ***gestalt principles*** of ***proximity*** and ***closure*** operate in the design? Can you make reference to design structures that utilize repeat motifs (wallpaper; border design; cultural motifs)? In what ways can you apply an understanding of grid structures (or plans) to everyday life?

A SERIAL EXPLORATION OF MOTIF AND STRUCTURE

Newspapers, magazines, and the Internet provide us with a vast array of visual information, which attracts us, repels us, and sometimes shocks us. In general, we are fascinated with all of this on a daily basis. Our emotional reactions to images are often centered in our recognition of the forms that they contain. The structures and sense of organization of any given image, however, can alter its impact and profoundly affect the ways in which it functions visually, conceptually, and emotionally. Certain images access physical and visual processes from which we derive pleasure. Patterns, with their rhythm, repetition, and organized structure, are examples of this type of image.

The pleasing, stable structure of pattern can also offer an opportunity to explore content. The basic visual component of a pattern is a motif. When content-based motifs are used, patterns can transcend the merely decorative and introduce thematic or conceptual issues to the artwork.

Traditionally, printmaking has been the dominant process used to create decorative pattern. The development of digital graphics programs, however, has instituted a truly facile means of generating form and pattern. They provide a very accessible way of quickly creating variety in structure, scale, and color.

OBJECTIVES

This project involves the creation of motifs and patterns within a digital graphic program. The objectives include the utilization of repetition and rhythm within formal compositional structures to create dynamic pattern designs.

MATERIALS

Electronic: A vector-based drawing program such as Adobe Illustrator; a raster-based drawing program such as Adobe Photoshop; mounting board; rubber cement; pen or utility knife

Traditional: Art erasers; acetate; paint; crayons; pencils; pastels; art papers; cutting tools

PROCEDURE

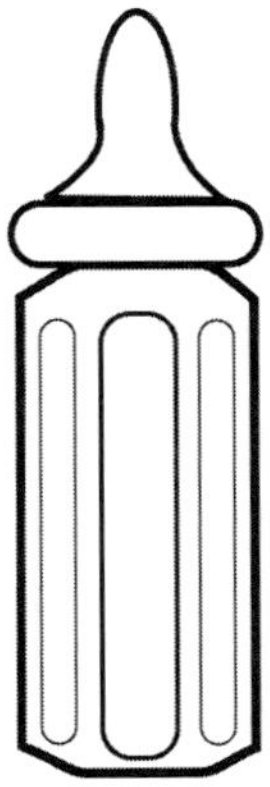

Figure 4.68

Electronic

Creating a Motif

Locate a photographic reference for the forms that you wish to utilize as motifs within your patterns. Keep these images visually accessible, either physically beside your computer or on your screen as scanned images. Working within a vector-based graphics program, utilize the shape and drawing tools to create simple motifs that reference your photographic images. Work with line only, changing stroke weight to vary the form. Focus on the creation of closed shapes, joining paths when necessary (Figure 4.68) When you are finished working, save your motif to your disc. Repeat the process to create a second motif form.

Creating a Regular Pattern

Regular patterns utilize a single motif that maintains its scale and orientation. Horizontal and vertical alignments are maintained within a simple formal structure. This type of pattern utilizes the most inactive compositional structure. Because of this, careful consideration needs to be given to other elements and relationships that can enhance and activate the overall design.

Begin by making a copy of your original motif into a new file of your own desired size. Choose a harmonious color scheme and apply color to closed shapes in the form of flat color, gradients, or patterns. Focus on the creation of contrast and activity within the forms and consider the use of differing ***chromatic values,*** black and white (Figure 4.69, color insert). It is important that you change the attributes of the motifs—that is, apply color, pattern and/or gradation—before they have been copied to create a pattern. Otherwise the time spent "filling in" shapes will be considerable. Leave the negative space shapes to be filled in after the pattern is completed.

On the same document as your now-colored motif or on a new file, set up a structure that will facilitate the creation of a formal compositional structure. This may be achieved by showing both **Rulers** and **Grids. Select** your motif, **Group** it, and **Copy** it. **Paste** it into your new file, repeating it and utilizing your grid to align it in regular intervals. Once the motifs have been aligned, complete the pattern by filling the negative space with any color, value, or pattern (that falls within your color scheme) that is desired.

Negative space can be worked with as a single shape that can be filled and arranged behind your layer of motifs or as a series of shapes created by closed negative space between motifs that are touching (Figures 4.70, 4.71 (color insert), 4.72 (color insert)). When your pattern is completed, **Save** your work onto your disc and **Print** a copy.

Changing Scale and Orientation: Working with Irregular Patterns

Irregular patterns utilize a single motif that may be altered in terms of scale and orientation. The alignment of forms within this structure may be altered with the stipulation that repetition must occur within the given format. This type of pattern utilizes a much more active compositional structure that may dictate more refined or less active color relationships.

Utilizing the same procedure as in the last pattern dealing with regular structure, create a second pattern that varies some of the prerequisites. Again, begin by working with a copy of one of your linear motifs. Choose a second harmonious color scheme and apply color to closed shapes in the form of flat color, gradients, or patterns. Focus on the creation of contrast and activity within the forms and consider the use of differing chromatic values, black and white. It is important, again, that you change the attributes of the motifs—that is, apply color, pattern, and/or gradation—before they have been copied to create a pattern so that excessive time is not spent "filling in" shapes throughout the image. Leave the negative space shapes to be filled in after the pattern is completed.

Select your entire motif and group the various pieces together. **Copy** and **Paste** your newly colored motif into a formal compositional structure to create a pattern. Utilize grids and rulers to help to align forms and create the structure. Complete the design by filling in the negative space shapes with desired colors, gradients, or patterns that fall within your given color scheme (Figures 4.73, 4.74 (color insert), 4.75 (color insert)). When you have completed the design, save your work onto your disc and print your pattern.

Combined Digital Patterns: Merging Vector- and Raster-Based Images

Combined patterns utilize a variety of motifs and alternating structures. Complexity often becomes extreme and consideration must be given to those other elements and relationships that produce relative stasis within an image.

Utilizing the digital patterns that you created in a digital graphics program, create a combined pattern that integrates photographic images. If you have not done so already, **Scan** photographs of your references into a raster-based graphics program. These may be the same references that you have been using or they may be radically different. You may use black-and-white or color photographs. **Save** your scanned photographs, now digital motifs, to your disc. **Rasterize** your patterns by opening up your vector-based patterns into the raster program. Create a new combined pattern by layering your drawn patterns with photographic images. You are still creating a pattern; the new layer(s) of images must be arranged in a formal structure that will overlap the underlying pattern. You may utilize whatever colors emerge naturally from this process (the original pattern and the actual colors of the photographic images) or you may alter the color scheme in any way that you desire. Try to use your intuitive color sense to create a harmonious color scheme. Consider merging the images and layers by manipulating the opacity of each of the layers when overlapping whole patterns, pieces of patterns, or motifs (Figure 4.76, 4.77 (color insert), 4.78 (color insert)). **Save** your work onto your disc and **Print** your pattern.

Traditional This project may be done as a traditional printmaking project. Motifs may be created as stamp prints or stencils utilizing basic materials such as soft art erasers and acetate. Compositional structures may need to be established utilizing penciled grids. Color may be applied utilizing paint, crayons, pencils, or pastels. The same conceptual and formal parameters apply to the problem.

PRESENTATION

Cut out your designs and mount on a single black or white board, creating margins and borders that best suit the images.

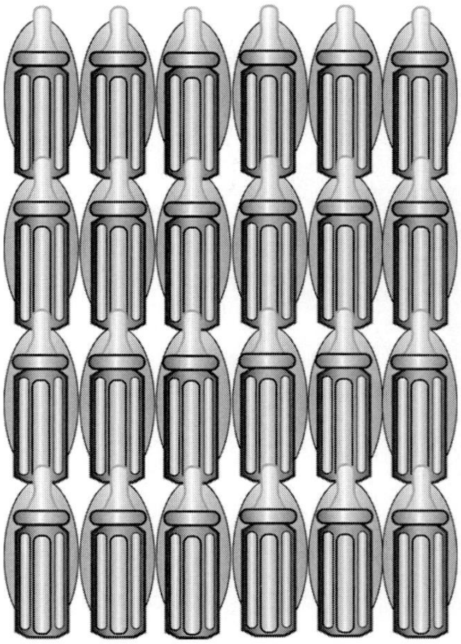

Figure 4.70

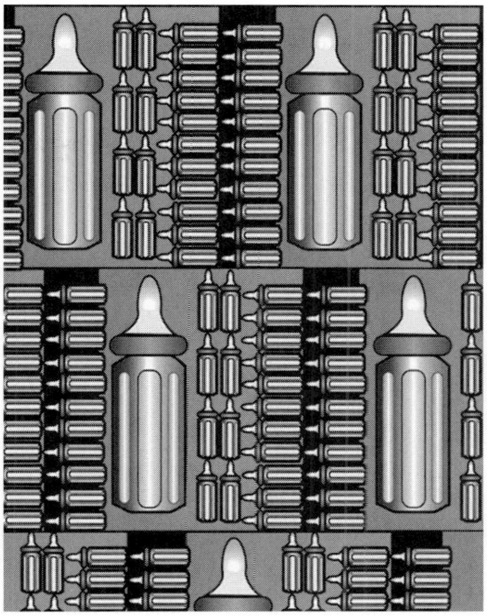

Figure 4.73

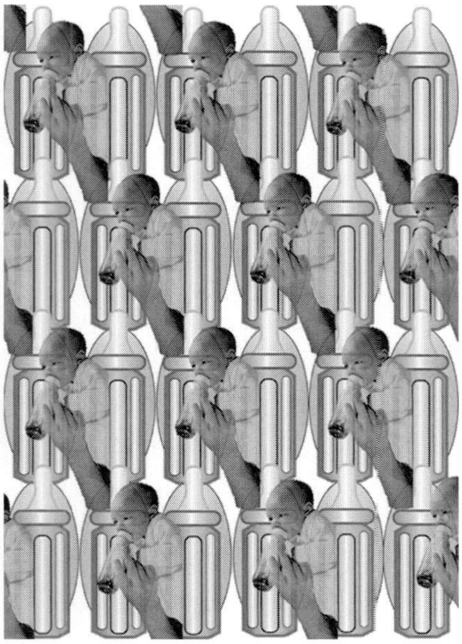

Figure 4.76

DISCUSSION

The possible solutions for this project may depend on experience and facility with the graphics programs, but also involve a number of formal variables. The critique should consider the issue of identity in regard to the motifs as a means of altering the function and content of any given pattern. Discussion should include the effect of scale on the legibility of the motifs and their dominance within the image and the role that complexity in structure plays in dictating the simplicity or complexity of other forms and relationships to create balance and unity within the completed image. The role that relative contrast of value and/or intensity can play in modifying any given color scheme also becomes an interesting point of discussion in a comparative review of the problem. These three patterns are but a few of the examples possible relative to pattern and motif. The presence of a variety of solutions provides instructive points of contrast for different visual effects.

RUN-TOGETHER PATTERN

We constantly seek order and meaning in our personal lives. Our conscious and subconscious selves reject chaos and dissolution, which run counter to the basic biological and chemical structure of our DNA. We use patterns at all levels of our being to satisfy this expression. Visual or artistic patterns have been used to order surfaces from prehistoric times to the present.

Patterns on clothing, window drapes, upholstery, and rugs are current ubiquitous examples. Random irregular patterns, irregular repeating patterns, rigid repeating patterns, and ***run-together patterns*** are different aspects of this visual way of ordering and decorating the surface.

OBJECTIVES

This project offers means of studying many run-together patterns quickly. It will also familiarize you with the use of raster computer programs if you are working electronically.

MATERIALS

Electronic: scanner; photographs and/ or Internet hook-up; computer; raster-based paint program such as Adobe Photoshop; laser printer; white or gray or black illustration board; rubber cement; utility knife.

Traditional: black-and-white photo or grayscale magazine photo; copy machine; previously listed assembly supplies.

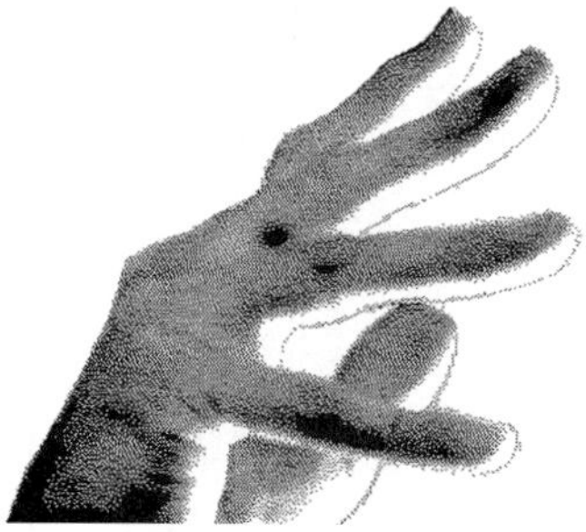

Figure 4.79

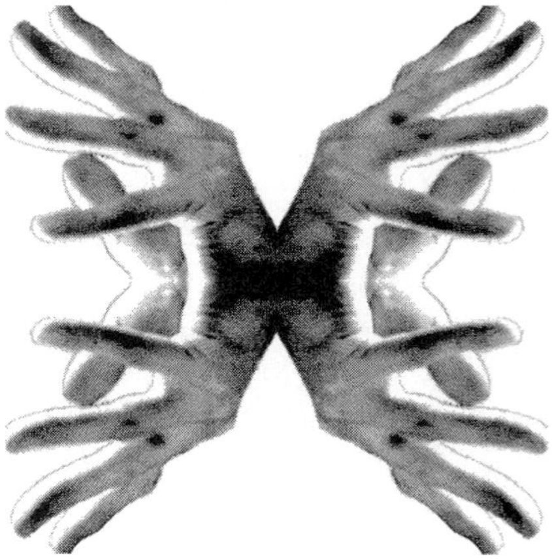

Figure 4.80

PROCEDURE

Electronic **Open** one of the photographic images you saved from the Internet or scanned from a magazine in a raster-based paint program. If the picture is in color convert it to a **Grayscale** image. Make a medium- to high-contrast version of the photograph. Save this by different file name so you can get back to your original version if you make an error.

With the **Selection Box Tool** select a perfect square out of the photo by holding down on the **Shift** key while making the selection box. Copy this selection in the computer's short-term memory. Next create a **New** page that is 6 inches square.

Display **Rulers** on the new page. Then **Paste** the square you copied from the photograph. After pasting the square picture move the picture to the upper lefthand corner of the format. Now draw a selection box around the picture. **Scale** while holding down on the **Shift** key to the 3 in. by 3 in. coordinate. Apply the transformation. **Copy** and **Paste** this selection again. Move it into another quarter of the format. Do this two more times to fill the 6-inch square format. Now use the **Rotate** and **Flip** menu choices on these four quarters to make an interlocked run-together tile. **Save As** tile number one or by some other such name.

Select the entire page and **Paste** into a new 6-inch square page. **Invert** this. This will give you a negative image to evaluate as well. You can use multiple copies of one or both of these 6-inch tiles to make a nine-tile run-together pattern design.

Make several versions of your run-together pattern design from these tiles on 18-inch square pages. Start by pasting a tile on one of these pages and move it to the upper lefthand corner of the page. **Copy** and **Paste** it into every other 6-inch square space on the format. Then **Paste** and **Invert** several others to see what effect it has. **Rotate** some of the squares to see what variations result. **Save** each by a different name. Pick out one to print.

You probably will have to resize the page to fit your printer. In Adobe Photoshop go to the **Image** menu and down to **Image Size.** Reduce the width and height to the size you

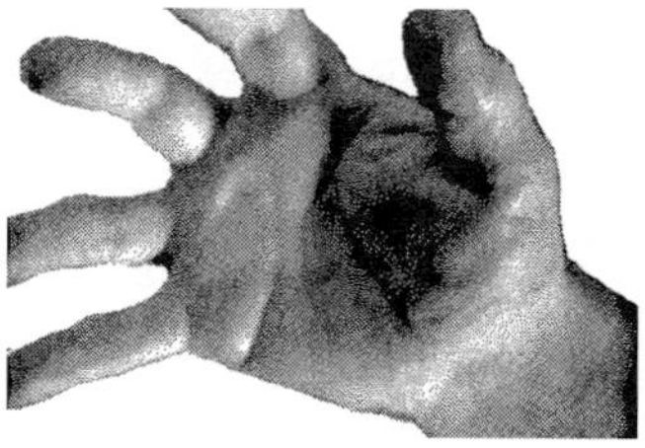

Figure 4.81

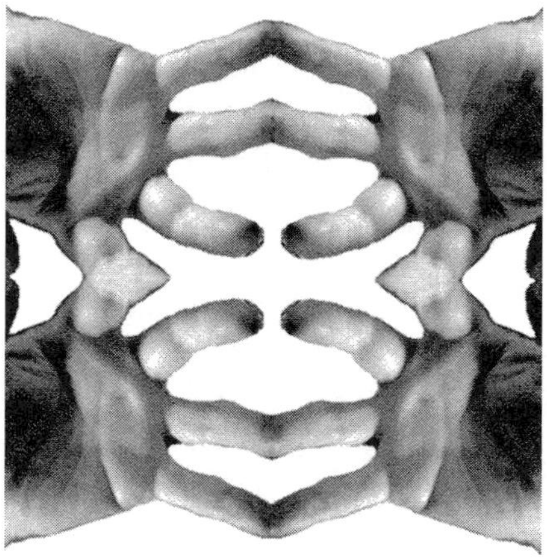

Figure 4.82

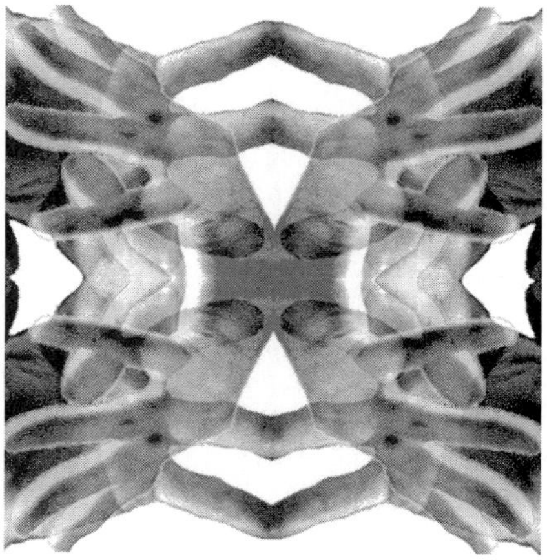

Figure 4.83

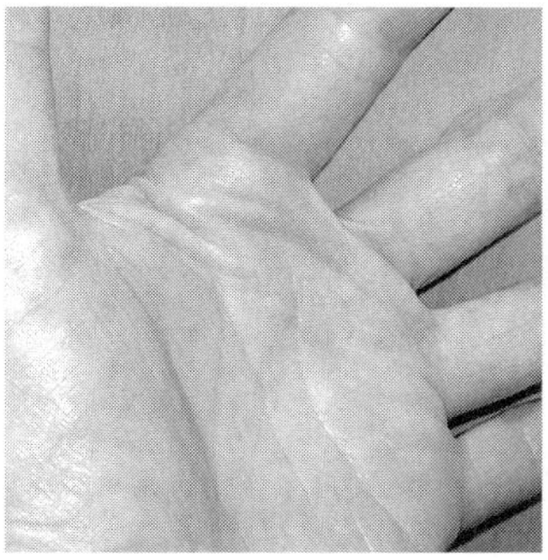

Figure 4.84

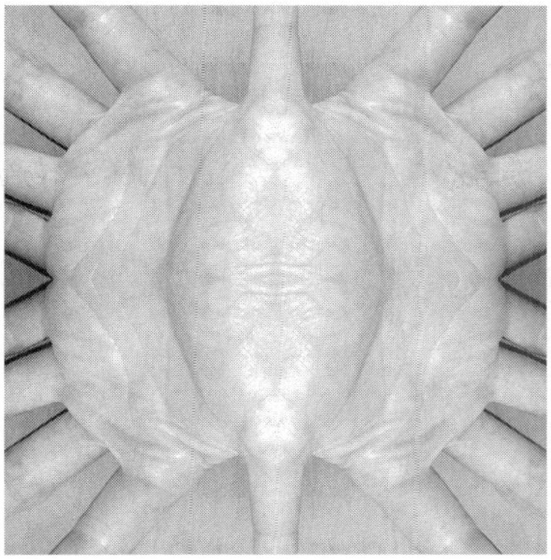

Figure 4.85

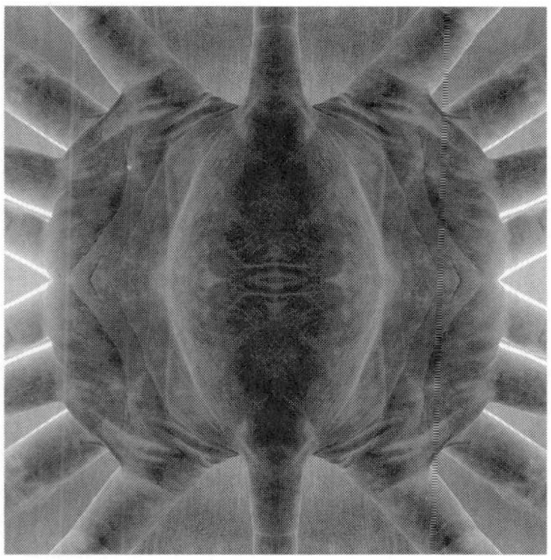

Figure 4.86

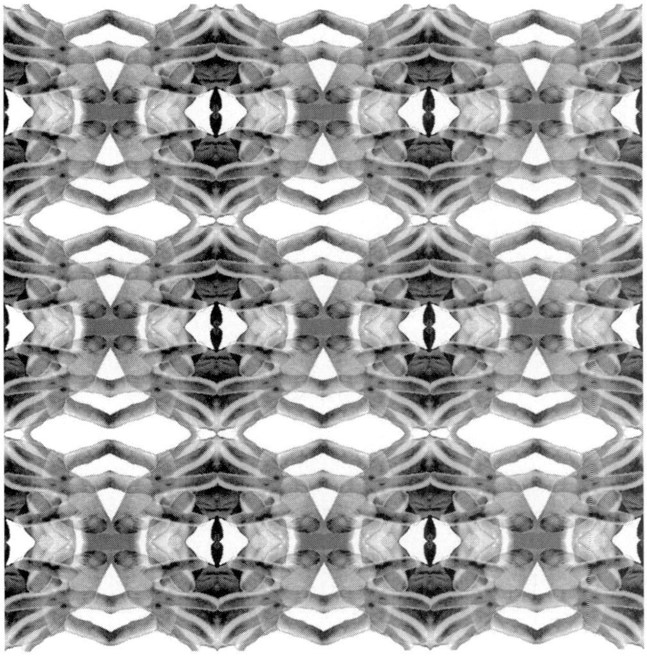

Figure 4.87

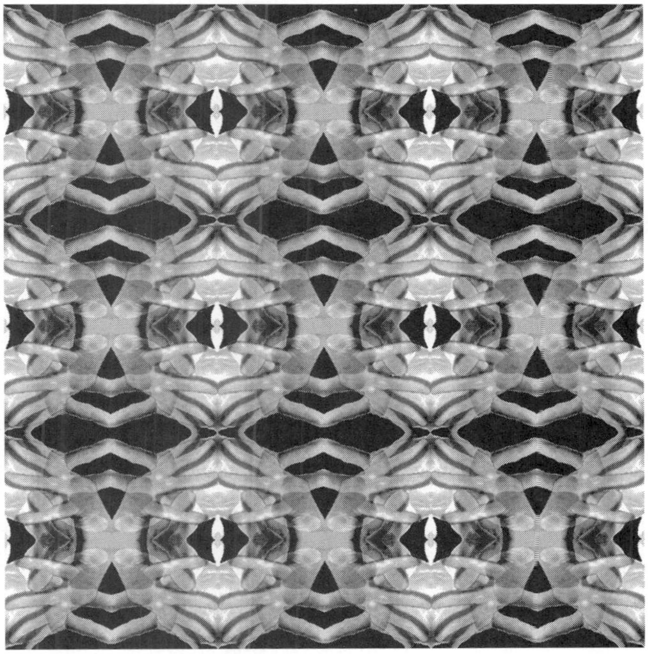

Figure 4.88

need and also at the same time raise the resolution as much as is necessary to keep the pixel dimensions number about the same as before resizing the format. It is very important that you do this before closing the image size window or your artwork will lose a great deal of detail. **Save** the resized piece by a different name. **Print** and mount this printout on illustration board.

Traditional Select a photograph with good focus quality and reasonable size. You need to crop a 3-inch square out of the image so that portions of the image run off the square on all four sides. Use a copy machine to make four copies of this 3-inch square. It is not possible to flip or invert the subject matter on a copy machine but you will be able to achieve a good result by rotating each square a quarter turn when assembling the initial four-part module. After you have assembled a 6-inch square from four of the 3-inch squares, use this as your master to copy nine squares. Cut these out and assemble on a piece of 19″ × 19″ illustration board with rubber cement.

DISCUSSION

If these patterns could be manipulated for use in the study of differing color situations, how might that effect our response to the patterns? How many differing solutions can you generate with one tile?

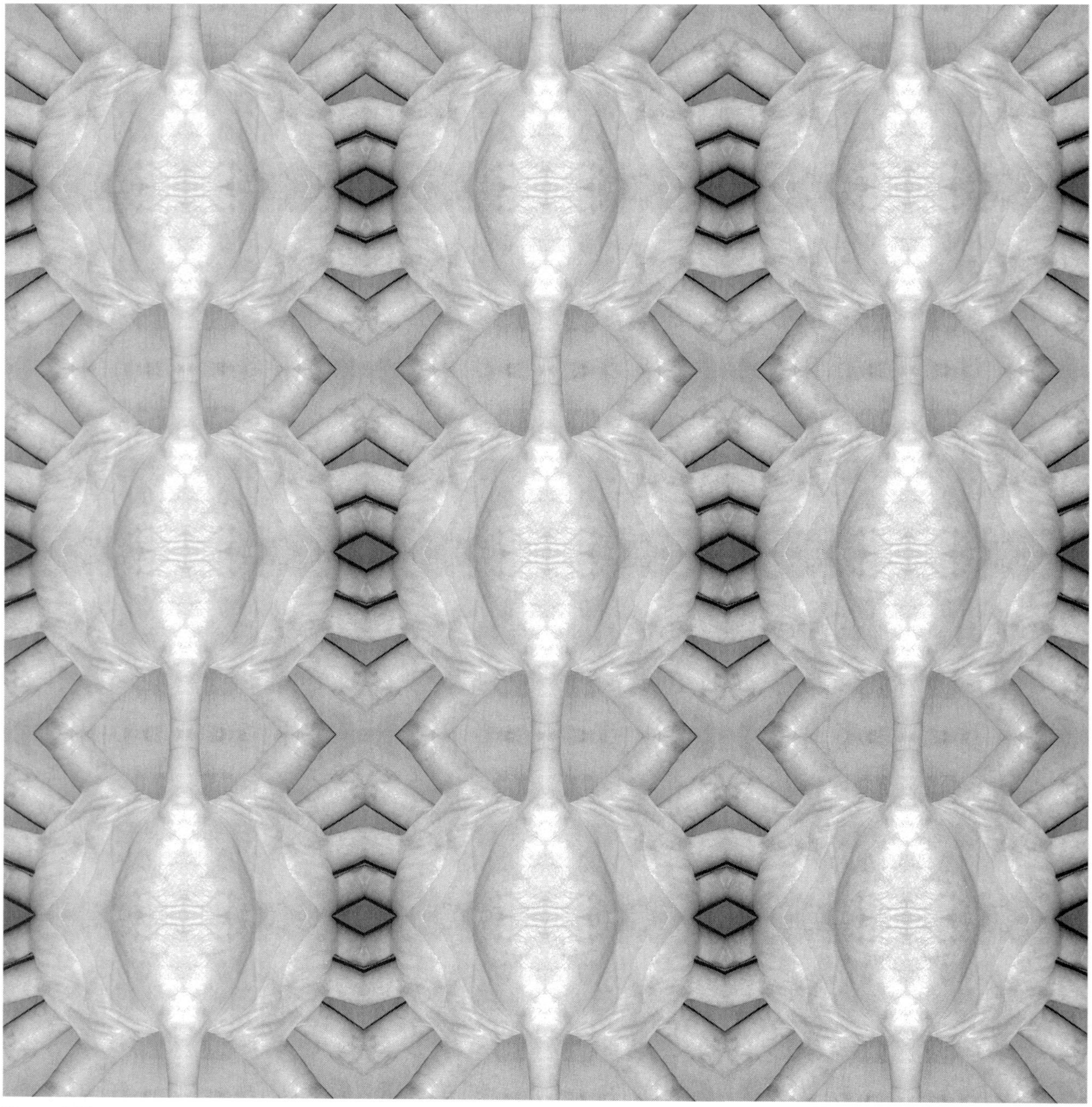

Figure 4.89

SPATIAL PATTERN

Designers, artists, architects, and craftsman have utilized the repeated grid structure as a dynamic means to create an overall design that achieves ***harmony, balance, symmetry, movement,*** and ***unity.*** A subset of this is ***pattern,*** which is the repetition of elements or the combination of elements in an easily recognized systematic organization.

While some patterns can be a collection of geometric units repeated in a formal mathematical arrangement, others are of informal irregular arrangement. The total effect of the relationships of differing light and dark areas within the pictorial field creates value pattern. Two factors are important in spatial pattern construction: the range of value gradation and the direction of implied movement. Gradation generates optical illusion, depth, and progression.

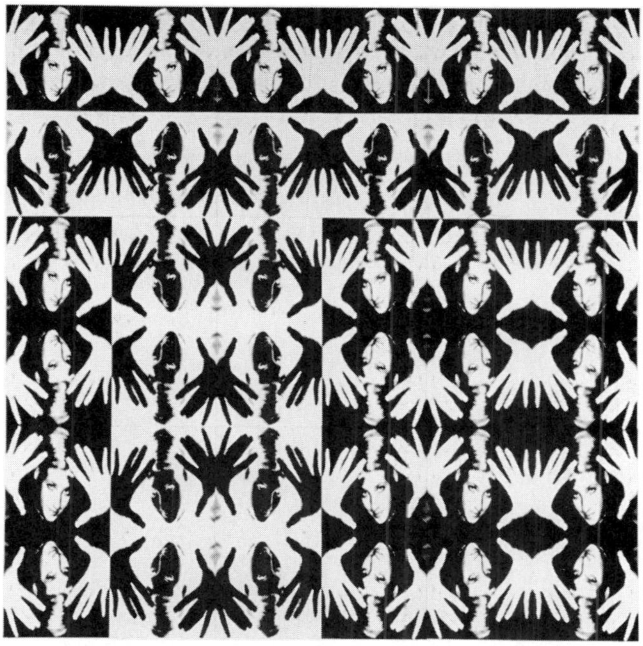

Figure 4.90 *Image by Brandi Boyce*

Rich surface articulation on architectural buildings may create spatial patterns and even a sense of motion. For example, Islamic architecture makes use of formal geometry and spatial pattern. Spatial movement illusions created by pattern structures often exhibit directional surface gradations that are either parallel, concentric, zigzag, or diagonal. Movement patterns with gradation are common in arts and crafts such as fabrics, rugs, ceramic Flemish tiles, quilts, American Indian baskets, Persian paintings, and Japanese prints.

OBJECTIVES

This project involves the study of a spatial pattern within a basic grid. The basic grid consists of equally spaced vertical and horizontal lines, crossing each other, resulting in equal unit subdivisions. A ***formal grid*** will be investigated with emphasis on shape, value, and range of ***gradation.*** A cropped image that has effective *chiaroscuro* will be studied as a modular unit. A module, which is a unit form, will be repeated and rotated in order to achieve a dramatic value pattern. Resource imagery will be acquired digitally by means of CD, digital camera, or a flatbed scanner. A secondary structure that utilizes further ***value*** and scale contrast will be investigated to increase spatial complexity into your overall grid structure.

MATERIALS

Electronic: Computer with a raster program; original photo images to be scanned; mounting board 16″ × 16″; glue; zip disc.

Traditional: gouache; acrylic paint; bristol board or plaster casts and a camera.

PROCEDURE

Electronic This project can be done completely on the computer using a raster program. Select a photo that has ***chiaroscuro*** and rich surface detail. (Figure 4.91) **Crop** your image to a square and use it as a ***unit of repetition*** (Figure 4.92). Create new formal relationships by repeating your module four times to create a more complex module (Figure 4.93). **Transform** the module by using rotation and flip features (Figure 4.94) Repeat this new module to create a large-scale grid. (Figures 4.95 and 4.96).

Further develop your grid by creating a border design as well as a central focal variation. You can alter scale of the module and **Paste** a micro pattern into your design. You can also use **Curves** or **Brightness Contrast** to alter value, create spatial depth and luminosity within your formal grid design. (Figure 4.97).

ALTERNATIVES AND VARIATIONS

This project can be executed by hand using gouache or acrylic on board. A similar project can also be created by making a 3D plaster mold of a textural surface unit, casting it and making multiple units, and photographing the final grid.

DISCUSSION

How does the rotation of the module affect the overall design? Explain how the value patterns or overall movement is impacted by the repeat formal structure. How has the original scanned image transformed? Is there a conceptual change or just a formal one? How has value and scale altered your composition?

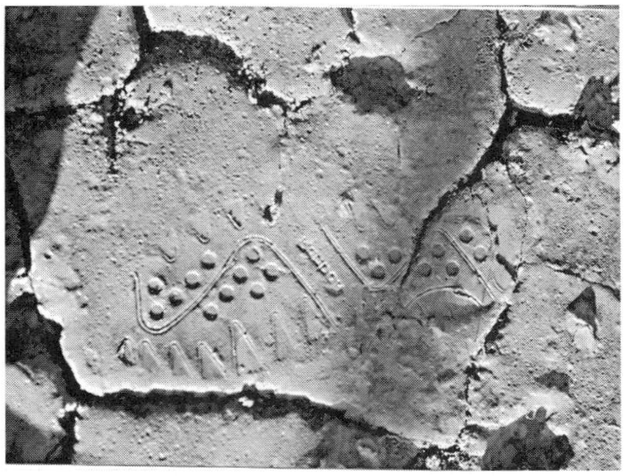

Figure 4.91 *Image by Alex Cole*

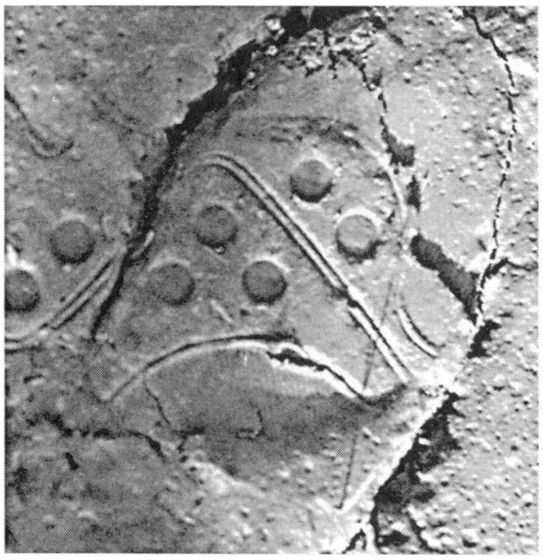

Figure 4.92 Unit form

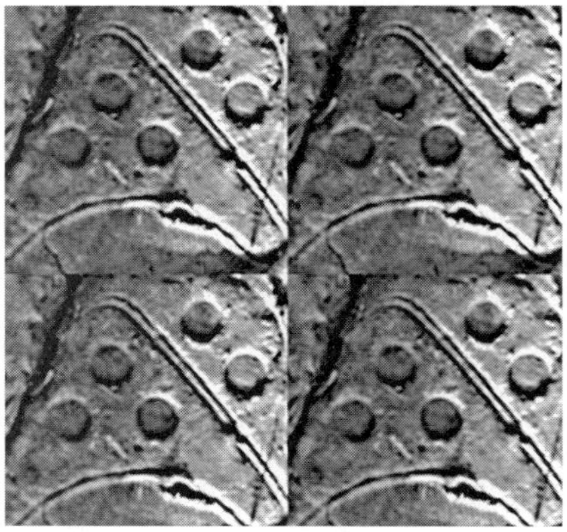

Figure 4.93 Four part

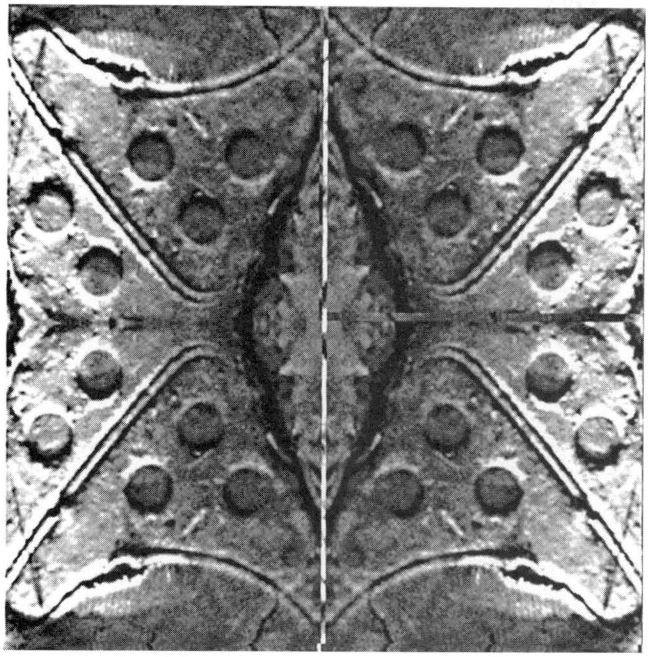

Figure 4.94 Rotation

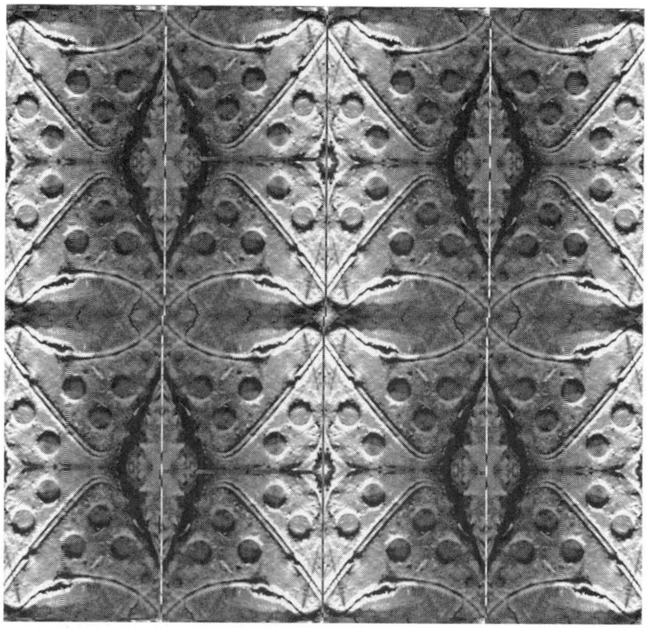

Figure 4.95

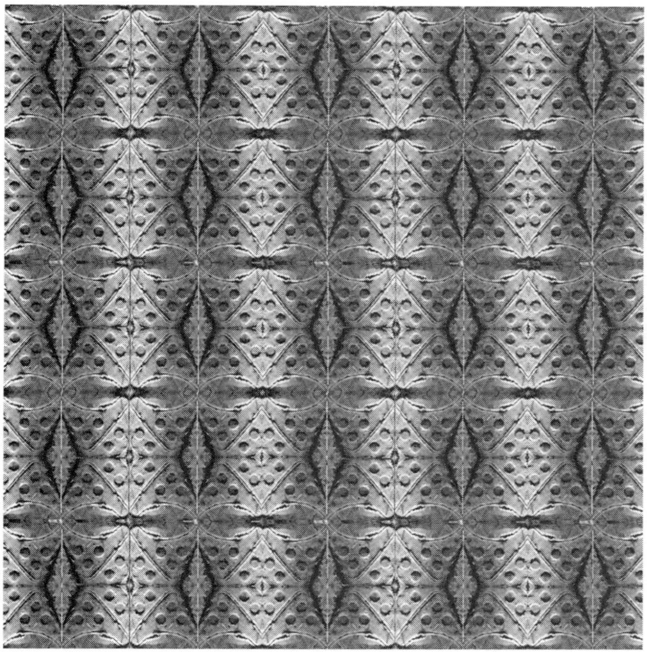

Figure 4.96

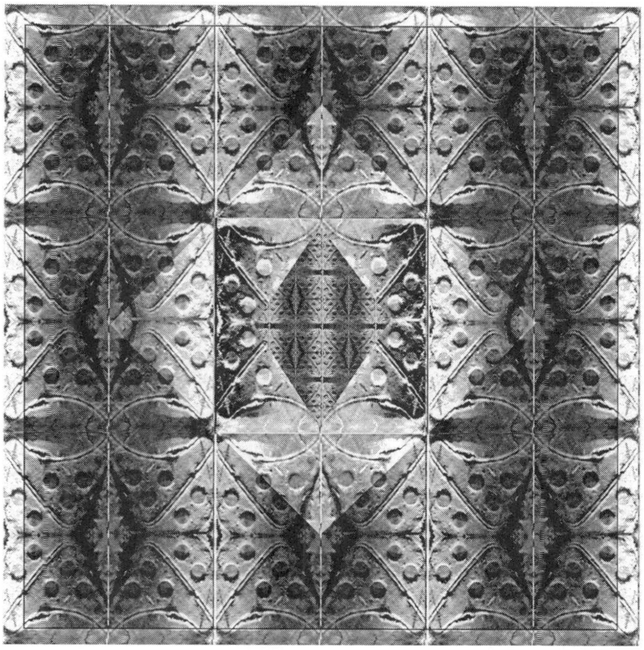

Figure 4.97

CHAPTER 5

THE DYNAMICS OF SURFACE

TEXTURE

Texture, described as the surface characteristics of an object, is the quality of a form that most appeals to our sense of touch. We can experience texture as ***real,*** through direct tactile response, or as ***implied,*** through illusionist devices that attempt to simulate the "look and feel" of a surface. Also, ***invented*** texture can be the result of a combination of materials and media that create unique and unusual qualities that do not mimic naturally occurring surfaces, yet reference them.

Real textures appeal directly to our sense of touch. Burlap, corduroy, sandpaper, and marble are examples of intriguing textures. The obvious tactile qualities of these everyday surfaces garner a response that is tied to personal experience. The day-to-day handling of materials and objects can establish emotional connections that will tend to be acknowledged and related to in artwork.

On the two-dimensional surface, ***simulated*** representations of textures depict actual surfaces and encourage a reference to real experiences. A connection made between the representation of a texture and its real counterpart heightens the visual experience and enhances the overall effect of an image. These optically experienced textures may not be as rich as the real thing, but still serve to dramatically engage the viewer and bring forth a more involved interaction with the image.

Value in texture refers to the light and dark characteristics of the overall patterns or repeated markings that comprise the textural effect. Some textures may have a pronounced dark surface that is the result of a dense or closed pattern structure, whereas others, by virtue of a subtle or open pattern structure, may seem more airy and light. ***Contrast*** and ***variety, rhythm, direction and movement, and repetition*** are all forces that come into play as texture and value come together to enliven an image, or are used to produce specific effects.

Although repetition of a marking or motif is an aspect of texture, the flat and more stylized characteristic of pattern is viewed as distinctly different from the tactile qualities that textures have to offer. It is often the scale of the repeating element and therefore its independence as a shape that distinguishes a pattern from a texture.

Tactile memory and the association of a tactile response within the context of a work of art is a powerful force that occurs between a viewer and an image. Texture can serve as a counterpoint or as an area of emphasis, and can constitute an important element in the construction of a two-dimensional image.

The following projects highlight tactile associations. Hands-on manipulations are important aspects of procedure in the first assignment, and textural implications with reference to text and image are presented in the second.

TEXTURAL TEXT

As we have explored in Chapter 3, *Letterforms, Numbers, and Symbols,* type is a pervasive, compelling, and dynamic visual form that functions in a variety of ways within a two-dimensional image. Fundamentally, type encompasses a variety of two-dimensional ***shapes*** whose characteristics and identity have been formed through interpretation by the human hand and later by standardized manufacturing and digital typographical technology. However, as the visual component of language, its function as a conveyer of content often supercedes its basic visual characteristics. Within a design, type should function as both a visual and a verbal form.

As a two-dimensional ***element,*** the impact, effectiveness, and legibility of type-based shapes are altered by the same variables as any other shapes. ***Value contrast, orientation,*** and changes in ***scale*** are key components that affect the strength and activity of typographical elements within a visual image. Of these, transitions in scale seem to have the greatest impact on the identity of these forms. Our visual ability to discern detail diminishes with distance. The legibility of type diminishes as scale decreases and/or viewing distance increases. Type-based shapes are transformed into tonal areas that have a slightly irregular distribution of value. Therefore, a reduction in scale transforms type into visual ***texture.***

OBJECTIVES

Create a design that transforms the surface and space of a pre-existing image by imposing a secondary layer of typographical texture.

MATERIALS

Electronic: Chromatic or achromatic image; flat bed scanner; a raster-based drawing program such as Adobe Photoshop; printer; acetate suitable for your printer; mounting and/or matting board; rubber cement; pen or utility knife

Traditional: Achromatic image; acetate, magic markers; pen and ink or paint; rub-on type; copy machine; acetate for copy machines; mounting and/or matting board; rubber cement; pen or utility knife

PROCEDURE

Electronic **Scan** or **Open** an achromatic digital image (Figure 5.1). Working within a raster-based program, create a **New Layer** on top of your original image. Use the **Type Tool** to create letters, numbers or words on this new layer. Value, scale, and typeface may be varied within a single image (Figures 5.2, 5.3, 5.4). Additional manipulations can be made by transforming shapes (rotating, flipping, changing scale, or changing proportions) as you compose. Forms may appear whole or they may be ***cropped*** by the edge of the format. Focus on the transitions that are occurring between the layers, utilizing ***grouping principles*** and ***balance*** as you create a new layer. This layer will merge with the underlying image to achieve a unified design.

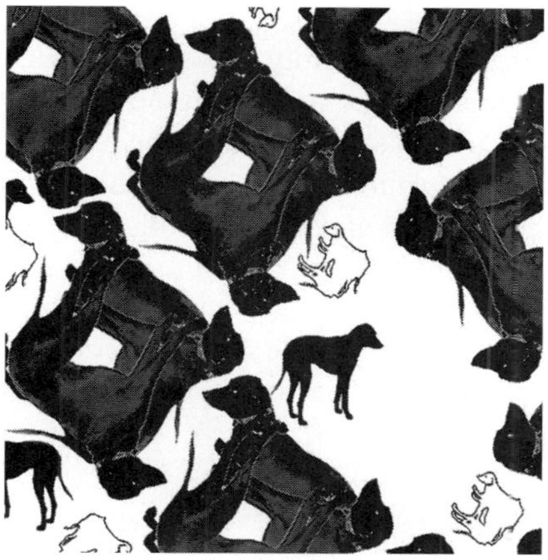

Figure 5.1

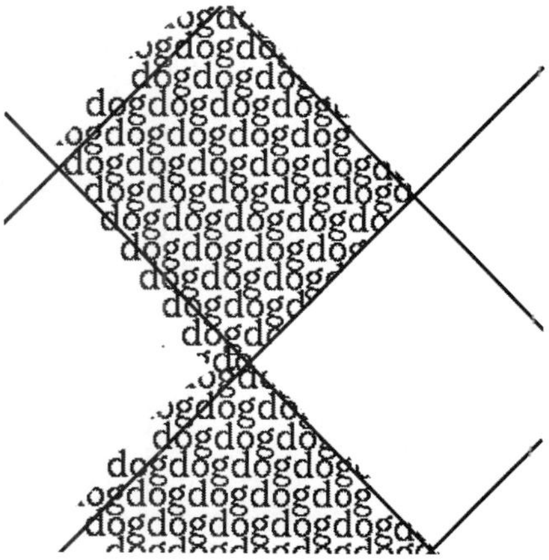

Figure 5.2

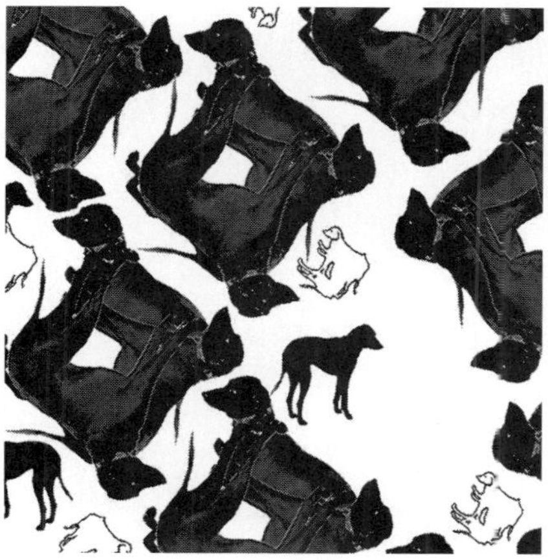

Figure 5.3

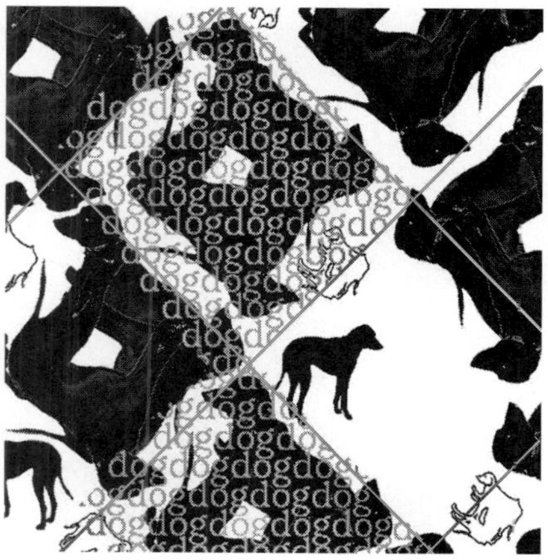

Figure 5.4

Choose letters that relate visually or conceptually to the original image as a means of enhancing the unity and visual strength of the new design. The choice of scale (point size) will alter the function of the type. A larger point size facilitates literal reading by identifying words and letters. Smaller point sizes diminish legibility and move type into the realm of texture. Carefully consider these effects and their impact on the final solution.

There will be two solutions to this problem. One solution will involve printing the textural overlay on acetate and physically superimposing it on your original image. The second solution will be created by merging the two layers to create a single print. The choice of printing support (paper versus acetate) will mediate the effect of value within the image. Laser writers do not have white ink. While white will be visible on your screen, it will not be visible on a transparent support (acetate). Light values on your screen are seen as a mixture of white and black pixels: Light values on paper will be created with less black ink.

When you have finished with your textural overlay, **Hide** your scanned image, **Merge Visible** layers, and **Print** the textural overlay on acetate. When the acetate print is completed, make your scanned layer visible, **Flatten** the textural overlay onto this layer, and **Print** the entire design out on paper (Figure 5.5).

For the final presentation lay the acetate printout over the original design and tape both to a support. The image area should be defined by a window mat cut to a size that best suit the needs of the design. Mount the merged digital image on a board with appropriate borders (Figure 5.6).

Traditional This project may be done as a studio problem without the computer. The transparent textural overlay can be created by applying magic marker, paint or ink, rub-on lettering to the surface of a sheet of acetate. Type may also be applied to a transparent support by copying type onto a sheet of acetate suitable for the copy machine. The same conceptual and formal parameters apply to the problem.

DISCUSSION

This project creates an opportunity to work with and transform a preexisting image (perhaps created for some other conceptual purpose) into a new image. Issues to be considered in critique and discussion should include the effect that the different supports impose on the image in regard to white elements. Additionally, the differences in material of the different supports provide the opportunity to discuss the impact of texture on the image, and

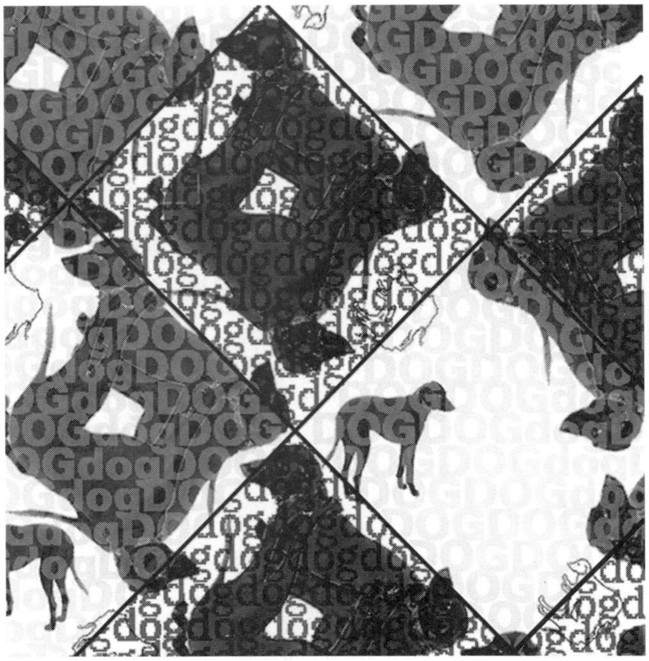

Figure 5.5

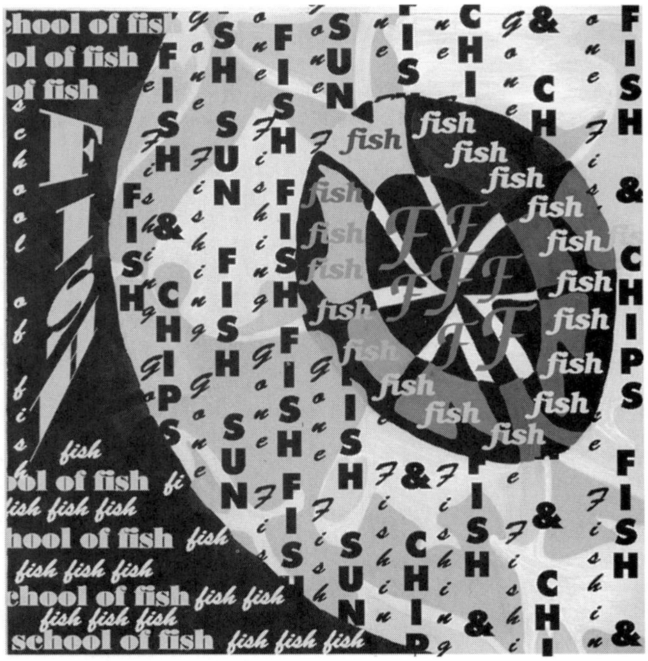

Figure 5.6 *Image by Allison Eastman*

even our cultural associations of "shiny" versus "dull." Discussion may also focus on the impact of text that retains its legibility and gestalt, which may alter the formal emphasis and conceptual content of the overall image.

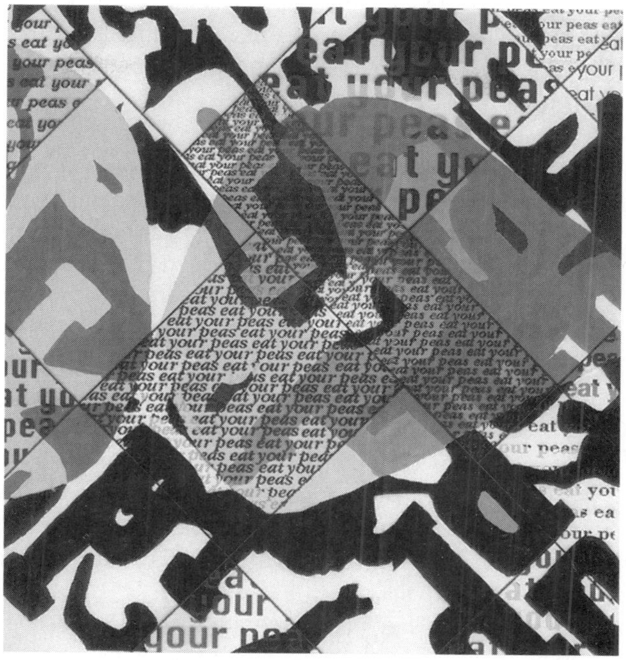

Figure 5.7 *Image by Brian Berlinski*

Figure 5.8 *Image by Mary Runser*

ASSIGNMENT A: TEXTURAL COLLAGE

The use of textural elements in an image can engage the viewer on many levels. Subtle references to real texture may be a catalyst in an image, generating a particular response because of tactile associations. Texture can enrich aspects of the image because of visual variety. Merging a texture-dominant image with a second image that has distinct representational elements is a way to capitalize on the strong visual characteristics of both. In this project, the legibility of realistic components should suggest enough information so that the image can be deciphered without complication. The converging of texture and "picture" can set up a dynamic that utilizes the inherent nature of each.

OBJECTIVES

In this assignment the student will combine the elements of texture and image to study the effects of juxtaposing contrasts. Emphasis and image dominance or subordination will be altered as students work with layers of information that can be easily rearranged with digital technology. Image manipulations on the computer will heighten basic strategies and provide for new and exciting possibilities for solution evolution and outcome. Fragmentation of pictorial elements will add to the level of complexity in the image, forcing students to make decisions about image clarity and coherence in the design.

MATERIALS

Electronic: computer; disk for storage; graphics program such as Adobe Photoshop; good-quality printer; various materials that have textural characteristics; color or black-and-white photocopy of a photograph or an image from an art historical text; illustration board

Traditional: black-and-white or color photocopy of a photograph or an image from an art historical text; illustration board; rubber cement; masking tape; black india ink (or colored inks if using a color copy); brushes; various papers like wax paper, tracing paper; rice papers; hand-made papers; foil; tissue papers; and texture rubbings

PROCEDURE

Electronic Begin this assignment by scanning real textures on a flatbed scanner. The scanner bed should be at least 8″ × 10″. Arrange a variety of textures on the scanner bed, making an effort to organize them thoughtfully. **Scan** at a resolution of 200 dpi, and **Save** to disk (Figure 5.9).

For your second image, choose a personal photograph or an image that has an art historical reference (from a book or reproduction). Both should be about 8″ × 10″. Figures, portraits, still lifes, or architectural elements are good subject matter. The imagery should be distinct and easily readable. **Scan** this image on a flatbed scanner at a resolution of 200 dpi and **Save** to disk.

Open up a graphics program such as Photoshop. Starting with your scanned photograph or artist's work, break up the image into at least two or three pieces with the breaks going from top to bottom. Imagine tearing the image so that it can be physically separated into distinct elements. To do this on the computer, first create a **New File** and name it. Now use a selection tool like the **Lasso,** and capture an area in your image. **Copy** and **Paste** that piece into the **New File**. Continue doing this for the other pieces of the image. You will essentially move to the next area on the image and capture that area, working across the window horizontally. Because you are copying and pasting into a **New File,** your copied elements will be placed on a new layer each time you paste them. You should now **Save** and name your **New File** because your assignment will all take place within this file (Figure 5.10).

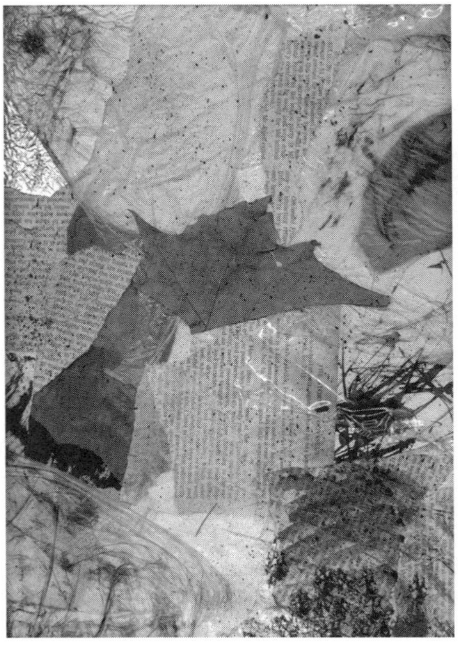

Figure 5.9

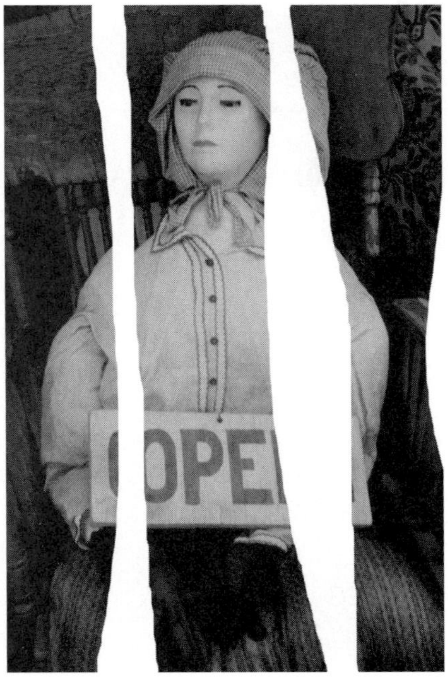

Figure 5.10

Open your scanned textures file and **Select All. Copy** and **Paste** this image into the **New File** that has the fragments of imagery in it. This again will come in as a new layer. You will now have a few layers with image fragments on them, a layer with texture information on it, and a blank background layer.

The goal at this point in the problem is to combine all these elements so they can stand as one. The textural elements should support the image fragments in a way that enhances the image, yet add visual interest and variety to it. Do this by using the blending modes to merge the various layers in different ways. Use the opacity sliders on the individual layers to decrease opacity so that one layer is dominant over another. Affect each layer using **Image** adjustments to create distinctly different qualities on each layer. Make copies of a layer by selecting it, and then going to the bottom of the Layers palette and clicking on the icon that looks like a box inside of a box. Use these copied layers to try other effects on those layers and then decide which ones you will use. You can turn layers on or off by clicking on the eye icon on the individual layers. This can help you see what your image will look like without a layer or layers, especially if you have a made copies of layers and have explored a lot. Move layers around on the layers palette by clicking, holding, and dragging and dropping them above or below other layers. Make sure you **Save** your work constantly. Flatten your image when you are done by going to the Layers menu and selecting **Flatten Image.** This will combine all your layers onto a background layer and decrease the size of your file. **Save** your image to disk by giving it a new name. Print out your image on good-quality paper and mount onto illustration board with a 2″ border (Figure 5.11). (See color section for Figures 5.11, 5.12 and 5.14).

Here is another example of a "torn" image in combination with the texture (Figure 5.12).

Traditional Using a photocopy (black-and-white or color) of an image (figure, portrait, still life, architectural elements), tear it from top to bottom into three segments. Paste these segments about an inch apart in a casual manner (they can be a little askew), onto a piece of illustration board that is about 12″ × 14″. Make a 1-1/2″ border all around. Brush rubber cement (with a dry brush approach) over the areas between the images and around the edges of the image. Let this dry completely. Once the rubber cement is dry, brush india ink that has been watered down a bit over these areas, being careful not to cover up much of the imagery. Blot up excess ink when necessary. Tear strips of different kinds of paper such as wax paper and tracing papers or hand-made papers and paste them down in a few places when the ink is dry. You can also add pieces of texture rubbings to the image. Texture rubbings are texture impressions that have been made by putting sketch paper over a real texture and rubbing over the surface of the paper with a soft pencil. Strips of masking tape or transparent tape can be adhered to the image in selected places. Add ink wash where needed to integrate tape, paper strips, and texture rubbings into the image. Working with ink and texture, continue to develop the imagery until the combination of all components come together in a successful solution.

DISCUSSION

In what ways do textural elements support the final image? Does the combination of image and texture create a more dynamic design? When does the image lose its effect? How do secondary characteristics such as color or value change the way that you understand the image? Do effects like fragmentation create movement in the image? How does it add to (or detract) from the success of the image?

ASSIGNMENT B: TEXTURE, RHYTHM, AND MOTION

The repetition of ***elements*** in a horizontal format can convey dynamic movement or subtle transitions. Repeated forms can set up a rhythmic structure that is useful in creating harmony in a two-dimensional image. The combination of texture, color, and a repeated component can create a complex ***visual field*** that engages the viewer on multiple levels.

OBJECTIVES

This assignment proceeds as the previous assignment, but varies in its intent. In this variation, students will also become aware of the ways in which the repetition of elements can be used to convey rhythm and movement in a design.

PROCEDURE

This project is created in the same manner as the *Textural Collage,* but it extends across a horizontal picture plane. The longer format of the board will support more repetitions of the fragmented image so that repeated aspects of the subject matter will create a rhythmic progression.

Electronic Proceed with the process as in Textural Collage, but create a format that is wider. For example, creating a **New** file that is 14 inches across and 9 inches down would provide for a horizontal format that would work for this assignment. Work with two files, a texture file and an image file. "Tear" and repeat elements of the image in a logical manner. Don't mix up or rearrange the way that the portrait, for example, is presented, just repeat it across the page two or three times with breaks in between.

Your texture scan should also be in a horizontal format. You can **Scan** on a larger flatbed scanner or make a few different scans that can be combined into the final image. **Save** all scans to disk and give them different names.

Again, make adjustments to the image and the texture layers. As in the *Textural Collage,* rearrange the hierarchy of layers to change the ways that layers interact with one another (Figure 5.14 (color insert)).

Flatten your image when you are done and **Save** it to disk. **Print** out on a large format printer using good-quality paper.

Traditional A traditional version of this variation would proceed with the same materials and processes as in the traditional Textural Collage, with the added variation of the horizontal repeated format.

DISCUSSION

Does the horizontal format change the nature of the image? In what ways do the repeated elements force a reading of the image?

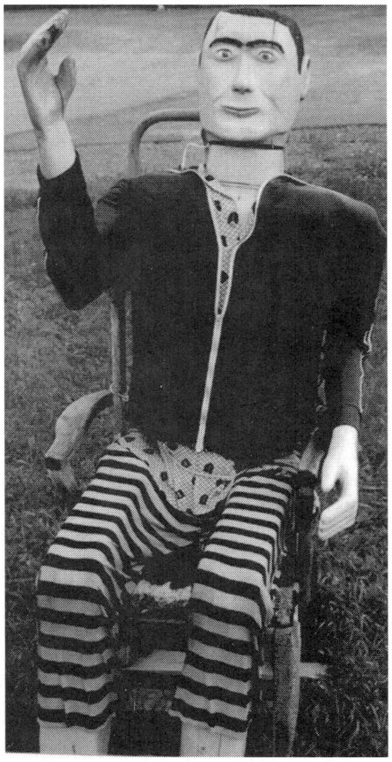

Figure 5.13

VALUE

Value refers not to color, but to the range of grays from black to white. Value is also one of the most direct ways in which we can represent the play of light over forms, or the illusion of a third dimension on the two-dimensional picture plane.

Grays that do not have any indication of a color are ***achromatic*** (without color) and are considered neutral grays. ***Chromatic*** grays contain a small amount of a color and will interact with the other elements in a design in a more complex way.

We are able to distinguish the forms in a design through a ***contrast of value.*** A white shape, for example, is more clearly perceived when placed against a darker background. Relative value, on the other hand, is the way we experience value in its environmental context. What may appear as white against a dark gray background could actually be a very light gray on a pure white background.

A high-contrast relationship is one in which the values are operating at the extremes of black and white, without a distribution of grays in between. This combination creates a very bold and graphic image. Subtle and systematic changes in value are regarded as ***tonal gradation,*** which suggests the illusion of space, drawing the viewer into the picture plane. The less distinct a value becomes, the more it recedes back into the picture plane. Tonal gradients in an image can also create a sense of ***luminosity*** that can suggest, in a naturalistic way, light filtering through space.

Transparency can also be indicated by value. By keeping the change in value consistent in the way every overlapped plane changes by degree of lightness or darkness, you can create the illusion of transparency on the two-dimensional surface.

Value weight is an effect in which the darkness or lightness of forms can influence ***balance*** in the image. The value of an element, in connection with ***scale,*** can create areas of ***emphasis.*** Dark forms tend to appear weightier than lighter valued ones. Placing a large form at the top of a picture plane will tend to visually press down from the top of the image, and may create a tenuous and overbearing feeling. A bold block of typeface within a body of lighter text can be eye-catching, and can be used as a way to focus attention or emphasize an area of information.

Value is a word tied to many meanings. We have looked at it in terms of gray scale and its implied spatial and illusionistic aspects. The concept of value will also serve as a natural introduction to color, as each color in the spectrum has its own light/dark value that corresponds to a position in a gray scale. Value may also be defined as worth, or measurement of how much economic or social validity something or someone has. This way of looking at the word "value" introduces possible personal evaluation and evolution.

VALUE IN TRANSITION: THE SELF AS SUBJECT

Portraiture as a subject for creation has a long history. Using oneself as the subject has been prevalent as long as man has been able to see his reflection. The self-portrait therefore becomes the perfect source for exploring an introduction to color. As we portray ourselves, we must also consider the manner of that portrayal, from the expression on our face to the color palette we select in order to capture the inner self we wish to project to the outside world.

THE SELF IMAGE IN SERIES

OBJECTIVES

The objectives of the three parts in this assignment are multi-purpose. At the outset, we will create a digital image, separating distinct levels of value to develop a contour study. This will enable us to understand not only the shapes of value but also the planes of the face. Once that base is established, develop a series of studies to increase our understanding of the relationship between value and color. As we move from an achromatic, or non-color solution, through a one-color, monochromatic study, finishing with a tri-chromatic, or three-hue palette, appropriate surrounding values will be employed to complete the gradation scales.

MATERIALS

Electronic: A raster-based software program, such as Adobe Photoshop; a photographic digital self-portrait; a printer or output device

Traditional: A photographic self-portrait; tracing paper; pencils; a 15″ × 20″ illustration board divided into four; bristol board; a set of gouache paint with white, black, primary and secondary colors; black ink; pen and brushes

PROCEDURE

As mentioned in the objectives, this assignment is a series of three solutions based on a contour study of the face. The following steps are the procedure you will follow for each of the studies in this series; Achromatic, Monochromatic, Tri-chromatic. Image capture and manipulation includes:

Contour development

Image placement on the page

Setting up the Gradation Scale

Filing the Gradation Scale

Coloring the Image

It is your choice as to whether the project will be completed in paint or on the computer. The important point is to understand the goals of each assignment and follow through on the concept. Traditional procedures will be interspersed with the electronic when applicable. If you are working electronically, remember to **Save As** the contour study so that it can be re-opened and used repeatedly in the series.

The final project will have four "plates"; the three studies mentioned previously and the finished contour. Each "plate," whether completed electronically or with traditional materials, needs to be large enough to support the image area and related gradation scale. Computer solutions can be printed on standard 8-1/2″ × 11″ paper. A quarter of the 15″ × 20″ illustration board is adequate for the painted solutions.

The first step in each plate is to complete the gradation scale, which guides the palette for the composition. The more attention you pay in developing the first scale—being accurate with the value range and consistent with the intervals—the easier it will be to have successful subsequent scales and solutions.

Electronic Image Capture We begin this project by generating our self-image photographically, which is open to interpretation. It is possible to begin the project with a traditional photograph that can be scanned into the computer, or you can use one of a number of devices to capture a digital portrait. What is most important is that you have an image that you can work from and a way in which you can develop a thorough contour of that image, describing the many shapes of value.

If you are using a digital camera, bring the camera view in close enough to allow the face to fill the frame of reference. Once you have been "captured" and saved, **Open** the image in an imaging program such as Adobe Photoshop. You have options as to how you choose to proceed.

Open the photographic image (Figure 5.15) in Adobe Photoshop. Go to the **Image Menu** and scroll down to **Image Size.** Adjust to approximately a 6″ × 8″ image size. When you **Constrain Proportions,** you can set either the width or the height, and the other dimension will change accordingly. **Resample Image.** When this is selected, you can change the image size and select the resolution independently. Use the lowest resolution that will still ensure a continuous tone on your printer. One of the first things you should do is convert the image, if in color, to a gray scale so that you can work with shapes of value and not be distracted by changes in color at this time. To do this you can go to the **Image Menu,** scrolling to **Mode** and selecting **Grayscale.** Discard the color information? [YES]. This will also reduce the file size. (RGB = 3x image size). **Save As,** *Grayscale* to allow you to return to the original if needed.

Return to the **Image Menu,** and this time scroll to **Adjust** then **Brightness/Contrast** (Figure 5.16). Move the controls to increase the clarity of distinct values in the image until you are happy with the results. **Save.** You can print the image at this point if you want to do the contour traditionally by tracing with pencil around the shapes of value on the print.

Electronic Contour Translating the image into distinct value levels from continuous tone will make it easier to define the contour. Return to the **Image Adjust Menu** and scroll to **Posterize.** Experiment with the number of levels you need to separate the image into distinct shapes of value, yet retain sufficient detail information. The lower the number, the flatter and more abstract or graphic the image will appear. A higher number of levels will give you an image of flat shapes but with greater resolution. Generally, you will use a minimum of [8] levels. What is correct will vary from one image to the next. **Save As,** *Posterize.*

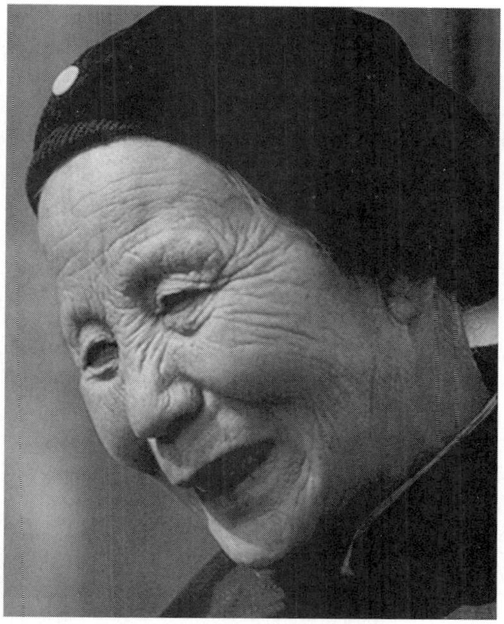

Figure 5.15 Original Grayscale image

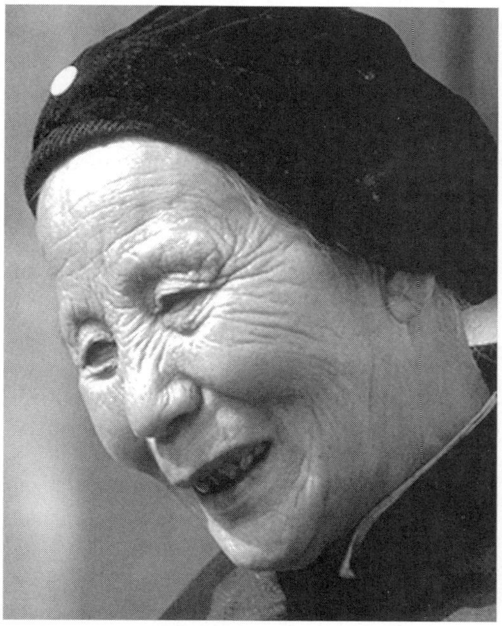

Figure 5.16 Bright/contrast

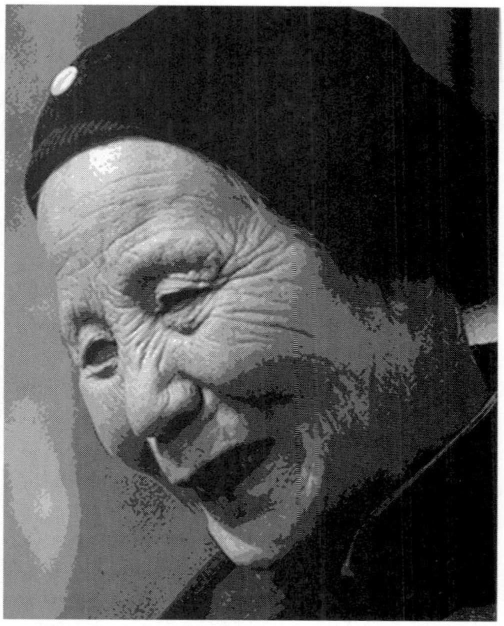

Figure 5.17

The first image (Figure 5.17) is an example of an eight-step posterization applied to the original grayscale image. The second image (Figure 5.18) is more refined, with an eight-step posterization applied to the image after brightness and contrast adjustments were completed.

Grayscale to Contour:

Working electronically, you can take advantage of the filters to create an "instant" contour. Under the Filter menu scroll down to Stylize and select Glowing Edges. Experiment with the correct settings to create a thorough yet clear contour. In the example we used:

Edge width: [3]

Edge brightness: [20]

Smoothness: [15]

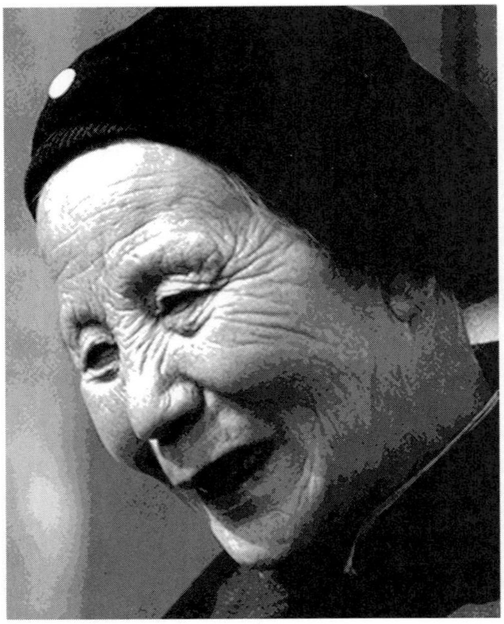

Figure 5.18

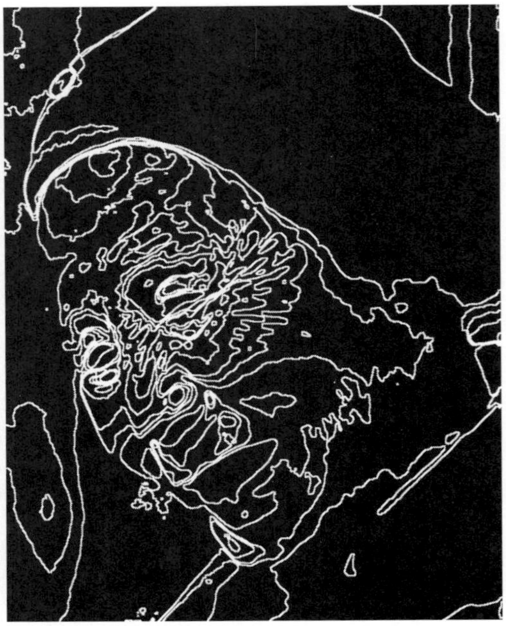

Figure 5.19 Glowing Edges

The results will be white lines on a black ground. (Figure 5.19)

Return to the **Image Menu** and **Invert** (Figure 5.20) to alter the contour. **Save As.** Use the **Zoom Tool** to zoom in to check for 'holes' in the contour lines. With the **Paintbrush Tool,** select a brush size equivalent to the contour lines. Move through the image, closing 'holes' where the value bleeds across objects (Figure 5.21). Adding lines personalizes the style of the line quality and improves image detail. You can also work back in to the lines selected by the computer, removing excessive line detail to improve image clarity with the **Eraser Tool. Save As,** *Contour* (Figure 5.22).

Traditional Contour After completing a contour study by tracing around the shapes of value on the printout or photograph, transfer the lines to a piece of illustration board. Remember to place the image toward the top of the board with sufficient room for the gradation scale below. Complete the study in ink, varying the line weights to emphasize the spatial location of the planes of the face.

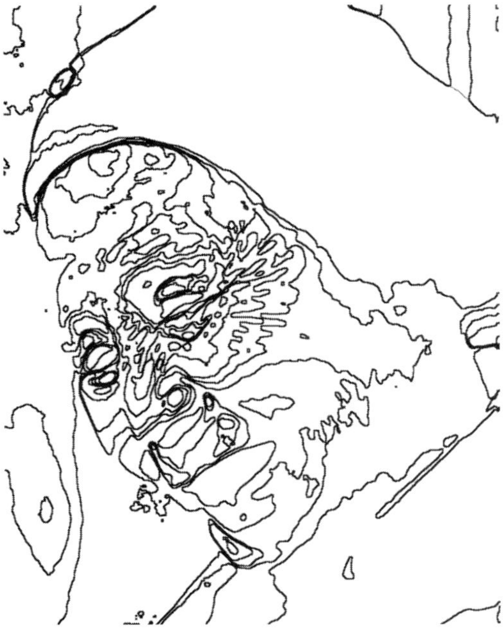

Figure 5.20 Invert

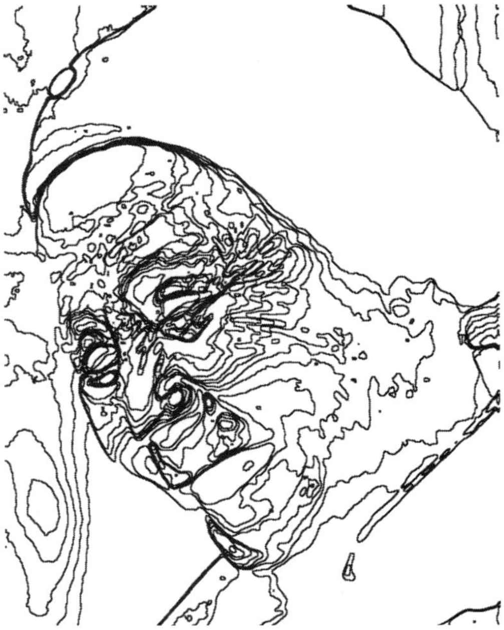

Figure 5.21 Contour

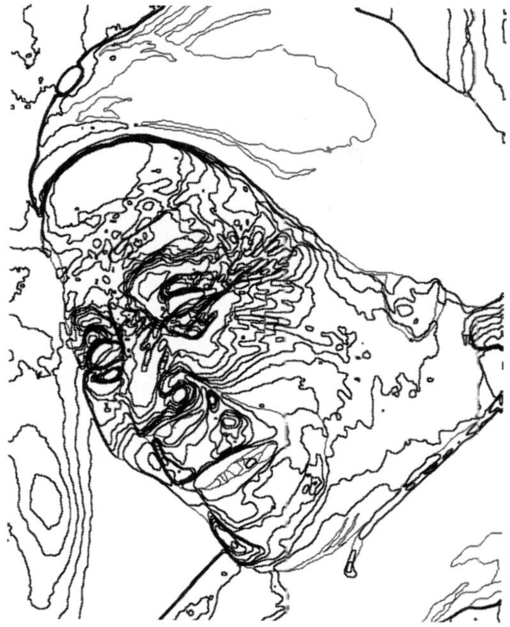

Figure 5.22 Refined contour

NOTE: If you chose to do your contour lines by hand, but wish to complete this assignment digitally, you can scan the contour solution, creating a digital file.

Add a Border Once the image is in contour line with all value removed, we will need to add a border to contain the shapes and complete the edge. You can either go to the **Tool** menu, selecting the **Marquee Tool** or the **Edit** menu and **Select All.** From the **Edit** menu go to the **Stroke Dialogue Box.** The following settings will stroke the edge of the marquee with the foreground color. **Save.**

Width [1]pixel

Location [center]

Opacity [100%]

Mode [normal] [OK]

Image Placement on the Page Before we add the gradation scale to the composition, we will need to increase the canvas size by going to the **Canvas Size,** dialogue box, using the following settings:

Width: [+2″]

Height: [+1.75″]

Anchor: [center]

Repeat to give yourself a larger bottom border in which to place the gradation scale.

Width: [same]

Height: [11″]

Anchor: [top row, center]

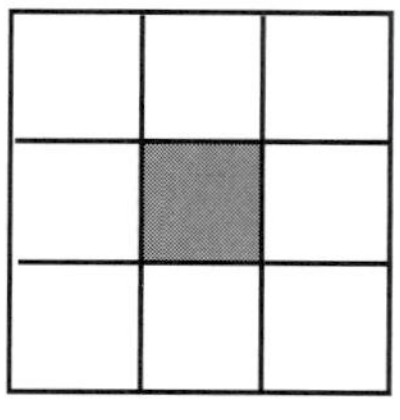

Figure 5.23

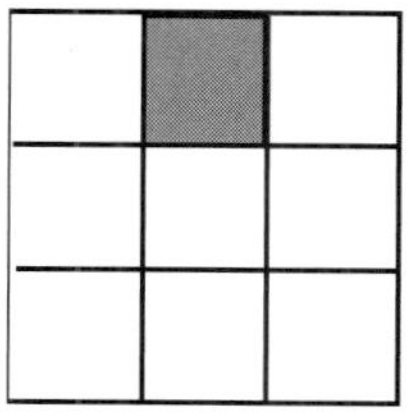

Figure 5.24 Canvas

Setting Up the Gradation Scale We will need to build the spaces for an eight-step scale, each rectangle .75″ × 1.25″. Go to the **Window** menu to **Show Navigator,** and use **Marquee Options** (visible when marquee tool is selected).

Style: [Fixed size]

Width: [108] pixels

Height: [180] pixels (=.75″ × 1.25″).

Use the crosshairs to set the marquee in place and click. Return to the **Stroke** Dialogue box.

Width: [1] pixel

Location: [center]

Opacity: [100%]

Mode: [normal] [OK]

These settings will stroke the edge of the marquee with the foreground color.

With the rectangle selected, **Copy** and **Paste.** The new box will appear in the image. Use the select tool to move it into place (Figure 5.25). Repeat this process until there are eight adjoining rectangles for the scale. When you view the **Layers** palette, you will see eight layers on top of the background, which contains the photographic image, currently in contour. **Save.**

To Fill the Gradation

VISUALLY: Select the layer of the rectangle to be filled. Adjust the foreground color. Double click on the foreground color box to get the **Color Picker.** Move the circle to the appropriate color and/or value. Click **[OK].** With the **Fill Tool** (spilling paint can), click in the gradation step you wish to fill with the foreground color and/or value (Figure 5.26).

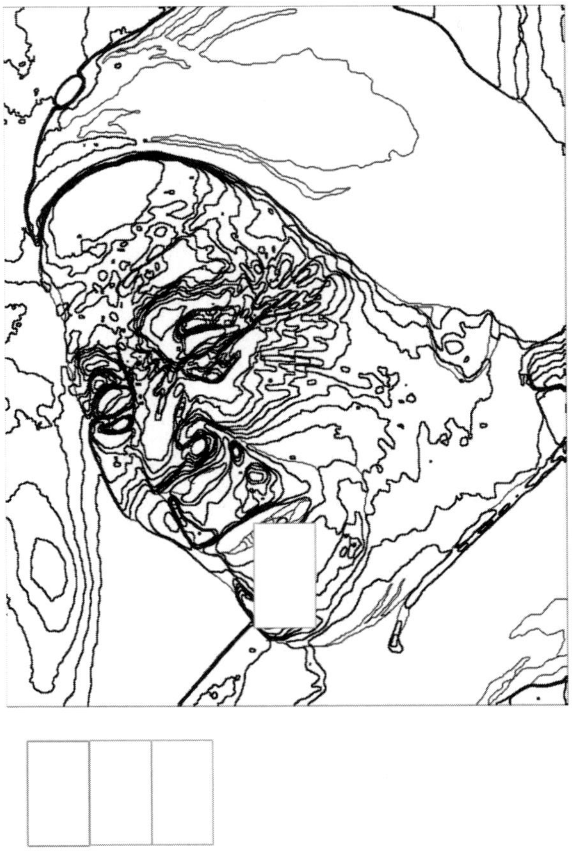

Figure 5.25 Addbox

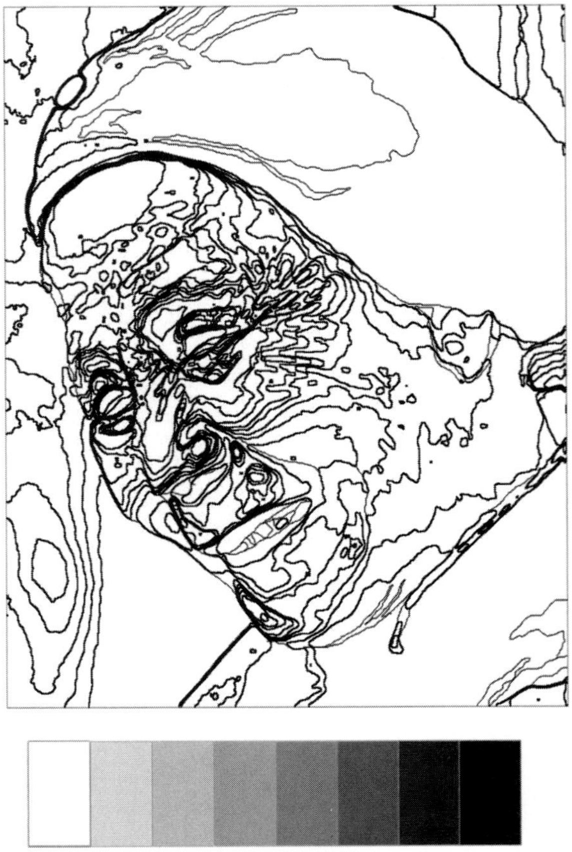

Figure 5.26 Achromatic gradation

NUMERICALLY: Double click on the foreground color box to get to the **Color Picker.** You will see four different ways the selected color is described. In the **HSB** category (Hue, Saturation, Brightness), only the [B] changes when addressing achromatic value.

White = H [0], S [0], B [100]

Black = H [0], S [0], B [0]

Divide the remaining steps to get a consistent interval of change. **Save As.**

Traditional Gradation Scale To paint a perfect, eight-step gradation is quite difficult. You will get more practice with paint and color mixing if you fill a sheet of bristol board with swatches of paint in subtle value steps. Cut out a .75″ × 1.5″ rectangle to use as a template. Trace the template onto various swatches and cut them out. Experiment with the correct interval or movement for an eight-step gradation that includes the white and black ends. When you are satisfied, mount the scale in the bottom border of the illustration board.

To Begin Coloring the Image With the background layer selected, use the **Eyedropper Tool** to select a value from the gradation scale. With this as the foreground color, select **Fill Tool** (spilling paint can) (Figure 5.27). Click in the space to be filled. (Hint: You can selectively "fill" the contour lines to convert them from black to the value of the adjacent shape.) NOTE: You can use more than the eight values in the scale. If you need a value that is lighter or darker, use the eyedropper to select the closest scale value. Double click on the foreground color to open the Color Picker. Adjust the value as needed; visually by moving the circle; numerically, by increasing or decreasing the B [#].

Traditional "Fill" Once the gradation steps are established, mix up quantities of the six gray values plus white and black. (HINT: 35mm, plastic film canisters work well to store the paint). Though you are not limited to the eight values in the scale when you "paint" the

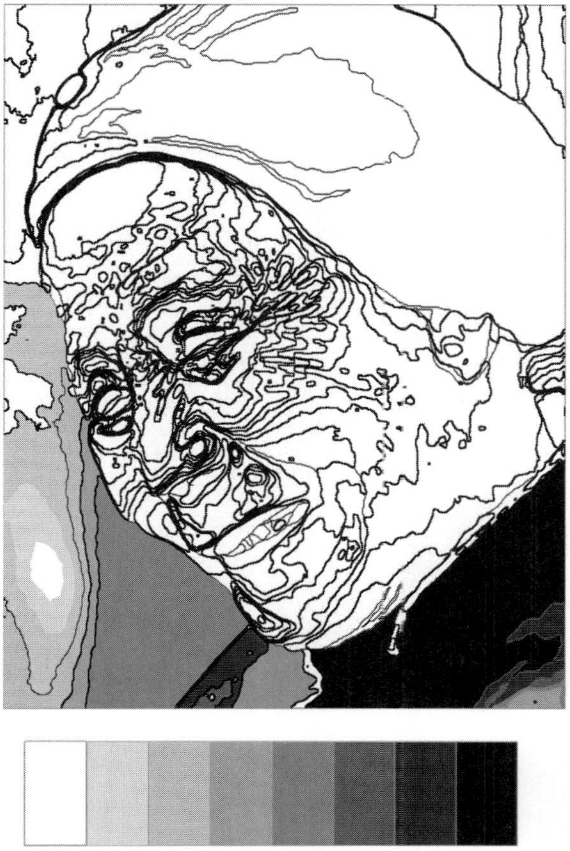

Figure 5.27 Fill achromatic study

portrait, the scale can serve as your guide to filling in the shapes of value. Begin painting into the contour shapes. The pre-mixed paint can be modified as needed when you develop the portrait further.

THE ACHROMATIC IMAGE

Achromatic means without color. Therefore, you are to develop an eight-step value scale from white to black, through gray. Using the eyedropper, you can pick up one of your value steps and place it in the foreground color box. With the **Paint Bucket Tool,** click in the appropriate spaces of your image to fill them with that value. Continue this way until you have created an interesting and reasonable achromatic portrait (Figure 5.28).

Consider the relationship of values within the image and the effect that changing the value key would have on a particular image. To see the effect of value keys more acutely, isolate segments of the composition that you feel would be served by having a different range of values. Consider how you could introduce three distinct value keys into this composition, adding a level of complexity to the image in the process (Figure 5.29). For example, your image might be served by having concentric rings identifying changes in value or you may find that imposing selective shapes might have a dramatic affect. The beauty of working electronically is that you can easily create these value changes by first making a selection then using the **Brightness/Contrast** control to adjust the value. You can also manipulate the curves or levels within a given area. Remember to **Save As,** *Achromatic.*

THE MONOCHROMATIC STUDY

If we analyze the word "monochromatic," we realize that mono = one, chroma = color, so this study will be completed with one color in addition to the black and white. Before you begin this study, consider what is communicated by the expression in the portrait and what color would best serve that communication. Does the image project cool, calm, and collected or hot and bothered? Did you have a favorite color as a child and does your attitude about a color make it the right choice?

Before you finalize your color choice, you need to consider the effect a gradation of value will have on that color. For example, you want your portrait to appear sultry and hot,

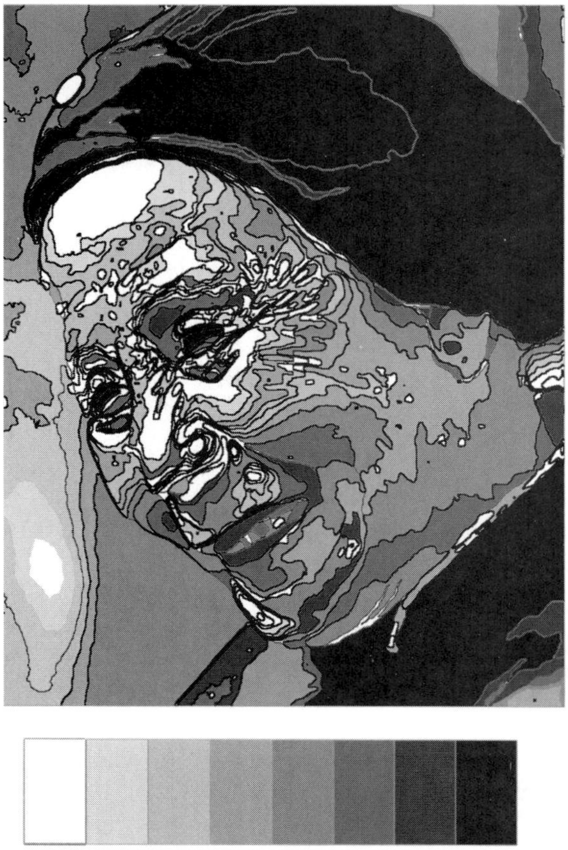

Figure 5.28 Achromatic portrait

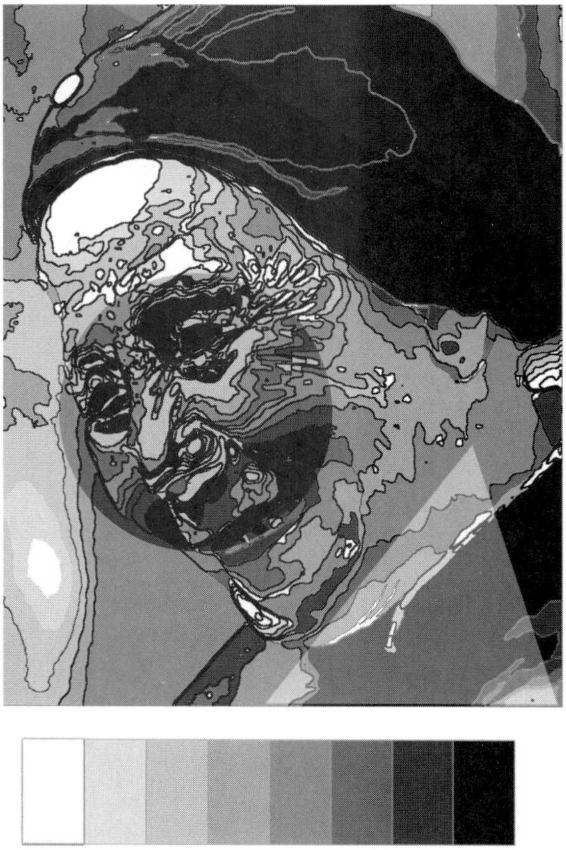

Figure 5.29 Value keys

red seems to be the logical choice because everyone knows that the cliche is to "paint the town red" when we are having a "hot time in the old town tonight." But what happens to red when you add white to create tints or black to create shades? The tints will be variations of pink. The shades might vary between maroon and brown, depending on the temperature of the red used.

Where in the image will light and bright colors fall, and in what proportion? Find the correct location for the pure hue in the value scale. What colors and how many value steps exist in the tints versus shades? When you analyze the amount of dark versus light in the image, you can project the effect color will have in the completed study.

The first step in the monochromatic study is to create the value scale in tints and shades of a color. Determine the innate value of the hue you selected, placing it in the correct location on the eight-step scale. Remember that most starting colors will not fall easily in the middle to give you an even number of tints and shades. Certain colors, such as yellow, are naturally light and might fall in the second or third step of your scale depending of course on the particular yellow. Violet is naturally dark and might fall in the seventh step of your scale. While it might seem a dark enough value to be in the eighth step, that spot is reserved for pure black. It also means that you will probably not need to mix any shades. On the positive side, dark areas of the image will glow with the chroma of a pure hue. Once the hue is correctly placed in the scale you can begin mixing the additional value steps. Keep in mind that this scale is composed of tints and shades, no tones. You need to mix white with pure hue for the tints, then mix shades from pure hue to black. Never change value by adding both white and black to the hue—this would give you tones and reduce the chroma, dulling the color further.

When you are ready to "paint by number" and complete the contour, remember that you are not limited to these eight value steps. Your scale is the guide for value distribution.

A TRI-CHROMATIC PORTRAIT

As in the previous studies, the first order of business is to create an eight- step scale from white to black. In this case, you will move through three different and distinct hues on the way. The colors should not be analogous, (that is, not next to each other on the color wheel). You must carefully select colors that are not the same innate value, needing the same step in the gradation scale. A few considerations when making your color choices might be:

1. Consider the value range in your image and whether you want to have more bright colors from lighter hues or brighter darks in the final image.
2. What effect would cooler colors in the light values have on your portrait?
3. What is the quality of the colors in the steps you mix between the pure hues?

See color section for Figure 5.30, 5.31, 5.32 showing several examples of possible tri-chromatic scales. Examine the constants, which are the selected hues, and where the mixtures occur.

CAMOUFLAGE PORTRAIT

The search for identity and meaning through portraiture brings art and culture face to face. Viewers flock to the Mona Lisa to experience beauty as well as enigma. A Zen monk in a meditative state reflects quiet humble spirituality while an African tribesman covered in tattoos embodies a proud forceful presence. Ancient and new, east and west, representation of the portrait can be expressive, powerful, and mysterious.

Value contrast and surface pattern are often used in photography, film, and painting. ***Chiaroscuro*** employs value as a means to create dramatic modeling of form. Rembrandt often used this concept in his paintings. If the value contrast is used in an even more dramatic sense, as happens naturally by dim firelight, the effect is referred to as ***tenebrism.*** Caravaggio created darker expressive compositions by using this look. Photographers have experimented with projecting light patterns onto the human figure to add a new context to their compositions. Other photographers and digital artists use minute contextual visual elements to recreate a larger photographic image. This is done by careful arrangement of the small color photos, taking advantage of value difference to blend the whole mosaic into a single picture. This idea surfaced long ago in the 1500s, when a painter named Archimboldo used organic elements such as tomatoes for cheeks, cherries for eyes, and peapods for eyebrows to paint portraits. Using small bits of color the Impressionists and the Pointillists created pictures almost in the form of mosaics. With the advent of computers and bitmapping, computer tools such as the paintbrush have become more versatile and are now loaded with tremendous bits of visual information just waiting to take shape and give referential meaning.

Adornment for the sake of decoration can add beauty, while adornment for the sake of contextual reference can modify and give new meaning to a portrait. In primitive societies, men believe that objects can have individual spirits and take on a spiritual presence (***animism***). African masks such as fertility, marriage, and funerary masks (Figure 5.34 and 5.35) often are filled with decorative sacred elements and are used in rituals to perform magic.

Overlapping a form with repeated visual elements tends to unify its surface. At times, a surface overlaid in such a fashion will function as ***camouflage*** or concealment. Just as one sees a chameleon or a lizard disguised in its natural environment, so too can a portrait become hidden from view by means of camouflage.

OBJECTIVES

This project involves several areas of study, including value, surface camouflage, fills, and various alterations of the self-image. First a portrait will be simplified into value shapes (see Value in Transition: The Self as Subject: Achromatic Portrait). Second, a personal image will be retrieved electronically, and given a redefined meaning. This image will be reduced, repeated, and developed into a ten-step value scale to be used as a surface fill. A realistic portrait likeness will be developed by means of careful step-by-step construction of surface fills that coincide with existing facial tones (Figure 5.36).

MATERIALS

Electronic: A raster-based program such as Adobe Photoshop; storage disk; mounting board; adhesive. Digital self-portrait and a personal image to be used as a repeat fill. (This image can be scanned from one of your own photos or obtained from a copyright-free picture CD library file.)

Traditional: Acrylic or gouache; brushes; bristol paper; drawing tools

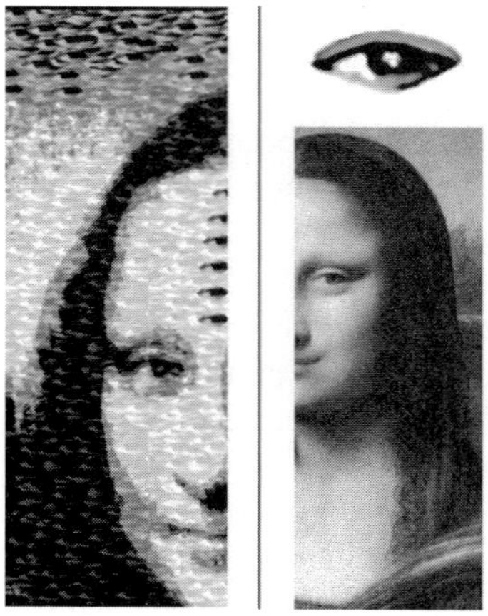

Figure 5.33

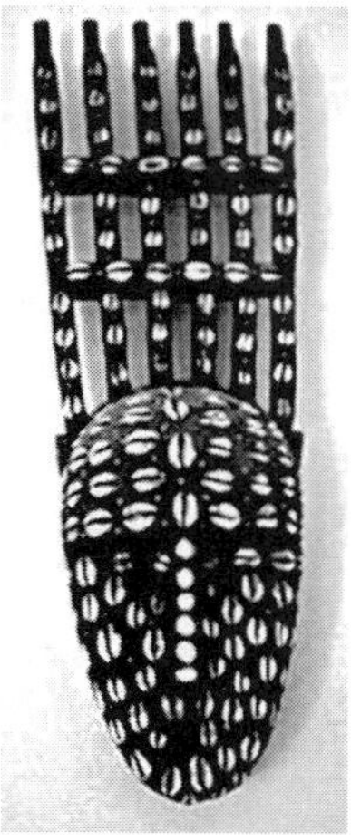

Figure 5.34

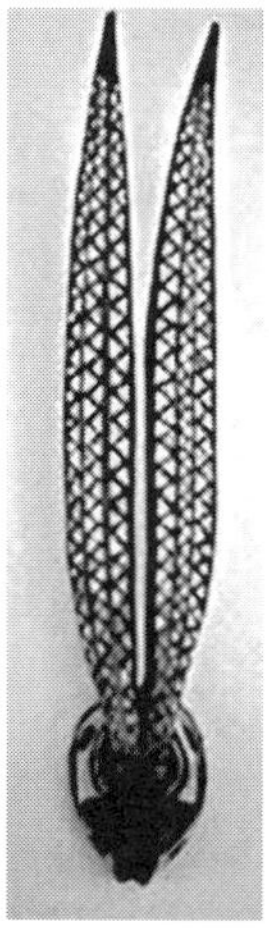

Figure 5.35

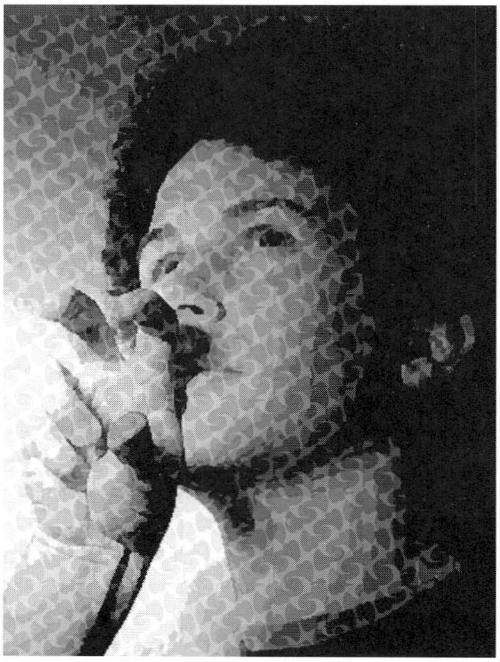

Figure 5.36 *Image by Pete Cardone*

PROCEDURE

Electronic This project can be done completely using a raster program. This project will utilize posterization, brightness contrast, pattern fills, copying, pasting, the magic wand tool, the pen tool and paths. This procedure will involve the following steps:

Posterizing a self-portrait

Capturing a contextual image

Creating a value scale with a repetitive element

Filling the portrait

Posterizing Your Portrait

Use a portrait that has full value range going from highlight to shadow. Choose a portrait that has chiarscuro side lighting and/or tenebrism, for dramatic effects.

Use a digital portrait or scanned photograph of yourself. **Save** your portrait with a resolution of 150dpi. Go to **Image, Mode** and convert to **Grayscale.** Then use **Auto Curves** and **Levels** to push your value range. Then go back to **Image** and **Adjust.** Scroll down to **Posterize** and create a ten-step posterization. This will reduce your portrait into ten basic values going from highlight to complete shadow. You may also experiment with different **posterization** settings to find a **bit depth** that creates a value separation that you like. The lower the number, the fewer value steps and the stronger the contrast **Save** your new posterized portrait as step one.

Capturing a Contextural Image

Use the flat bed scanner, the slide scanner or an image from a CD archive for the repeat image. Extract a part of the image such as a scissors (Figure 5.37) or a fish by using the pen tool as a selection device.

First go to the **File** menu and **Open** the image in your raster program. Next, go to the **Window** menu. Scroll down to **Palettes,** go to **Show Paths,** and select a **Pen Tool** to use. In magnified view (use the **Navigator** palette) you can surround the object by creating a path of "clicked " points. Next, click on the arrow on the top right of your Path and Pen Palette (in Adobe Photoshop) and **Save** your path and give it a name. Click again on the arrow to the right of your path Palette and scroll down to **Make Selection.** You now have created marching ants around your object and turned it into a precise selection. **Copy** your object and **Paste** it onto a new 8″ × 10″ page.

Creating a Value Scale with a Repetitive Element

Adjust the scale of your newly captured image by going to **Edit** and scrolling down to **Transform** and selecting **Scale.** Hold down on the **Shift Key** to constrain your

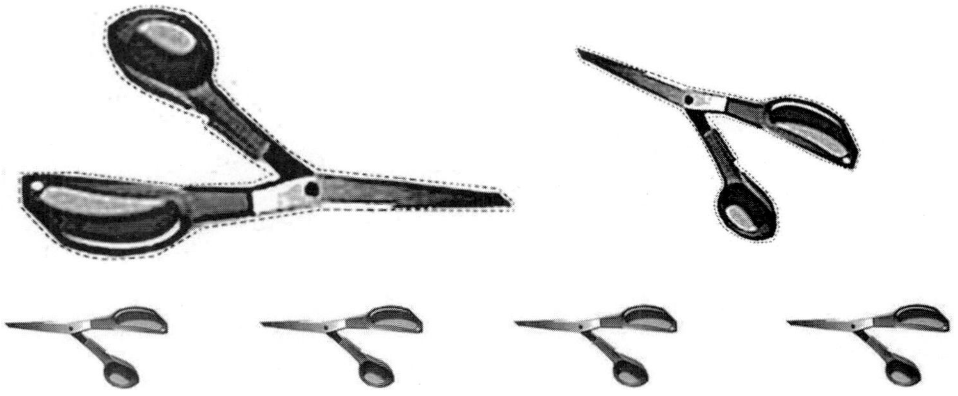

Figure 5.37

proportions. Click with your hammer inside the image when the size is to your liking. Remember to **Save** often! **Copy** and **Paste** your image many times. You may **Rotate** and **Flip** as well. **Fill** a small area with this image to create a dense pattern. Use the **Rectangular Marquee Tool** to select an area of your new pattern. **Copy** your new rectangle ten times going down the page. Create a ***value scale.*** Adjust each rectangle in terms of the values of your posterized portrait. Go to image, scroll down to adjust, and select **Brightness/ Contrast.** Continue to adjust your values going from light to dark. **Save** this as value scale boxes (Figure 5.38).

Filling the Portrait

Using the **Magic Wand Tool,** select an area of your portrait. Remember to adjust the **Tolerance** of your magic wand tool. Adjust the **Tolerance** to eight. The lower number means a smaller area of selection. Go back to your value scale boxes and select one of the rectangular pattern fills that matches the value of your portrait. Go to **Edit** and **Copy** and scroll down to **Paste Into.** You now have a repeat image fill pasted onto your portrait only in the selected area. Repeat this process until you have entirely filled your portrait by value zone (Figure 5.39).

You may also be able to fill your portrait by means of creating a pattern. Go to **Edit** and **Copy** and **Define Pattern.** Go back to **Edit** and to **Fill** and **Select Pattern** instead of foreground color. Note, when you use the **Paste Into** command, you will be creating a layer. Watch to see that you return to the **Background Layer** each time you select with the **Magic Wand Tool. Save** often.

Traditional Keeping in mind the same conceptual and formal parameters, create a painted ***monchromatic*** self-portrait. Isolate two shape areas of value and exagerate the values by using a ***high*** and ***low value key.*** Fill these keys with small image motifs that correspond in value. Exaggerate the values to express mood and draw attention to the added visual elements.

ALTERNATIVES AND VARIATIONS

Convert the portrait to **Grayscale** and then to the **Duotone** mode and create a color portrait. You may also return to the **RGB** mode to add color.

Explore portraiture in 3D by creating a plaster facemask.

Collage value patterns to the facemask.

DISCUSSION

How effective is the use of value to achieve realistic gradation? Is there a consistent light source? How has value and surface fill altered you portrait? What is the unit form of your pattern? Explain the contextural significance of the fill. Comment of the idea of decoration, obliteration, and transformation with regard to your portrait (Figure 5.40).

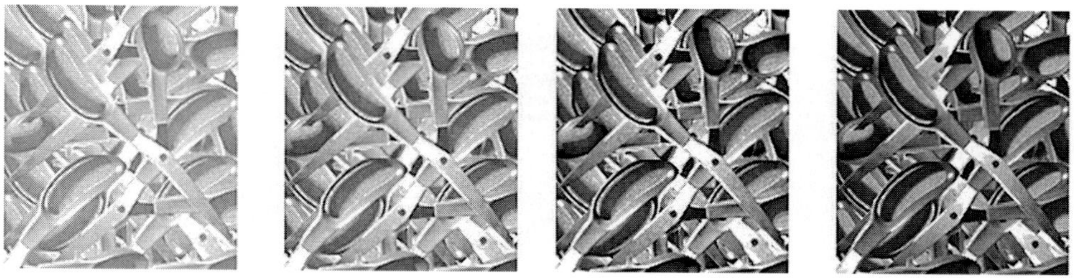

Figure 5.38

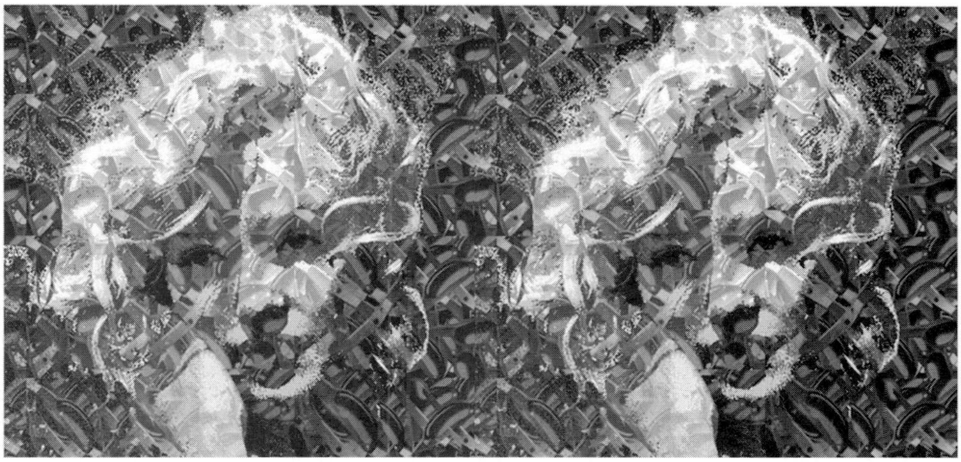

Figure 5.39

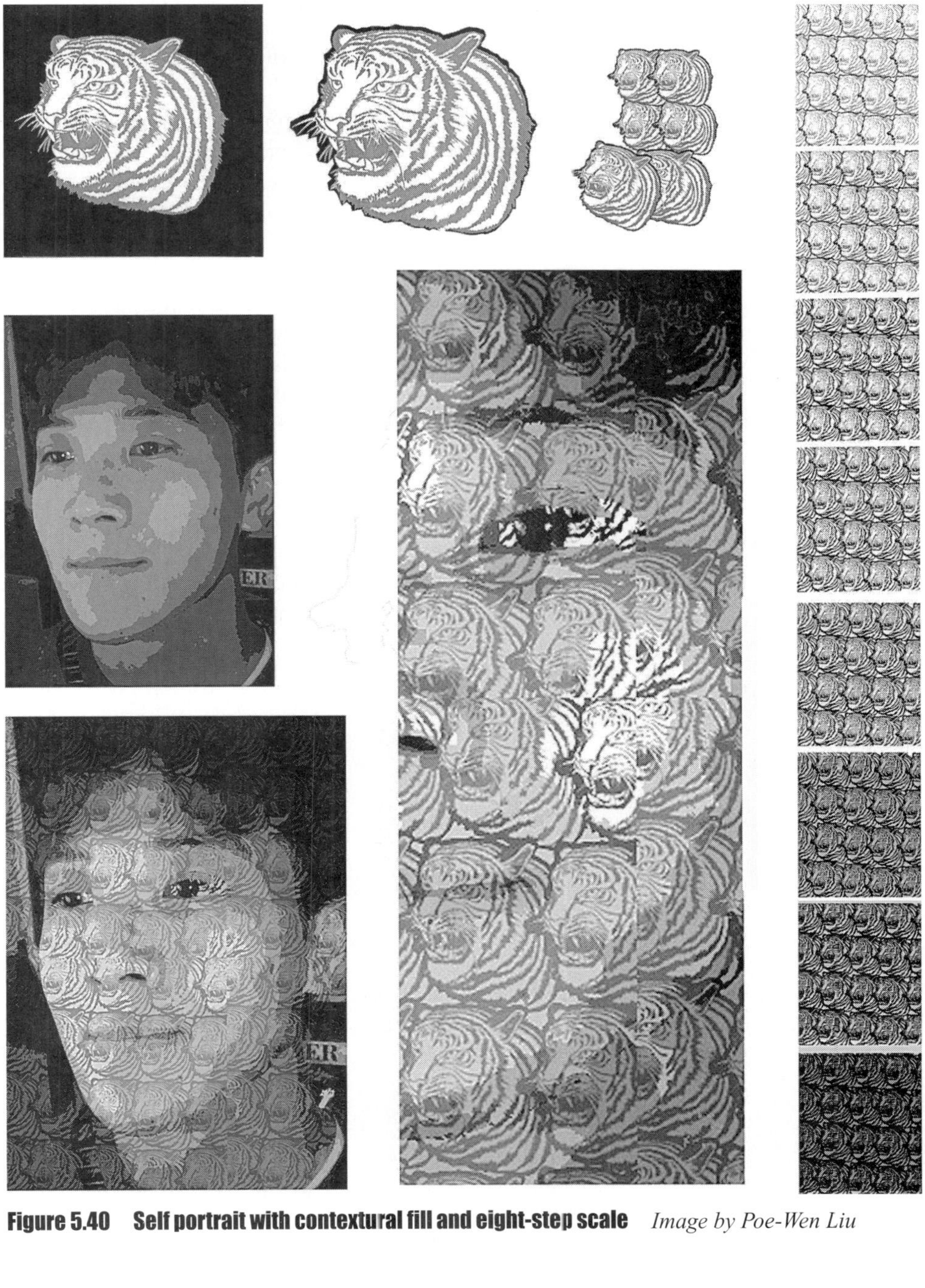

Figure 5.40 Self portrait with contextural fill and eight-step scale *Image by Poe-Wen Liu*

THE "BODY" PORTRAIT

The figure is a common subject for artists. From Rembrandt to Picasso to Chuck Close, artists have used the figure to describe human nature and expound on it. Artists have found innumerable ways to use the figure to express themselves as well. Standard head and shoulders portraits can give insight into more intimate aspects of an individual. A full-figure presentation can be more evasive, or focus on other attributes such as pose and ***gesture. Self-portraiture*** is a very alluring type of portraiture because the artist is unveiled, challenging the viewer to read nuances and glances that reveal attitudes and beliefs.

OBJECTIVES

The goal of this assignment is to introduce students to the subject of portraiture and to study color and value issues utilizing a combination of digital technology and traditional techniques.

MATERIALS

Electronic: Digital camera; computer; graphics program such as Adobe Photoshop; high-quality ink jet printer; illustration board

Traditional: Gouache; brushes; illustration board

PROCEDURE

In this study, a full-body portrait will be used as the basis for exploring issues regarding portraiture and the more fundamental issues of color and value. The use of a digital camera will allow for quick image-capture so students can bring their image into a graphics program quickly. They will be able to translate portions of it in different ways, or use the technology to assist in aspects of the assignment when it might be done in a more traditional manner.

The portrait will be taken in three parts (head and shoulders, torso, knees and feet). Each segment will be treated differently but presented the same size. As a final presentation, all portraits will be displayed as a mural with head and shoulders as the topmost section, the torso as the middle section and knees and feet as the bottom section. They will be pushed up next to each other without any space in between. As a humorous twist to the mural, the various sections can be mixed up and combined to create "new" composite student body portraits.

You should think about the ways in which you can invest this portrait with personality and character. The poses you take, and any adornments (hats, scarves, humorous glasses) will begin to suggest something about you. Look at photographer portraits, painter's portraits, and any artist's work that deals with the figure to help you conceptualize your portrait.

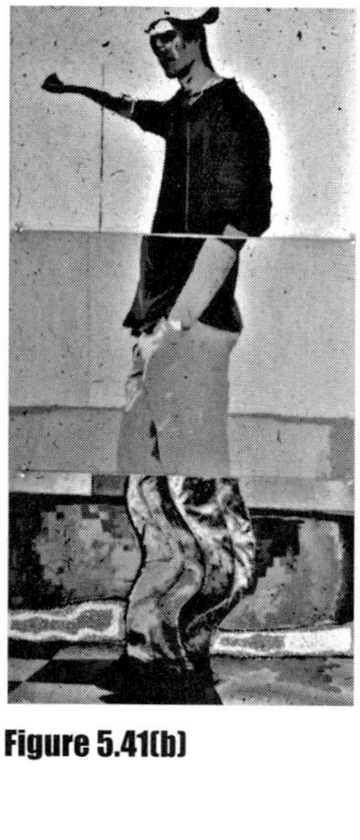

Figure 5.41(b)

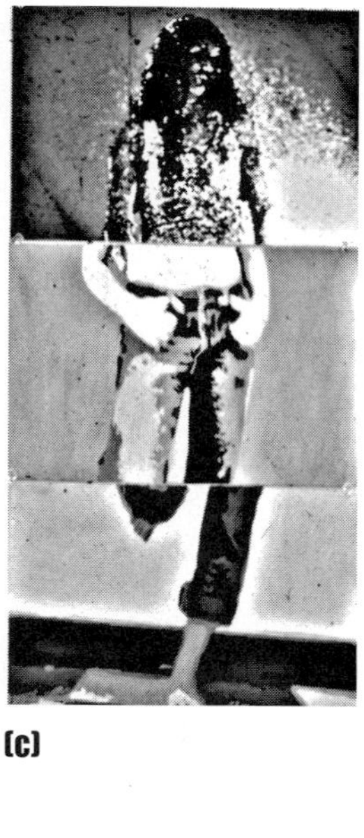

(c)

Electronic

Taking the Portrait with the Digital Camera

We will be using the digital camera to take these photographs. Choose whether you want a high-resolution image or a low-resolution image. The higher the resolution the larger the file. If you have a newer system it should be able to handle a bigger file. The higher resolution the image the more information you will be able to use and the crisper your translation will be.

Format

All segments should be equal in size so that when they are printed out they will align correctly. You should decide on the size digital files you want and adjust them on the computer. Scaling down will work but scaling up will resample the image (the graphics program will add pixel information and degrade the file). In the traditional/digital version this would not be a problem for the black-and-white printouts because they will be painted over, but for the segment that will be printed out as a color digital image you will want to keep the image as intact as possible. Each camera will bring in an image that is its own distinct size and format. With the camera we use, the file came in as an approximately 7″ × 9″ file, which we scaled up to approximately 10″ × 13″. If the scaling up is not dramatically different from the original you should not have a problem.

Once you have the digital images on your disk, you will be treating the image in three different ways: one file will be translated to a grayscale image; one file will be translated into a monochromatic image; and one file will be manipulated with the graphics program.

Changing the Files to Monochromatic Color and Grayscale

Open the file (portrait segment) that you would like to translate into a grayscale image. Go to **Image** and **Mode** and choose Grayscale. You will be asked if you want to discard color information. Select OK. Now go to the **Filters** menu and select the **Artistic Cutout** filter, move the **Levels** slider to 8 values, and select OK. This will allow you to see the way value is translated into black, white, and grays. The artistic cutout filter creates a simple breakup of values (like a paint-by-number style), so it is easier to see the ways in which value works in an image to suggest light falling on a three-dimensional form. Save this file (**Save As**) and give it a new name.

Next **Open** the file that you want to translate into a monochromatic version. Go to **Image** and then **Adjust** and **Hue/Saturation**. Click on the monochrome box and use the sliders to adjust the hue and lightness and saturation of the translation. Say OK and then go back to **Filters** and **Select** the **Artistic Cutout** filter and move the levels slider to 8. Say OK. You should now have an image that shows you what it would look like if it was presented in only black, white, and one color.

Your third translation will be a manipulation using a graphics program such as Adobe Photoshop. You will be able to change the image in any way that you like, but should not lose the sense that it is a segment of a body. Experiment with image adjustments and selections to create a unique image.

Print out each image onto good-quality paper and mount on illustration board. The board should be cut the same size as the print (mount flush to edge, no borders).

Traditional (with digital components) This version is a combination of digital and traditional techniques. In this example the digital camera allows for quick image capture and manipulation of the images to assist in the color and value study that follows.

Open up the body segment file you would like to translate into grayscale. Go to **Image** and **Mode** and change to **Grayscale** (discard color information). Now go to **Filter** and select **Artistic Cutout.** Move the slider to 8 levels and select OK. **Save** this file with a new name. **Print** the file out and paste it down to illustration board using rubber cement. Make sure you have coated all of the back of your image and then coated the whole area that it will be mounted to. Let the rubber cement dry and then paste the two together. Mix up an eight-step value scale in gray (start with white and end with black) using an opaque, water-based paint such as gouache. Proceed to translate the image into a grayscale painted image, painting the image directly on top of the printout. Use the value area shapes as the guides that correspond to the eight values that you have mixed up in paint.

Choose another segment and change the **Mode** to **Grayscale.** Choose the **Artistic Cutout** filter and translate into 8 levels. **Print** out a black-and-white print of this image. Mount on illustration board and trim to edge. To create a ***monochromatic*** painted image, choose one color and mix up an eight-step value scale using only white and black to change the lightness or darkness of the color. Paint directly onto the printout. Make sure you correspond the color values of paint with the values of white to black that are on the printout. The lightest tint of the color would be painted in the white areas, and the darkest shade of the color would be painted in the black areas. Keep paint fluid, but not too wet, to ensure a flat, opaque covering.

For the final segment use a graphics program to manipulate the image without losing the sense of the body. Experiment with the variety of **Image** adjustments and **Filter** manipulations that can be used to create a unique transformation of this segment of the portrait. Consider how your color choices will work when the three pieces are put back together for the mural. **Print** this out on glossy paper, trim, and mount onto illustration board.

Presentation and Printing

If you have a large format printer you can print these out at their original size without a problem. If you have a smaller format printer you can divide the image in half and save each half as a separate file. Mount the two halves together on the illustration board. To eliminate the possibility of the paper curling at the mid-section where they are joined, you can get a photocopy of the smaller printout and scale up on a copier that will give you a larger copy. The photocopy will then be used for the grayscale and the monochromatic translations. For the color digital printout you will have to find a printer that will print a larger format print. If all else fails, print out the image to the largest size possible on your printer and work with that scale instead of a larger one.

DISCUSSION

How were aspects of personality depicted through gesture or choice of costume or body adornment? Does the mural presentation of this assignment dictate how you respond to the portraits? What artist references can you come up with that work with the figure in similar ways? What do we learn about value and color as represented in this assignment?

THE DUOTONE SELF

Imagine an antique sepia-toned portrait or a deep blue-toned picture of a sailing vessel. Rich in color and tonal range, these beautiful mood-setting two-toned photographic prints are commonly known as duotones.

The use of duotones, tritones, and quadtones is popular in the commercial printing industry as a means to create dense images with strong highlights, shadows, and added color effects. In the digital environment, a duotone is actually made up of two similar continuous grayscale images that are colored with a custom ink set to a corresponding curve. Before printing a digital duotone, all continuous tone grayscale images are converted into tiny dots known as halftones. Each halftone is printed with a designated custom ink and combined together to produce a fully colored image. (Figure 5.42 (color insert))

OBJECTIVES

This project has multiple objectives. The first objective is to use psychological color and the rich value range of a classical duotone as a means for personal expression. The second objective is to be able to use formal color schemes such as a split complement or a tetrad scheme when the image is converted to a quadtone. Within the quadtone, you will learn how to use custom colors and curves to separate color and value. The third objective is to visualize your inner self.

The first part of this project is about how you can enhance images and create duotone and quadtone panels. The second part of this project involves the use of small intimate windows within each of the duotone panels. Each window reveals another "inner snapshot" of yourself in subject and color variation. Each color variation will involve the relationship of color harmony and contrast to hue, value, and chroma. (Figure 5.43 (color insert))

MATERIALS

Electronic: Raster-based program such as Adobe Photoshop; portrait images; autobiographical images; matte boards; utility knife; adhesive; archival tape

Traditional: paint; bristol; matte board; tape; utility knife; adhesive; personal images and self-portraits

PROCEDURE

Electronic This duotone project has three main steps. The goal is to create an eight panel self-portrait project with eight hidden windows. The panels and windows are to reveal your inner and outer self. These steps are:

Create the classical duotones portrait panels

Create the posterized quadtones portrait panels

Create the window snapshots of varying hue, chroma and value

Creating a Classical Duotone

Select full tonal range digital self-portraits. These can be scanned in from original photographs or can be digital photos. Digital photos should be continuous tone color or grayscale images that each have 256 bits of information per inch. Go to **Mode** and change any color photos from **RGB** to **Grayscale** mode. From **Grayscale** select the **Duotone Mode** and select two custom inks. In order to produce a fully saturated image, the inks are set in descending order: darkest at the top and lightest at the bottom (Figure 5.44(a)). Each ink has a corresponding curve to enhance the shadows in the black ink curves and alter the highlights and tints in the mid value ink curve (Figure 5.44(b)). These two ink settings can be further separated in a **Multi-Channel** mode so that each individual channel can be viewed. (Figure 5.42 (color insert))

Using the **Duotone** mode in Photoshop create three color portraits that work together as a triptych. Create a duotone, a tritone and a quadtone. In order to work with the dutone mode convert your portrait from **RGB** mode to **Grayscale** and from **Grayscale** to the **Duotone** mode. Select two ink colors (Pantone black and another rich color ink as the second hue) for your duotone. These duotones should have a feel of their richness and harmony of color and value.

Creating a Posterized Quadtone

Construct another self-portrait, this time move from the duotones setting to the **Quadtone** setting. Now you will have four inks to choose from in descending order of dark to light. Select each ink by clicking in each ink box. The graphs along side each ink selection will need to be altered as well as manipulating the dragging points on the lines (Figure 5.44(b)). Push the tonal richness to its extreme by adjusting the graphs. Adjust the curves this time so that your grayscale image appears posterized. The first curve (Custom Black) should stay primarily in the top right where shadows are formed. The second curve should move over a bit from the right for a darker ink setting. The third setting should be a mid to lighter value and the curve should form an arc in the center of the graph. The final highlight setting should adjust the curve to the left side of the screen to emphasize highlights. To utilize a **Quadtone,** select four Pantone color inks. The darkest one at the top being black and moving down to the lightest on the fourth color selection. You can then take your adjusted grayscale images and go back to **Image** and then **Mode** and choose **Muti-Channel** mode. Here you can view you grayscales in individual chanels and even print each chanel out as a

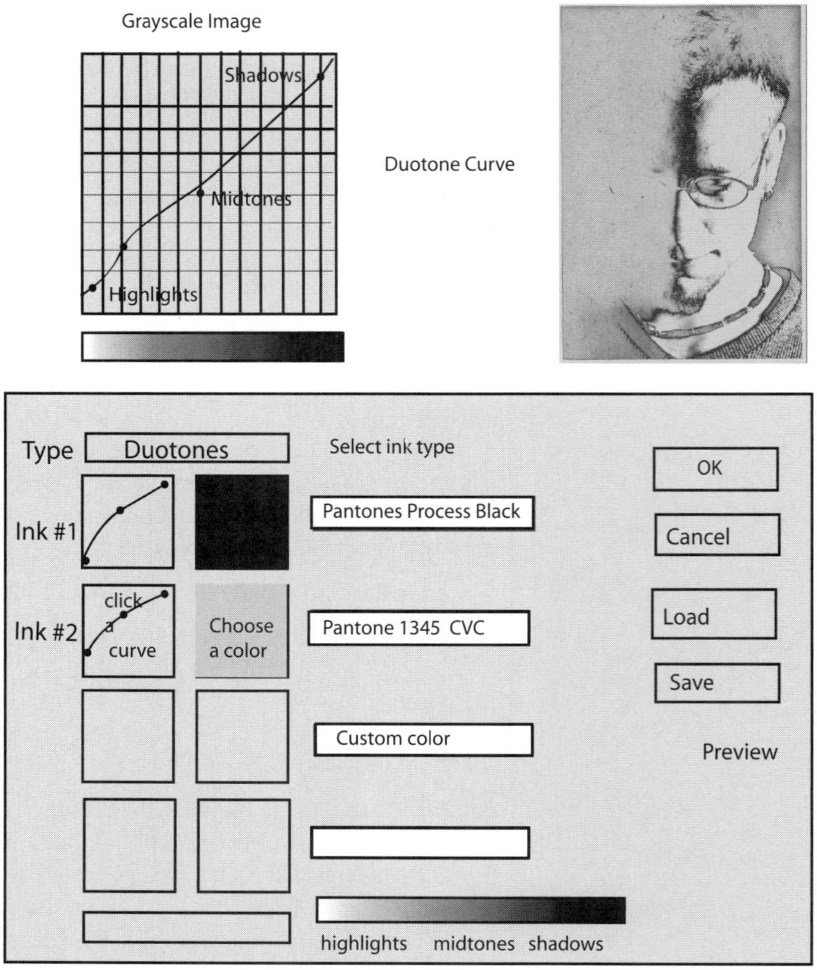

Figure 5.44(a) Choosing the inks and curves for the duotone setting

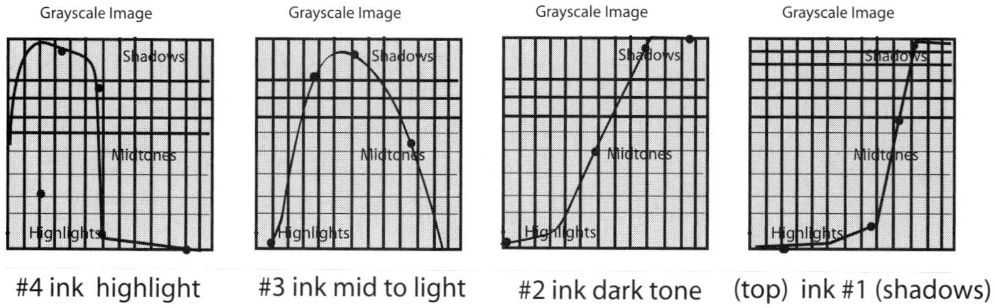

Figure 5.44(b) Adjusting the curves for the quadtone grayscale images

separate image. You can also then print out the combination of all the images together to see the final version.

Creating Windows That Are Hue, Value and Chroma Variations

Using the **RGB** mode, add five small windows with snapshot "autobiographical" imagery . . . reflections about you and your interests, family, and friends. Each window should be a different color permutation in terms of using harmony and contrast of ***hue, value*** and ***chroma.*** Construct the windows with "doors" much like the format of an advent calendar (Figure 5.45 (color insert)). Work with symbolic color and integrate theme and content with color. Explore a folded structural format to combine panels and windows together to create a unique self-portrait (Figure 5.46 and 5.47 (color insert)).

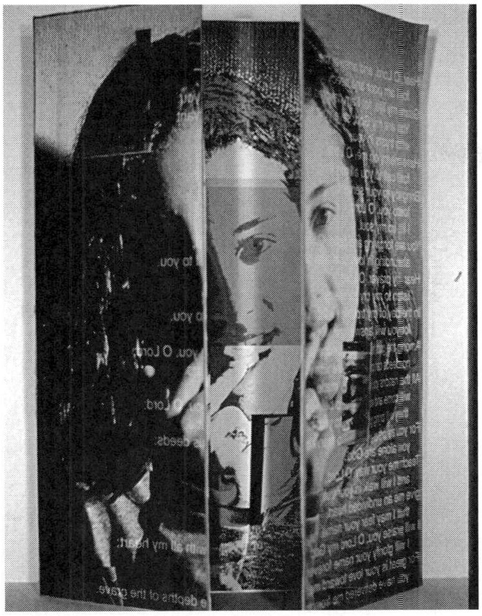

Figure 5.46 *Image by Isobel Werner*

Traditional Take each window snapshot and create a color variation in terms of harmony and contrast in relationship to an image's ***hue, value,*** and ***chroma.*** Refer to Chapter 6 on color for information on the properties of color. Reduce each image to simplified values such as a ten-step value scale and draw out your images accordingly. Or you can combine electronic with traditional procedure and take your digital images and go to **Image Adjust** and then **Posterize** your image. Then paint, scan, and place each window into the duotone panels.

ALTERNATIVES AND VARIATIONS

To add further variety to your portraits combine a **"portrait stamp pattern"** to one or more of the panels. Select an image with the **Rectangular Marquee;** and under edit, define your image as a pattern. Then fill any selected area with your newly created pattern. The color self-portrait prints may utilize duotones, tritones, and/or quadtones.

DISCUSSION

Do the panels of the portrait work together? Explain in terms of color theory. Are the values enriched? How closely do the values of the original portrait match the duotone portrait? Is the portrait composition visually pleasing? If not, why? Consider color balance, overall movement, background space, and value. How do the five windows work compositionally with the portrait panels? As a self-portrait reflection, what ideas come to mind with the personal window images? What kinds of feelings are evoked? Is the visual content in keeping with the medium as well as the compositional structure (Figure 5.48 (color insert)). What is strong about this triptych? What areas still need improvement?

CHAPTER 6

A WORLD IN COLOR

FACETS OF COLOR: AN INTRODUCTION TO THEORY AND PERCEPTION

Color is the most complex fundamental element of design. It functions both physically and psychologically and can be used to visually communicate a complex, rich blend of information. Color design principles involve and often depend on formal, contextual relationships. Our understanding of color is also formed through our personal experiences and cultural backgrounds. This filters the formal chromatic effects and endows color with the ability to communicate feelings and ideas without words. Because there is so much information, on a variety of levels, when studying color theory, a dynamic body of knowledge emerges that can be applied equally well to traditional art, design, photography, and electronic media.

Within our physical environments, color functions as a property of light and can only be experienced in the presence of light. White light is composed of seven colors that are revealed when it passes through prismatic glass or a mist of water (rainbows). The study of color theory is based on our understanding of this ***additive system*** (Figure 6.1, color insert) of spectral colors and their interactions. TV and computer monitors utilize the additive system known as the ***RGB color system*** to define and create colored images by projecting light onto a monitor screen. As artists and designers, however, the use of light as a medium can be limiting. ***Pigments*** found in paints, inks, and dyes have been developed to mimic the colors in white light while providing a material substance for manipulation. Pigments comprise the ***subtractive system*** (Figure 6.2, color insert) of color, in which the theoretical combination of all colors yields black or the absence of light. The CMYK system is a newer subset of the subtractive system and is used by the printing industry.

Regardless of its source, our perception of color is dependent on the interaction of light with our eyes. Light, a form of electromagnetic energy that is visible to the eye, travels through the atmosphere, hitting the surfaces of forms as it moves. These chromatic rays are either absorbed by an object or reflected from it (Figure 6.3, color insert).

Reflected light rays enter our eyes and are transformed by the rods and cones in the retina into electrochemical energy. This information then travels to the sight centers of the brain, where it is decoded to identify color. Not all surfaces are perceived to have color: Black objects absorb all light rays, returning no spectral colors to our eyes, while white surfaces reflect all colors in the spectrum, combining them to create white. Regardless of the perceived color or the individual involved, this process is consistent in human visual perception (Figure 6.4, color insert).

Individual comprehension, however, is modified by our history and experience, imposing psychological filters that create our own unique perceptual palette of colors. Additionally, the history and experience of a society or culture may produce emotional or symbolic associations with particular colors, thus altering their impact and perception (Figure 6.5, color insert).

It is easy to see or perceive color, but to have a full grasp and appreciation of the phenomena you must study its attributes and interactions. The ***qualities*** of color are basic properties that may be changed or altered within a visual sample. ***Hue*** designates the name of a color and indicates its position in the spectrum of white light. Hue also refers to the relative relationship of a color to its basic components. Red, pink, maroon and rose are different colors that all emanate from the same "red" hue.

Value is another quality that refers to the lightness or darkness of a color and has a number of manifestations. ***Local value*** is the perceived value of a color in the visual world. ***Chromatic value*** is the lightness or darkness of a color that has been achieved through manipulation. ***Tints*** are light values of a color created by the addition of white and ***shades*** are dark chromatic values resulting from the addition of black. ***Inherent value*** refers to the relative value of a color in its pure state. Yellow has a very light inherent value, while violet has a very dark intrinsic value. The creation of tonal groupings to establish value keys can also be undertaken with colors. This may be used in the manipulation of overall feeling or mood within a chromatic image. ***Intensity*** is a quality that deals with the brightness and purity of a color. ***High-intensity*** colors are pure and unmodified by any other color or value. ***Low-intensity*** colors are those that have been dulled by the addition of black, gray, or another color.

The fourth quality of color is ***temperature.*** This quality refers to the warmth or coolness of any given color. Visual interaction with colors such as red, orange, and yellow results in an increase in our circulatory blood pressure, actually creating the physical impression of warmth. Perceptually, these warm colors tend to advance, expand, and emerge in space. Observing colors such as blue, green, and violet lowers our blood pressure, actually creating the physical impression of cold. Visually, cool colors tend to contract and recede into space. Changes in chromatic temperature within visual images can profoundly alter the perception of space, depth, and volume.

Our understanding of color is further enhanced by its classification and organization into various groupings or schemes. Early taxonomy of colors began by referencing their visual source in the spectrum of light. In the 17th century, Sir Isaac Newton developed a model for the progression of hues within white light. His arrangement of twelve colors within a circular format produced the ***color wheel,*** a basic design reference. This organization of hues creates three basic categories of colors whose relationships are established along regular mathematical intervals. The ***primary*** colors (Figure 6.6, color insert) are those that cannot be made by mixing any other colors together. In the additive system of light, such as the RGB system found on computer monitors, these colors are red, green, and blue. Although the CMYK system used in the color printing industry uses Cyan, Magenta, and yellow as primary colors, the basic primary colors found within the subtractive system of pigments are red, yellow, and blue. They are placed equidistant from each other on the color wheel. Bisecting the spaces between primaries are the ***secondary*** colors (Figure 6.7, color insert), produced by mixing their two neighboring primaries. ***Tertiary*** colors (Figure 6.8, color insert), which fill in the six remaining slots on the color wheel, are the sum of their adjacent primary and secondary colors. The primary color precedes the secondary in the names of each of these colors. The color wheel provides a clean and rational means of understanding color. In reality, the success of Newton's model required a bit of creative problem solving as red-violet does not exist in the spectrum of white light. Over time, a number of artists and designers have modified and reconfigured this basic structure to produce a number of two- and three-dimensional versions.

Regardless of the model, the formal structure and mathematical divisions of the color wheel also function to create physical relationships between colors whose juxtaposition is visually pleasing. ***Harmonious color schemes*** are created by colors that may be adjacent to each other on the color wheel (***analogous colors***) or across and equidistant from each other on the color wheel (***complementary colors***) or found on the corners of triangles or squares drawn within the color wheel (***triads*** and ***tetrads***), to name a few. The concept of color harmony is also involved in decisions regarding relative quantities of one color to another within an image. ***Color ratios,*** devised by Goethe, deal with the relative proportions of primaries to their complements. In this system, each color is evaluated in terms of its value and luminosity. Two juxtaposed colors must be present in equivalent proportions to maintain their intensity. Yellow, for instance, was assigned a nine while violet was assigned a three, dictating that violet must appear in three times as great an area as yellow to maintain its visual brightness.

As with almost every other aspect of our lives and experiences, our perception of color depends on the context in which it is seen. Changes in the hue, intensity, value, temperature, and size of an area of a color can alter the attributes of a superimposed or juxtaposed area of color. ***Simultaneous contrast*** involves a contextual relationship in which a color imposes its complement on another color that is placed next to it. This contrast is the result of activity within the light receptors of the eye. The rods and cones of the retina exist in a state of repose when they are exposed to neutral grey. By visually imposing the opposite of what they are viewing on an adjacent area, they are able to visually neutralize a color and stabilize their activity.

Ultimately, color's relative nature is illusive and complex and its perception is highly relative to the environment. Its meaning within images is often personal and dependent on association and context. Despite scientific explanation, our perception of and response to color can remain somewhat of a mystery, defying logic and moving to a higher plane of pure mystical expression.

TWELVE-HUE SCALES

OBJECTIVES

As we begin our entry into the world of color, we need to gain an understanding of how color can be generated in different media, electronic as well as traditional. The goal of this exercise is to develop color scales in a variety of media to form a basis for comparison. A color scale created from a commercial color system, such as Color Aide, will serve as a guide for the mixing of color in traditional materials, which in turn can be referenced for color mixing on the computer.

While there are a variety of color systems, a twelve-hue scale of primary, secondary, and tertiary colors is the goal. In review, the ***primary colors*** of red, yellow, and blue form the basis for all of the color mixing in this particular system. Consider each primary a point on an equilateral triangle. Mixing adjacent primary colors creates a ***secondary color.*** The third-level or ***tertiary colors*** are created when you mix each primary with the adjacent secondary color. Although the color hierarchy and organization remains the same, the qualities of each color will change as you switch equipment and media. Colors generated with phosphors on a monitor will appear differently than those created by paint with pigment or found in other sources.

MATERIALS

Electronic: Either raster- or vector-based software such as Adobe Photoshop or Illustrator; printer or other output system.

Traditional: Bristol and illustration board; mixing tray; a set of gouache paint with good mixing capability; brushes; Color Aide or other color reference system.

PROCEDURE

As we have done with previous exercises requiring a gradation, you will create a scale composed of 1″ × 1-1/2″ rectangles, assembled into 1″ × 13″ band. Because the traditional wheel is rolled out into a line, the thirteenth step allows you to begin and end in the same color to show a continuum.

The first exploration will be in paint, learning how to mix color to achieve the purity of the hues expected in this scale. What you may discover is that what works in theory might not work as effectively with pigment. In theory, we should be able to mix yellow and red to create a perfect orange and use the same red to create a vibrant purple when mixed with blue. However, paint is not always that flexible. You may find that you need to have available both a warm red and cool red to effectively mix colors at opposite temperature ends of the scale. This is to ensure that you retain a high level of ***intensity*** of color, or ***chroma,*** in all of the secondary and tertiary mixtures.

It is recommended that you begin with the primaries and establish a base of what you consider to be "true" colors. For some, it might be helpful to think back to "crayola crayon" days as an effective place to start. Once the three primary colors are created, mix the secondary colors that fall in between before attempting the tertiary colors. As you work your way down the color hierarchy, consider not only your perception of "true," but also the value of each color that you create. The goal is to create a reasonably smooth transition around the wheel. Keep in mind that between yellow and red there are an infinite number of possibilities for yellow-orange through degrees of orange to the range of red-oranges. It is up to you to determine which yellow-orange, orange, or red-orange is most appropriate to keep the scale moving smoothly. Remember, you are trying to create a "wheel" of the twelve major hues and must retain a high level of chroma or intensity of color to reflect the purity of each hue.

Electronic The completed scale in pigment can be used as a reference for color mixing on the computer. We see color on the monitor through phosphors and light rather than pigment. That alone can be a difficult transition. An added complication is the difference in color between what we see on the monitor versus what we find in print. It is helpful to know before beginning any project what the expectation is and whether the work will ultimately be in print or remain on the screen. Because the goal of this exercise is to prepare you for subsequent color projects that will be printed, you will need to explore electronic color mixtures and print color tests to achieve the expected results (Figure 6.9, color insert).

Students can decide whether it is more effective to work in a raster program such as Adobe Photoshop or a vector program such as Adobe illustrator. You can begin with a circle or some form of a twelve-sided object that can easily be divided into equal segments. If you prefer, a linear scale is equally effective. Review the procedure for developing an electronic gradation scale described in the *Self Image in Series* in Chapter 5.

A VISUAL EXPLANATION OF COLOR THEORY

OBJECTIVES

As expressed in the title, the goal of this assignment is to create a visual explanation of color theory. Instead of random or individual explorations of the attributes of color, you will consider hue, value, and chroma within the context of a single but comprehensive image or design. The final image might be representational, imaginary, or a completely abstract composition. The format and subject matter are less critical than the successful application of color theory to the chosen format for effective communication.

MATERIALS

Electronic: A raster- or vector-based software program such as Adobe Photoshop or Illustrator, with full color capabilities; a printer or other output system

Traditional: Illustration board; mixing tray; a set of gouache paint with good mixing capability; brushes

PROCEDURE

As stated previously, there are three primary areas of concern—hue, value, and chroma or intensity—when we discuss attributes of color. To help the viewer understand the distinct differences and importance of these issues, you will need to include the following five considerations.

Hue

1. **The twelve major hues.** Remember that hue describes a "family" of colors and is color in its purest state. Consider the placement of these colors to effectively address issues of space, location, and form in your composition. You may also want to consider the hierarchy of the twelve hues, and designate the differing importance of primary versus secondary and tertiary colors. The hues should be placed in the composition to enable the viewer to understand the generation of color (that is, because orange is a mixture of red and yellow, it should be placed between these two colors), making the sequence of colors critical.

Value

2. **"Sets" of Tints and Shades.** To help the viewer understand issues of value, which is the relative lightness or darkness of color, you will include a "set" of tints and a "set" of shades. A "set" is a gradation in at least five steps. For the tints, the gradation will move from white to the color or colors selected. The gradation of shades of a color will be mixed with black in varying amounts. Whether you complete one gradation of each type or several should be determined by what would best for the composition. You should also consider the effect that a smooth gradation can have on a composition to show light and form. In addition, the gradation might be more effective in greater than five steps, which is the minimum.

Chroma

3. **Gradation of Tones.** To help present issues of intensity, the student will include, at minimum, two additional types of gradations. One will be a set of tones and the other a complementary neutralization. Tones may be described as grayed colors. There are, however, many ways to gray out a color. For the purposes of this exercise you will do a gradation from a gray to a color. What is important to consider is the appropriate gray to use as the beginning point. If you use a gray that is of a different value than your selected color, the gradation will reflect a change of value in addition to the intensity change. It is therefore important to begin by mixing a gray that is of the same value as the selected color and a gradation between the two. With the value consistent, the change is one of increased dullness rather than a change in lightness or darkness.

4. **A Complementary Neutralization.** In earlier discussions of the color wheel, we learned that colors that fall directly across from each other are said to be compliments of each other. The reason they are said to complement each other is that within each set of compliments all colors exists. Yellow and violet are across from each other on the wheel. Yellow is a primary, while violet is a secondary color, composed of the other two primary colors, red and blue. If you could mix all color in pigment you would theoretically reach black, while color in light returns to white. Each set of compliments has its own particular affect and attribute when used next to each other. When mixed together however, they will neutralize each other because they grow closer to being all color. For this part of the assignment, carefully select which set of compliments to use and consider where to apply this particular transition. Most combined complements create a

neutral brown in the middle but the quality of that brown varies by which set of complements is used.

With all of the preceding inclusions, carefully consider where you apply each of the gradations. Are they to be a random set of lines or transitions, or can they effectively use light and create a sense of space, form, temperature, atmosphere, etc? Whether your composition is representational or abstract, color must be placed to effectively communicate the visual environment.

5. **Harmony and Discord.** One additional set of issues to be considered in the image is the representation of a color harmony and a color discord. Those of you with musical training might recognize these terms. When Johannes Itten was working on his theories of color at the Bauhaus, he brought his training in music to the discussion. As a result, many of the terms we use currently have a musical analogy. In music, a harmony is pleasant to the ears, and in the case of art, it should be pleasant to the eyes. Harmonies are often generated by evenly spaced intervals to create the pleasant combination of sounds. A discord, on the other hand, can be grating because of the sometimes awkward relationships of the notes, or in this case, the colors. In design, as in music, there is a place for the unpleasant or not beautiful. Imagine selecting a group of colors that are at even intervals around the color wheel or in logical combinations. Compare that grouping to a selection of colors that fall at random points on the color wheel and are also of different values and intensities. Which grouping of colors would be discordant to you versus harmonious? Applying the harmony/discord selections to your "poster" might be as simple as placing three elements together with harmonious colors and three elements together with discordant colors somewhere in your composition. Analogous colors, those colors that fall next to each other around the wheel, are easily harmonious. In this assignment, however, you are expected to search beyond an analogous harmony (Figure 6.10 and 6.11, color insert).

COLOR, LIGHT, AND SPACE

The spatial attributes of color are important characteristics to artists and designers. The perception that warm colors advance and cool colors recede has traditionally been used to expand the limitations of the two-dimensional picture plane. This spatial reference continues to be used today as a contributor to image enhancement.

Combined with other spatial indicators that have been discussed earlier (scale, overlapping, placement, etc.), color can expand the picture plane and mimic aspects of three-dimensional reality. In this assignment, the creation of the illusion of space through the manipulation of color, and light and shadow characteristics in an image, can be an effective strategy.

OBJECTIVES

The goal of this assignment is to create a design (Figure 6.12, color insert) that uses fundamental elements as objects that float in space. ***Points, lines,*** and ***planes*** are organized into a working design, and in carefully chosen places, their cast shadows are used to create the illusion of space on the two-dimensional plane. Exploring the spatial attributes of color and discovering the logic of light and space are important aspects of this inquiry.

MATERIALS

Electronic: Computer; graphics program such as Adobe Photoshop; good-quality ink jet printer; glossy printer paper; illustration board; rubber cement

Traditional: color aid paper; rubber cement; illustration board; scissors; #11 mat knife; sketchbook; pencils

PROCEDURE

To begin this project, explore design options for a number of ideas. Points (about the size of a paper punch and not necessarily round) and lines (longer than they are wide) will contrast with the larger planes for design variety. Vary the way that you are using these elements in relationship to placement and direction. Also, consider the fact that some of these elements will have cast shadows and that the shapes of the shadows will become elements in the design as well.

Electronic Using a graphics program such as Adobe Photoshop, begin by creating one or two color base planes as a background layer for your design. Keep the colors of these planes fairly light so that any cast shadows that are created can be seen as they overlay them (it is difficult to see a cast or drop shadow on a dark color so your illusion will be compromised).

Create shapes on the computer that are based on points, lines, or planes, utilizing tool functions such as selections and fills, or painting functions that allow you to create your objects. All of these elements are to be viewed as if they were cut from a piece of paper, and as if floating in space.

Your choice of color for the forms should come from your understanding of how we perceive color in space. Use characteristics such as ***color temperature*** and ***value*** to push and pull the forms in space. You can also cut out elements of some of the objects by selecting areas and deleting them. This will allow other layers to show through and will exaggerate the illusion of space. (Figure 6.13, color insert).

Create cast shadows for the forms by selecting each layer individually, and going to the **Layer** options on the **Menu Bar.** Go to a function like **Layer** then **Layer Style** and **Drop Shadow.** Adjust for opacity, angle distance, and blur. Continue to create new points, lines, and planes, organizing their placement and choosing which ones will cast a shadow. Place each new element on a layer of its own so that you can eliminate it if it is not working in the design. Turn off individual layers so you can see which layers work with each other.

Because these elements are considered to be flat forms floating in space, the illusion of depth will be based on the creation of a moderate spatial effect through the creation of cast shadows.

DISCUSSION

How is color used to enhance the spatial illusion in the design? In what ways have the elements been manipulated to control the sense of space? How effective are the cast shadows in accentuating the spatial illusion in the design?

A NATURAL SOURCE

Science and art are flip sides of human cultural accomplishment. Artists and scientists have looked to the natural world as a great source of inspiration, compelled to examine the beauty of natural elements while understanding the structure and composition of organic growth. We are drawn to the natural world because it is aesthetically pleasing, finding comfort in its structure and stimulation in the colors we find there. The ornamental feathers of a peacock or the vibrancy of tropical fish capture our attention. We marvel at the repetition of decorative shapes and the strong, graphic presentation, formed without human direction.

Nature, as the primary source of emulation, has varied across art historical time. Early Greek and Roman sculpture examined human form, while artists of the Renaissance, such as Michelangelo Buonarotti, took the representation of musculature and form to new heights of perfection. Representations of leaves have found their way three-dimensionally into the capitals of columns and are painted repeatedly as the borders of two-dimensional pages.

Nature can move beyond being only a resource in art to become subject matter or the actual content in works of art or artistic investigation. Artists have wanted to represent the natural world, often interpreting their perception of representation through the cultural filter of their time. Artists of the nineteenth century moved out of the studio to examine the play of color and light in the natural world. These Impressionists changed the way paint is used on a canvas and the perception of colors in a shadow cast on the water or in the grass forever.

Which colors we use and how they are applied changes across time and with personal experience. Artists use combinations of colors for a variety of reasons, at times dealing with objective representation, unless the goal is a subjective expression. Picasso, for example, moved through periods of blue and rose, casting an emotional response on the imagery.

Where do you begin assembling a palette of colors with which to communicate? For the answer to this, we will look to the natural world as an initial source for combinations to reference.

OBJECTIVES

A natural object will serve as a source of information for both form and color in the development of a three-part series, color pattern study. As a controlled experiment, the same palette and non-focal pattern will be used to create differences in the images through the interaction of color and design principles. Using proportion and placement, the goal is to develop contrasts in hue, value, intensity, and image type. To reach this goal, process is important, requiring that you explore multiple variations at each step of the procedure. The finished project will include:

Several drawings of the natural object

A palette of ten colors found in the natural object

At least three black-and-white pattern explorations

At least three color pattern studies

MATERIALS

Electronic: A raster-based program such as Adobe Photoshop; a scanner; a color printer or other output device; a natural object or objects; drawing materials

Traditional: Drawing materials; illustration board; gouache paint; brushes, transfer paper, ruler

PROCEDURE

There are several steps that are followed whether you choose to work electronically, traditionally, or with a combination of the two.

Natural object selection

Drawing the object

The unit of repetition

Pattern development

Palette discovery

Image transformation through color

Conclusion

Natural Object Selection Select a natural object as a source for both form and color. Consider objects with surface detail that provide added interest. Structural protrusions, such as the spikes of the shell or the progressive bumps on the starfish, act dynamically in the composition (Figure 6.14). Though flat, decorations organized around the shell in pattern-like movements or randomly splashed on the surface can also be used to great effect (Figure 6.15).

Sand-dollars, on the other hand, are circular in nature. Consider the effect of a circle in repetition and whether it would generate sufficient dynamic interest. (Figure 6.16) Using circular elements in combination has greater potential. The "edge" these sand-dollars have over a typical circular outline are the negative "cutouts" and incised "star" motif that will add a level of interest in the pattern.

Another consideration in selecting the natural object is the degree of ***color.*** A sand-dollar, which is essentially ***achromatic***, might not be the best color source. A second natural object can be used to generate your palette, because a representational outcome is not one of the project goals.

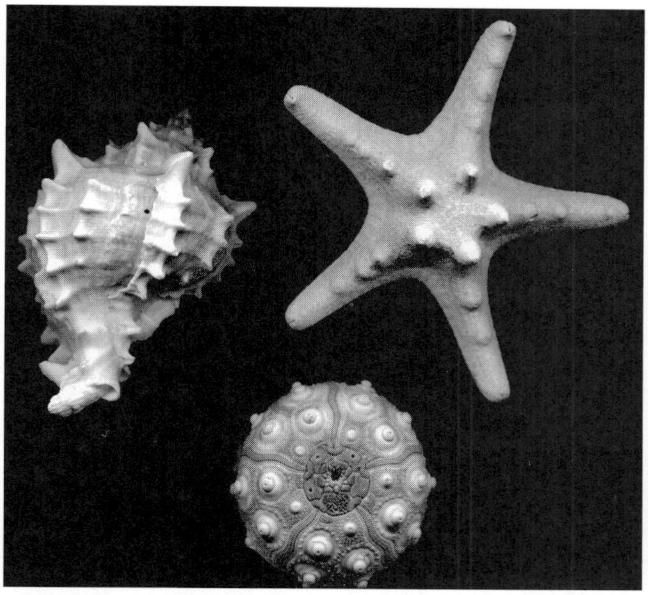

Figure 6.14

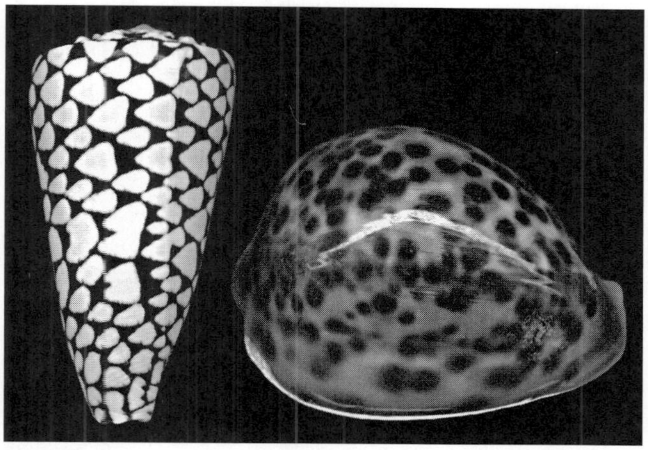

Figure 6.15

Drawing the Object Complete several drawings of the natural object from different views to discover different attributes (Figure 6.17). Ultimately, it is most effective if the object is translated into a line drawing. ***Contour line*** can be used to describe the areas of value as well as areas of form. The line study should be thorough, and capture both external contour and internal details, whether structural or surface decoration. The object becomes a "cartoon" that can be colored in selectively. While the initial drawings of the object might be representational, they can abstract in the process of development.

The drawings can be done on paper and should explore not only different views of the object, but different media and drawing styles. They can be continually refined to reach the contour line needed for this project (Figure 6.18).

For those working electronically, initial drawings on paper can be scanned into the computer. They can also be used as a reference when drawing directly on the computer using a vector- or raster-based program.

While drawing is significant as part of the process of discovery, scanning the natural object is certainly an option. The object should be scanned in **Grayscale,** as in the case of this shell, (Figure 6.19), or converted to **Grayscale** when the file is opened in a raster program such as Adobe Photoshop. If you begin with a photographic **Scan,** you can take advantage of the image manipulation capabilities of the software to reduce the image to a thorough contour. Review the procedure for creating an electronic contour described in the *The Self-Image in Series* in Chapter 5.

The Unit of Repetition The drawings can be complex and elaborate (Figure 6.20) or simplified and abstracted (Figure 6.21). Both approaches can be successful in the project if you consider the scale of the object (Figure 6.22). A more complex drawing can be used at a larger size, with fewer repetitions in the pattern, to generate sufficient interest and independent areas to color (Figure 6.23).

Consider what an appropriate frame of reference would be for a single object to promote maximum interaction when placed in repetition. Explore different structures, element relationships, and placement as you develop several pattern experiments. (Figure 6.24)

Decide which view or views of the object you plan to use. With the **Magic Wand,** click on the black line to select the object. If there are isolated contour lines that are not captured with this initial selection, hold down the **Shift Key** (which allows you to add to a selection) while you click on the remaining black lines until the entire contour drawing is selected. **Copy** the selection so that it can be repeated when you **Paste.** The beauty of doing

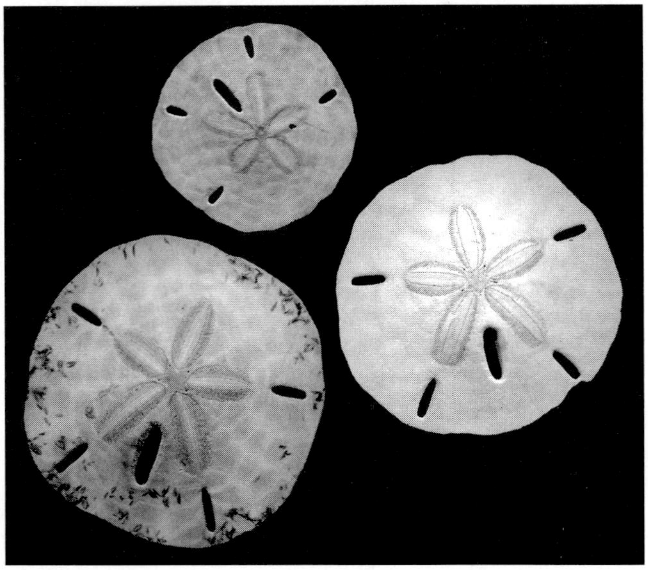

Figure 6.16

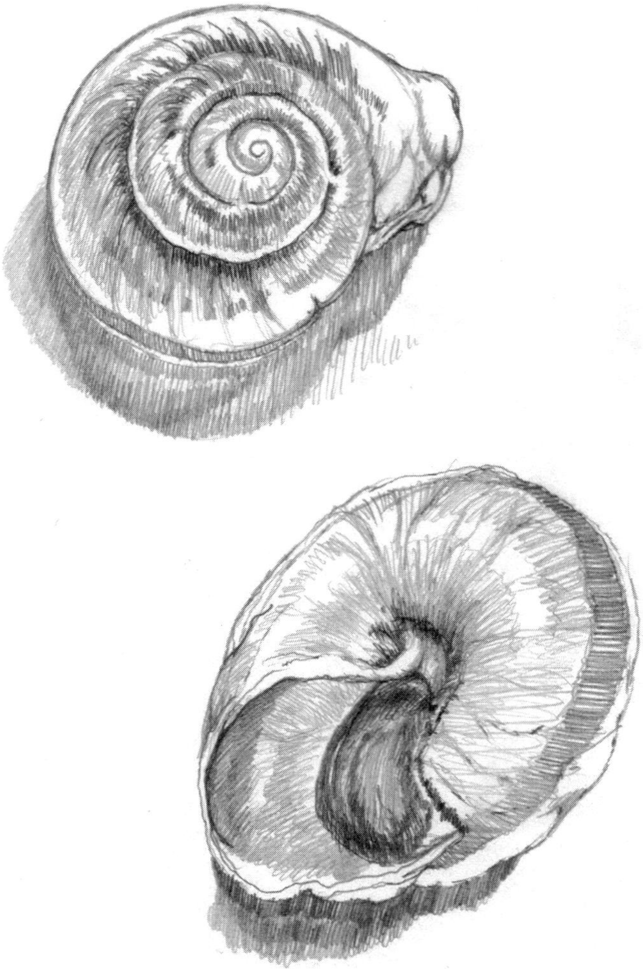

Figure 6.17

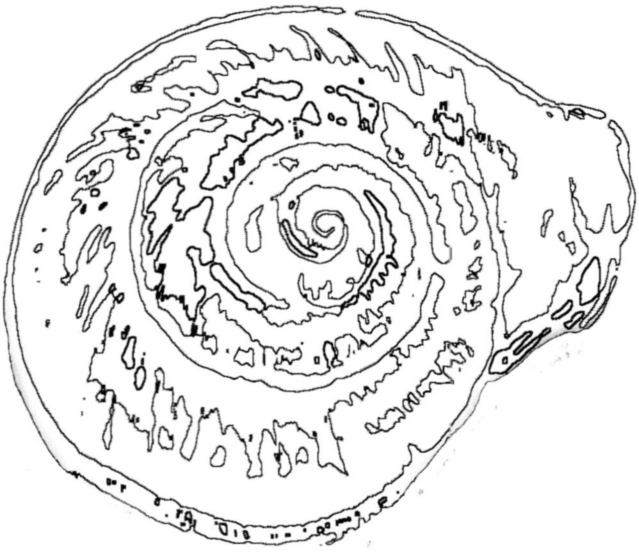

Figure 6.18

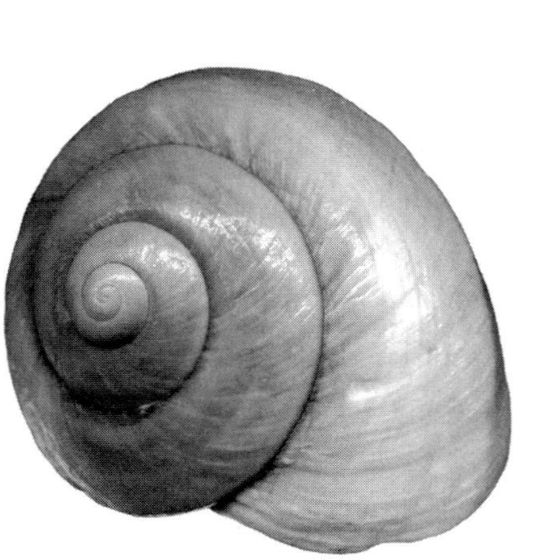

Figure 6.19

this assignment on the computer is that it is easy to scale, reduce, overlap, flip, and transpose, essentially manipulating the object in as exciting a fashion as you choose without increased time or labor.

With traditional materials, you can transfer the contour directly to the illustration board. Trace the drawing first onto a vellum or tracing paper. You can rub graphite onto the

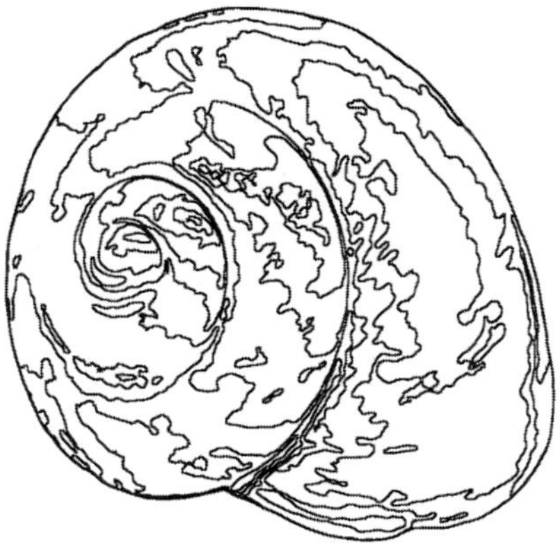

Figure 6.20

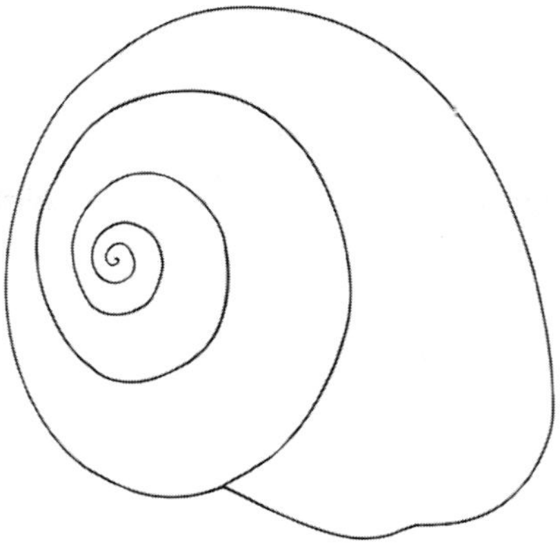

Figure 6.21

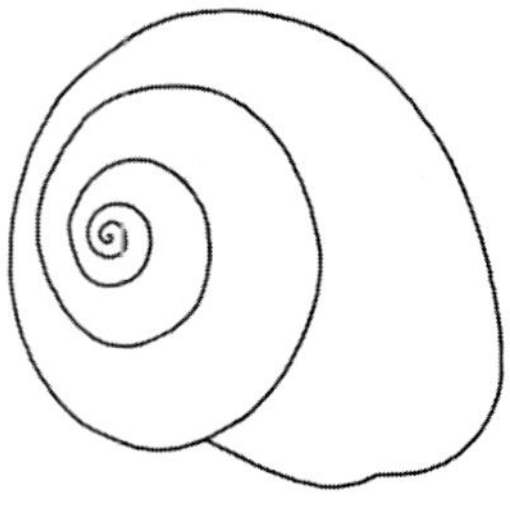

Figure 6.22

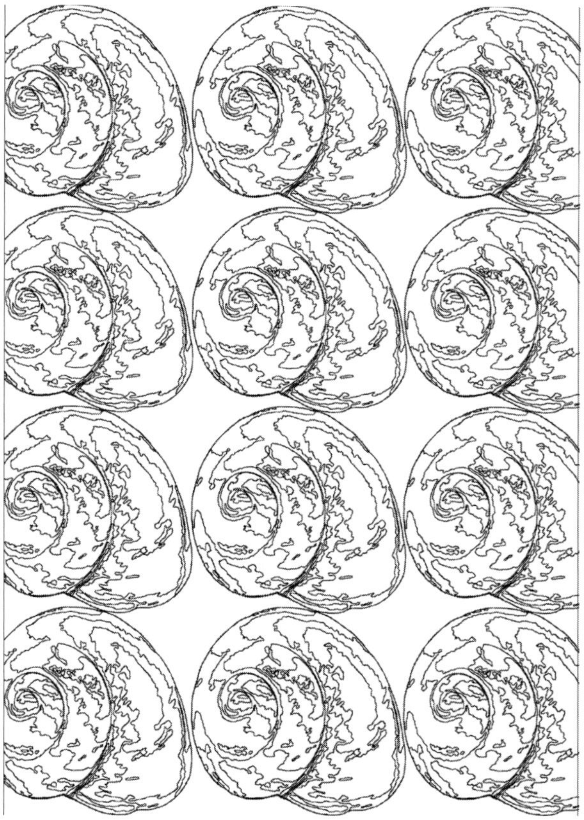

Figure 6.23

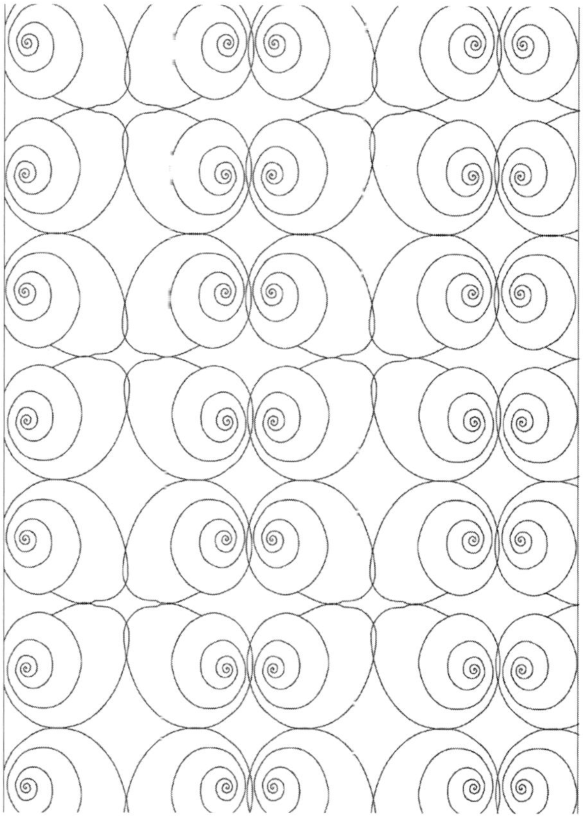

Figure 6.24

back of your tracing, or use a sheet of transfer paper, like graphite paper placed between the tracing and the illustration board. Draw over all of your lines to transfer the image.

Pattern Development If you are planning a non-computer solution, you will need to trace the object repeatedly to fill the board with pattern. To guide the placement of the object you should measure and draw the structure you plan to follow. The pattern should be completed in a clean ink line. Working electronically, the contour object that is drawn, saved, selected, and copied can be easily pasted as needed. With this ease of repetition, the expectation is that you will create at least three, well-designed, interesting, ***nonfocal patterns.*** Each pattern should fill the standard 8.5″ × 11″ page.

To begin the pattern experiments, you will need a new page. Under the **File menu,** scroll down to **New,** at which point a dialogue box will appear. Set the width to [7.5″], the height to [10.5″] and the resolution at [300] pixels/inch.

When you **Paste,** the object you selected and copied previously will be placed on the page. With the **Move Tool** in the **Tools** palette you can place the object where you want it to be on the page. When you select **Show Layers** under the **Window** menu, notice that this shell is on Layer 1, above the **Background. Paste** again and a second shell appears on Layer 2, which you can move into position. Each time you **Paste,** the new shell will appear on a new layer. This will allow you to continually manipulate each pasted shell independently until you are satisfied with the result. When you have created the pattern you want, go to the **Layer** window and **Flatten** the image. This will put everything onto one layer and reduce the file size. **Hint:** If you are setting up a pattern in horizontal rows, you can **Merge Down** the layers of the first row into one layer. **Duplicate Layer** and move the duplicated row into position. Continue this way until the page is filled. **Save As,** *Pattern 1* (Figure 6.25).

Repeat this entire procedure to complete Patterns 2 and 3. Experiment with different structures, movements, directions, and pattern types. Take advantage of the **Transform** functions under the **Edit** menu to **Flip** and **Rotate** the shapes, to create interesting and dynamic surfaces. Remember, the patterns at this stage must remain nonfocal to give you the greatest flexibility to create significant change when you complete the project in color. (Figures 6.26 and 6.27)

Palette Discovery The next step in establishing the baseline for this experiment is to develop the palette with which you are going to work. Begin by mixing and matching at least ten different colors that are found in the natural object. Remember, you may use two different natural objects for the assignment, one for form and the other for the color that must come from a natural source. When matching color you are not looking for ten different hues. Identify ten different colors that display similarities and contrasts in hue, value, and intensity. It is through the relationship of the colors that you will control the space and emphasis in your patterned surfaces. Once the colors are established, organize them into a "gradation," finding relational connections between the colors. Through this organization you will start to understand how the colors can support each other in the creation of an image.

If you are working in paint, use gouache to mix the colors, painting rectangular "chips" on bristol that can be cut out and assembled. When the final palette is determined,

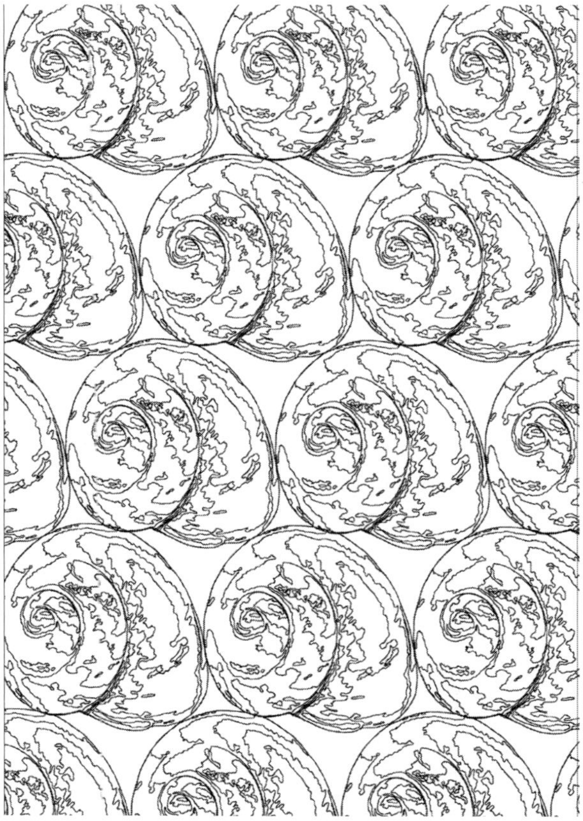

Figure 6.25

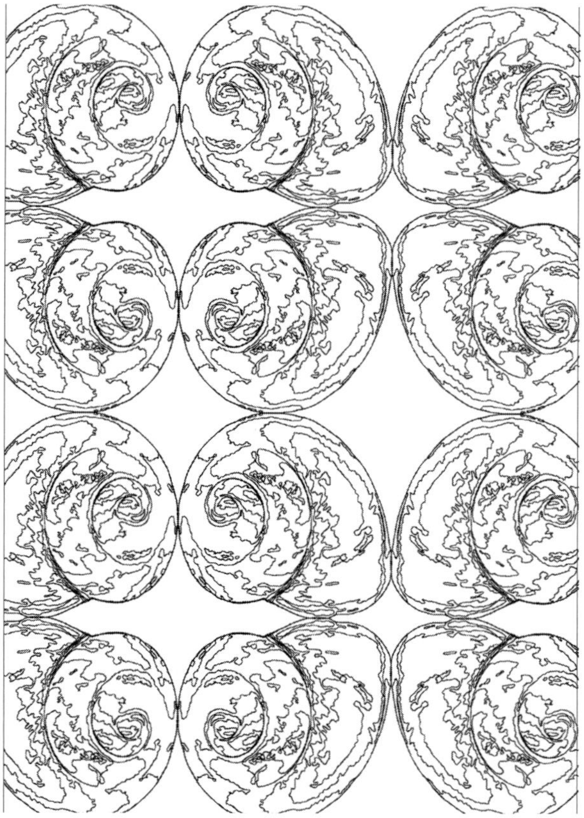

Figure 6.26

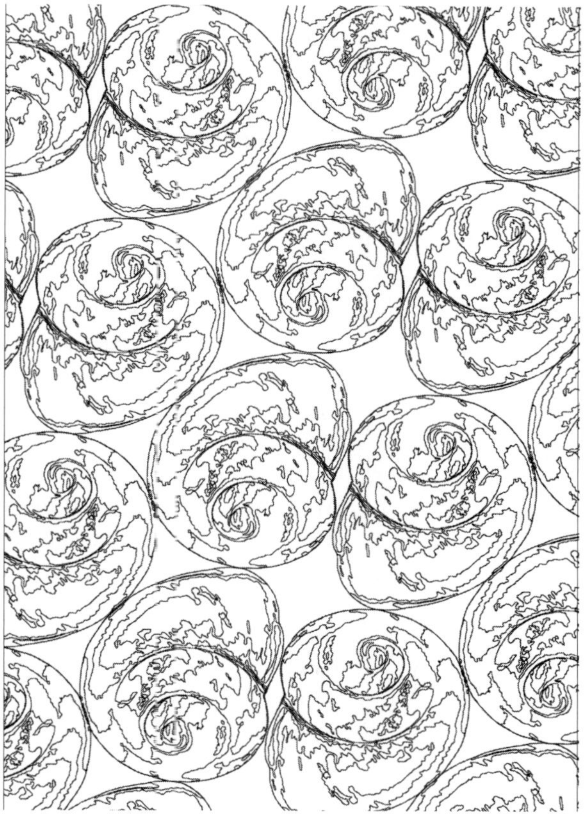

Figure 6.27

mix and save sufficient quantities of each color to cover three different color studies that use the identical palette.

Begin the electronic palette with a **New** page. Set the width to [10″], the height to [1.5″] and the resolution at [300] pixels/inch. Select **Marquee Tool** and use **Marquee Options** with the following settings to create the 1″ × 1.5″ "chips":

Feather: [0]

Style: [Fixed size]

Width: [300] pixels

Height: [450] pixels

Place the active rectangle in the first spot on the left. Show **Stroke** under the **Window** menu. Set the **Weight** to [1] pixel, and click, [Okay]. This will make the outline of the marquee visible with the foreground color. Continue placing rectangles until the 10″ palette is divided into ten spaces that can be filled with color (Figure 6.28).

The **Mode** has been set to **Grayscale** for the earlier black-and-white parts of the project. Go to the **Image** menu and scroll down to **Mode** to return to **RGB** color. Double-click on the **Foreground Color** box to open the **Color Picker.** Use the slider to select the general hue to want to begin with. Once the hue fills the gradated square, move the circle to select the appropriate level of value and intensity to match a color in your natural

Figure 6.28

object. This created color will appear in the **Foreground Color** box of the **Tool** menu. With the **Paint Bucket Tool** click in the box to be filled.

If you need to alter a rectangle that has been filled with color, use the **Eyedropper Tool** to place it back in the **foreground color** box. Make additional modifications in the **Color Picker** and over-fill the color rectangle in your scale. When you have filled all ten rectangles and you are satisfied with the placement and relationship of the colors, **Save As,** *The Scale* (Figure 6.29, color insert)

Image Transformation Through Color Once again, the primary objective of this project is to investigate how to radically change an image through the placement of color. To maintain control of the experiment, you will use the same ten colors in your palette and the same basic pattern for all three color explorations to complete the assignment. Select the pattern study you consider the most interesting and dynamic, with the greatest potential for change.

Open the pattern you plan to use and pull down the **Image** menu, scrolling down to **Mode** and selecting **RGB** to access the color. Re-open the palette you have saved, moving it to a part of the screen where you can continually access the colors. With the **Eyedropper,** click on one of the colors in your scale to place it in the **Foreground Color** box in the **Tool** menu. The **Paint Bucket Tool** can now be used to fill shapes in your pattern.

Because you flattened the image, all shapes are on a single background layer. You can fill on the background layer, over-filling shapes when you want to change a color. If you prefer, you can create new layers for each color for added flexibility and re-flatten the image when you are finished.

At this point, the object is part of a complex pattern. Whether the object maintains its identity is not important. As you begin to place color in all shapes of the pattern, consider the color relationships you are establishing. What happens when two colors of equal value are placed next to each other versus colors of strong contrast? How can you use chroma effectively to bring out parts of the image or to vary the temperature of the study? You must use all ten colors in each of the studies to maintain control. Consider all the variables at your disposal to make each surface appear radically different by varying the proportion and placement of color. Through color connections and contrasts, different elements in the pattern combine at times and separate at others. What appears to repeat might be altered as you create changes in scale, movement, and direction. While one study remains a nonfocal pattern, another could display areas of emphasis or a single focal point. Strive to create overall changes in hue, value, and chroma. (Figure 6.30, Figure 6.31, Figure 6.32, color insert).

DISCUSSION

What will be evaluated is your ability to create three, well-designed, interesting and exciting surfaces from a single pattern. The quantity and quality of image change created through the recognition and use of design issues is the goal. The contrast of color will also be examined, looking at the quantity and quality of hue, value, and chroma change by the manipulation of color issues. Varying the palette or the pattern is unacceptable. Attention should be paid to good craftsmanship, whether you are working with traditional or digital media. The three studies should be printed out on a color printer along with the computer palette and the three black-and-white, nonfocal patterns.

AN ISSUE OF PROPORTION

CONTROLLING EMPHASIS THROUGH COLOR RELATIONSHIPS

Color can be used to call attention to areas of an image through various color groupings, and the individual parts can be visually coordinated through fundamental color relationships. As we have seen in the previous project, *A Natural Source,* similarities and/or contrasts in value, intensity, placement, and the amount of color are all important aspects of color interaction in an image. When creating a pattern, knowledge of color characteristics can aid in presenting clearly defined color relationships distinguishing elements of the structure one from another.

As a variation to *A Natural Source,* color issues in this assignment will be explored through the process of appropriation, physical color mixing and matching, and applied color theory through the principles of fundamental color harmonies.

OBJECTIVES

In this assignment a pattern structure will be created that can be used to carry out a controlled study of color, value, and intensity changes. Students will use three copies of the same pattern design to explore the ways in which color can be manipulated for changing effects. Using a found color palette from a scanned natural object or digital file as a point of departure, you will create a design, rearrange color relationships to shift emphasis, and manage a palette using a chosen color harmony. As a result, it will become evident that even limited color organization and choice can lead to infinite variations.

MATERIALS

Electronic: Graphics program such as Photoshop; computer; good-quality printer; printer paper (regular and glossy); illustration board; gouache; brushes; mixing containers; water container

Traditional: Tracing paper; pencils; illustration board; gouache; brushes; mixing containers; water container

PROCEDURE

This project is a combination of electronic and traditional processes.

Electronic With a graphics program on the computer, create a tile design that can be repeated within a grid structure. To create this tile, **Scan** a natural object or image from a book or magazine (an insect shape, for example) or download a natural form from a web page (Figure 6.33).

Make this element 2″ × 2″ and using the graphics program, create a four-step value translation by using the **Artistic Cutout** filter adjusted to 4 levels.

Repeat this element in an 8″ × 8″ or 8″ × 10″ grid, set up in a graphics program on the computer. Utilize the **Cut, Paste** and **Transform** capabilities of the program to **Repeat, Rotate** and **Flip** the tile to create a pattern design that builds on the characteristics of the form (Figure 6.34). At this point, you could also change colors, and manipulate values and intensities to move areas of emphasis from one structural element to the other.

Use selection devices such as **Select/Color Range** to select designated color areas and change colors with the **Edit-Fill** option. When you have a successful pattern design, **Save** it onto your disk.

Print out one version in color and two in black-and-white. Trim all printouts and present all on illustration board side by side (no gaps between prints), with a 2″ border on top, sides, and bottom. Use rubber cement to adhere your prints to the board.

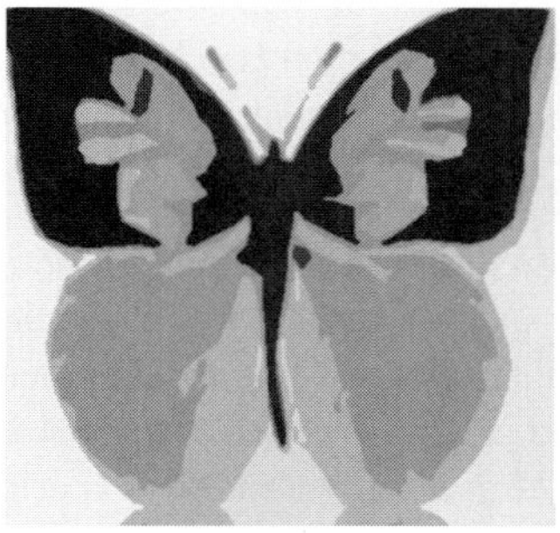

Figure 6.33

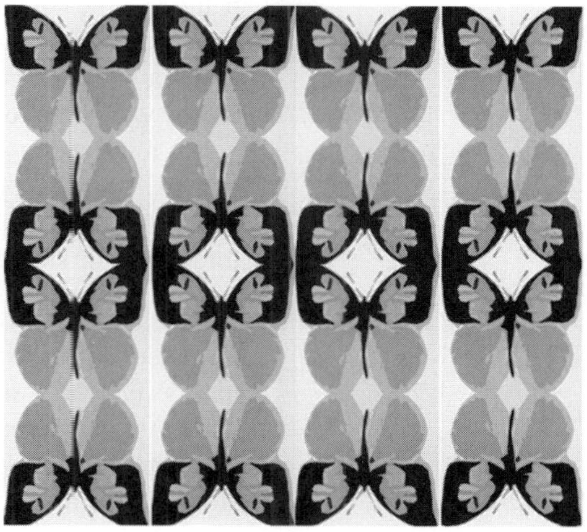

Figure 6.34

Using gouache and brush, mix a palette of colors using the color print as your guide. Using the same colors as in the print, paint in different components in the black-and-white printout next to it. The four-step breakdown will allow for simple shapes of value that you can translate into flat areas of color. Be as true to the colors on the printout as possible.

The goal will be to try to make the same pattern structure look like a different one, even though the same colors are being used. Create areas of structural associations through color and value similarities, and separate areas through color differences (Figure 6.35, color insert).

In the third pattern printout, use a palette of color utilizing a common color harmony such as ***primary, secondary, triadic, analogous, complimentary,*** or ***warm*** or ***cool*** color groupings and/or contrasts. Your palette should include values of your color choices for a variety of contrast effects. In this exploration you are working with a completely new ***palette*** of colors, and your goal should be to create a new and engaging color grouping (Figure 6.36, color insert).

When painting, keep paints liquid but not watery. Paint your chosen area of color directly onto the printout. Your final presentation will be a triptych of the three images (Figure 6.37, color insert).

Electronic Version Without the Traditional Component If you would rather do the total project on the computer, you can continue to manipulate color relationships electronically. Using the pattern you have created, selectively change color distribution (without changing the original palette) by moving colors around the design. You can select areas a number of ways. You could begin by selecting areas of the design with the **Magic Wand** and filling with color, or by using the **Color Range** command under the **Selection** menu. For the third pattern, change the original to a **Grayscale** image by going to **Image,** then **Mode** and **Grayscale.** After the color has been removed, change the **Mode** back to **RGB** color. Proceed to fill selected areas with colors that have been chosen according to a fundamental color harmony (primary, secondary, tertiary, complimentary, analogous, etc.) and then print out all three and mount flush next to each other on illustration board.

Traditional Create a tile design, derived from a natural form, within a 2″ square. Use imagery from books or magazines or images you have downloaded from the web. Trace the forms, simplifying them to basic linear elements. Trace and transfer this design into a grid structure, mirroring, rotating, and repeating, to create a pattern design.

Make three copies of the design. Trim and paste onto illustration board side by side (no gaps between copies), with a 2″ border on top, sides, and bottom. Use rubber cement to adhere your prints to the board.

With gouache and brush, mix a palette of colors using a found image as your guide. Using the same colors as in the image, paint a color version of the pattern for the first exploration. On the second copy, using the same colors, paint different components of the pattern (same colors but put into different places). The goal will be to try to make the same pattern structure look like a different one. For the last exploration, use a palette of color utilizing a common color harmony such as primary, secondary, triadic, analogous, complimentary, or warm or cool color groupings and/or contrasts.

Your palette should include values of your color choices for variety of contrast effects. Try to create the look of a totally different pattern here as well, even though the pattern structure is the same as in the other two images. Create areas of structural associations through color similarities, and separate areas through differences.

DISCUSSION

Can color contrasts and/or similarities emphasize or de-emphasize components of the pattern design? How do the spatial characteristics of color come into play? Viewing the three variations next to each other allows for contrast and comparison. What aspects of the original pattern have changed and why? What role does intensity play in the pattern designs? How can we relate what we see in these color experiments to the more complex world of ***visual communication***?

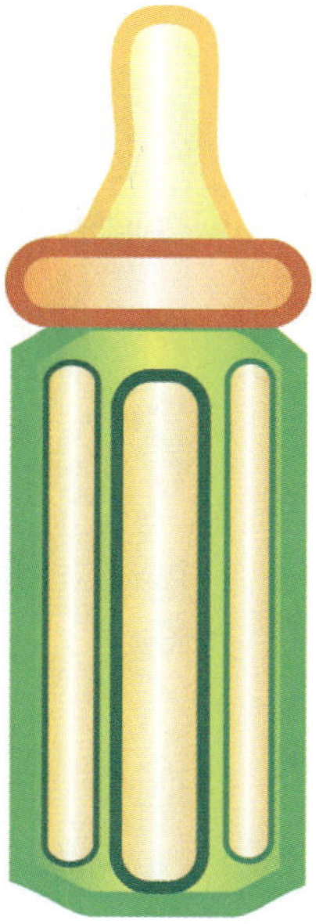

FIGURE 4.69

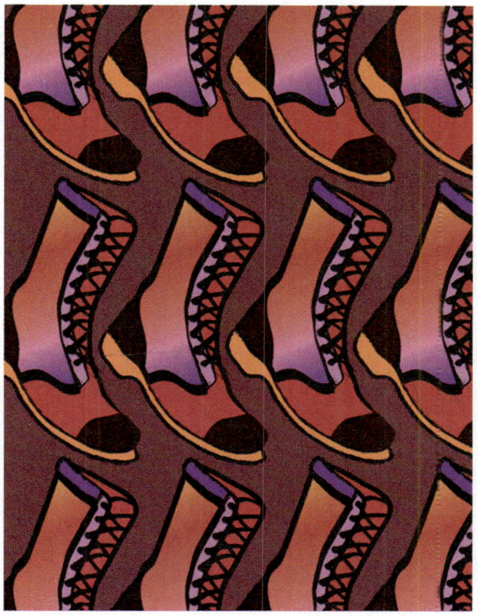

FIGURE 4.71

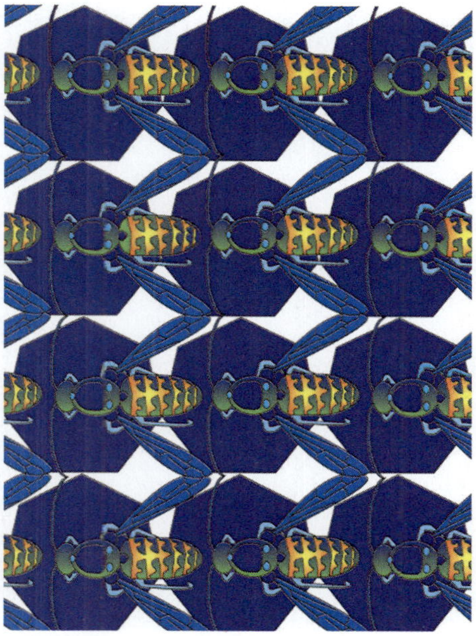

FIGURE 4.72

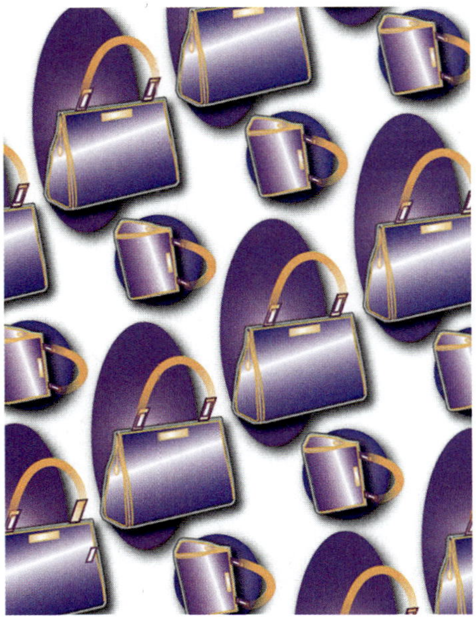

FIGURE 4.74

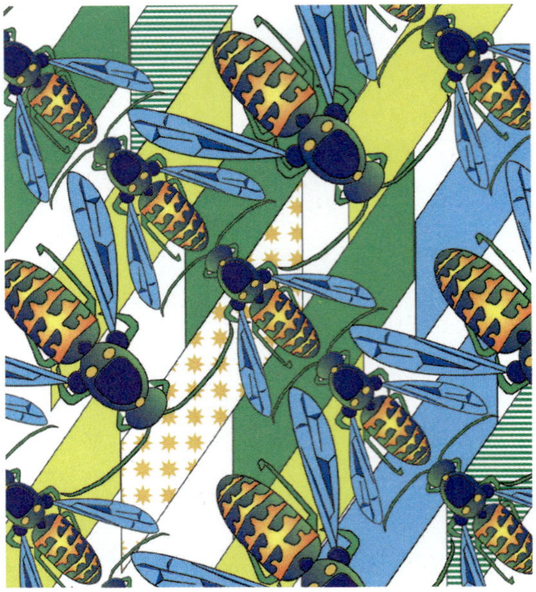

FIGURE 4.75

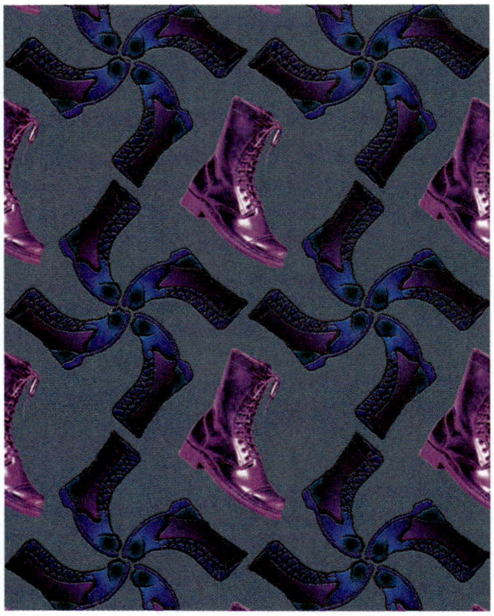

FIGURE 4.77

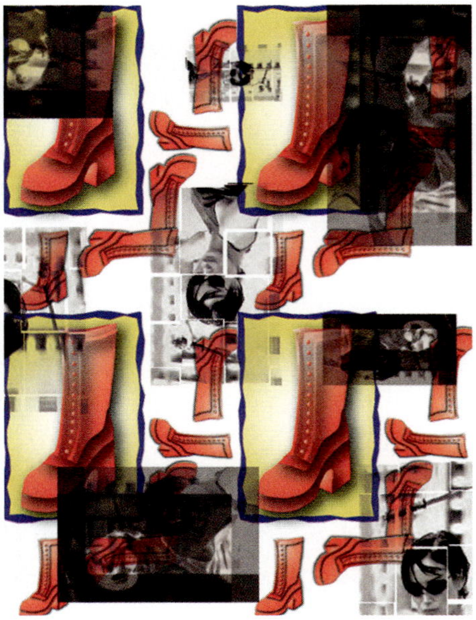

FIGURE 4.78

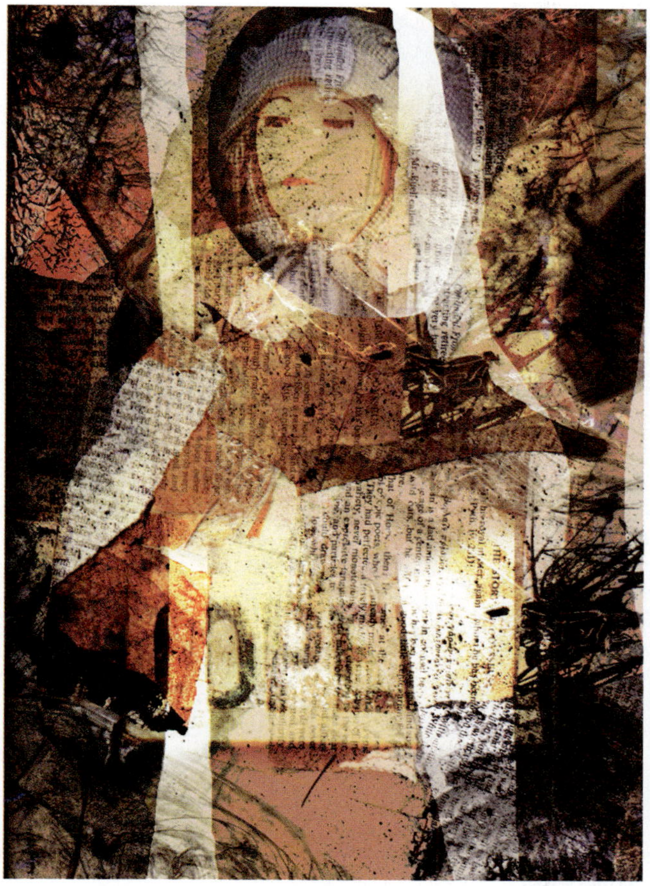

FIGURE 5.11

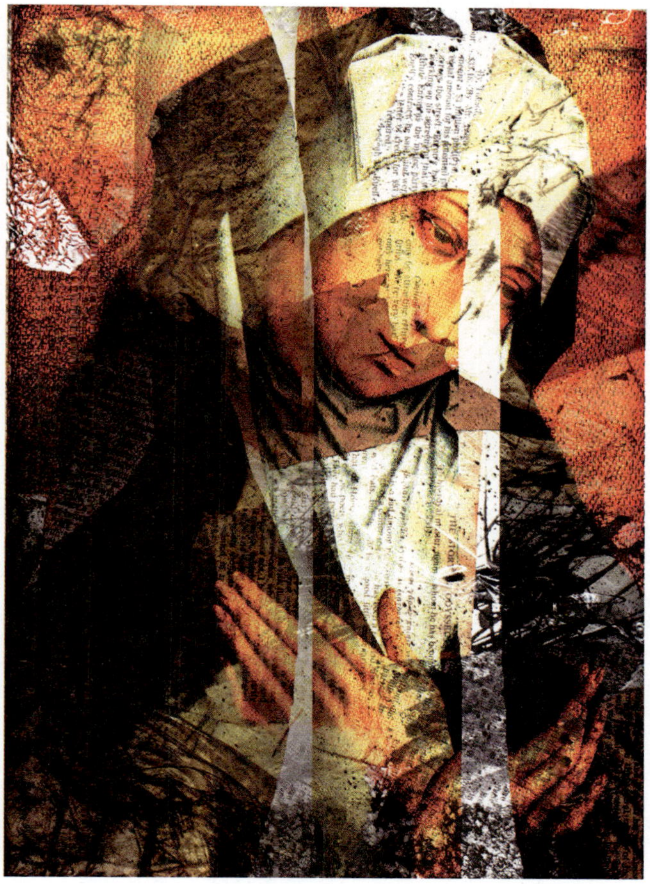

FIGURE 5.12

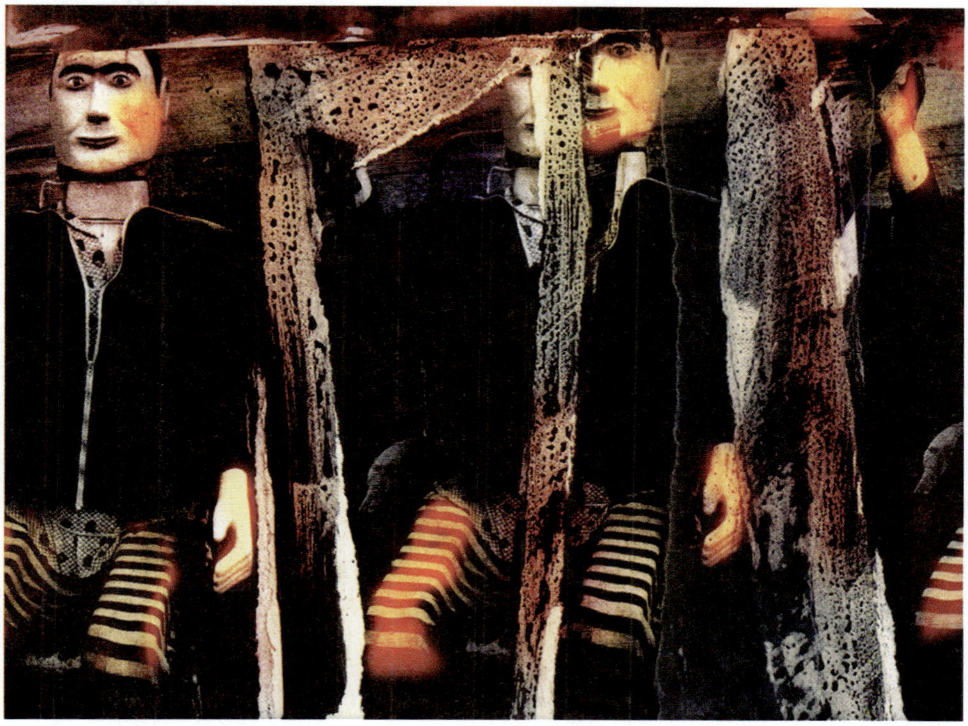

FIGURE 5.14

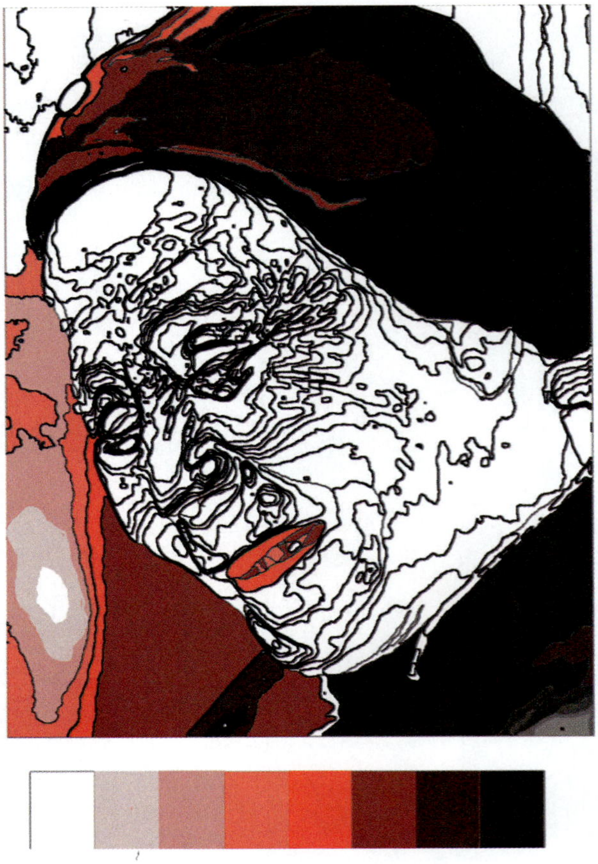

FIGURE 5.30

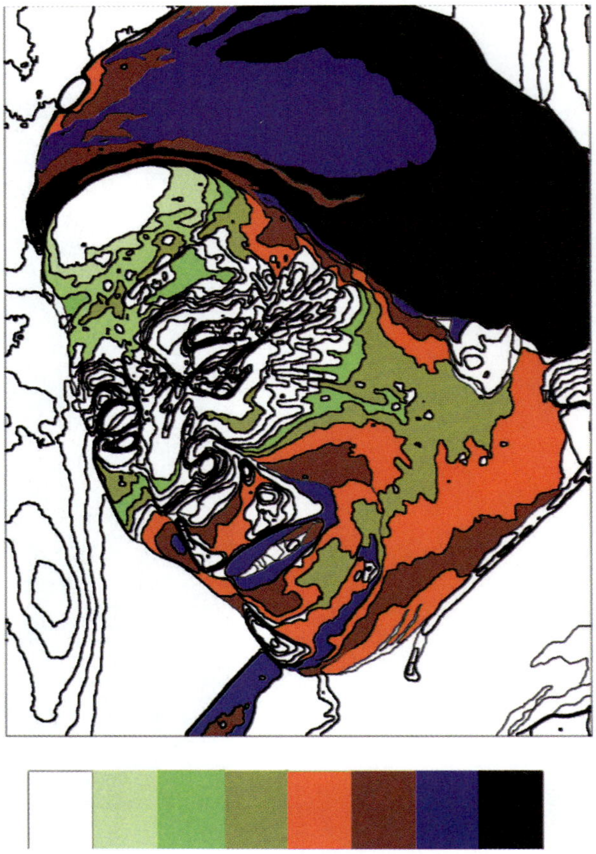

FIGURE 5.31

W	Yellow	Yellow MIX Orange	MIX Orange Red	Red HUE	MIX Red Violet	Purple HUE	B

W	TINT YO	YO HUE	MIX YO BG	BG HUE	RV HUE	SHADE RV	B

W	TINT YG	YG HUE	MIX YG RO	RO HUE	MIX RO P	P	B

W	TINT YG	YG HUE	MIX YG RO	RO HUE	MIX RO P	P	

FIGURE 5.32

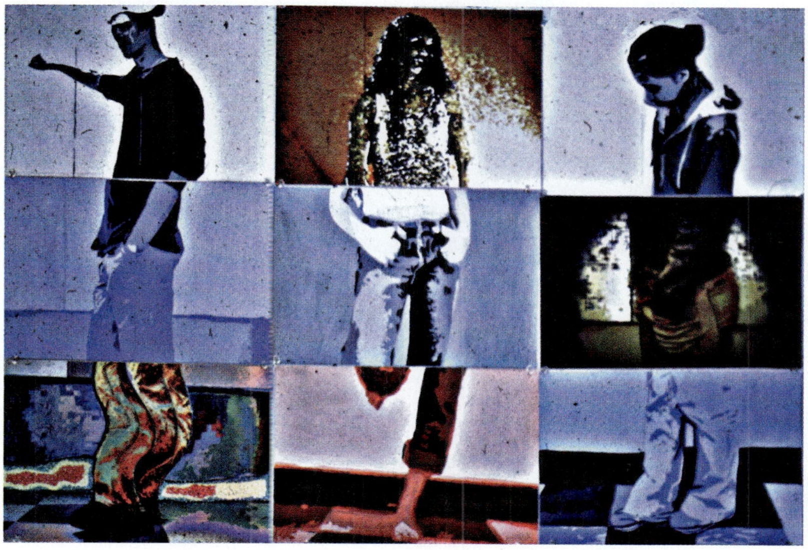

FIGURE 5.41A

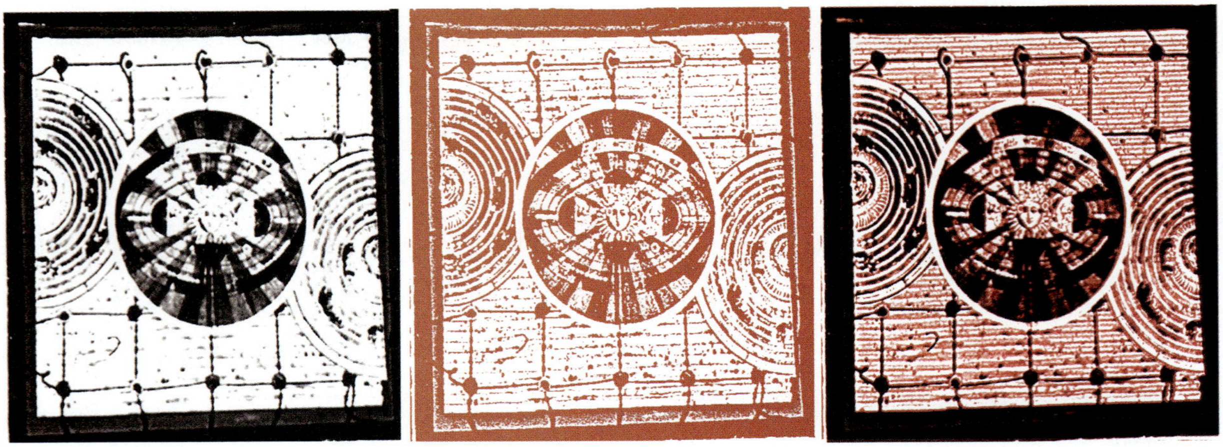

FIGURE 5.42

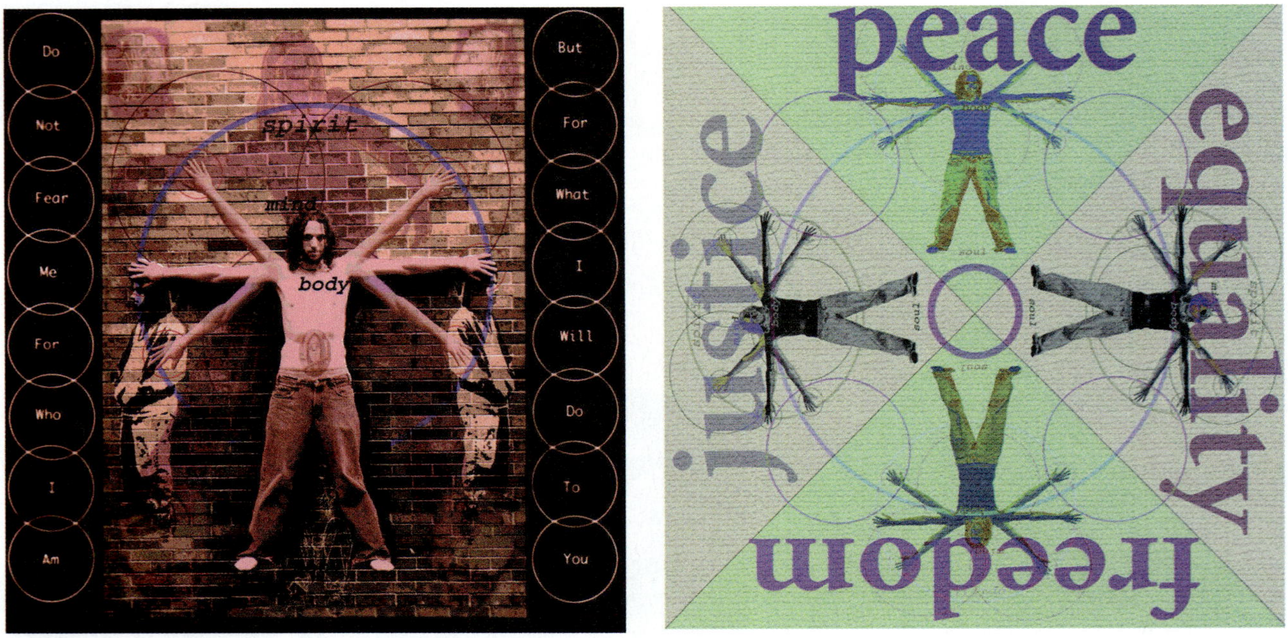

FIGURE 5.43

Additive System

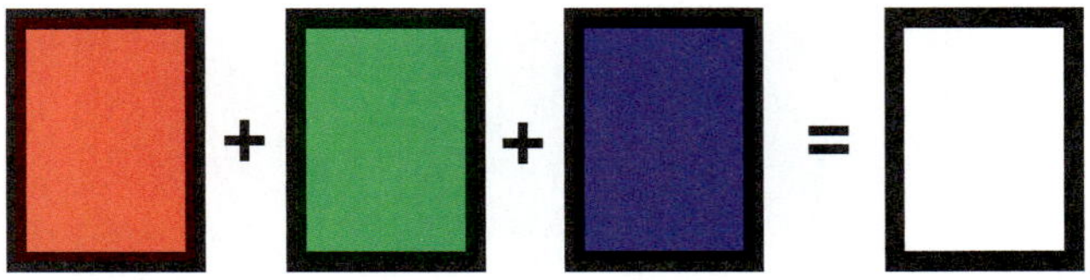

FIGURE 6.1

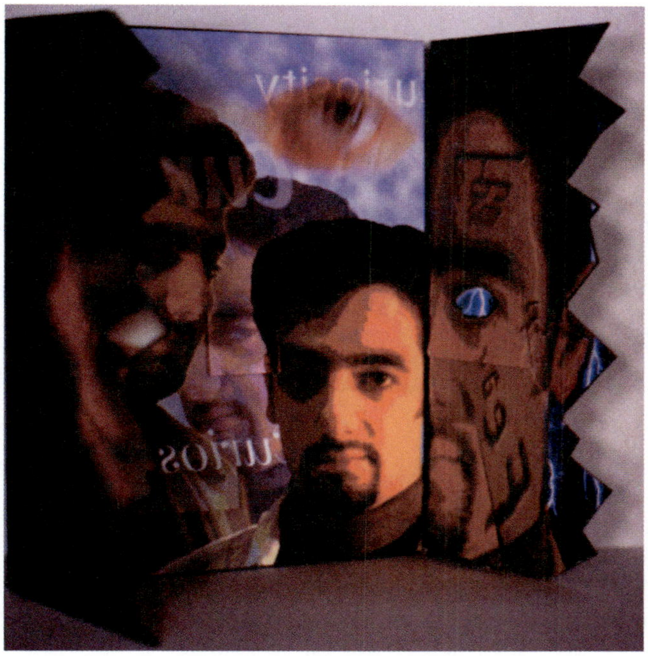

FIGURE 5.45

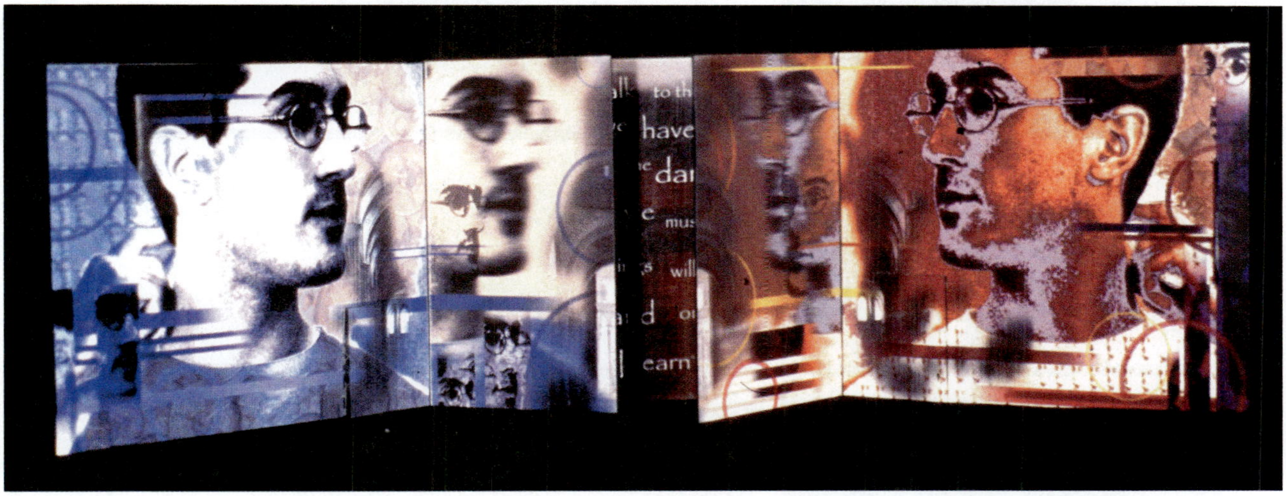

FIGURE 5.47

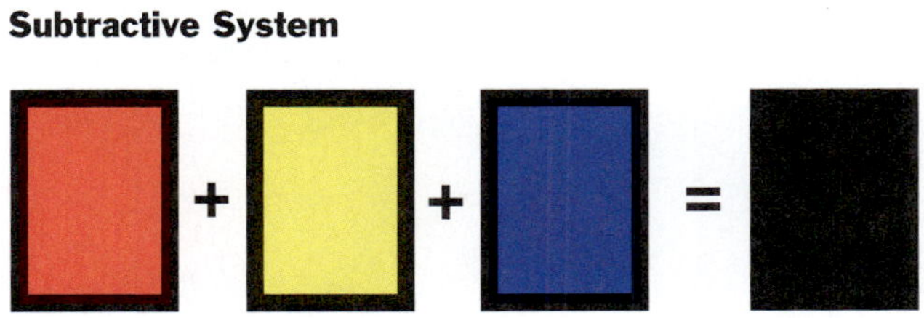

FIGURE 6.2

How we see color

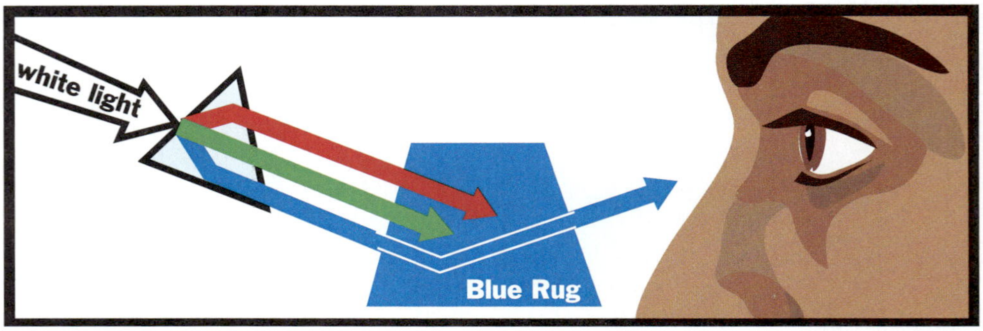

FIGURE 6.3

Physical qualities of color

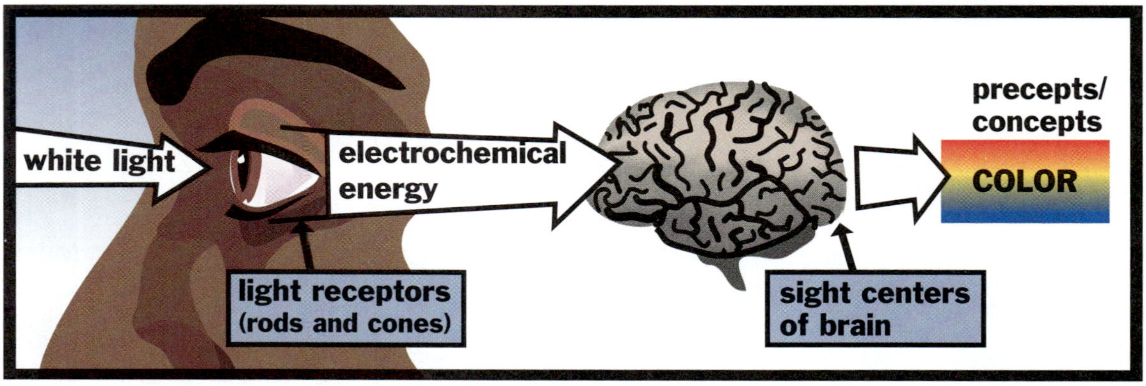

FIGURE 6.4

Emotional/Cultural associations of color

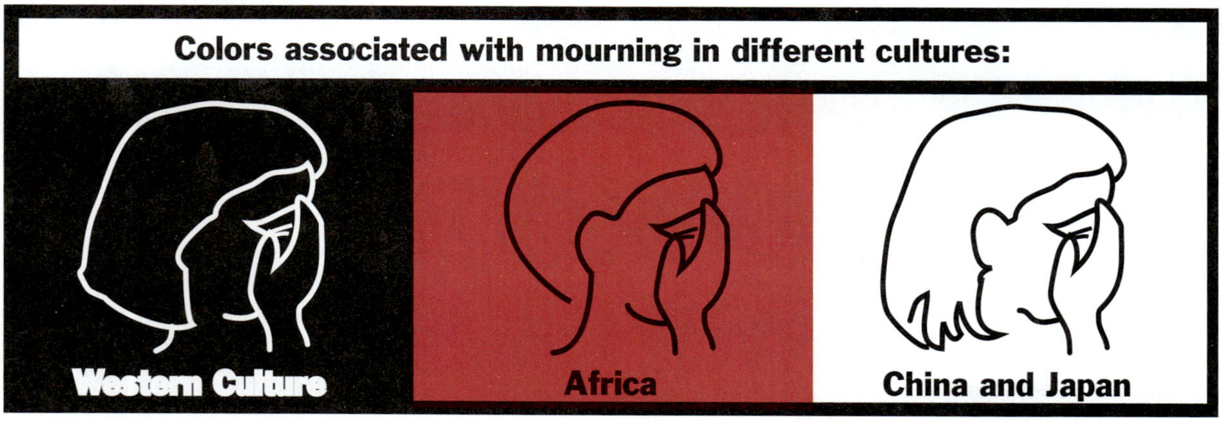

FIGURE 6.5

Color Wheel: Primary Colors

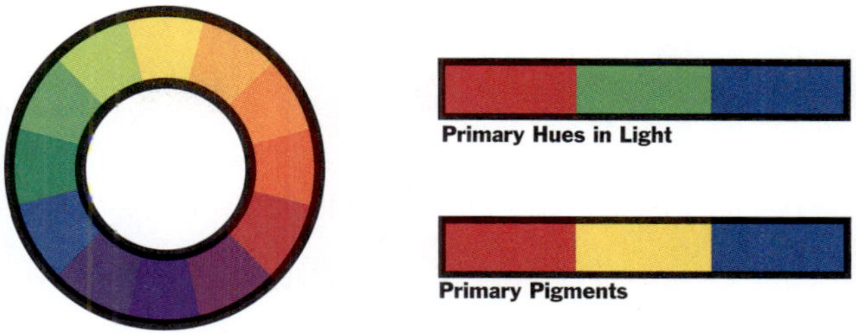

FIGURE 6.6

Secondary Hues

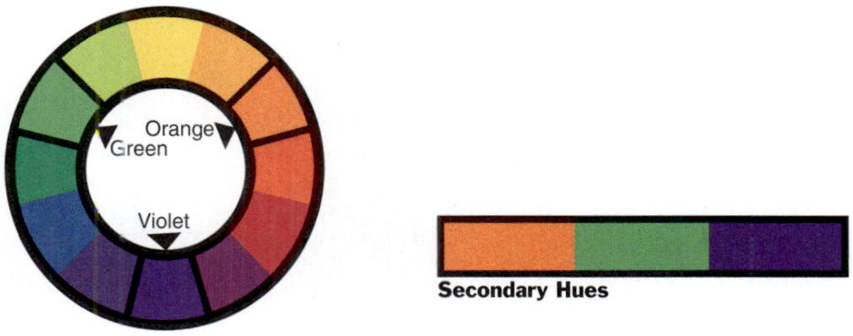

FIGURE 6.7

Tertiary Hues

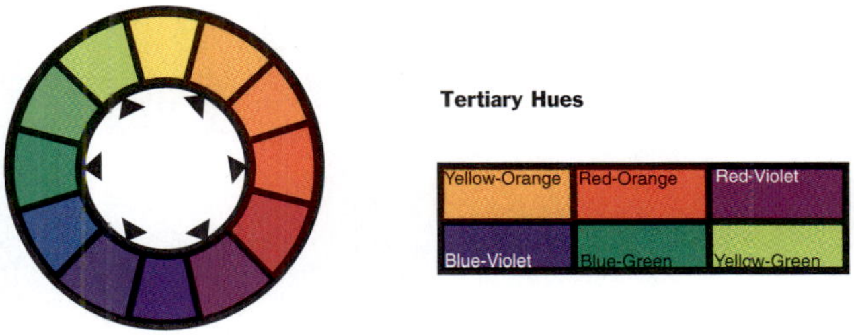

FIGURE 6.8

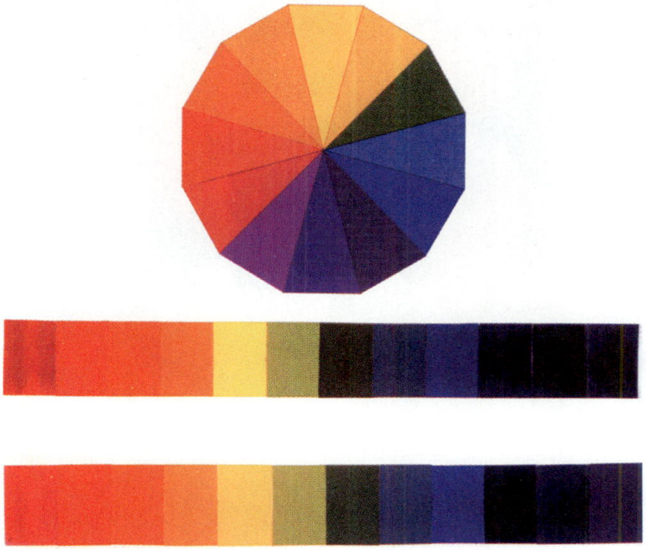

FIGURE 6.9

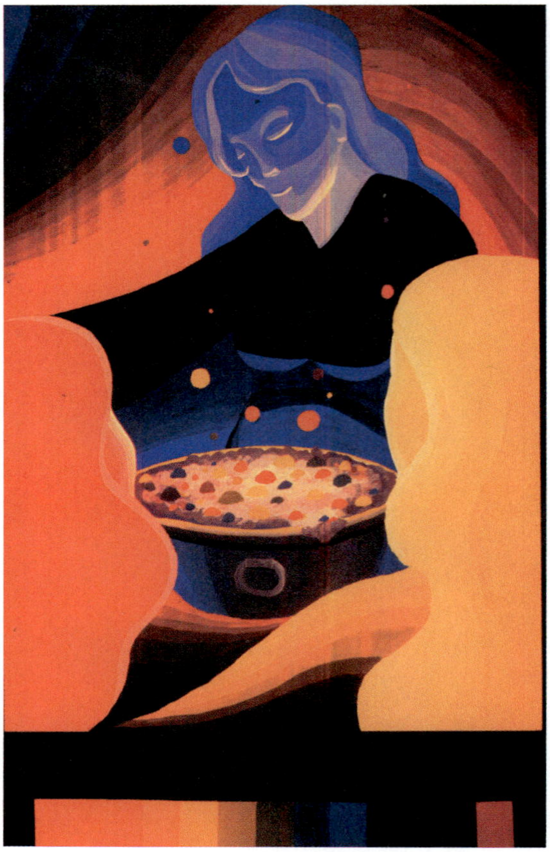

FIGURE 6.10

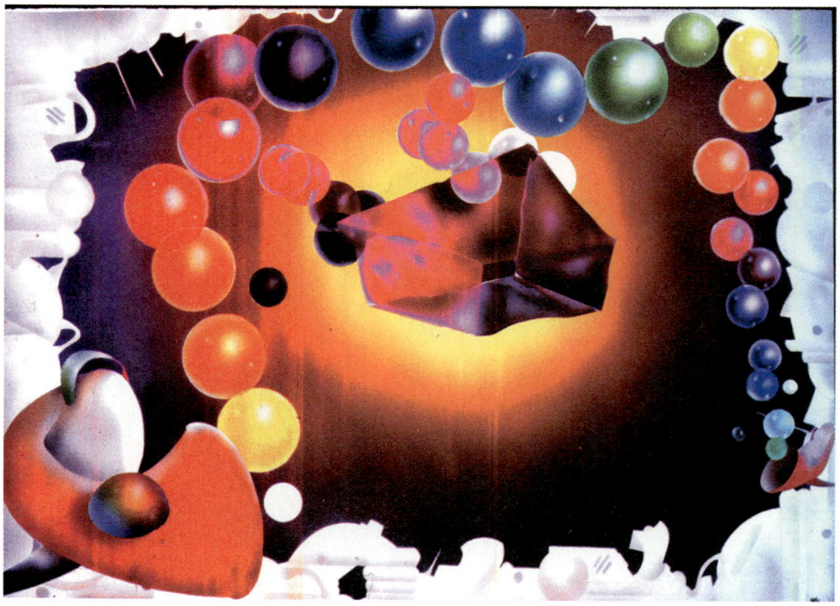

FIGURE 6.11

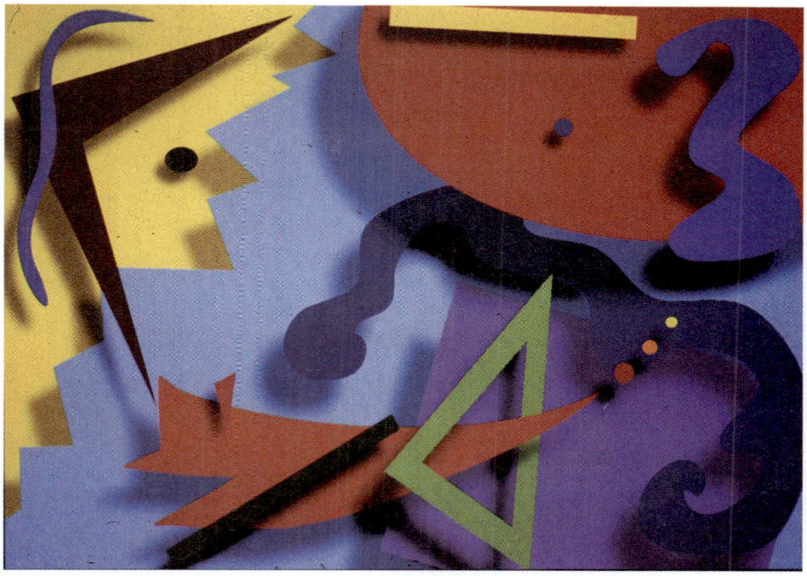

FIGURE 6.12

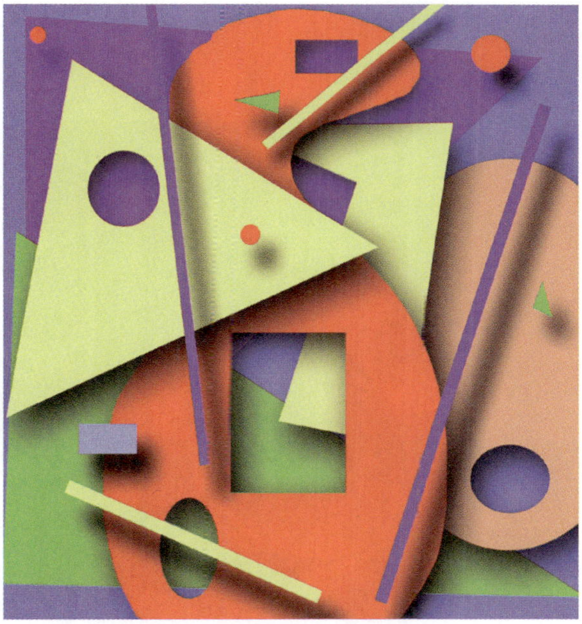

FIGURE 6.13

FIGURE 6.29

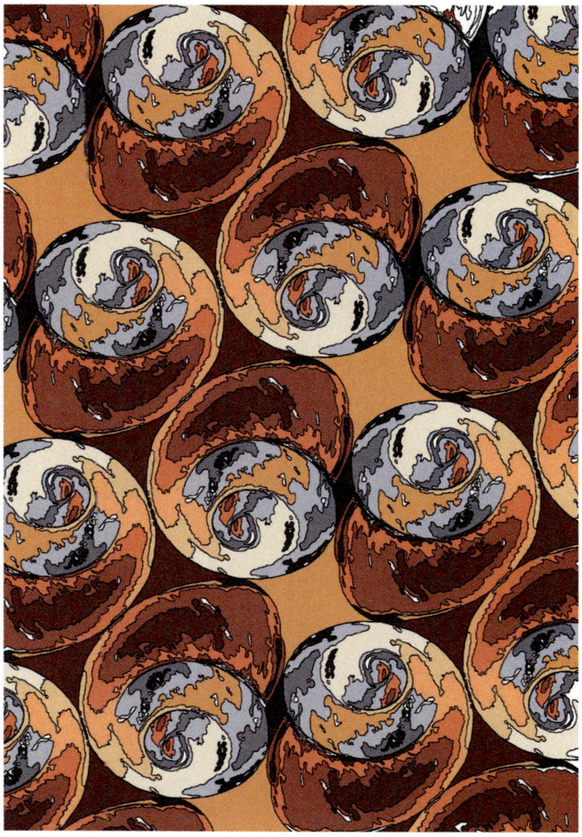

FIGURE 6.30

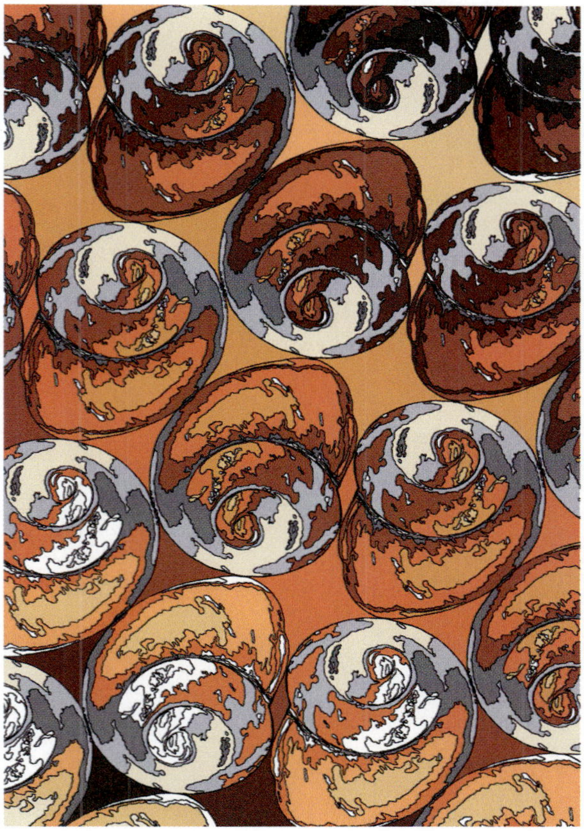

FIGURE 6.31

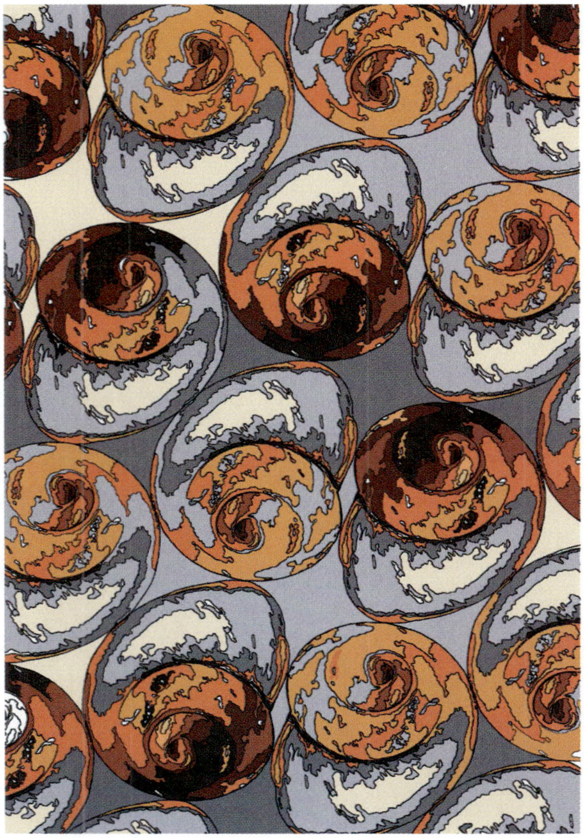

FIGURE 6.32

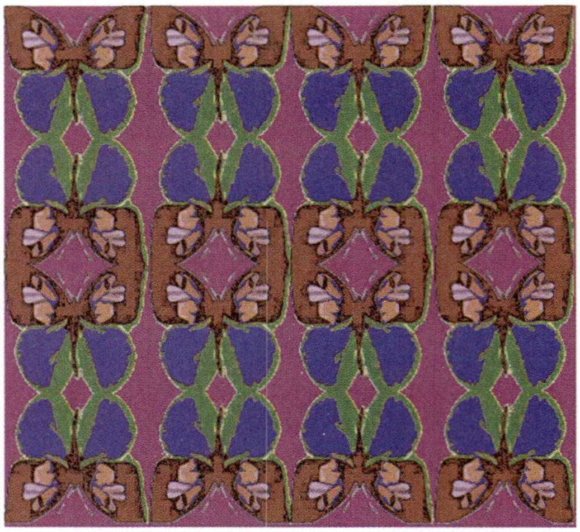

FIGURE 6.35

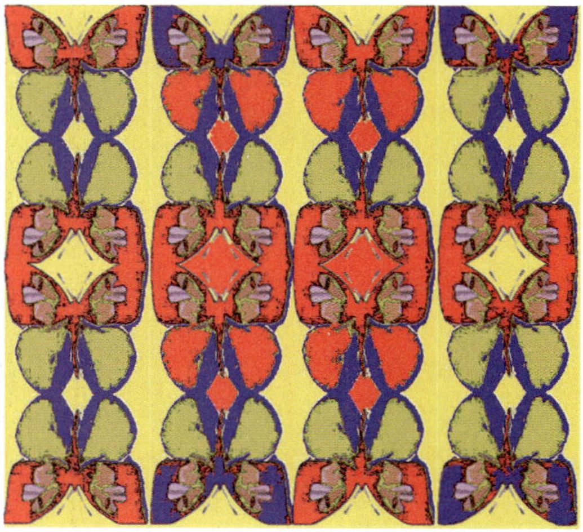

FIGURE 6.36

FIGURE 6.37

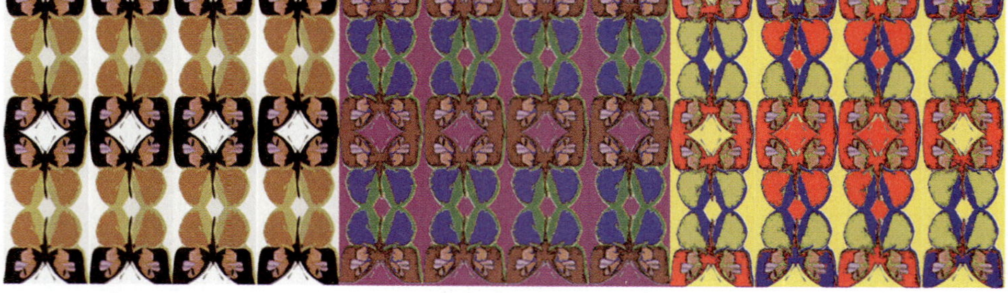

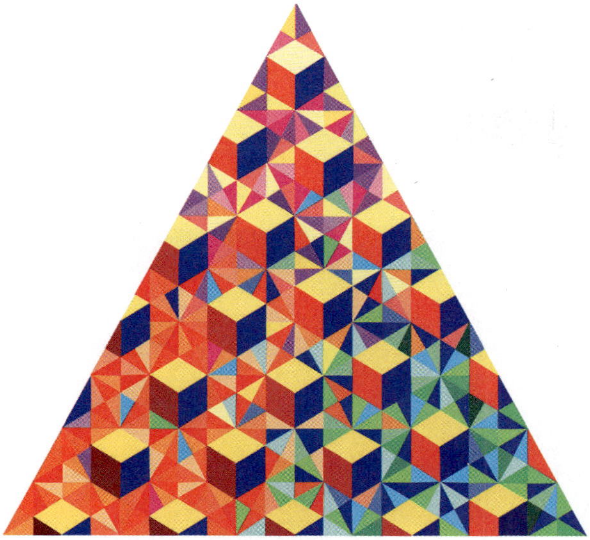

FIGURE 6.39

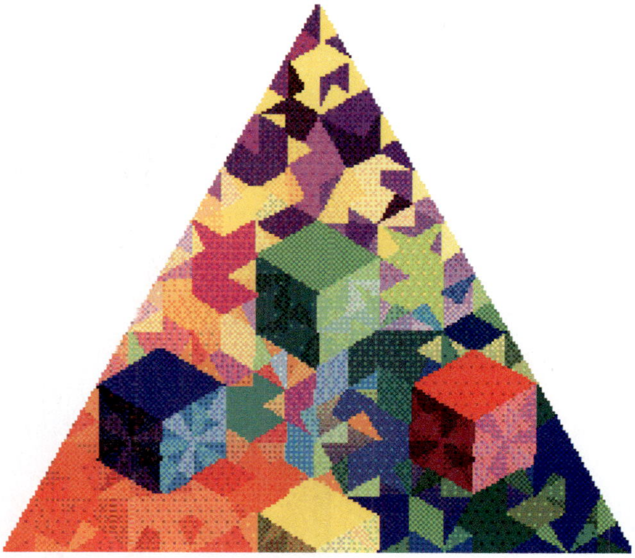

FIGURE 6.42

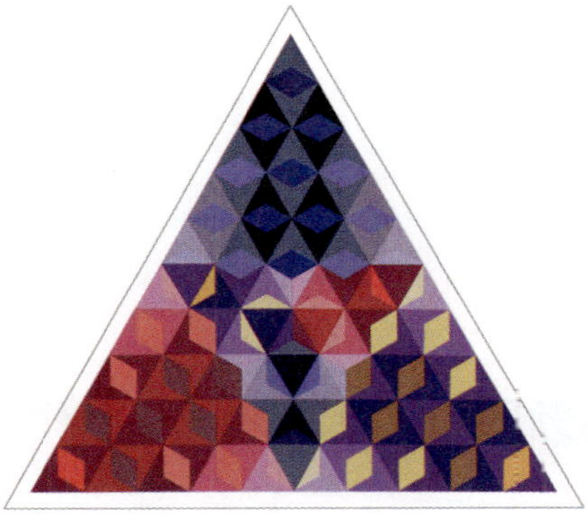

FIGURE 6.43

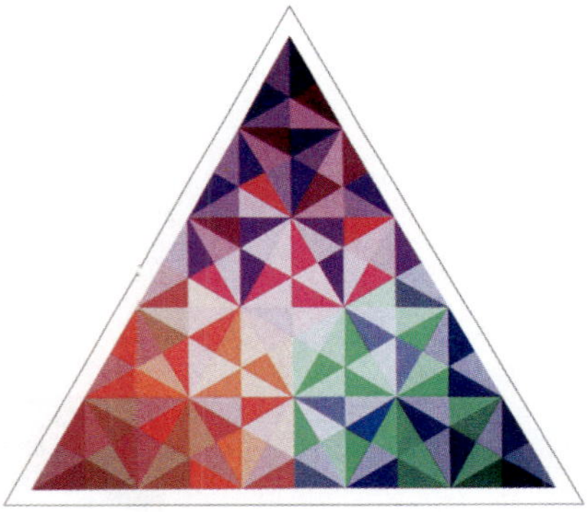

FIGURE 6.44

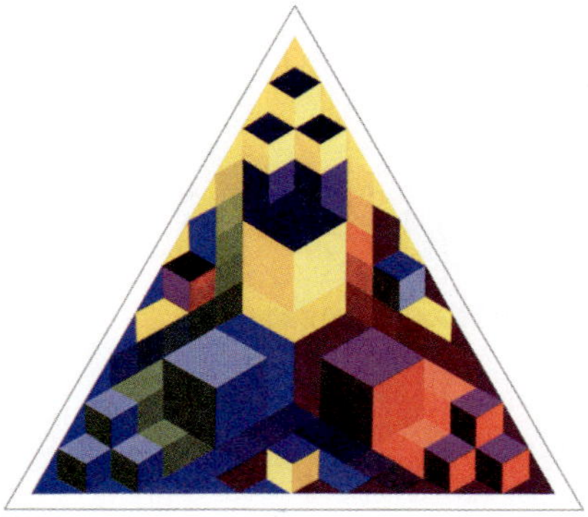

FIGURE 6.45

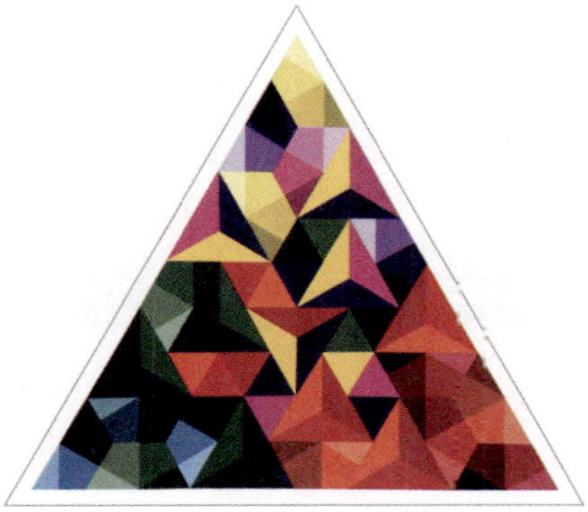

FIGURE 6.46

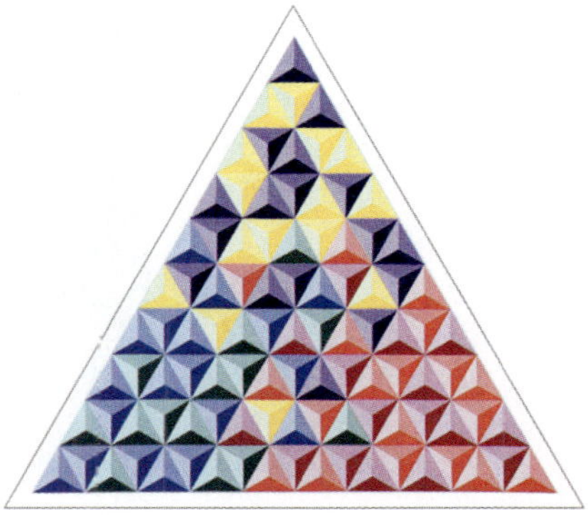

FIGURE 6.47

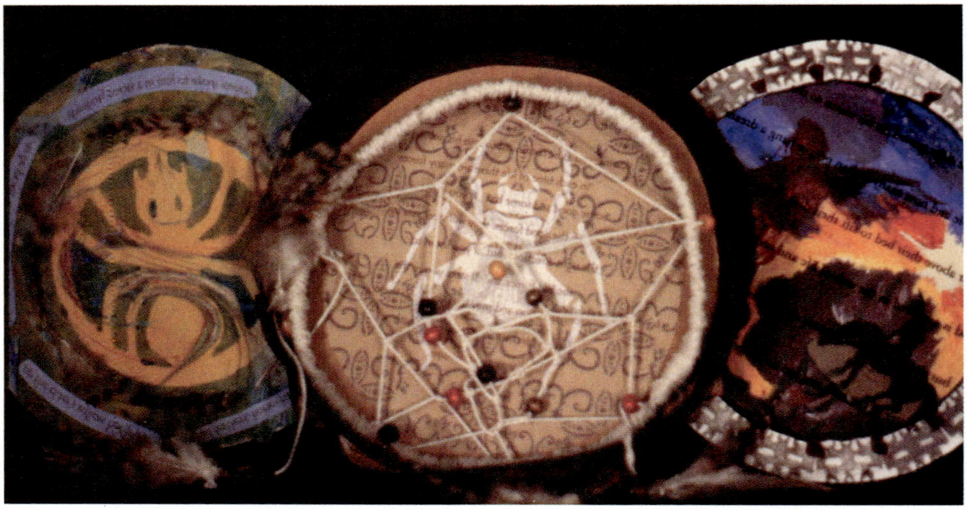

FIGURE 7.2

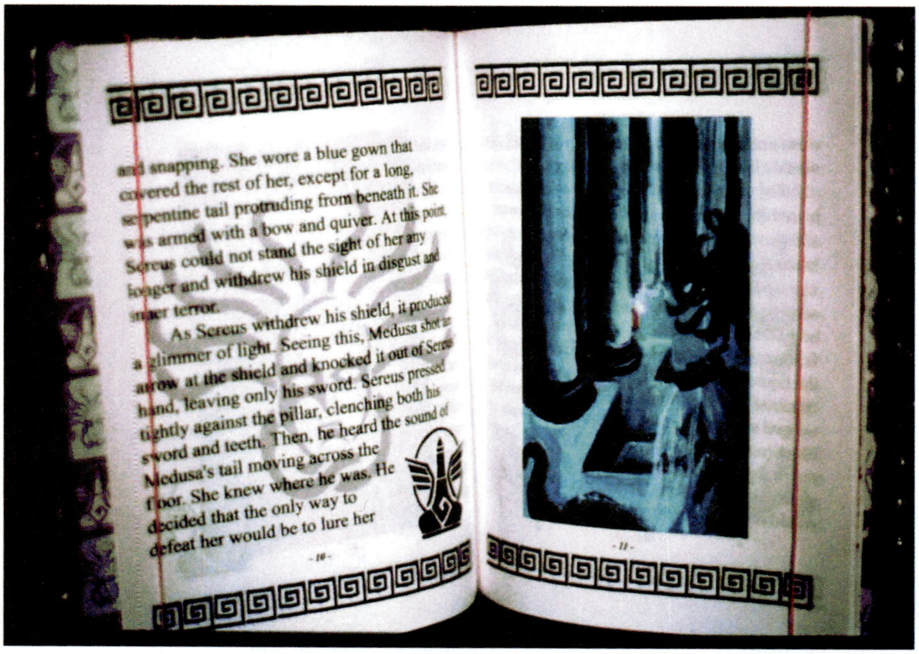

FIGURE 7.4

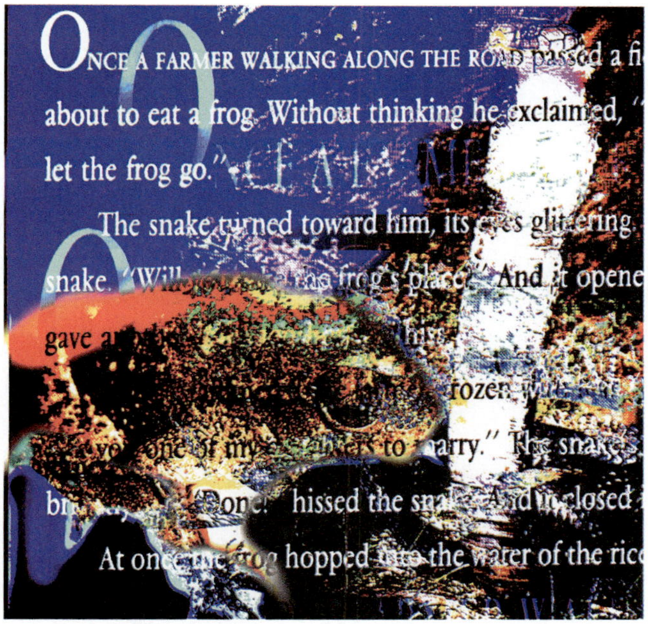

FIGURE 7.8

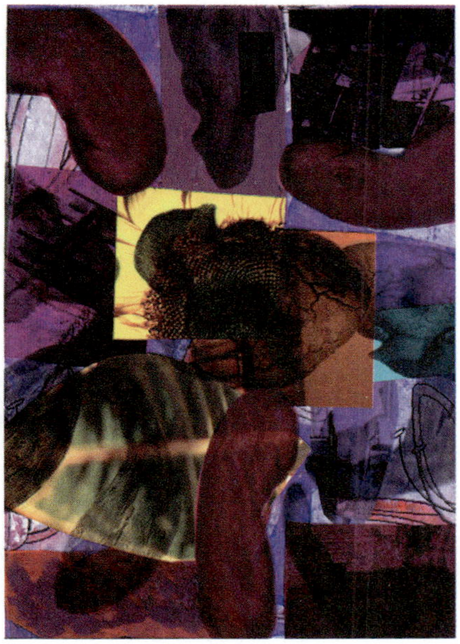

FIGURE 7.11

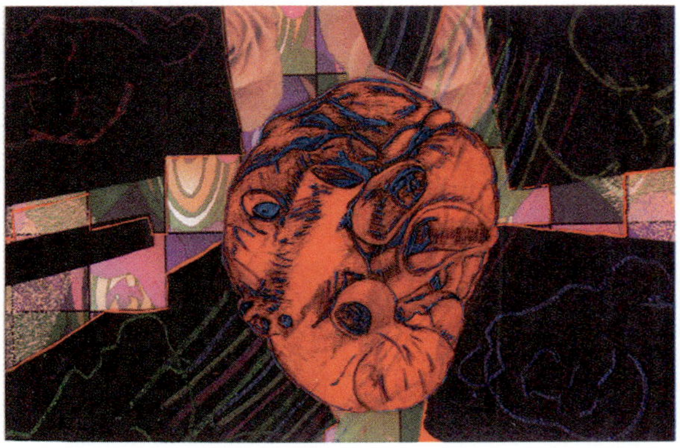

FIGURE 7.12

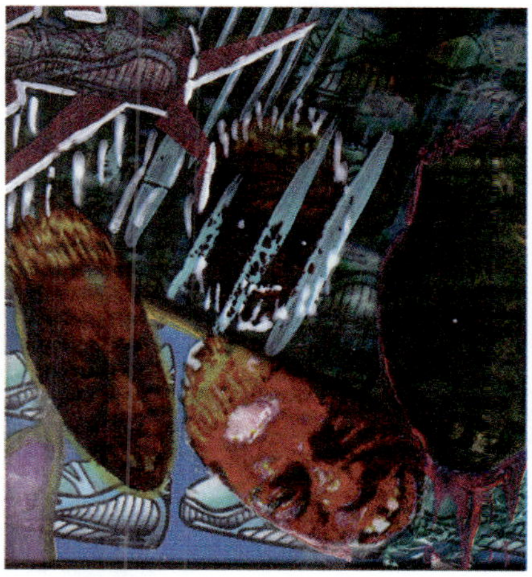

FIGURE 7.13

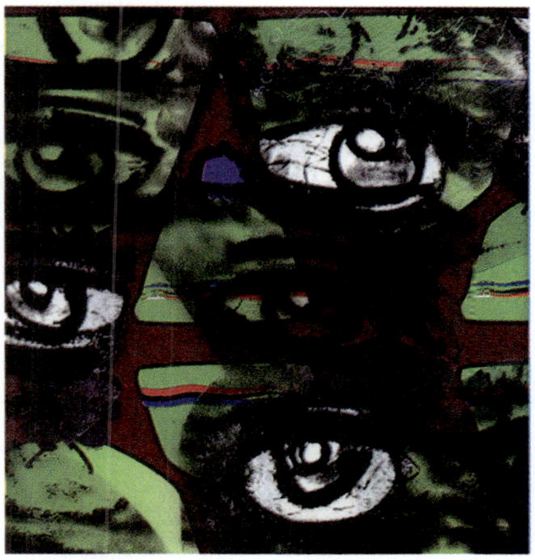

FIGURE 7.14

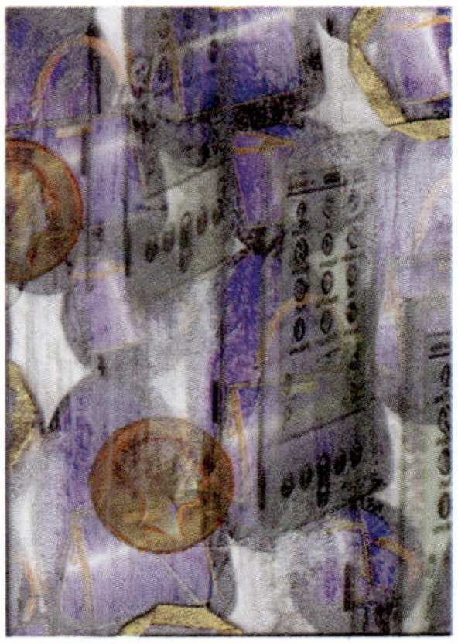

FIGURE 7.15

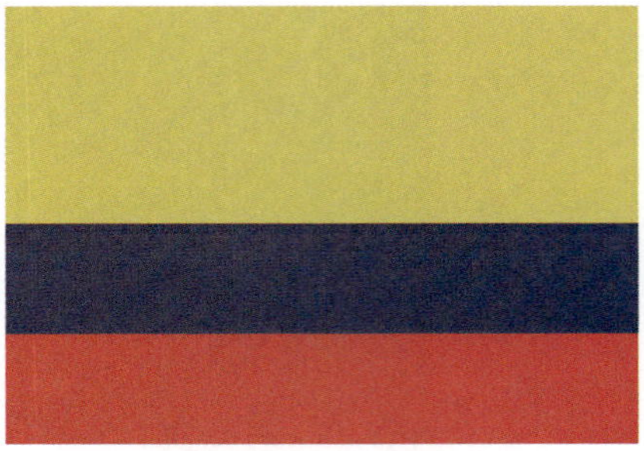

FIGURE 7.16

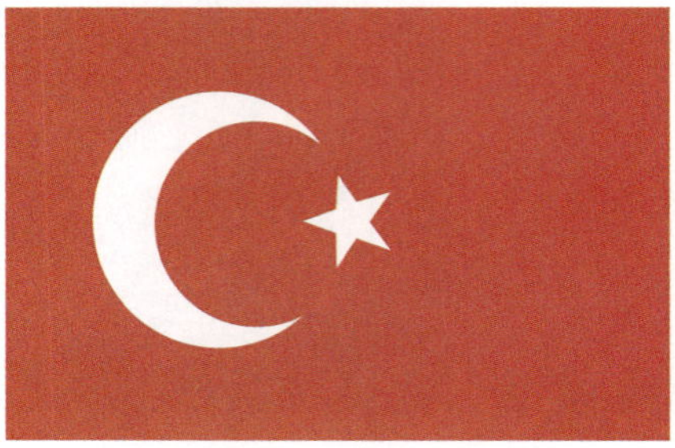

FIGURE 7.17

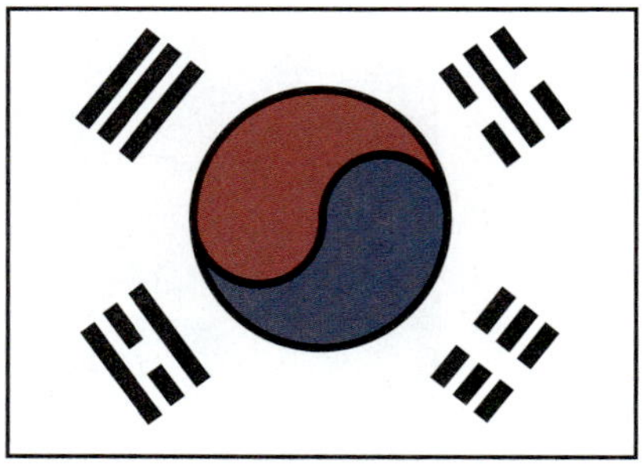

FIGURE 7.18

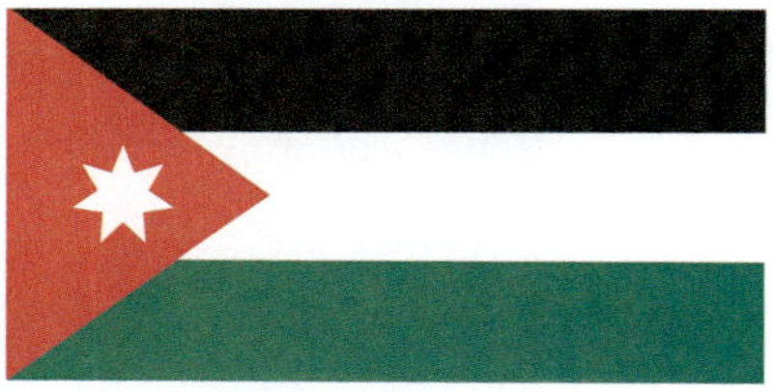

FIGURE 7.19

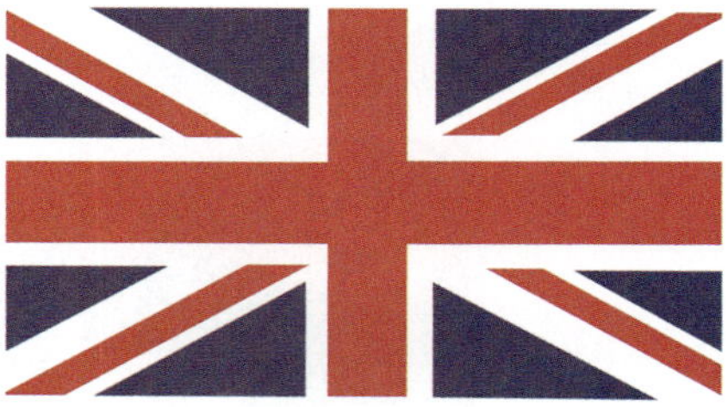

FIGURE 7.20

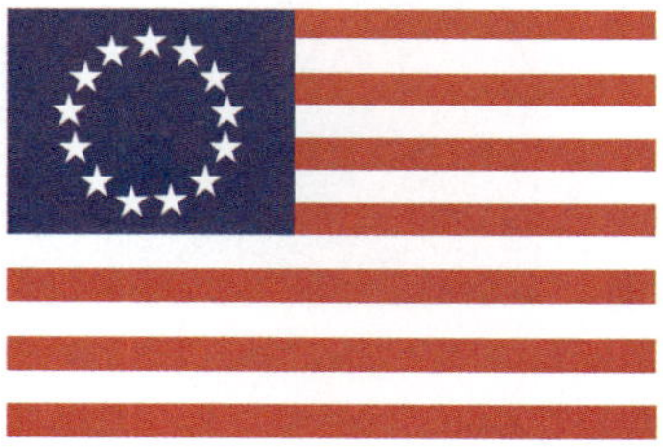

FIGURE 7.21

FIGURE 7.44

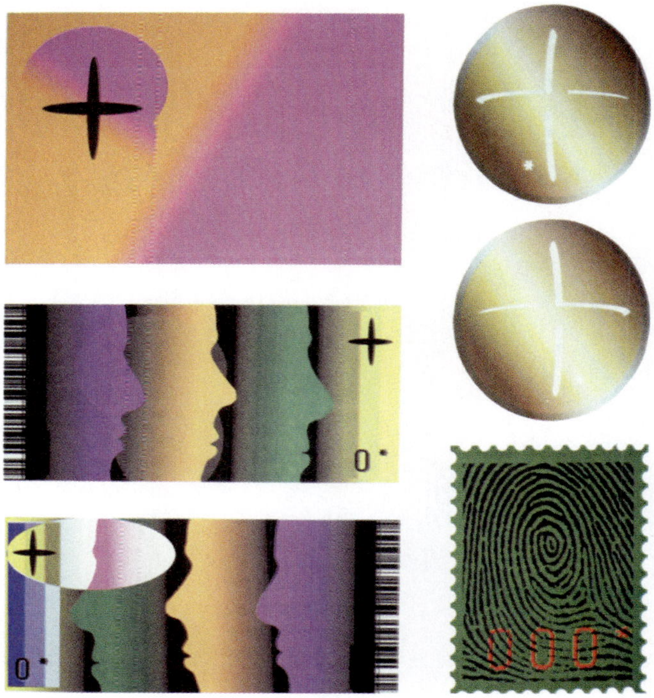

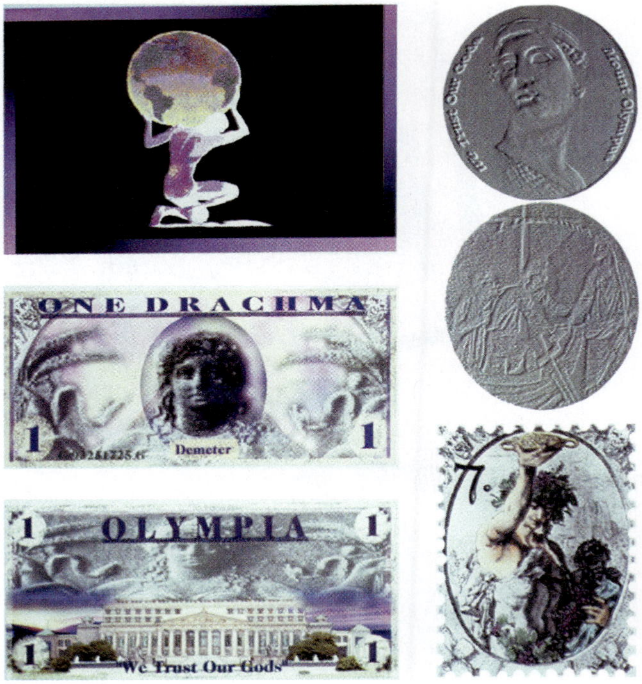

FIGURE 7.46

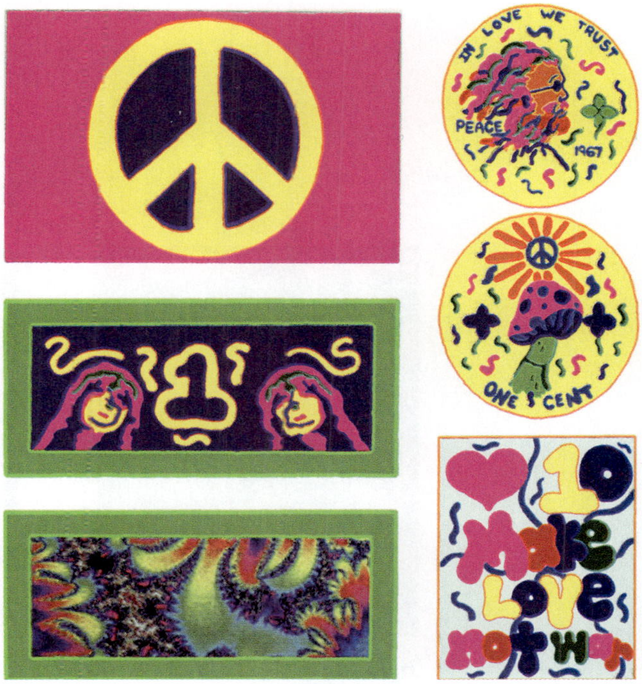

FIGURE 7.45

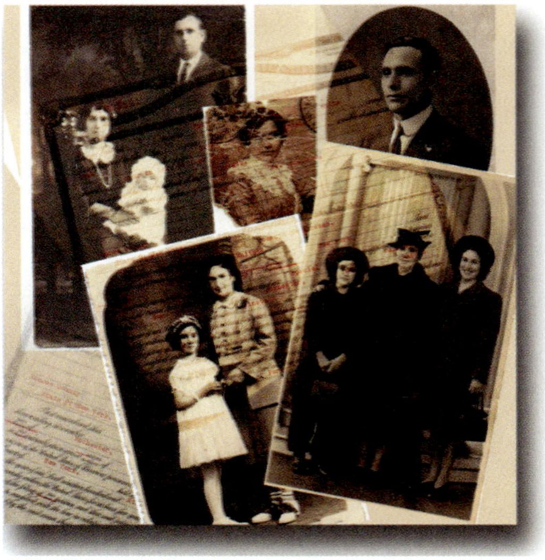

FIGURE 7.48

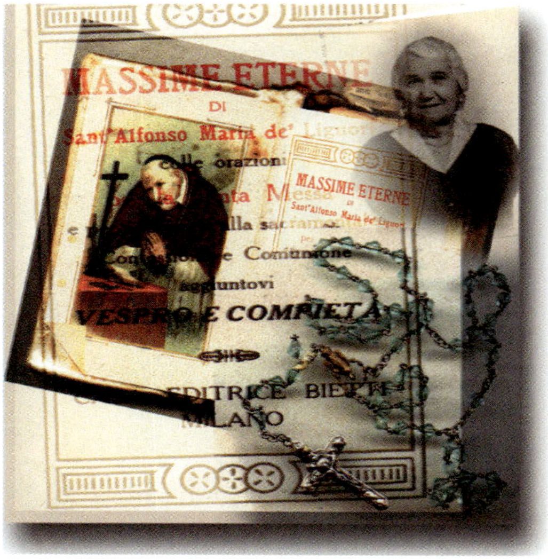

FIGURE 7.49

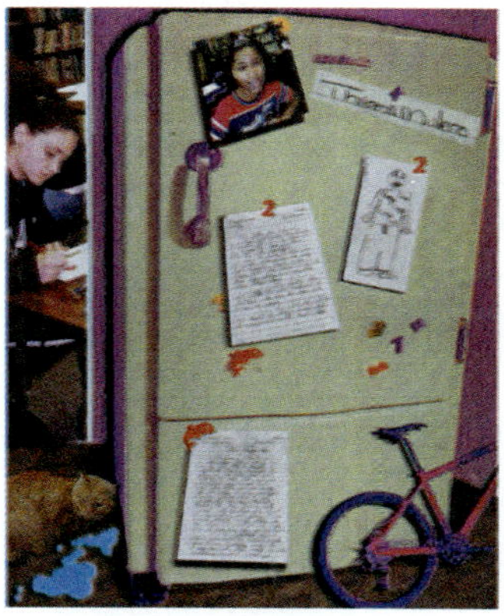

FIGURE 7.51A

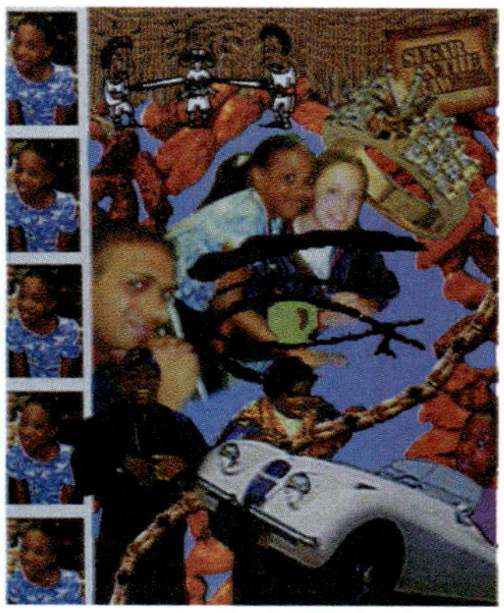

FIGURE 7.51B

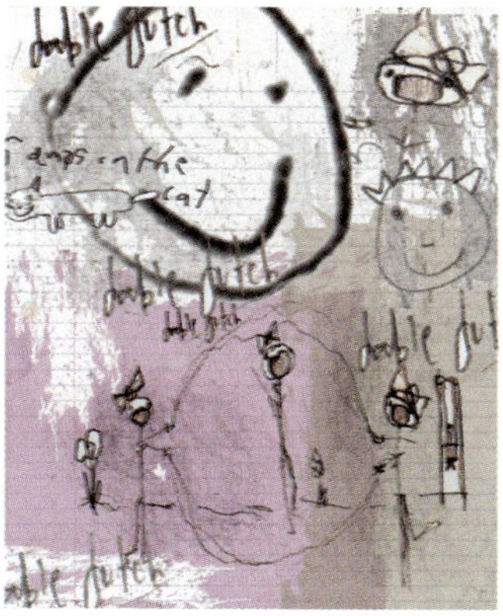

FIGURE 7.51C

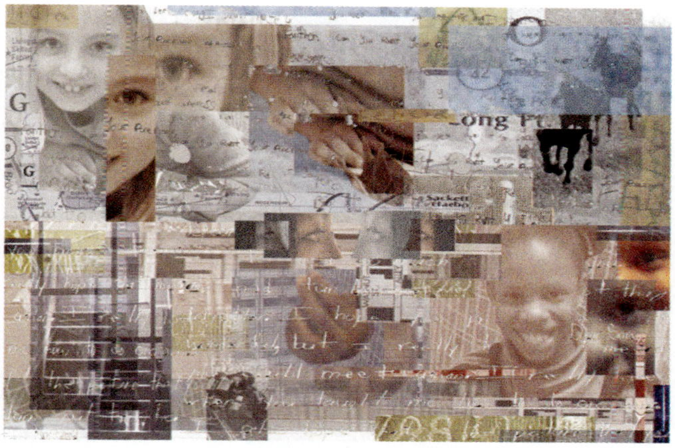

FIGURE 7.52

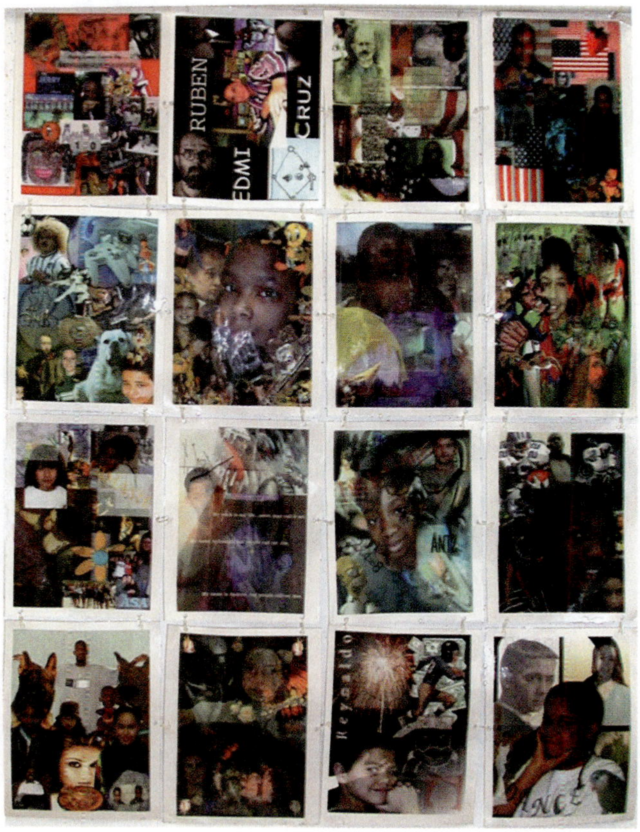

FIGURE 7.53

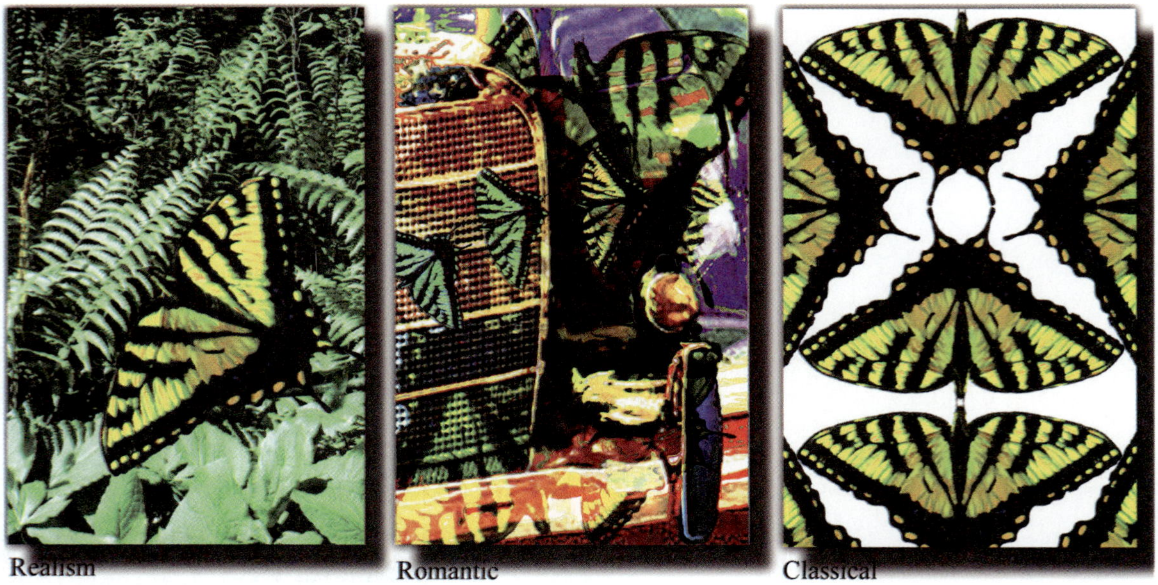

FIGURE 8.1

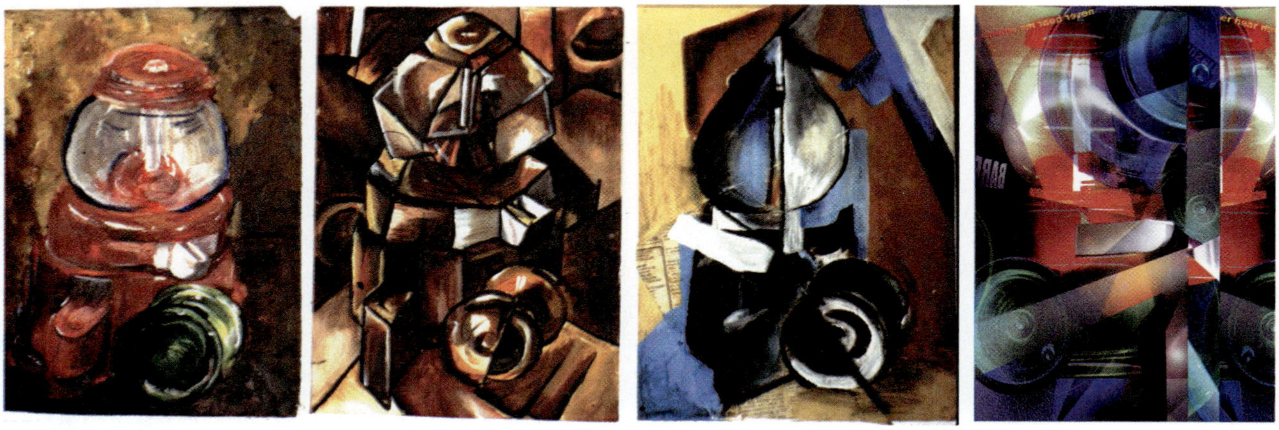

FIGURE 8.3

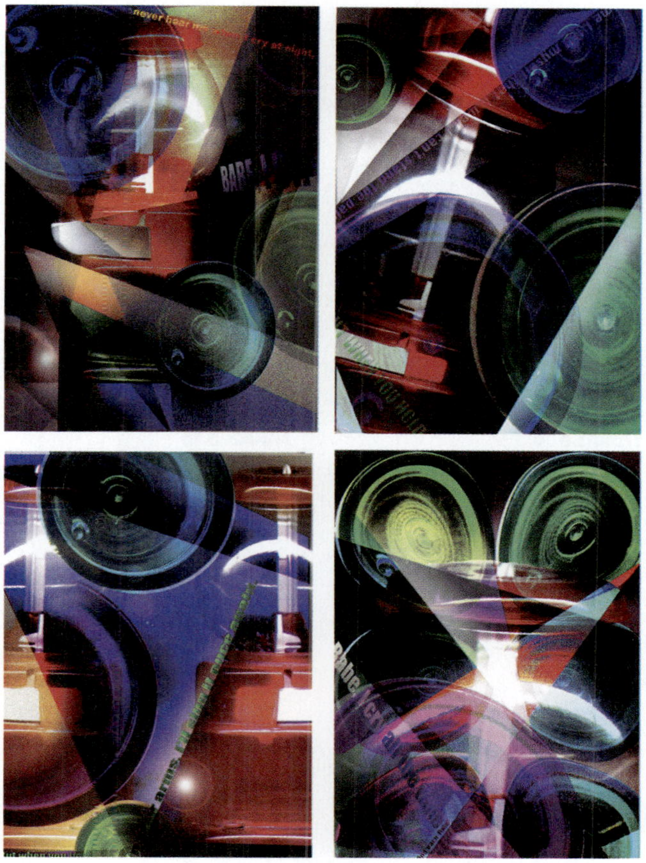

FIGURE 8.5

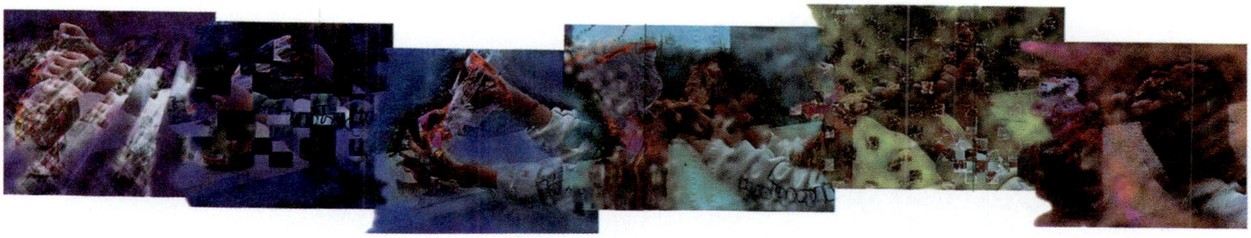

FIGURE 8.16

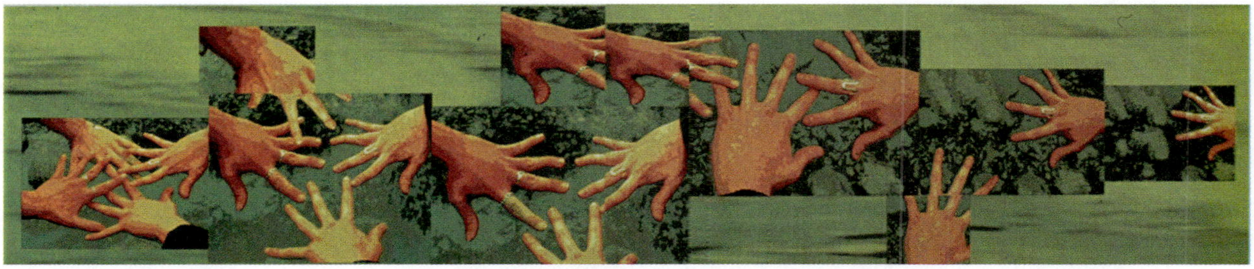

FIGURE 8.17

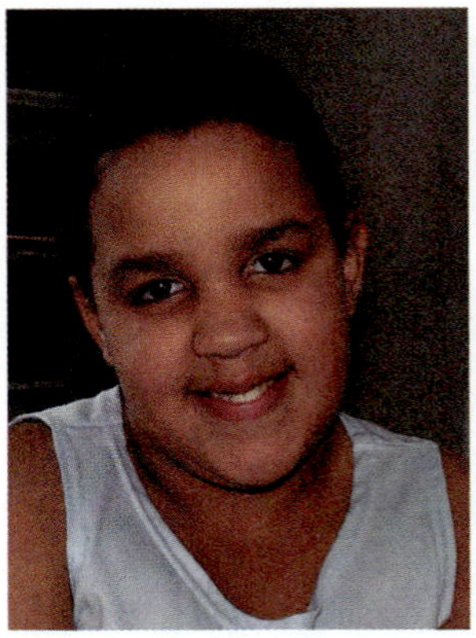

FIGURE 8.18

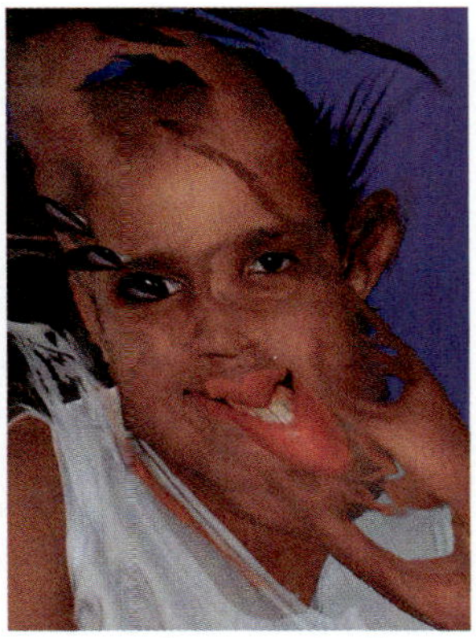

FIGURE 8.19

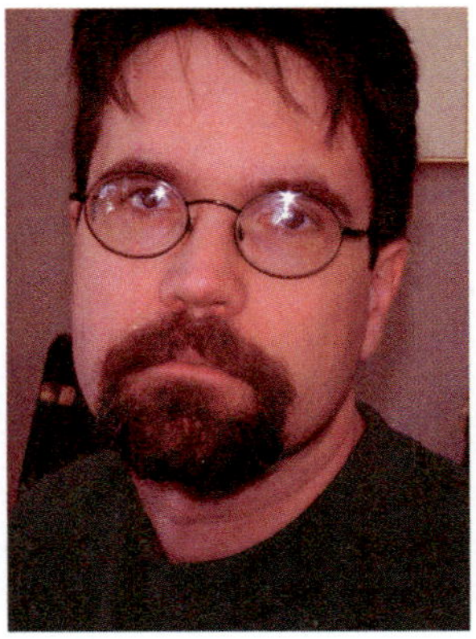

FIGURE 8.20

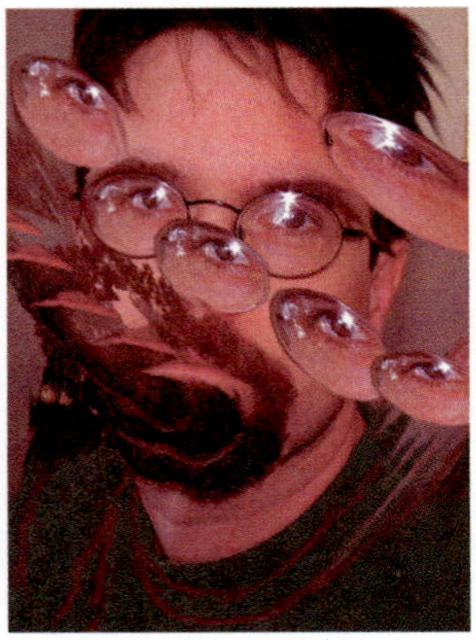

FIGURE 8.21

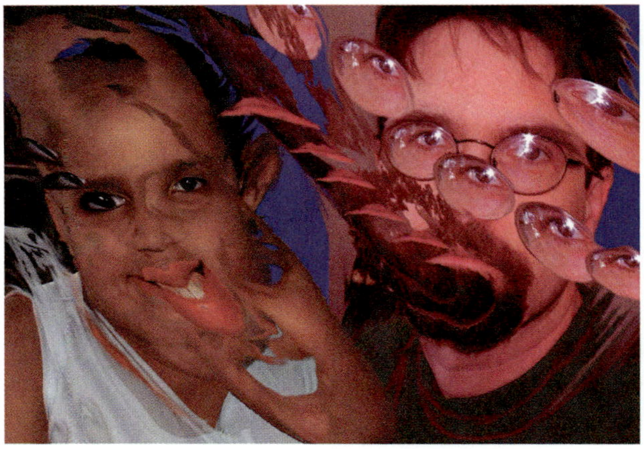

FIGURE 8.22

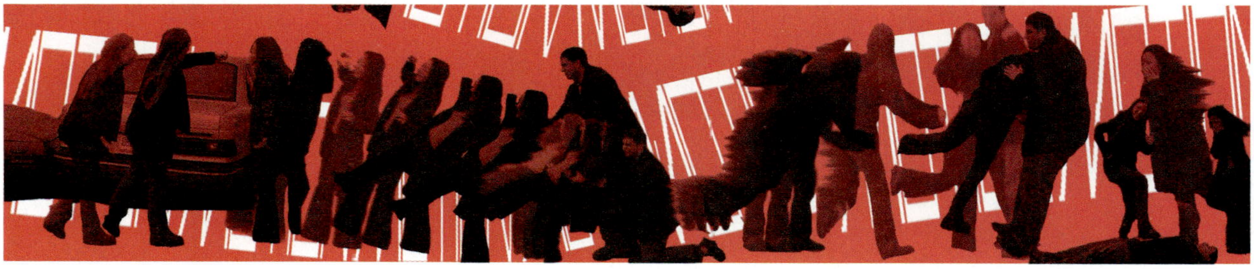

FIGURE 8.23

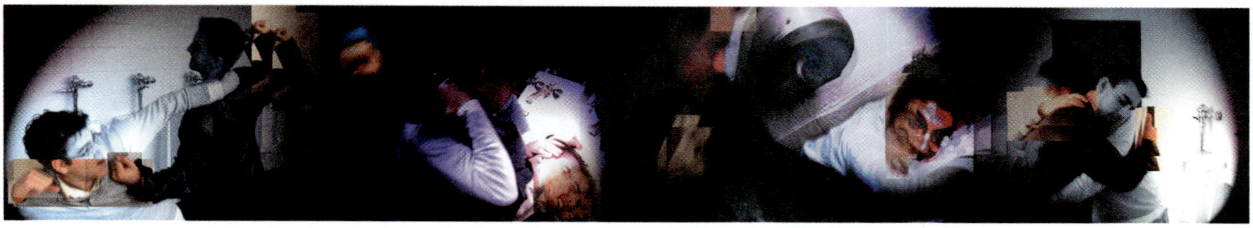

FIGURE 8.24

TEMPERATURE DESIGN

The triangle has been used from prehistoric to present time for decorating and enlivening the surfaces of our living spaces. If isolated, these triangles appear to be shards broken off of a larger whole body, whereas assembled triangles interlock with their neighbors to make a continuous pattern field. Such a unit is an ideal structure to use for studying the effects and psychology of color.

Most people have definite color preferences. Included within this personal color taste is a conscious or unconscious response to apparent color temperature. Is a hue sample warm or is it cool? Past experiences from early childhood dictate most of these color responses.

The most common choices for warm hues are red, red-orange, or orange but green and yellow are often referred to as warm as well. The common choice for a cool color is blue, blue-green, blue-violet, or green. Colors that are referred to as neutral in temperature might variously be yellow, violet, magenta, or green.

OBJECTIVES

This project allows you to study color temperature issues, pattern building with an equilateral triangle grid, and will help in developing color skills.

MATERIALS

Electronic: A vector drawing (Adobe Illustrator) and a raster painting (Adobe Photoshop) program with computer and quality-color printer.

Traditional: Double-weight cold press illustration board; pencil; T square; ruler; 30/60/90 degree triangle; utility knife; gouache or tempera paint; drafting tape; brushes; palette knife; paint palette

PROCEDURE

Build the color composition from the three points of the triangle. Use the logic that one of those points is warm, another is cool, and the third is neutral in temperature. Somewhere, probably in the center, all the colors should be juxtaposed to each other. Use two cool hues, two warm hues, two neutral hues and tints and saturation variations of them as needed for the composition. Please work non-objectively. See the color Figure 6.39, 6.40, 6.42–6.47 examples.

Electronic An equilateral triangle grid must first be constructed. For efficiency purposes, one person could make this grid and then share the file with others (it takes about three hours to draw this grid). Make this grid in a vector-based program such as Adobe Illustrator that has a layers feature. Set the **stroke** (line) thickness as thin as possible. Set the page in landscape orientation and the grid spacing at 1/16th inch (.06 inches) in the **Guide & Grid** preferences. Activate **Show Grid, Snap To Grid,** and **Show Rulers.**

Align the rulers to the upper left corner of the printable surface of the page. Find the **Polygon Tool** (in Adobe Illustrator click and hold down on the **Circle Tool** until the polygon tool appears) and select it. When the **Sides** and **Radius** (size) option appears (in Adobe Illustrator click once on the page to make this appear) type in "three" sides and set radius (size) to "5". Carefully scale this up to a 10-inch base line while holding down the **Shift Key.**

Draw a 10-inch line and at each inch draw a short perpendicular cross line. **Select** this line and all its perpendiculars (holding down the **Shift Key**) and then go up to the **Object** menu and **Group** this. This is now your "ten-space ruler". **Cut** this ruler from the first layer and **Paste** it on a **New Layer.**

Deactivate the first layer. Move your "ten-space ruler" carefully onto the baseline of your equilateral triangle. Then **Paste** another copy of it and **Rotate** to meet the right side. Do the same for the left side so that a carefully placed guide is on all three sides. Take pains to get this right! Use the **Magnifying Glass.** If your rulers are a little short or long make certain that the aberration meets at the top point of the triangle evenly. Select all three rulers (holding down the shift key) and group them and apply a color to the **Stroke** line.

Activate both layers and **Select All** and hold down on the **Shift Key** while scaling the baseline to 9-1/8 inch and the height to 7-7/8 inch (that is the standard maximum printable area). Then deactivate the ruler layer and activate the first layer so your grid will be on that layer. Select black for the **Stroke** (line) and set the **Weight** at 0.25. Use the **Pen** to commence drawing the grid by carefully joining the points on your "ten-space rulers" as in Figure 6.38. After drawing the first set of ten lines you can **Select** them and **Group** them and then **Copy** and **Paste** them back into a **New Layer. Rotate** and/or **Mirror** this group to meet another side of the triangle at the proper angle. Do this step a second time to create the third set of lines. **Select** individual lines with the white (hollow) **Direct Selection Tool** to fine tune where the line ends meet the side of the triangle. Do this in magnified view.

When all lines of the grid are drawn and properly positioned, hide all the grid layers and activate the ruler layer and **Delete** it. Then show and activate the grid layers so that you can **Flatten** them into one layer. After saving the finished grid you're ready to import it into a raster-based program (Adobe Photoshop).

Open your raster-based program with a layers feature and make a **New** page that is 8-1/2″ by 11″ with white fill. Now **Paste** or **Import** the grid that you made in the draw program onto this page to make a **New Layer.** Then make a third layer to work on (title it "work layer"). Use the **Magic Wand Tool** with the **Options** set at 32 and **Anti-Aliased** checked on and use **All Layers** checked on. This is very important! In the layers palette highlight the work layer and block the other two layers.

Use the magic wand to **Select** various shapes in the grid work. Hold down on the **Shift Key** to make multiple selections. After the areas you want to color are selected, proceed to select a hue with the **Color Picker** and go down to **Fill** under **Edit.** You can also use the **Gradient Tool** if your program is so equipped—select foreground and background color then click on the design where you want the foreground color deposited and draw a line with the gradient tool to where you want your selected areas to fill with the background color. Release the mouse button and see what the gradient looks like—change by refilling with other colors (Figure 6.39, color insert).

Select new areas and proceed to fill out the design on the grid framework. Deactivate the grid layer occasionally to hide the distracting black grid lines so you can see if the shapes are working well. Don't worry about the thin white grid lines running through the larger shapes. These will be eradicated later. You can reselect areas that need more work and utilize the color picker or one of the color slider palettes found in "high end" paint programs. After the design is finished **Save** your artwork! Now **Hide Grid** and make sure the working layer is active. Then go to the layer menu and **Duplicate** that layer. Move this "duplication layer" in the layer palette so that it is positioned underneath the original working layer. Now hide all but this new copy. Use a **Filter** on it to drastically blur it, blending the white grid lines away. Try the **Gaussian Blur** set at about 7 pixels. Any white spots left can then be easily closed up with a smudging tool. Now show the original working layer on top of the blurred layer. All the white grid lines should be gone. **Merge** these two layers and **Delete** the black grid lines. **Save** the image. Now cover the excess gaussian blur around the outside edges of the large triangle. Draw crisp white lines with the **Stroke Weight** option set at about 12 to do this (Figure 6.40). **Save** the image again.

You are now ready to **Print** the art. Several variations could be designed and printed out on a color ink jet printer and dry mounted to single-weight illustration board.

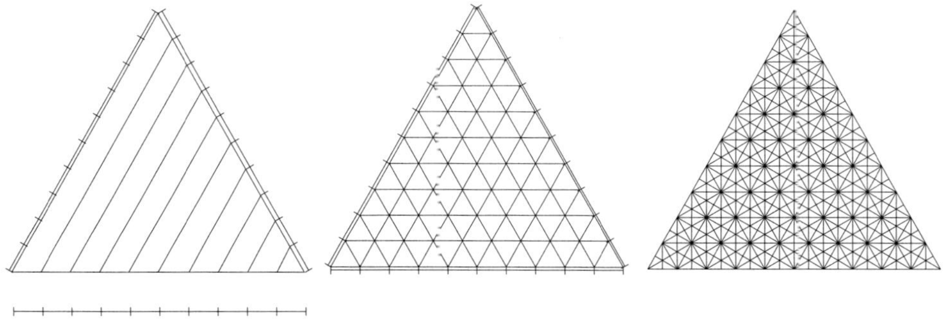

Figure 6.38

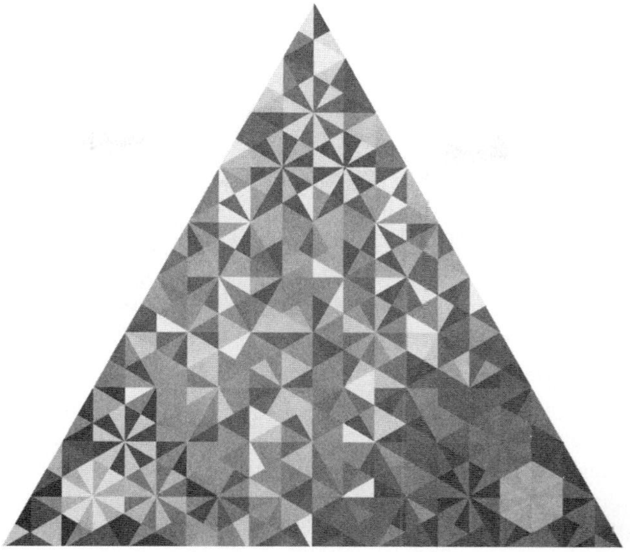

Figure 6.40

Traditional On a piece of 20″ × 30″ white cold-press double-weight illustration board, lay out an equilateral triangle in pencil that is 22″ to a side. Center a 20″ equilateral triangle within the first as illustrated in the diagram (Figure 6.41). Next construct 2-inch-sided equilateral triangles within the format (10 to a side). Divide these further in halves or sixths as needed for your composition. Then cut out the 22″ triangle. Use gouache or tempera paint and drafting tape for crisp clean edges.

DISCUSSION

This pattern grid could just as well be used to study other color effects such as complementary contrast or color emotion. Does the pattern regularity or irregularity affect our perception of the color effects? If so, how? What kind of qualitative differences occur between the hand-painted and computer-generated versions of this assignment? The finished triangles can be used to create a large wall-sized display by fitting the triangles together as tiles (Figures 6.42 through 6.47, color insert).

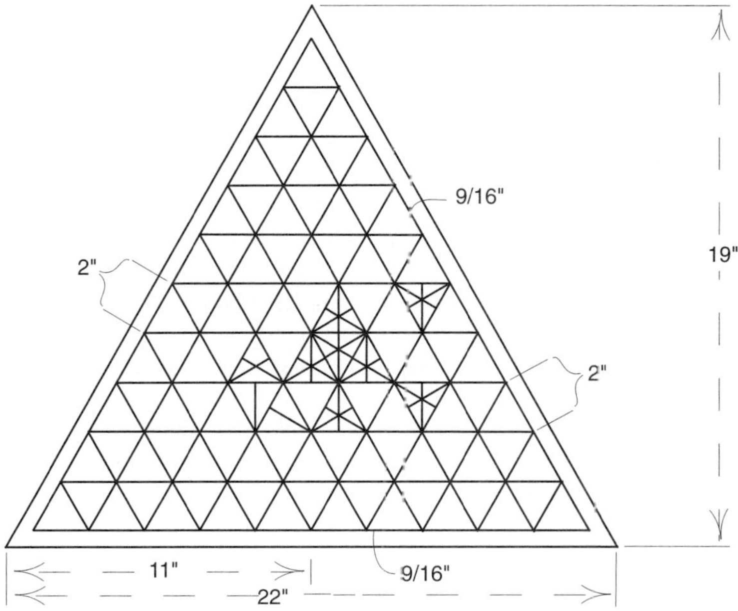

Figure 6.41

CHAPTER 7

DYNAMIC INTERCHANGE: INVESTIGATIONS

In a vast world full of news and events, those stories that attract our attention are ones that deal clearly with relevant information about an event, person or thing. Visually, the same criteria can apply. Being visually literate is critical to an informed understanding of society and culture. It transcends the limitations of the written word and allows us to decode the myriad bits of visual information around us. This can be a daunting task. Every day we are required to literally sort through stacks of visual images that demand our attention. These images can be loaded with superficial, yet subliminal messages or they may be dense with important overt content. For us to put them into some kind of order takes skill as well as savvy.

In Chapter 7 investigations are presented as an aspect of the creative process that address more complex relationships in visual communication. Creating images that rely on references or innuendo, that respond to existing themes, or that ask new questions are important processes in the visual arts. As you build upon fundamental concepts, these assignments require research of information to support your ideas. What has been explored previously becomes the building blocks for continued image development. The art of visual literacy is always a dynamic interchange. These next projects suggest some strategies for tackling the more involved concepts that are a result of this dialogue.

VISUAL MYTHOLOGY

A ***symbol*** is a word or image that means more than the obvious. It goes beyond the apparent and enters the realm of ambiguity and mystery. Symbols help us begin to understand the world around us through implication and suggestion. Symbols make us think beyond the constructs of our ordinary visual references.

Symbolic imagery (Figure 7.1) has been used in many cultures to enhance important ceremonial events or to explain various phenomenon such as the origin of man or his customs and religious beliefs. According to Jungian Psychology, archetypal symbols, which may include universal elements, arrive from the unconscious without any allusion to the natural world. These forms are often found in unrelated cultures.

Myths are stories that contain symbolic representations and communicate widely held beliefs that are essential to the understanding of a culture. There are cultures today that continue to use the method of storytelling, or the retelling of tales, as a way to instruct and pass on information that has been handed down from generation to generation.

Cultural diffusion takes place when cultural traits or patterns spread from one culture to another. This inclination has influenced contemporary artists and designers, and cultural references have become important sources for them.

OBJECTIVES

Students will create a visual artist's book that will be a collection of symbols, patterns, and imagery. The imagery they develop will use as its inspiration the rich symbolic language of various cultures (Figure 7.2, color insert). A personal narrative based on the characteristics of traditional mythology will support this combination of elements. Image development may be referential or personal, with the goal being a dynamic combination of abstract elements and symbolic forms.

MATERIALS

Electronic: A vector- and/or a raster-based graphics program such as Adobe Illustrator and Adobe Photoshop; scanned actual references; illustration board; paper; objects with textural surfaces

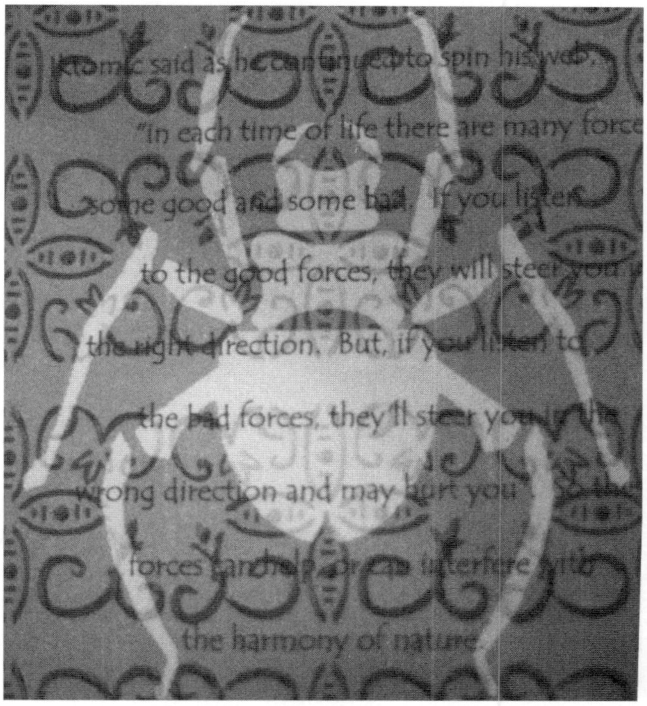

Figure 7.1
Image by Sarah Broadhead

Traditional: Paint; stencils; various paper textures; found cultural references; inks; brushes; other mixed media of choice

PROCEDURE

This project involves a number of steps; as follows:

Researching myths as they pertain to a specific culture

Creating a narrative based on the characteristics of traditional mythology

Creation of five symbols as visual imagery to include in an "artist book"

Designing the artist book structure so that it works with your personal myth

Weaving text, symbols, patterns, and texture into this book

Researching Mythology The first step in this project is to research myths from the culture you have chosen. Use the library, the Internet, or your personal collection to find information. Study the ways that myths communicate universal themes.

Writing the Narrative Using your research as a starting point, write a brief narrative that captures the essence of traditional myth structures. For example, myths may have a historical basis or attempt to explain a phenomenon of nature. Stories of gods, heroes, tricksters, or warriors are common. Begin by setting a time and place and describing a situation. Resolve the narrative through character development and/or a transformation of some kind.

Electronic In a sketchbook, begin by sketching out ideas for your book structure and sketch or write down ideas for imagery. Think about the ways that you are might combine imagery and materials and develop symbols that can be used in the book. Using a graphics program such as Adobe Photoshop or Illustrator, create a number of symbols (Figure 7.3) that will give rich meaning to your myth. These symbols can weave through the visual narrative. Develop a variety of symbols that interrelate. Develop a ***pattern*** using one or two of these symbols as the motif. Consider the ways that these symbols can reflect your personal connection to the story. (Figure 7.4, color insert)

Create other imagery by scanning various textures and using them to combine with visual images that you have collected. These combined images can be manipulated on the computer so that color and style, for example, are relating to your myth. Utilize the capabilities of the software to merge imagery or to scale or distort existing information. Personal illustrations or photographs can be integrated into your book. These can be brought into the computer as well, and changed to suit the mood and style of the book.

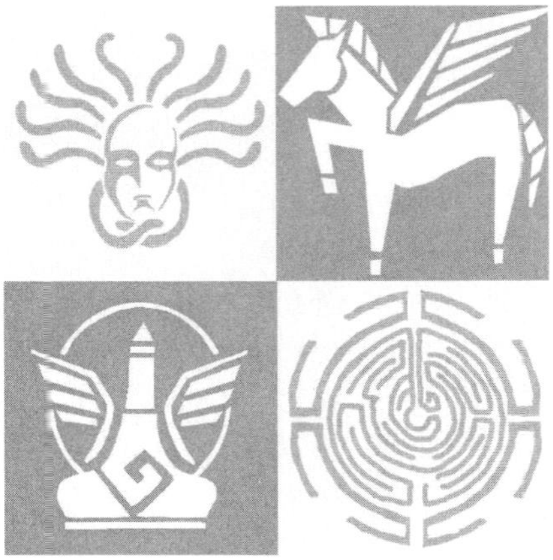

Figure 7.3

As you develop the imagery for the book, you will also begin to design its structure. Study various book structures, looking at children's books, pop-up books, limited edition books, and die-cut processes. Researching artists' books, in particular, will help you to understand the unique character of this medium. Consider the shape and dimensions of the book in relationship to your narrative (Figure 7.5, color insert) and whether the book cover should be incorporated. Your design must reflect the character of your narrative and should capture the essence of your idea.

Traditional Using the same conceptual and formal parameters as the electronic procedure, use traditional art materials to execute this assignment. (Figure 7.6)

PRESENTATION

As you assemble the book, pay attention to craftsmanship. Make sure you use appropriate adhesives and glues to create strong bonds. The structure should be durable and easily accessible.

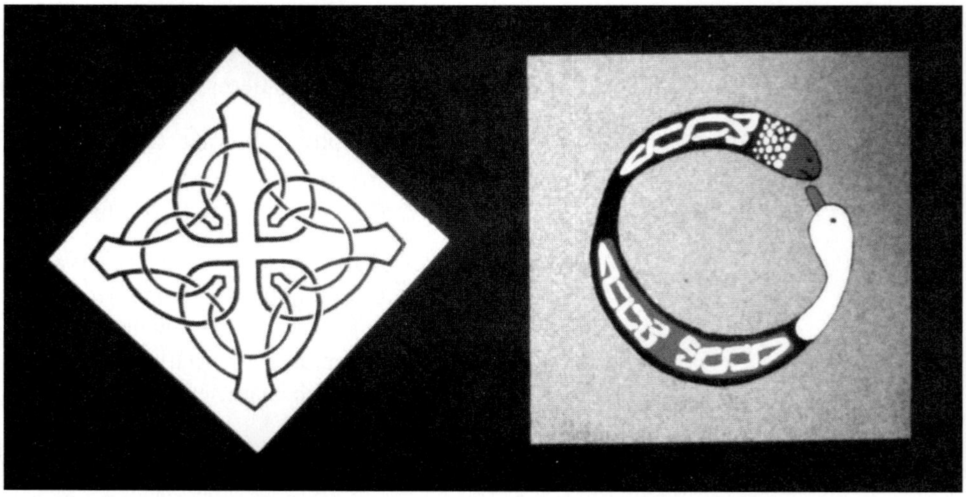

Figure 7.6 *Figures by Christy Camfield-Carson*

FOLKTALES: WORD AND IMAGE

Folktales can be rich resources for imagery. The characters and places that they conjure up can be jumping-off points for a design. Art history is full of images that have been inspired by these texts, and children's literature continues to be a repository of tales that have been told. Using stories as a source for inspiration is an age-old technique, but the results can be personal and evocative.

OBJECTIVES

This assignment intends to increase students' awareness of literature as a source for image-making. Students will respond to the written story and develop imagery that uses the content of the folktale, and the actual words in the text, as inspiration for their work. They will explore the ways that text and image can work together to create an interesting design. Inventive applications of type and creative combinations of images are important aspects of this project.

MATERIALS

Electronic: A raster-based program such as Adobe Photoshop; scanner; clear acetate transparency sheets for your color printer; good-quality printer; scanned and printed-out text and imagery; printer paper; illustration board; rubber cement

Traditional: Pencils; inks; paints (gouache or acrylics); acetate sheets (clear); various papers; illustration board; rubber cement

PROCEDURE

Create a design using a folktale as the source for an image. The folktale may be from any culture or time period. Actual words from the folktale will be used in the design as a way to make direct reference to the text. As opposed to illustrating the tale, you will be creating imagery that relates to the subject matter. Words and images will work together to heighten the impact of the story to which they refer.

Creating a Text File for Your Design Create a "text" element for your design by using an actual passage, phrase, or words, from the folktale that you have chosen. You can repeat your chosen text as many times as you like. Some approaches to creating textural information include scanning directly from the book or typing in the passages directly. In a raster-based program such as Adobe Photoshop you can **Open** a **New File** and use the **Type Tool** to type directly into the file. After you type in any text you will need to go to **Layer** on the **Layer** menu, and then choose **Rasterize** and **Text.** This will rasterize your type layer so you can manipulate it like the image layers. If you have access, load some interesting, additional fonts on your computer. Experiment with the variety of styles, playing around with size difference. Use the transform functions (**Edit** menu and then **Transform**) in the program to distort the individual letters, words, or whole bodies of text.

If you would like to, you can integrate hand-made text with the computer text by creating original text on illustration or bristol board and then scanning it into the computer. Text can be hand-written with gouache or other media (oil pastels; india ink; or acrylic would work). Stencils can be used to trace or spray paint through onto bristol board, and then scanned. You could also use the computer to type out the passage, print it, and then draw back into the text. Rescan this into a digital file and manipulate it again. If you like, this image can be printed onto a transparency sheet and used as an overlay in your design. Explore as many possibilities as you can.

If you want to combine files, you will have to **Open** each file and then **Copy** and **Paste** into an existing file. Any pasted imagery will come in as a new layer and can be manipulated separately. **Save** any work that you do on the computer.

Creating an Image File for Your Design The next step is to integrate imagery with the text. While imagery should relate to the folktale, it need not be too literal. The imagery can be created directly in a graphics program or scanned in and then manipulated. You can scan in your own drawings and photographs. Copyright-free imagery can also be appropriated. Pieces or segments from other image sources such as magazines or books can be scanned and brought into the computer.

Each time you **Open** a file and then **Copy** and **Paste,** your image will come in as a new layer in the active file. The advantage of layers in a graphics program such as Photoshop is that it will allow you to create transparent effects and blend layers in interesting ways. Think about how you will integrate the combination of images if you have numerous layers.

Merging Text and Image The final image will be an integration of text and image. **Open** up whatever files you would like to combine together. You will need to bring these files together by copying and pasting into one file. The copy and paste commands bring in whole files if the entire image is selected. Try using the **Lasso** tool or the **Marquee** selection tools to capture only parts of the image. You also can capture part of the image using the **Quick Mask** mode and **Gradient** tool to get a subtle transition between images. To do this, go to the icon for **Quick Mask** mode on the bottom of the tools palette (white circle in the middle of a gray rectangle). Select this mode and then go to the **Gradient Tool.** Make sure the foreground color is black and the background color is white. Select the file that you want to capture and click on the image at the point that you would like to start a gradation. This process will put a red mask over your image. Now quit the **Quick Mask** mode by clicking on its icon again. Your image will show the "marching ants" selection. Go to the **Move Tool** and then click on the image inside the selection. You can now click and drag (hold the mouse down) and drop this selection onto another file. The side of the image that had the lightest masked area will be the area that looks faded and that merges in a subtle way with the other file.

Be creative and think of many ways to manipulate the concept of integrating type with imagery (Figure 7.7). Once you have established an image, use the computer to continue to changing or enhancing the solution (Figure 7.8, color insert). Use **Image** adjustments such as **Curves, Brightness/Contrast,** and so on to change aspects of the image. **Save** all changes under a new name so that other files are not written over.

The final image should be able to convey the content of the folktale through the combination of image and text. Remember that the text does not need to remain readable. It is a starting point to be used as needed for the resolution of the image.

If you have one image, mount the printout onto illustration board with a 2″ border all around. If you are overlaying an acetate sheet with imagery over a (printout) base image, tape it at the top. A window mat over the whole image will conceal and flatten the layers.

Traditional This project can be done with traditional materials. Follow the conceptual guidelines of the electronic version but use various materials to create text and image, and experiment with various ways to combine them.

Explorations with media could include:

- write the passage in black ink then create an image on tracing paper or acetate or even wax paper and paste it over the text, playing with the concept of transparency; color could be washed over the words; the words could be blurred in some way.

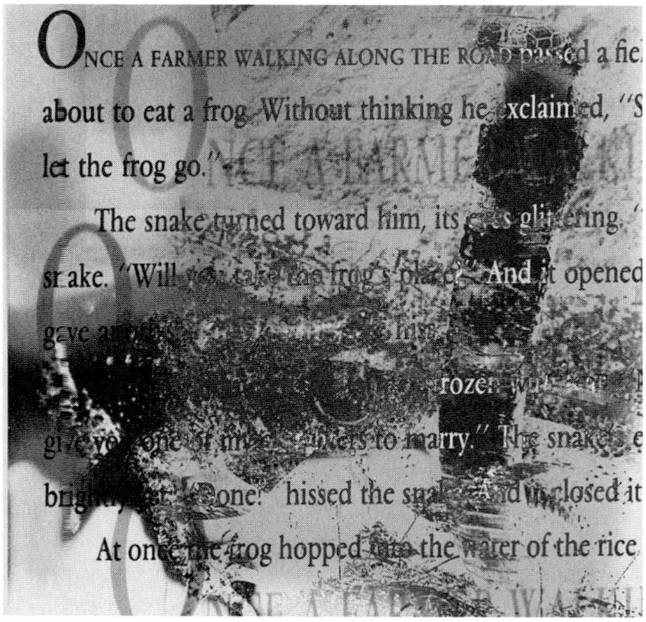

Figure 7.7

- Make black and white copies of the words . . . enlarge them so they are almost unreadable. Make black and white copies of visuals that relate to the folktale. Collage them onto the text. Use more copies of the text to collage back on top of the imagery. Use black plaka, or india ink to work back into the images and the text.
- Write the text on clear acetate and then overlay that on top of imagery that relates to the folktale or collage or paint imagery on clear acetate and overlay that on the illustration board that has the text written on it. Scan all this into the computer and manipulate some more.
- Write the text on bristol board and then cut out some of the words a letter at a time. Lay your other images under the letters so you can see them through the letters. Lay other visuals on top of the text; or use the cut-out letters as a stencil that you can spray paint through.
- Lay down "layers" of the word passage by collaging torn pieces of it on top of one another. Collage other information into this.

Mount the final image onto illustration board with a 2″ border all around.

DISCUSSION

How did the story inspire the images? What dictated the imagery or what led you to your solution? Are the words readable, or do they act as abstract elements in the image? How was the issue of text and image resolved in regard to the ***subordination*** and/or ***dominance*** of particular elements?

MERGING DIVERGENT IMAGERY

We live in an age of immense complexity where information, events, and objects perpetually move, change hands, transform, and co-exist within our surrounding environments. The processes of layering and juxtaposition have generated a paradigm of chaos that in fact defines our contemporary lives and everyday existence. Logically, this model of reality also exists within the art world where subject, media, and approach have become stratified, blurring boundaries and forcing a redefinition of traditional disciplines and models of working. Within individual works of art, this layering of information can be seen as an internal echo of the external nature of our lives.

Designers strive to organize information in order to achieve successful visual communication. They work to harmonize the cacophony of visual information that exists within our external environments by merging and unifying visual data. Divergent images may be unified in a number of ways including the establishment of conceptual links and the use of media and transparency as formal means of achieving visual fusion. Ultimately the juxtaposition of divergent elements offers a vast resource of forms and solutions by altering the context in which individual forms are seen and creating new meanings for those elements.

OBJECTIVES

The objectives of this problem involve the utilization of the computer as a means of sketching and visualizing superimposed images and the use of ***transparency*** as a means of merging images. The series will use a formal structure such as ***pattern*** with a stable compositional structure, as a base on which juxtaposition and the establishment of areas of ***dominance*** and ***subordination*** can be readily achieved. The goal is to create a series of juxtaposed images that are merged conceptually and visually.

MATERIALS

Electronic: Photographic or graphic images; a raster-based program such as Adobe Photoshop; flat bed scanner; a printer or other output device; acetate suitable for your type of printer; mounting board; rubber cement; pen or utility knife

Traditional: Photographic or graphic images; copy machine and acetate suitable for a copy machine; colored acetate sheets (clear book covers; colored plastic wrap; lighting gels; paint; gel medium; collage materials; mounting board; rubber cement; pen or utility knife

PROCEDURE

Electronic

Preparatory Work There is some preparatory work that needs to be done before you begin this project, specifically finding suitable images and **scanning** them onto a disc (Figure 7.9). In order to find a commonality, you will be juxtaposing the forms found in your patterns with new images that are visually divergent but conceptually related. For instance, if your pattern uses flower ***motifs,*** you can deal with the concept of flowers as the reproductive organs of plants and juxtapose them with human organs. Motifs that represent relics can be juxtaposed with images related to reliquaries, and so on. These alternative forms will provide divergent visual images that can be scanned into the computer environment. Your own drawings or preexisting photographs of the chosen forms can be used. You may also choose a form represented in a variety of ways or you may choose a variety of forms. These images may or may not relate visually to your pattern motifs.

Digital Sketching—Combining Imagery and Working Out Some Visual Ideas Using your patterns as the background for each image in the series, layer the divergent images on top of the patterns. Utilize a raster-based program such as Photoshop to sketch and problem solve as well as to produce part of the final visual solution.

Begin by opening up one of your patterns into the program. Create a **New Layer** on top of your pattern. **Open** up your scanned images into the program and **Copy** and **Paste** them onto the layer over your pattern, moving them into desired positions. Experiment with changing the scale, rotating, overlapping, cropping and otherwise transforming the ***shapes*** on this secondary level in order to achieve an interesting visual integration. The color and fill of any of your forms can be readily altered, as can the opacity of any of the individual layers (thus altering color and value relationships). Scanned textures and surfaces may also be integrated into your work. Patterns follow rigidly ***formal structures*** and the integration of additional imagery may break or transform this rigidity by introducing secondary ***semiformal*** or ***informal structures.*** Compositional organization is dependent on the use of ***pause*** and ***emphasis/focal points*** and areas of relative inactivity. Your patterns are, for the most part, very active and have now been further activated by the juxtaposition of additional imagery and identifiable forms. Utilize color, texture, form, and transparency to reinterpret the surface and the space to create areas that are ***dominant*** and ***subordinate.*** An additional issue to consider involves the impact that the ***texture*** of the acetate will have on the image.

When you are finished, make the layer containing your original pattern invisible. This is achieved by clicking off of the eyeball icon in the **Layers** palette next to your image. **Save** the overlay that you have created, **Merge Visible,** and **Print** it on acetate out of the appropriate printer (laser or color)(Figure 7.10). Repeat this process with each of your scanned patterns.

Tape or glue your pattern to a piece of bristol board. Consider hinging the transparency by taping it to the pattern along a single edge so that you can easily lift it to make changes or additions without altering its orientation. At this point, the edges of your design do not need to be clean. You may actually glue or tape things together along the edges to adhere the layers. Be aware that any tape or glue in the center of the image becomes a visual part of the finished design (Figure 7.11, color insert).

Once your images are completed, cut a series of window mats that will complete the pieces. This process will allow you to reassess the formats for your images as well as hide the edges of the original layers. Utilizing scraps of paper or bristol board, create a window frame around your finished design. Carefully consider ***positive and negative space*** relationships as well as visual tension and the forces within the format as you are moving the pieces of paper around your image. Once you have established a visually successful format for your image, measure the opening that you have created for your image (Figures 7.12,

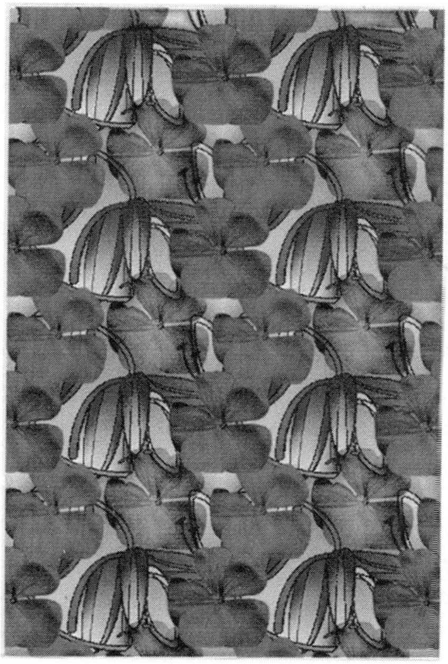

Figure 7.9 *Image by Karen Lin*

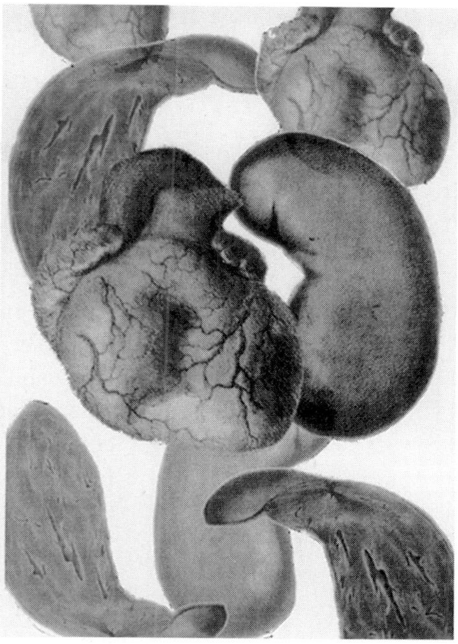

Figure 7.10 *Image by Karen Lin*

7.13, 7.14, 7.15, color insert). Determine a value or color (careful!) for the border of your image. Cut a window mat for your design and hinge it to the back mounting board to which the design is adhered.

Traditional This project may be done as a ***collage*** problem without the computer. The transparent layer over the pattern can be handmade with paint and collage materials. Surface tension, which causes wet media to bead on the plastic surface, can be broken by adding small amounts of hand soap to paint and ink This will allow wet media to stick to the surface of the acetate. The same conceptual and formal parameters apply to the problem.

ALTERNATIVES

This design may be done entirely as a computer project. Layers of related images are developed independently and then merged to produce the finished solution. This way of working explores the manipulation and visual combination of information within a digital environment. The beauty of the tactile interaction with media and space, however, is eliminated with this approach.

Another alternative involves the use of computer patterns and the transparent printouts of their correlated forms to create new designs that combine both images through the use of layering. Initially you will simply be placing the transparencies over the patterns to create the same relationships that you were seeing within the raster based program. The tangible separation of the layers, however, will allow you to integrate additional media to both enrich the surface and reinterpret the emphasis of the image. Transparency becomes an integral part of this project, altering the color, space, and clarity of the image. The same formal and conceptual parameters apply to the problem.

DISCUSSION

This project affords the opportunity for intense media experimentation in the creation of a group of related works. The critique may include a discussion of how the function and ***content*** of any given design may be altered by the dominance of one element over another and the ways in which altering the ***context*** of any given form can change its content.

NATIONAL EXPRESSION

No person is totally isolated. Even an inmate consigned to solitary confinement receives food, water, and shelter and is guarded in rotation by other human beings. We are social beings with a craving for acceptance by our own peers. We have sexual drives that attract us toward or repel us away from other individuals. We desire to feel safe in our environment when in contact with other people. We desire to express our opinions and/or dominate or follow others. These considerations, among many others, give rise to the social orders we call government. The most primitive tribal groups exhibit the same need for social structure as found in any modern European "technocracy."

As history develops within a tribal or political social order, a set of defining ***myths*** and ***symbols*** emerges to identify the common experience of the members. These symbols decorate flags, pennants, shields, and banners for identification purposes. As technological sophistication increases, coinage, paper money, and postage stamps also enter the common cultural experience.

The kind of design that is acceptable and usable for a flag differs from that of currency and stamps. Flags generally are designed to be seen and recognized from some distance. (See Flag Figures 7.16–7.21 in the section of color illustrations.) Therefore bright colors and simple distinctive geometric shapes are standard. The intimate viewing distance for money and stamps usually dictates an emphasis on sharply focused detail. Careful consideration of the placement and legibility of type and numbers that don't overpower the pictorial images and associated decorative boundary frames is also important.

Money and, to some degree, postage stamps share another common historical design constraint that is far more important than their diminutive size. They have "cash value" and therefore have to be designed to discourage counterfeiting. Coins have the longest history in this regard. Gold, silver, and copper are relatively soft and easily marked by hammering with a hard iron stamp to indicate the value of a specific piece of precious metal. Over the years this method developed into the tradition of fine low-relief sculpture that adorns our present coinage. Careful design of the edges of the precious metal coin is critical to maintaining its value. These coins not only had to discourage counterfeiting but also deliberate shaving and filing of the edges. You can still see this tradition continued on today's coins even though they no longer contain enough precious metal to be worth the effort of a thief. Check the edges of the United States quarter or Canadian nickel.

The threat of counterfeiting paper money is even greater than that of coinage. Consequently paper money has a history of highly complex design executed on specially made,

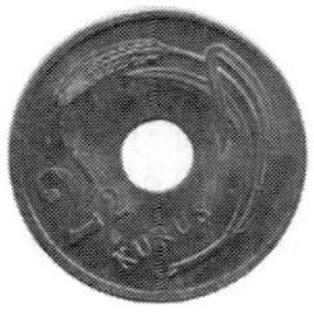

Figure 7.22

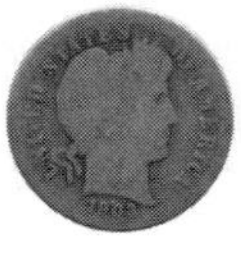

Figure 7.23

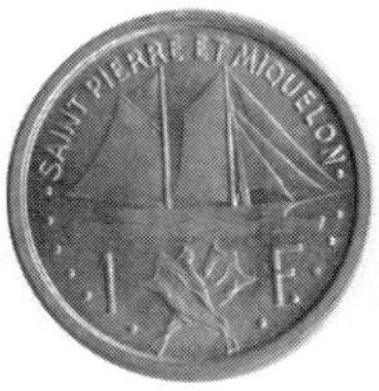

Figure 7.24

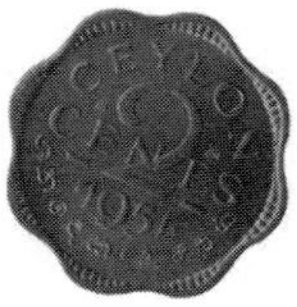

Figure 7.25

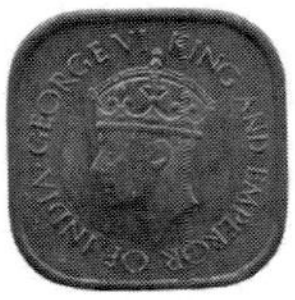

Figure 7.26

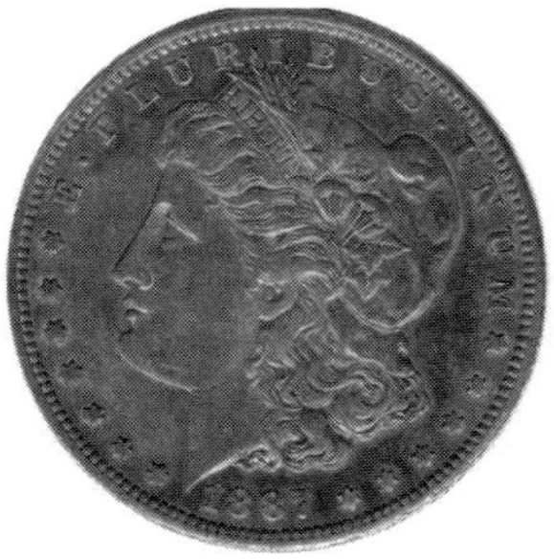

Figure 7.27

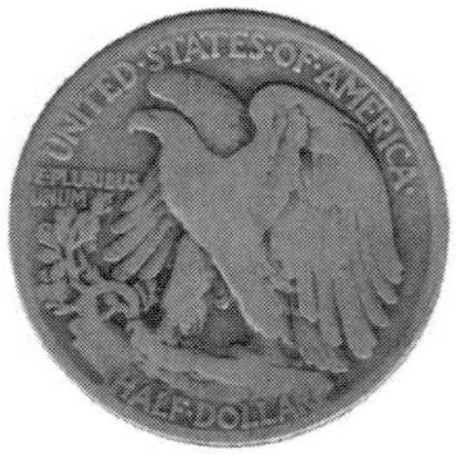

Figure 7.28

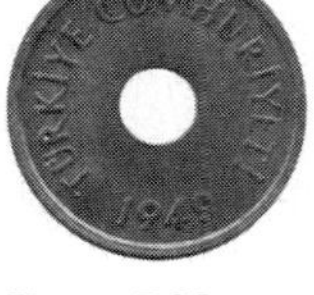

Figure 7.29

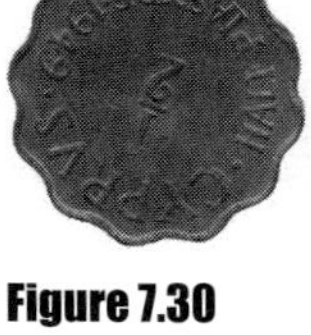

Figure 7.30

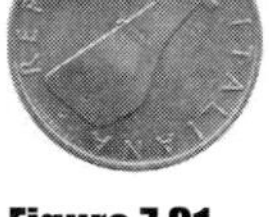

Figure 7.31

tough watermarked papers. With the advances in digital technology it is now no longer possible to just use intricate engraved designs and watermarks to foil counterfeiting. Other invisible coding is embedded in the special paper that our currency is printed on to verify the value of the paper currency in circulation. (See paper money Figures 7.32–7.35).

Today, postage stamps are less tied to the political life of nations and more directed at raising money. Many third-world countries have beautiful stamps designed and printed in the United States, Europe, Japan or in other developed countries. Most of these sheets of stamps are sold to collectors to raise funds to help support their respective economies. The proliferation of exotic stamps is used by the United States postal system for much the same purpose. (See postage stamp Figures 7.36–7.42).

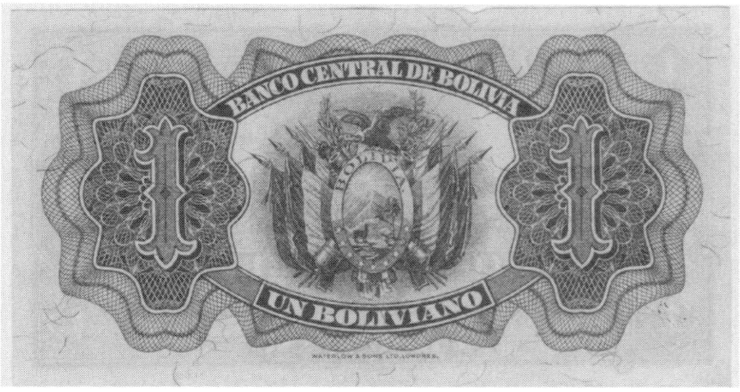

Figure 7.32

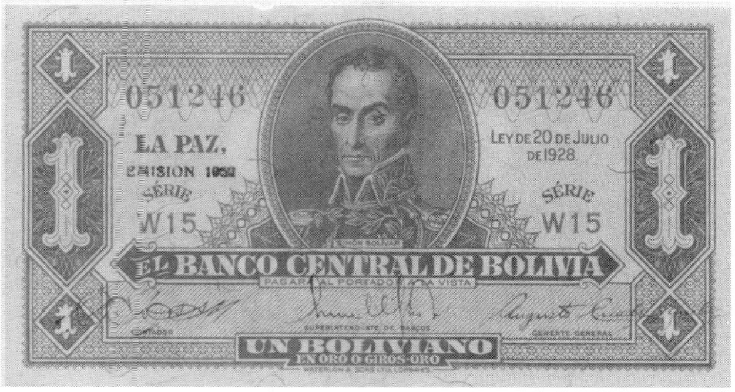

Figure 7.33

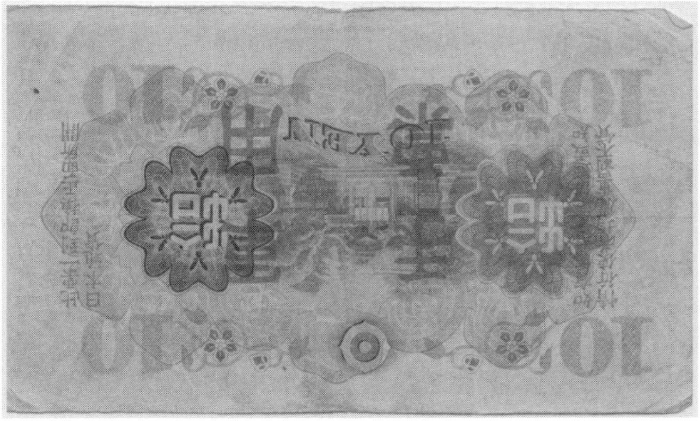

Figure 7.34

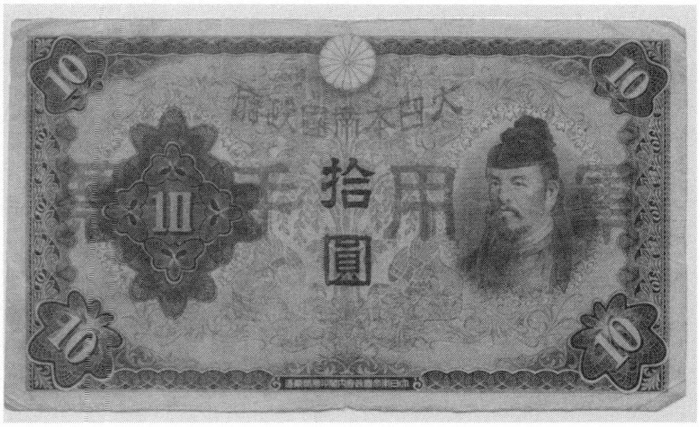

Figure 7.35

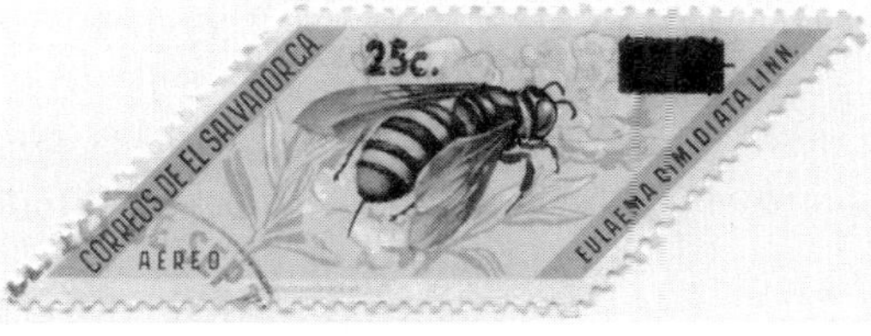

Figure 7.36

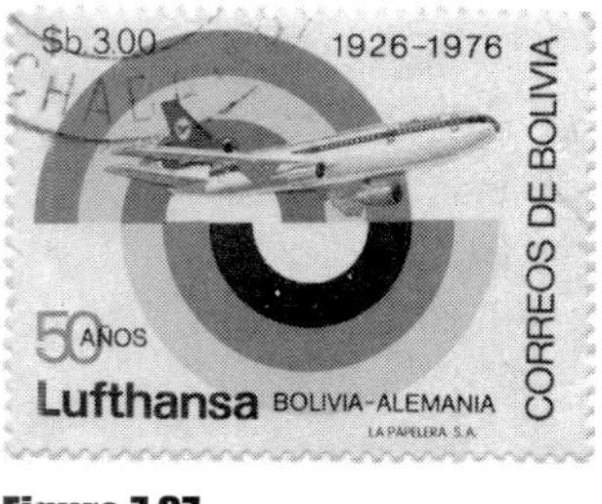

Figure 7.37

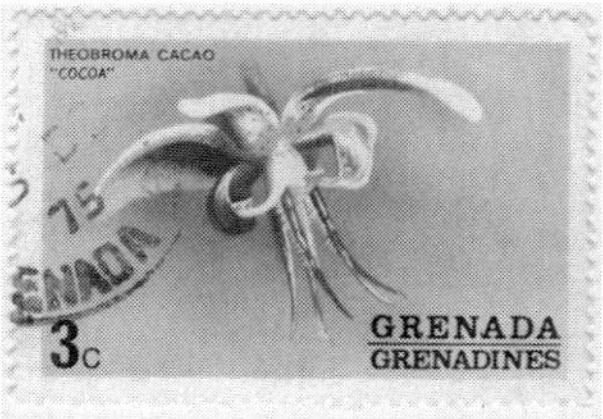

Figure 7.38

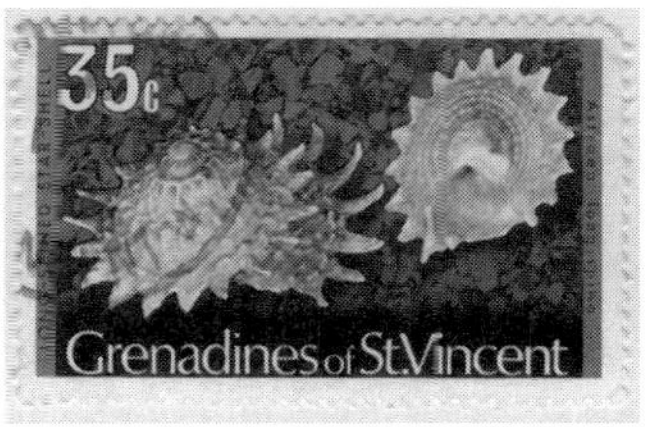

Figure 7.39

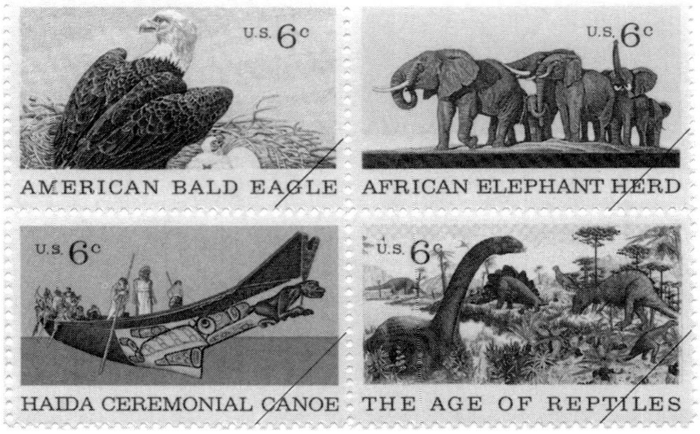

Figure 7.40

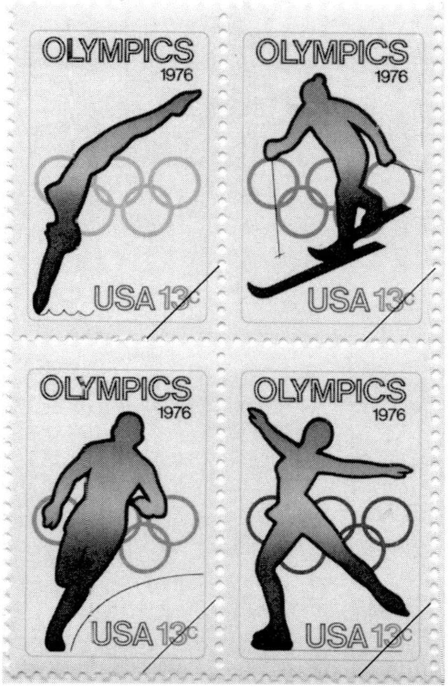

Figure 7.41

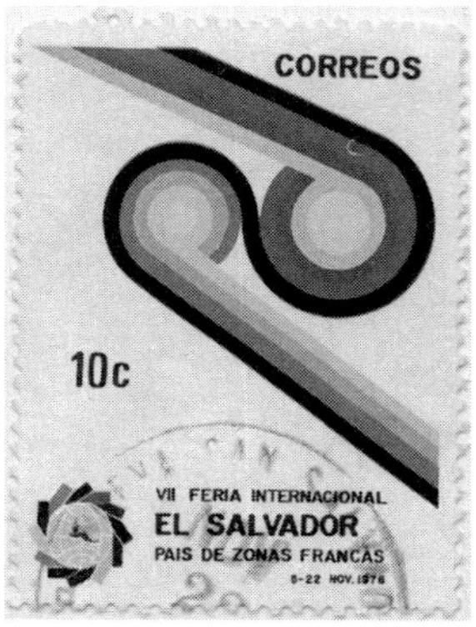

Figure 7.42

OBJECTIVES

This project focuses on designing a set of dissimilar serial objects (flag, currency, and stamp) in relationship to cultural phenomenon. (See example Figures 7.44–7.46 in the color illustration section.)

MATERIALS

Electronic: White illustration board; a raster program such as Adobe Photoshop and/or a vector program such as Adobe Illustrator; color printer; ruler; utility knife; rubber cement

Traditional: White illustration board; paint; brushes; color pencils; ink; art paper; magazine photos; ruler; utility knife; rubber cement

PROCEDURE

Research a real country, investigating its history, geography, and religions. Look for its visual symbols and verbal slogans as they relate to a sense of national identity throughout its history. In the United States, for example, our heritage has spawned stars, the numeral 13, the eagle, and a religious motto as well as our national patriots and famous architectural monuments. Using this information as an example, design a fictional country or place and assign a set of "historical" attributes and "political personnel." Make a series of national or political elements that go with this invented country. The objects that you will design for this country are as follows:

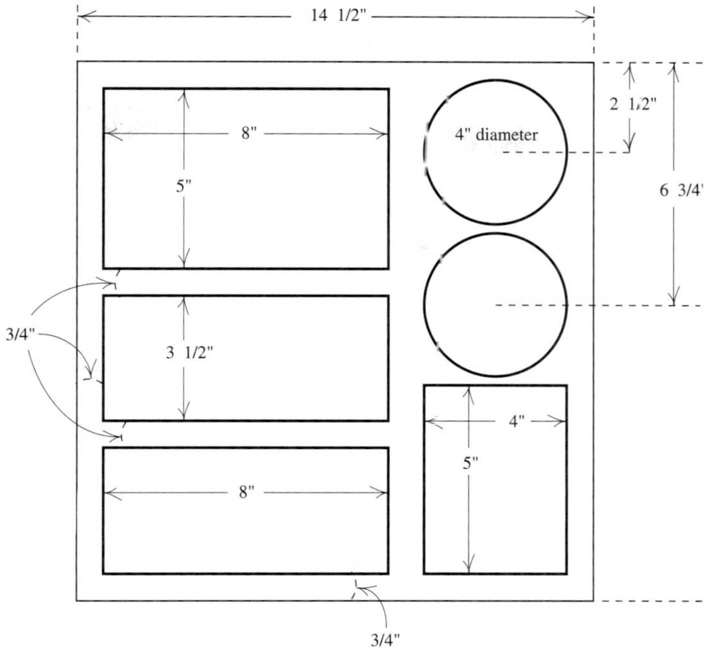

Figure 7.43

Flag: 5″ by 8″ in color with no lettering or minimal lettering if necessary.

Paper currency: 8″ by 3-1/2″ in color, designing both front and back. One side must include at least one portrait of an important person from the country's history.

Coin currency: 4″ diameter in metallic colors such as gold and silver or use shades gray. Show both obverse (front) and reverse (back) sides, with one side having at least one portrait of a person from the country.

Postage stamp: 5″ by 4″ in color designed to include the perforated edges. Use any subject from the country.

Electronic Design these individual formats on the computer using any sophisticated raster or vector program or combination of the two. Assemble as indicated in the diagram (Figure 7.43) on a single, large computer page and print out on a large glossy sheet. If you are working with a small printer, do the individual parts on separate pages and piece them together on the illustration board with rubber cement.

Traditional Work directly on the 15″ by 14-1/2″ piece of illustration board in mixed media, perhaps working with different media in different formats. Colored pencil, acrylic paint, tempera paint, cut paper, magazine collage, and ink are all possible choices of media.

DISCUSSION

How well does the choice of decorative effects, colors, symbols, monuments, and "patriot" portraits relay a sense of cultural reality? What constitutes the difference between display pennant and flag design? How are seals different in design from coins? What problems are encountered designing paper money versus postage stamps?

ALTERNATIVES

Develop an imaginary history of rivalry between two tribal societies. Design symbols, crests, and battle flags for these opposing tribes. Consider designing symbols of identity for a distant future time that amalgamates several current cultures on the world stage today.

PAST-TIME CHRONICLING HISTORY THROUGH SEQUENCE AND NARRATIVE

Historical events have long formed the subject materiel for designers and illustrators. Engaging subject matter or past political commentary has motivated artists to create imagery that draws on their connections to people or events in the past. In this assignment the creation of a series of images that are related in subject as well as technique will tie the works together. By establishing a ***narrative*** through related imagery, or creating a carefully orchestrated group of images, an aspect of the story can be told and allow for a more comprehensive understanding of the topic at hand.

OBJECTIVES

In this assignment students will become familiar with visual strategies that can be used to tie separate images together and present them as one "voice." They will be introduced to the concept of a time-based narrative, and will establish a cohesive stylistic strategy that works in concert with the thematic intent of the imagery.

MATERIALS

Electronic: Computer; graphics program such as Adobe Photoshop; scanner; printer paper; sketchbook; research materials; storage disk; photos, artwork, and other materials to scan

Traditional: Paint; pencils; drawing paper; illustration board; pastels; charcoal, and other appropriate media

PROCEDURE

In this project students will create a series of three images that use a historic event, historical figure, or an issue of historical significance as the ***subject matter.*** The series of images must be related not only in subject, but also in the way the images are treated. It will be obvious from the ***style*** that the images are done in, that they are part of a related group. The handling of different techniques and effects should enhance the imagery and be thoughtfully considered in relationship to the overall visual presentation (Figure 7.47).

Electronic In your sketchbook, develop your idea through rough sketches that convey the way you would like to present the three images. Try to represent the purpose of each image. Create a strong grouping of three images that hold together and convey information about your subject (i.e., one image of a civil war soldier in uniform; a second image of the battlefield; a third image of medals of honor in a memorial to the soldier). Try out a number of ideas and record them in your sketchbook.

Collect information about your topic. Assorted visuals from books and magazines can be used as long as they are considerably changed from their originals in your final work. Your own drawings, prints, and paintings or photographs can be used, or you might want to present a collage of found images. Importing images that you have created in paint programs is another possibility. Researching your subject is critical. You must be able to convey clear and accurate information on your topic. Begin to establish the style you want to use for all three. Scan all visuals and bring them into your program to create the final image (Figure 7.48, color insert).

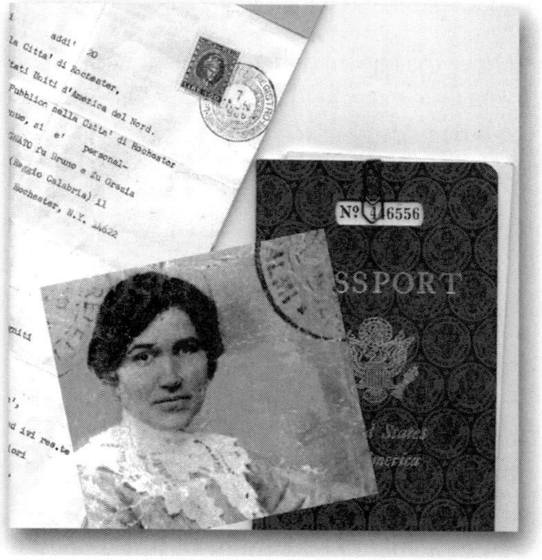

Figure 7.47

Consider:

The dominant color or tonal qualities in the images (would a monochromatic color scheme work for the images? why?)

The continuity of the "style" depicted in all three works (i.e.1960s color and/or style effects or images that relate to that period in history).

Edges or borders—how might they be treated to create a specific quality (i.e. vignettes or faded out edges) (Figure 7.49, color insert).

Utilize a graphics program that has **Actions,** or a similar function, to automate the commands that can be used on all images. A command such as **Actions** allows you to apply the same series of commands you have chosen to create one image, to other images of your choosing. After you create one image and have the commands saved as Actions you should be able to apply those commands to other images that you create so that they will have the same look or treatment. Try to keep the visual information that you are using (such as scanned imagery or downloaded imagery) consistent in its file type, resolution, and size, and so on.) Think about the visual organization of the image . . . should one element be dominant? . . . are you creating a montage or a realistic depiction of space?

Print out the three images on paper of your choosing. Decide if you want glossy paper or paper that has a more matte quality. If you can print on rag paper or good-quality art paper, try experimenting with the texture and color of the paper. Trim and mount images to illustration board or window-mat them if desired.

Traditional Use selected art materials to create the sequence of three images. Follow the conceptual guidelines of the electronic version but allow the handling of the materials, and aesthetic decisions such as color palette and style to combine with the imagery to tie the images together.

DISCUSSION

How has technique tied the images together? Has the technique been used effectively? Can your viewer learn something from the group of images? Has a narrative been established in any way, or do the three images combine to create a statement. Do stylistic devices come into play as a way to unite images?

PLAYING WITH THE PARADIGM: A COMMUNITY-BASED COLLABORATIVE

In the course of studying ***elements*** and ***principles,*** methods of organization and the manifestations of ***space*** and ***time*** relevant to two-dimensional design, one of the most critical aspects of art making in general is often omitted. This concept is the one that involves who you are and what you are becoming, which is an artist. Society's view of an artist is often that of an isolated person, sometimes thought of as a hero, creating art that involves a self-expression that is often separated from a social conscience. This paradigm or model, though not intrinsic to art making throughout history, is nonetheless one that prevails in our culture today. (Figure 7.50)

Our views of what art is and how it functions are continually changing and expanding. Social and cultural transitions and the interface of the Internet transform and expand our ways of seeing, defining, and realizing visual form. The growth of digital technology

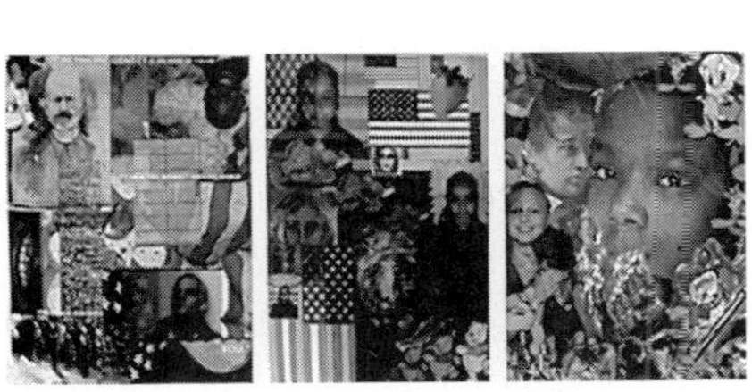

Figure 7.50

has not only affected how we manipulate imagery, but also has altered the conceptual and visual base for the creation of form. The role of the artist in society has evolved along with these changes. As time progresses, many groups of artists are reassessing their roles within society and the basis for the generation of their work. Cultural and social transitions have generated a desire to create a direct dialogue with the community from which these changes emanate. This community-based model of an artist examines his or her role in relationship to self and community. This is the connective paradigm, and involves the exploration by an artist of the relationship of his or her work to social issues and the community in general. Students are at the center of this approach, acting as both learners and mentors within the process. The locus of creativity moves from the individual to a dialogic, collaborative, interactive, and interdependent center. The connective aesthetic addresses social, psychological, political, aesthetic, and ethical issues that lie at the center of the interactive process. This project will utilize this paradigm and involve an interface between the personal cultural expectations of both you the artist and other members of your larger community.

OBJECTIVES

This project involves the creation of a digital design in collaboration with a person in your community. It involves the creation of images that will be digitally produced, conceptually linked, and eventually unified within a larger format. The goal is to explore the implications of an issue through personal history, personal interpretation, and an exploration of the impact of the issue within the community in which you now live.

This project will investigate and explore the concept of identity as it has been molded and defined by family history, commonality of experience within the larger community, and personal viewpoint. You will explore the concept of identity through the writings and thoughts of another member of your community, striving to define a sense of self and your own personal perspective and relationship to these ideas.

MATERIALS

Electronic: Source book/sketchbook/notebook; a digital camera; an application or card/disc drive to transfer the images to a computer; a raster-based drawing program such as Adobe Photoshop; color printer; mounting board; rubber cement; pen or utility knife; laminating film; transparent packing tape

Traditional: Source book/sketchbook/notebook; a camera; drawing paper; drawing supplies such as pencil; colored pencil; crayons; watercolor paints and pastels; mounting board; rubber cement; pen or utility knife; laminating film; transparent packing tape

PROCEDURE

Once a connection with a member of the community has been established, the project may be directly linked to the curriculum/interests/events with which that particular person or group is working. Identity is but one of the subjects that may be dealt with. Community participants may not need to participate initially on a visual level; their responses may be purely verbal. Collaborators can create a series of stories that chronicle important events in each of their lives. These stories may be shared and critiqued with others within their institutions or residences, revealing how family history has contributed to each person's identity, the commonality of experience that is shared by the community, how the individual's personality affects viewpoint, and how these layers come together in a continuing story. Your role in this project will be multi-faceted. You will be acting as an archeologist of sorts, recovering, studying, and organizing some of the emotional and physical artifacts of an individual's life. In addition, you will be making connections in terms of a commonality of experience by finding similar or related events in your own life, making the dialogue tangible within the work that you are creating.

A Source Book Document any and all visual and/or verbal information that you are researching or generating. This may include notes, Xerox copies of text or images that you research, drawings, collage sketches, and an ongoing diary of observations relative to the project. This work must be turned in as a neat, unified book on pages of the same size that are bound (stapling is fine) together. Beginning with a preexisting sketchpad can be beneficial.

The Collaborative Design You will create a design that involves the merging of appropriated imagery, your own designs, text, and photographs. The form of this design will not be new: This is a ***collage*** that will involve the merging of divergent imagery within a digital image. What will be new is that you will be interviewing a partner about his/her perception of self, for example, how and why they have established a sense of identity, and then using this information within your own work. The conceptual and visual solution will be collaborative rather than individually generated.

The Research Using the Internet, research a contemporary model for the connective and community-based paradigm of artistic expression. Tim Rollins and KOS (Kids of Survival) is an example of an established group working within this paradigm. This information may be accessed through a number of search engines and may include a variety of sites. Include any personal/subjective, objective, and/or written response to this information within your source book. Read any literature or stories that are read and discussed by your community partner. Record any responses to these readings within your source book.

Generating the Basis for a Community Interface Read the stories created by the collaborators with which you are working. Using them as a reference, generate a list of questions that would help you to understand how other members of the community use personal history as a means of understanding. Consider what questions you will need to ask to clearly understand how another person creates a sense of self that is both conceptual and visual. In addition, you will be crossing generational divisions. Because your collaborator in the community may be different in both age and experience, your language and comprehension will be very different from theirs at this point, and you must take this into consideration when asking questions. If desired, work in groups to generate these questions. Write down your finished list in your sketchbook, leaving spaces for answers during your interview.

The Dialogue Visit with and interview your community partner. You will collect information in several ways, including the writing down of answers to your previously generated questions in your source book. Photograph the person with whom you are working. Have your partner create drawings related to the interview in your source book.

Because you are asking this person to expose themselves through the sharing of their writing and artwork, your interaction and the resulting dialogue may be enhanced by sharing some of your own work. Bring drawings or any other easily portable images to show your partner.

Explore your own responses to the interview. Brainstorm and write down some ideas regarding personal history and its relationship to identity in your source book. Using yourself as a reference, consider personal history, familial and cultural context, educational understanding, and individual point of view in relationship to the idea. Consider those elements, forms, and objects that would best communicate those ideas. Have a photograph taken of yourself so that your physical form can also be incorporated into the final image.

Electronic Create a digital collage that integrates your collaborative partner's image, their collaborative partner's writing and drawings, your own image and/or imagery related to personal history, and any and all images that will help you to formally, conceptually, and visually merge the forms. The concept that you will be utilizing to construct this project is one that was discussed earlier: Archaeology. The root of the word archeology is the Greek Arche, mean both "beginning" and "power." Utilize the formal and conceptual strategy of layering to dig below the surface and create meaning between the stories, the individuals, the families, and the community in which they interact and live.

The ***format*** size for this image will be dictated by the printers that you have available. Consider how ***line, shape, value, texture, color, compositional structure, movement, balance,*** and the use of ***scale*** (life size, larger than life size, smaller than life size) can best communicate your ideas. Symbolic forms may be utilized and the actual style of the image manipulated. As with all visual images, ***grouping principles*** and ***balance*** are key issues that will need to be considered in the unification of the image. This is a problem that involves the need to merge a diversity of visual images. ***Color*** and ***transparency*** will be key elements in the creation of ***unity.*** Any and all images or elements needed to successfully complete the design may be added at any point in the creative process (Figure 7.51(a) 7.51(b) 7.51(c) and 7.52, color insert). When you have completed your image, **Save** your image and **Print** it in color.

If time and funding allows, provide the opportunity to have one or more in-process critiques with collaborating partners. This allows each participant to contribute to the development of the work and assures that the visual meaning is truly collaborative. This process may be done in person or through email, by sending images as attachments and then discussing their impact in verbal form.

Traditional This project may be done as a collage project, merging images from a variety of sources and unifying them with repetition, media, and transparency. The same conceptual and formal parameters apply.

ALTERNATIVES

The concept of community can be interpreted in a vast number of ways. This project may be centered within a single classroom or within a single institution, focusing on the individuals that comprise the more immediate and intimate community. Commonalties of age, experience, and language will modify a variety of the approaches, but the ultimate goal of generating imagery that responds to issues of community through a collaborative process may be readily achieved.

PRESENTATION

The final format for this project can be any one of a number of options. Images may be arranged within a grid or "quilt" format or organized to move within a book. Decisions regarding the format might take into consideration the physical exhibition spaces available within the residences or workplaces of the collaborating partners. In almost all cases, laminating or dry mounting the images will assure greater longevity. All adult participants in this project should meet and decide on a final format size, including borders for all of the images. Mounting the images on lightweight bristol board before lamination gives a bit of desired rigidity to the lightweight computer prints. The space on the back of the images provides an opportunity and location to include originals or copies of the stories and drawings generated by the collaborators.

Regardless of the final format, all images must be laid out before being attached to each other and arranged to create a large, unified composition of related designs. Once the final arrangement is determined, individual designs may be connected to each other. For a quilt format, each design should be trimmed to include an extra lip of plastic around all four edges (make sure that it is the same size border for all participants). Holes are punched in these edges and the designs are connected utilizing small plastic cable connectors. Be aware that placement of each image within the overall grid will determine which sides require holes (images along edges do not need holes on the outside edges) and a template for punching holes will assure a unified arrangement. The final quilt can be hung from cable connector loops threaded through a simple wooden rod (Figure 7.53, color insert). For book formats, individual images can be connected with clear packing tape, applied to the front and back of the spaces between images.

RESOLUTION

Although the final format for this project will be singular, the component pieces will vary tremendously. Critique should include a discussion of the nature of the collaborative process and its impact on the process as well as the finished product. Discussion should also include the impact of representational imagery (especially portraits) on the acceptance and understanding of visual images to those not involved in the visual arts. Finally, thought should be given to the enthusiastic acceptance of visual art works, regardless of their forms, compositions, or internal relationships, that directly address the concerns of the community rather than the singular desires of the artistic creator.

CHAPTER 8

DYNAMIC INTERCHANGE: TRANSFORMATIONS

The ways in which we transform visual, verbal, and conceptual information enrich our daily lives. Transformation of information can be readily observed in the nuances of negotiation between political world leaders. Each opponent believes that his or her point of view is best or correct or logical. As time passes and events occur the issues and data start to look slightly different to the opponents and compromise becomes feasible. Viewpoints have been modified or transformed.

In the field of linguistics, language is viewed as a living cultural entity constantly transforming and morphing through time. The English language is a prime example of this continual morphing and addition of words. Sample the existing works of Chaucer and then compare that to Shakespeare and/or King James English and then contemplate the current American idiom and it becomes evident that radical transformation has happened through the centuries. Only dead or largely non-spoken languages such as Latin do not benefit by this transformation.

When an artist looks at a still life and contemplates making a painting of the arrangement he or she must transform the observed subjects into two dimensional shapes scaled up or down to fit on a piece of canvas. At all levels of "data transfer," transformations occur. As the artist draws or paints preliminary lines and shapes on the format, liberties may be taken with respect to the actual positions of the objects in the still life to achieve greater compositional affect. Some or all of the shapes may be abstracted. The very brushstrokes and paint texture can radically alter the subject. Often color is manipulated to further enhance the composition. All of these working decisions and interpretations cause transformations.

We transform all data that comes before us whether it is verbal or visual. Each of us has a viewpoint that is somewhat different from his or her peers. The facts are always open to interpretation. As we move through time and space we edit this information with a personal viewpoint, sifting data to fit our mold and re-project it out into the broader world. In Chapter 8 various means of developing and refining these transformational skills are showcased.

PHILOSOPHICAL STYLE

Style is the quality or manner of how you do something and how this quality appears during and after making a thing or event. Our genetic code and our environment make us each individually somewhat different, directing us toward a ***personal style.*** Style can be a conscious effort of laying "imitation" or "borrowed" personalities over the person's indigenous self. An actor or celebrity projecting an artificial or public persona that differs radically from his or her own self is an example of this. Artists in some branches of illustration rely on a chameleon-like style, borrowing to make their living. The most obvious example of this is in cartoon animation, where a team of artists work to realize one artist's styled cartoon character throughout a complex story line.

Various groups of people tend to project an overriding "ethnic" style that reflects the ancient roots of their culture. Oriental, Islamic, Greco-Roman, Egyptian, and Western European art are all easily distinguished from each other as ***cultural styles.***

Culture changes throughout time as new information and events affect groups of people. These cultural shifts affect everything from their method of creating things to their preference in how they should appear. This gives rise to historical styles within the broader cultural style. In Western European art the styles of Romanesque, Gothic, Renaissance, Baroque, and Impressionism are excellent examples of ***historical style.***

Another way of understanding style is to consider the philosophical base from which the art springs by analyzing the overall resulting visual effect of the art. Considering style in this way allows one to see common themes that cut through all cultures, time-periods, and individual artistic skill. Three main ***philosophical styles*** can be distinguished:

> ***Realism*** is the attempt to record what the artist and his or her companions believe to be an accurate representation of reality. The result may range from photographic to somewhat abstract, depending on cultural conventions and the artist's personal style. This style cuts through all cultures and historical periods and has a wide audience appreciation from culture to culture.
>
> ***Classical*** style concentrates on refined order. Placing things in rows or mathematical sequence is indicative. The human figure is measured to meet idealized proportions. Motion or its implication is measured and appears controlled. This style may involve taking structure apart and reassembling forms for visual analysis. Dictatorial societies and leaders often prefer it. Much of the art of the ancient world cultures has strong elements of classicism.
>
> ***Romantic*** style exhibits diminished intellectual order and rising emotive effects. The artwork appeals to us through our emotions rather than our intellectual abilities. This type of art attempts to engulf us directly into its story, plot, or tableau. The emotions run the gamut from sentimentality to horror or even terror. Ironically, a Victorian valentine and a horror movie are both considered romantic.

OBJECTIVES

The purpose of this project is the study of style from a philosophical point of view. Select a common subject or theme and express it in the three differing styles using abstraction of form, redefinition of subject, and/ or context manipulation.

MATERIALS

Electronic: A quality raster program such as Adobe Photoshop or vector program such as Adobe Illustrator; a quality ink jet printer; three pieces of illustration board; ruler; pencil; rubber cement; a utility knife

Traditional: Any media may be used. Use same assembly materials as for "electronic."

PROCEDURE: ELECTRONIC AND TRADITIONAL

Pick several contemporary subjects or topics that interest you. Gather information and visuals from library sources and/or the Internet. Think about how this material could be categorized stylistically. Decide which subject or topic has the most potential for style manipulation. Then design a series of three compositions about it that differentiate realism, romanticism, and classicism. Use the same size format for each composition. These compositions are not to be thought of as advertisements per se but rather compositions using a contemporary subject or topic to show it in three stylistic aspects. Do not use unnecessary verbiage. The concept should be evident by nonverbal clues. See (Figure 8.1 in the color illustration section and Figure 8.2).

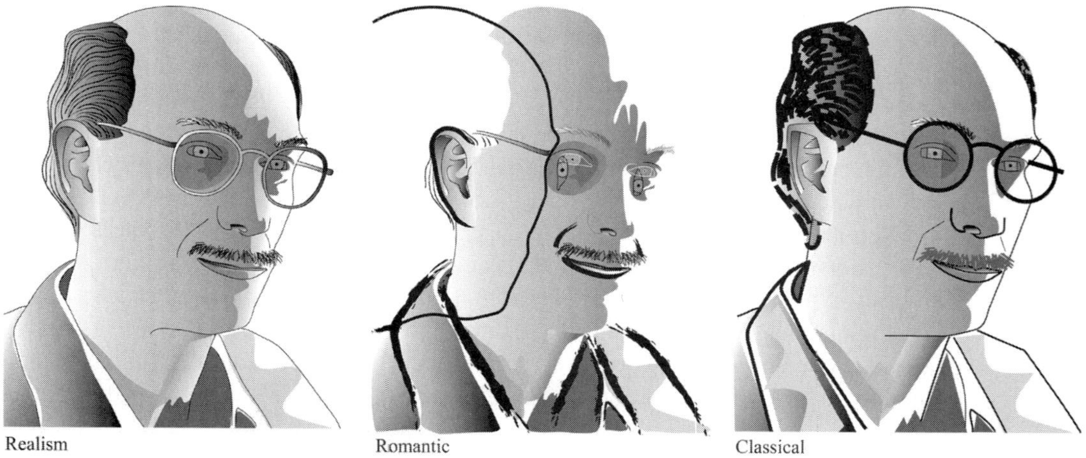

Realism   Romantic   Classical

Figure 8.2

DISCUSSION

How a topic or subject is presented affects the perception of the audience. Stylistic nuances are a powerful tool in the hands of an artist or designer who is aware of them. Consider the advantages and disadvantages in utilizing these three philosophical styles to influence your audience toward a positive or negative opinion. Which style is most often used in advertising?

How do the philosophical styles differ from historical styles? And when do they converge? How does your own personal style affect philosophical style? When is photography not realism?

ALTERED STILL LIFE

Still-life composition has been an important subject for artists throughout history. During the seventeenth century, the Dutch Masters produced exquisite still-life paintings. These opulent pictures contained lavish tableau arrangements of flowers, fruits, material treasures, and artifacts. The objects seem to be bathed in light that reveals texture, volume, and space within the picture plane.

Around 1910, artists such as Picasso and Braque (influenced by Cezanne's Post-Impressionist paintings) created paintings that fragmented and reconstructed still-life images, utilizing numerous perspective views, in which "disorder created order." Through this they invented Analytical Cubism. Soon after this Picasso and Braque explored the addition of found textured materials to their paintings and Synthetic Cubism emerged. During this period, Analytical and Synthetic Cubism influenced many artists. These artists were all participants in this new vision of "translating the world in many different perspectives." Paintings with multiple views and altered perspective and overlapping fragmented and distorted shapes epitomize the art of this period.

Today, numerous artists and photographers working with still life are concerned with formal issues of composition as well as portraying the expressive nature of the subject matter. Artists have investigated altering the still life by changing context, use of layering, superimposition, and digital manipulation.

OBJECTIVES

This project involves the study of four still-life variations: representational, analytic, synthetic, and altered still life. Students will create four related designs of a still life: a realistic, an analytic, a synthetic, and an altered still life (See color insert Figure 8.3). The subject matter, still-life setup, and still-life compositions will be inspired by cubist ideas of using everyday objects, fractured multi-view space, inclined planes, movement, found materials and textures, and selected use of color and value.

MATERIALS

Electronic: Digital camera; a raster-based program such as Adobe Photoshop; everyday still-life objects; found materials and textures; glass; mirrors; gels; screens; mounting boards; adhesive

Traditional: Everyday still-life objects; paint; found materials and textures; illustration boards; brushes; adhesive

PROCEDURE

Electronic

Creating a Representational Still Life

To create a representational still-life composition, photograph your still-life objects with a digital camera. Arrange individual objects on an inclined plane and light each subject with some highlight and shadow. Shoot several views of each of the objects along the same axis. Consider the lighting and angle of view. Download your images in a raster-based program such as Photoshop. Go to **Image** and scroll down to **Adjust** and then **posterize** your compositions.

Creating an Analytic Still Life

For an analytic cubist composition, show multiple views of the still-life object at the same time in the composition. Simplify and fragment your subject into simple geometric shapes. Use overlapping shapes and some transparency.

Take your **Posterized** representational images and fragment them. You can cut and paste sections of your still life showing multi-views. Combine portions of your imagery from the several views and angles. Create layers of superimposed shapes using such tools as the **Magic Wand** and **Pen Tool** to select portions of the individual objects. Use the **Transform** menu and **Edit** menu **(Copy** and **Paste** commands) to create overlaps and superimposition. Use the **Opacity** option in the **Layers** palette to create shallow depth.

Creating a Synthetic Still Life

For the synthetic cubist collage scan textures, patterns, and found materials. Using these materials and the fragmented simplified shapes of your subject matter, compose an electronic collage with shallow space.

Combine flattened simplified posterized views of your subject with your scanned textures and found materials. Overlap, transparency, and linear superimposition can be achieved using the **Layer** palette and the **Edit** menu. The **Quick Mask Tool, Blur Tool,** and **Transform** menu can be used as well to select portions, fragment shapes, and dissolve edges.

Creating an Altered Still Life

In addition to working with the objects of your original still life, you must add elements that alter the 3D perspective of your image. Different types of glass, screen, paper, mirrors, and translucent materials might be used when photographing your subject. By using found materials including translucent fabric, screen, etc. you may physically alter your images and increase texture variation.

Shoot more pictures of your still life this time, using additional objects such as mirrors, screening, translucent materials, and gels, to alter your still life. Download these new images and use superimposition, layering, shifting space, multiple imagery, and digital manipulation to transform your composition. Use the edit functions and **Layer** adjustments and the **Tool** menu to transform and alter the 3D perspective of your still life. You may also alter sharp to soft focus to show shifting depth as well as vary scale.

Mount the following four images for presentation: Representational Still-Life composition, Cubist Analytical Composition with multiple perspectives, Synthetic Cubist Collage with found materials, and a new Altered Still Life.

Traditional Using the same formal and conceptual parameters of the electronic procedure, use paint and found materials to create several versions of the still life (Figure 8.4).

ALTERNATIVES AND VARIATIONS

You are to add additional elements to your still life that will support a compound composition. This composition should provide enough information to create a ***triptych*** or a ***quadrant*** composition (see color insert Figure 8.5). Students will create numerous panels to produce one completed composition. The final image can take on a traditional shape such as horizontal and vertical or you may go nontraditional and explore other formats such as diagonal or a tondo. Don't lose the integrity of the still life, though. Remember in ***gestalt***: the whole is greater than the sum of its parts.

Create a number of variations. The size of each panel is no less than 8″ × 8″. Mount each panel on a board and arrange the panels in a format that is in keeping with the content, expression, and formal qualities of your individual panels (Figure 8.6). Remember to keep the overall imagery unified.

DISCUSSION

How do the first three compositions—representational, analytic, and synthetic—reflect the spirit of cubism? (reference Figure 8.4) Do all three compositions work as three variations on a theme? What are the unifying elements and principles within the three variations? In the final triptych or quadrant composition, how does gestalt apply to the overall composition? How do these panels reflect a more contemporary context?

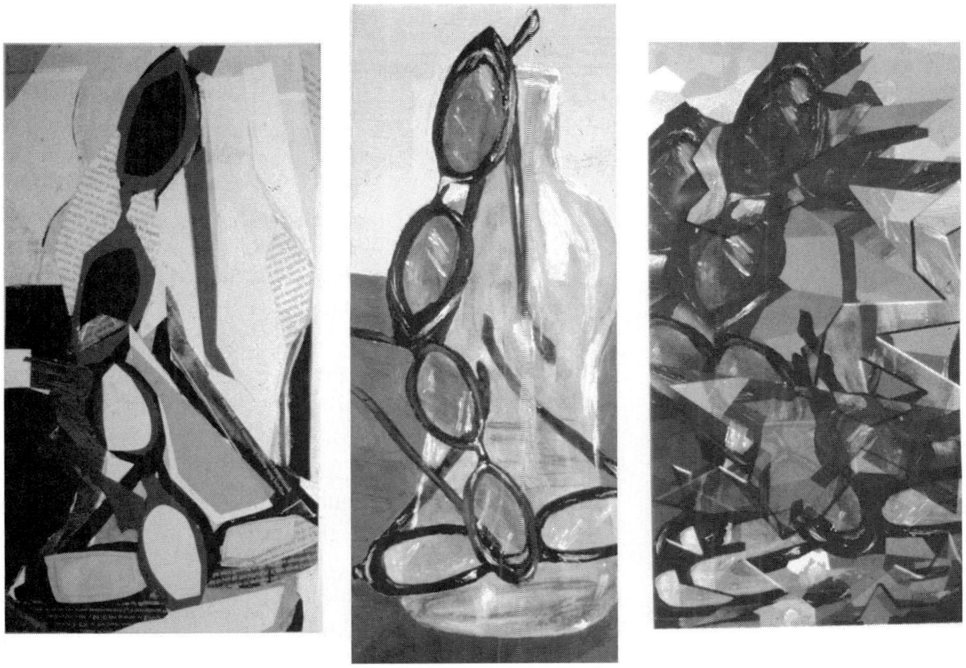

Figure 8.4 *Image by Brandi Boyce*

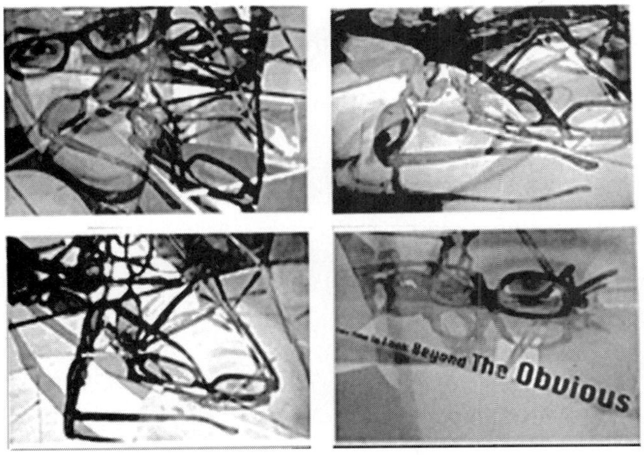

Figure 8.6 *Image by Brandi Boyce*

LETTER PROGRESSIONS

We experience our lives in a three-dimensional space. It is natural for us to refer to the width and height of an object and also to think about how thick or deep it is. In modern physics it has been noted that our universe probably has several more dimensions that are tightly wrapped into atomic structure. This may account for the apparent illogic at the sub-particle level and the mysterious dark matter that astronomers have long been looking for to support or disprove various theories of cosmology.

In our everyday existence, we experience another dimension that we do not usually think of as a dimension—time. It is common to all that we see and whatever happens. In fact the word "happen" implies the passage of time. Events progress through time and space.

Music and film are two art forms that deal extensively with time/sequence-related creative issues. The traditional visual arts (painting, drawing, and sculpture) often work through progressive ***sequence*** as well. The narrative history painting of the 19th-century academicians or current cartoon strips of the Sunday paper come to mind first. Interesting complex sculpture tableaus on the Civil War battlefields of the United States reflect various idealized heroic narratives.

OBJECTIVES

Working with nine formats, you will develop your sensitivity to the visual concept of progressive sequence. This project also provides for your investigation of letterforms as a nonverbal element in the picture plane.

MATERIALS

Electronic: A computer with a vector-based drawing program such as Adobe Illustrator; a high-quality printer; illustration board; a ruler; utility knife; rubber cement

Traditional: Quality black-and-white art paper; pencil; erasers; black ink; illustration board; a ruler; utility knife; rubber cement

PROCEDURE

Design an interesting sequence of nine 6″ squares. Use only letters from your name. None of the squares should be verbally readable. The letterforms are to be thought of as shapes only. Distort and/or enlarge letters progressively. Rotating the letters will give many possibilities. Consider using the letters as stacking blocks. Use a minimum of three letters in each square of the sequence. Small white letters work well over top of large black letters.

Electronic Open your vector-based program such as Adobe Illustrator. Set the **Units and Rulers** to inches. Set up the page with **Rulers** and **Grid** and **Snap To Grid.** To establish the proper format you first need to set your **Stroke Color** as black and the **Fill** color as none. Also select a relatively thin **Stroke Weight.** Now, select the **Rectangle Tool** and draw an exact 6-inch square. After drawing the square turn off the **Snap To Grid** and reset the **Fill** to black.

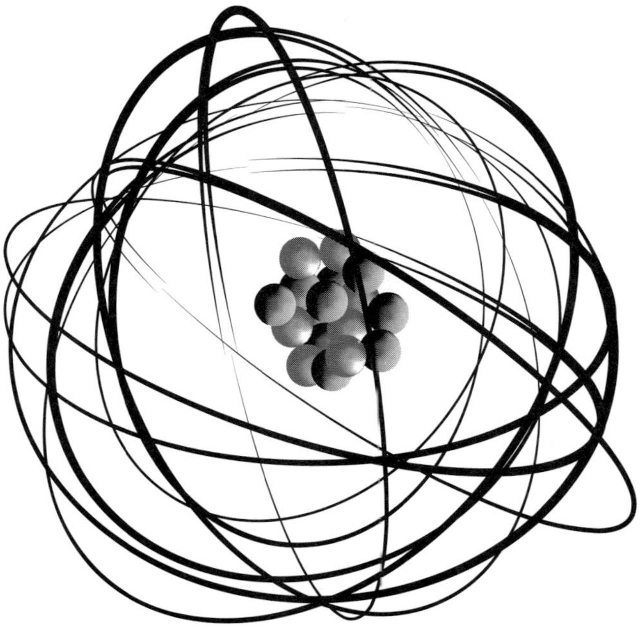

Figure 8.7 Early 20th-Century Model of an Atom

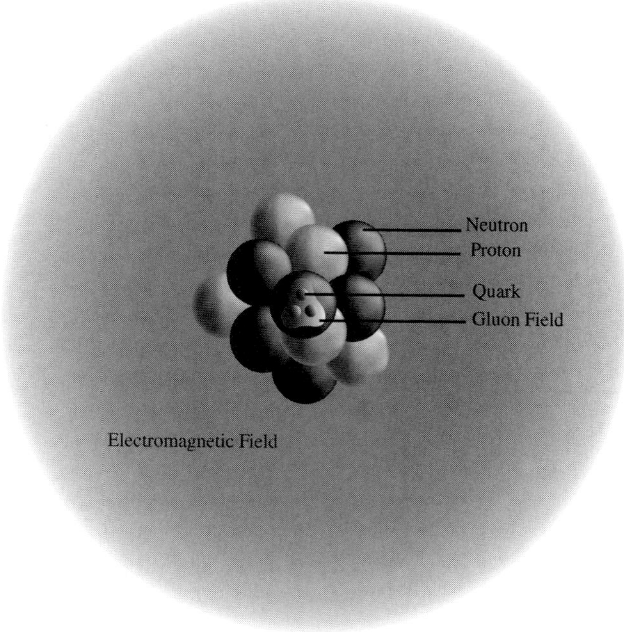

Figure 8.8 Late 20th-Century Model of an Atom

Begin investigation of the text or **Type Tool** and its associated menus. Start by selecting one of the **Fonts** from the menu. Open up the **Font Size** menu and select the largest type size on the list or select "other" and assign a large size such as 300 or 500 point. Click on the **Type Tool** in the **Tool** palette. The cursor arrow turns into an **I-Beam** or insertion bar. Position this somewhere inside your 6-in. square format and click. Type only one letter! Now, go to the tool palette and click on the **Selection Tool** arrow. Click on the typed letter. Experiment with this selection arrow for moving the letter around in the format. Find the **Transformation** menu and experiment with **Scale, Rotate, Sheer,** and **Reflect** options in the program.

Push the letter partly off of the format. To erase the part hanging off, create a white rectangle with the **Rectangle Tool** in the tool palette. Set the line or **Stroke Fill** as white and the **Fill** as white. Simply start to draw the box at the format edge and cover up the portion of the letter extending beyond the format.

Consider using gradient-filled background shapes if your program has such a feature. A gradient many also be used on the type letters if you convert them to objects so that they are no longer recognized by the program simply as type. In Adobe Illustrator this is done by selecting the letter and then going to the **Type** menu and down to **Create Outlines.** If you want to use the text tool's shape and path following features you must first use the **Pencil** or **Pen** or **Shape Tool** to create a **Path.**

When you have completed the design with three more letters, number this sequence square outside of the format in the upper lefthand corner so that the printer will not cut it off. Now **Save** your design.

Before proceeding to the next step of the sequence you need to **select all** and then **Copy.** Make sure you **Copy** after selecting.

Now, set up a **New** page like the first one. Then go to **Edit** and **Paste.** Make alterations to the pasted artwork on this new page to build the second step in the progression. The first change should be the sequence number that you typed outside the format—simply **Select** it with the **Type Tool** and change it.

Please note: To move and change letters that are stacked on top of each other go to the **Object** menu and down to **Arrange,** where you will find the **Bring To Front** and **Send To Back** commands. With multiple layers you might have to select 5 or 6 things and send them to the back before you can finally select the letter that you wish to manipulate.

If you prefer to print all of the designs on a single sheet of paper, set your print size as large as your printer will allow and then **Paste** each of the 9 squares on this new page. **Scale** each of them so that they all fit in the printing area, forming an even square. You may have to **Select All** and change all of the **Stroke** lines to minimum size if the outlines of letters fatten too much. The finished 6-inch squares can also be printed individually and mounted with rubber cement using the dry into dry method on a 20-inch square piece of single-weight illustration board, either white or black. Carefully cut the squares out and mark the board with three-quarter inch borders at the edge and a quarter inch between all the squares. See Figure 8.10.

Traditional Lay out the individual squares in pencil. Develop all distortions, rotations, and spacing manipulations in light pencil line. Work with cut paper and/ or ink to finish the artwork. You can work directly on the illustration board or on quality 6″ white paper squares that are then rubber cemented to the illustration board as laid out in Figure 8.10.

DISCUSSION

Reading skills are very important for most people in the world and particularly for those of us in Western culture. Our public and private schools are judged on how well their students read and write. Ironically, little thought is given to the visual meaning and form of letter characters used to build this mental phenomena that we call reading and writing. Each letter is a highly abstracted picture borrowed from some past culture that developed it. These pictures all had a specific descriptive meaning. Gradually they became subverted to stand for phonetic sound having no relationship whatever to their original pictures. In this project you have appropriated these symbols and used them out of their verbal context. Does this detract from the letterforms or does it enhance them as shapes? Would someone not knowing the context of this project comprehend the project outcome?

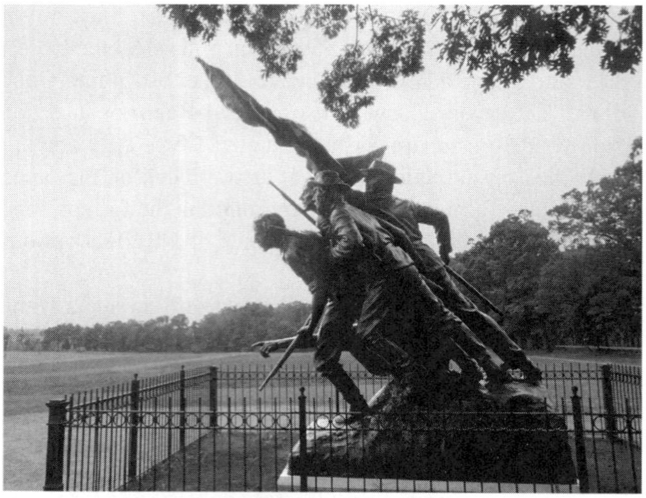

Figure 8.9 Gettysburg Battlefield Park, Pennsylvania, North Carolina Monument, Seminary Ridge by Gutzon Borglum, Dedicated 1929.

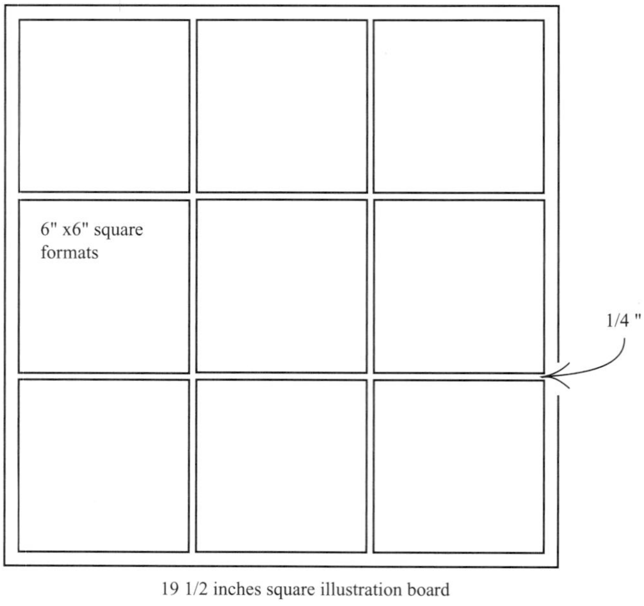

Figure 8.10

A sequence can be done with figurative elements or geometric shapes with or without the computer. How would that affect the end look and meaning of the art? Would using more than nine steps in your sequence be better? How about using differing format shapes through the sequence? Which sequences done for this assignment are most easily understood as sequential and why? What characterizes the art that is difficult to see sequentially?

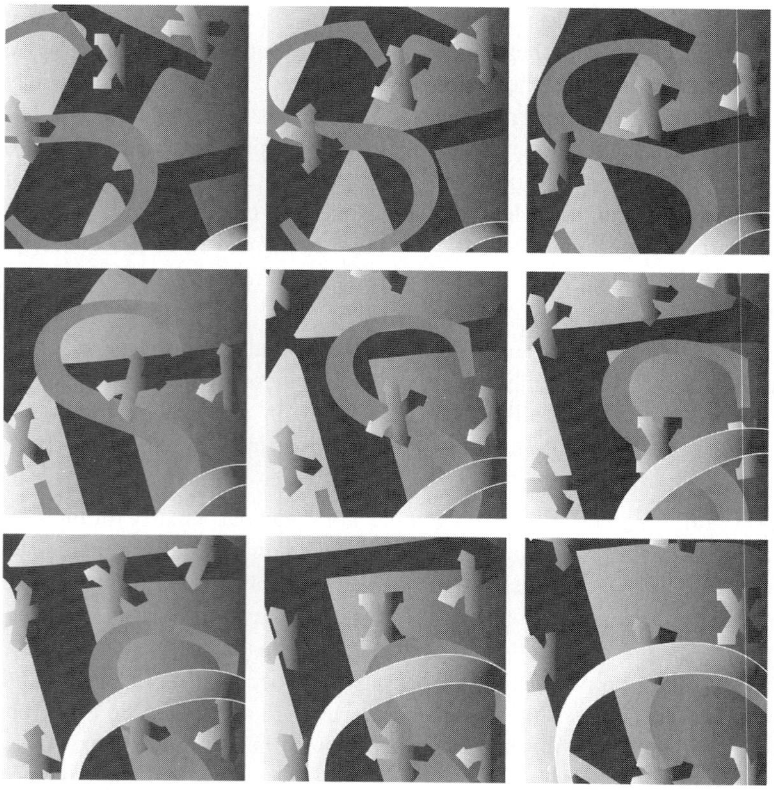

Figure 8.11

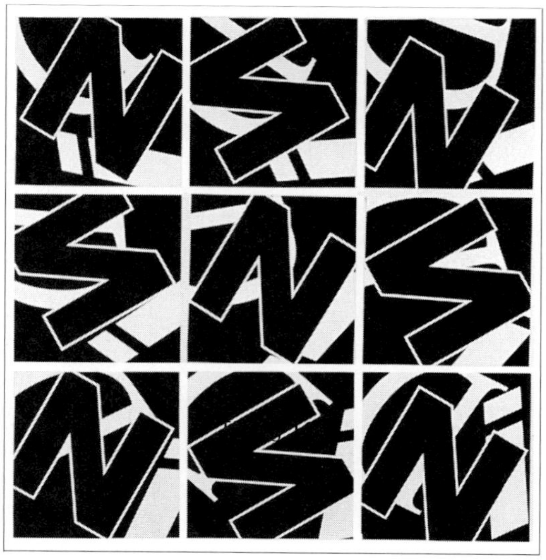

Figure 8.12 *Image by Danielle Tourgee*

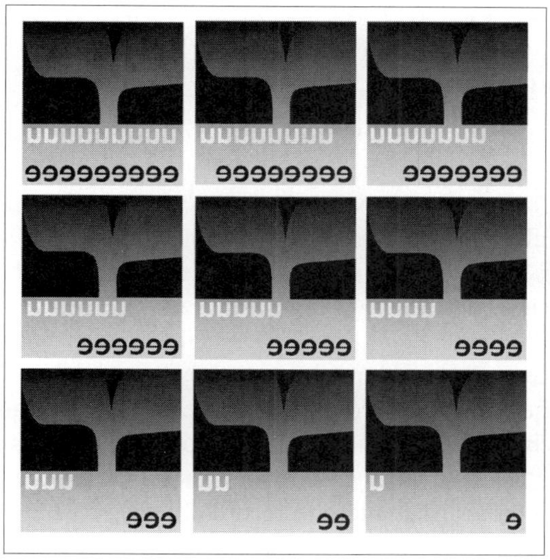

Figure 8.13 *Image by Kenneth Hocker*

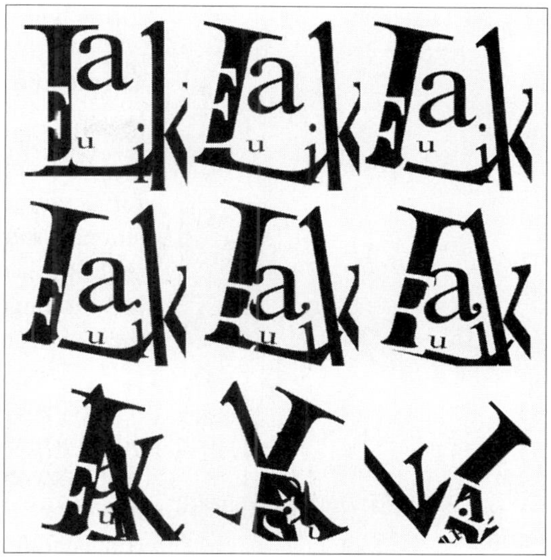

Figure 8.14 *Image by Lauren Ceike*

SEQUENCES: EXPERIMENTING WITH TIME, CHANGE AND MOTION

Our experiences with events in the world are vast and multidimensional. We vicariously experience religious warfare and natural disasters in many parts of the world. On television, we see sporting events and the weather taking place in distant locations as well as within our local communities. The reality of these "experiences" and our understanding of them are based on the documentation of actual events. Photography and video provide us with vestiges of actual happenings that substitute for experience and become a paradigm for reality. Indeed, our exposure to almost all forms of visual art occurs through documentation; Photography is the reality, not the actual work or event itself. Many artists, such as those involved with installation and performance art, are dependent on the use of documentation to communicate with an audience. Documentation allows images and events to transcend location while capturing those intangible aspects of the process of creation itself: the passage of time, the occurrence of change, and the action of motion.

Within the two-dimensional plane, time, change, and motion are made tangible through the use of sequential transition. ***Sequence*** is a design form that utilizes illusion to replicate those intangible aspects that are at the core of our perception of reality. It facilitates the use of properties of movement and change in the inherently ***static*** environment of the picture plane. Conceptually, this project deals with the ways in which we experience life and come to understand what is real.

OBJECTIVES

This project involves the creation of a series of six designs, which are related and unified through the concept of sequential change and the use of digital media. The genesis of these designs will be photographic documentation of any desired forms, objects, or people participating in an interaction with the surrounding environment. This project will explore the creation of a series of images that utilizes formal and conceptual commonalties. The series will also involve the creation of a site-specific scene or happening and the use of digital photography as a means of recording ***transient*** events. The photographs will be manipulated and transformed to create a sequential series of related images.

MATERIALS

Electronic: A digital camera; an application or card/disc drive to transfer the images to a computer; a raster-based drawing program such as Adobe Photoshop; laser printer; mounting board; rubber cement; pen or utility knife

Traditional: Preexisting photographs; Color Aid papers; paint; brushes; pastels; colored pencils; various collage materials; mounting board; rubber cement; pen or utility knife

PROCEDURE

Electronic

Create and Capture Images

Utilizing any and all found and/or collected materials that you can gather, the surrounding environment and other people create an installation or event that arranges and organizes forms within an environmental space. Carefully consider all ***design principles*** and compositional issues while you are creating an interesting and dynamic series of images. This part of the project is meant to encompass and embrace the concept of transience; nothing has to last for longer than it takes you to take a picture. As you record your images, further refine the composition through the lens of the camera and preview your images.

These images will become part of a six-step sequential series. To prime the pump, as it were, you will be utilizing the concepts of time, change, and motion as you are recording your images. Each of you will take a series of four photographs. You may take the photographs to record the step-by-step process of creating your piece (time and change) or you may move around the finished piece to record all of facets of the three-dimensional form (time and motion), or you can do a combination of both. You may work in groups of two or three people, but each individual should take his/her own pictures. Try to plan which approach you will utilize to document your images before you begin.

In addition, you will need to include a ***remnant*** of your performance. Collect forms found on site—weeds, junk, branches, etc.—that may be scanned and used in conjunction with your sequence. Consider choosing materials that will not rot or smell, as you may need to hold onto them for a period of time.

Creating the Sequence

Create a sequence that involves the manipulation of photographic images through the process of ***collage.*** This sequence must have six distinct and closely interrelated parts (formats). Choose two types of sequences with which to manipulate your original image. Elements may add or subtract characteristics as they progress through space. Forms may change position, direction, or size to indicate transitional alterations that take place across time. Forms may even transform within a given space, undergoing a metamorphosis from one thing to another. Within a sequence, however, it must be understood that the ability to clearly discern any transition is dependent on changes that occur in regular or incremental quantities or intervals. Distortion may also be utilized as an agent of change within the sequence. The viability of this option lies in its power to transform an element so that it functions in a unique way within the image. Distorting forms because it can be done within a digital environment is not viable justification for the use of filters and transformation functions.

Utilize color as an integral element within your design. It may appear as a sequential element (being gradually added, subtracted, or transformed within the series) or it may be a consistent element throughout the sequence. It must, however, be different or altered from the color seen in your original scanned image.

Incorporate the remnant collected from your documented event. **Scan** the form or forms and **Paste** them into place as desired. Consider working on top of the picture plane to manipulate spatial illusion. Other options for this problem include the use of text as a visual element within the series. The power of the gestalt and its ability to direct content must be carefully considered when making decisions involving the scale and orientation of the type. This problem affords the opportunity to utilize a vast selection of created, appropriated, realistic, and non-objective elements (Figure 8.15, and Figures 8.16, 8.17, color insert).

As you will be dealing with a number of relatively complex color images, consider the storage capacity of your disc(s) and reduce the size of the image to accommodate this capacity if necessary.

Traditional This project may be done as a studio problem without the computer. Any and all materials and processes may be utilized with the limitation being that photographic

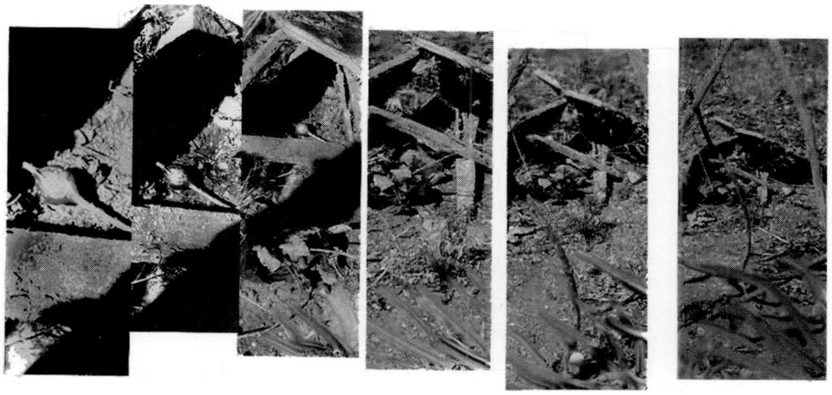

Figure 8.15 *Image by Greg Yoder*

images will need to be documented through a sequential transition in order to be utilized within the design. The same conceptual and formal parameters apply to the problem.

PRESENTATION

Cut out your designs and mount on a single black or white board, considering margins and borders that best suit the images.

RESOLUTION

This project affords participants the opportunity to physically interact with each other and their environments. Location and actors may be repetitive within different images, but transitions and manipulations within the digital environment will afford a vast array of solutions. A variety of formal issues may be considered during critique and discussion. Margins and ***intervals*** between images serve as a means of controlling the speed at which the images may be read and impact the viewers' ability to discern change. Sequential transitions involve movement through time that is linear. Orienting a sequential image along a linear path can facilitate a clear reading of the activity that is occurring. Sequences need not move in one direction from one thing or state to another. They may begin in the center of an action, move to the end and then back again to a middle position. Additionally, issues involving balance and unity must be considered for the sequence as a whole as well as for individual compositions.

ILLUSIONISTIC MOTION

Our perceptions of physical, emotional, and conceptual reality are formed by our continuous interactions with rather intangible elements of our existence. Time, or the fourth dimension, is the irreversible continuum in which our lives move. Change is the fundamental condition of this transitional existence, and motion the way that we experience and understand the three-dimensional reality of the world around us. Although none of these elements of time, change, and motion can be experienced actually within the realm of two-dimensional design, they may be experienced illusionistically on and behind the surface of the ***picture plane.***

Motion may be seen as the most tangible of these three ***elements,*** facilitating the occurrence of change over the continuum of time. The illusion of motion on a two-dimensional plane may be created in a variety of ways. Images and forms, particularly human forms that are positioned in such a way that we recognize their instability, evoke a ***kinesthetic response*** or ***empathy*** within our own bodies. Our memories and experiences allow us to "feel" the movement that is captured in two-dimensional form. ***Fuzzy*** or ***blurred contours*** suggest the movement of forms through space by simulating the visual impossibility of focusing on the contours of elements that move quickly through our field of vision. So too, repeating a form within a single ***format*** can give the illusion of viewing a figure in the process of movement. Forms that are somehow distorted or exaggerated can give the illusion of change occurring through the process of motion. This particular effect is dependent on our perception that things have departed from what we understand to be "normal."

Certain compositional relationships can also result in an increased sense of motion within an image. ***Heightened contrast*** can increase the power and activity of certain forms and create ***focal points*** that forcefully direct the eye. A strong sense of ***directional movement*** or ***tension*** within a design can enhance the overall sense of visual animation. The use of ***gradients*** can impose movement by directing the eye to travel across a series of gradual transitions in size, value, or texture.

Motion is a key factor in our understanding of the world that we inhabit. As infants, our ability to roll over profoundly changes our understanding of the world that we inhabit. So too, learning to crawl, walk, and run provides us with an ever-increasing comprehension of the space and forms that surround us. As a key component in our understanding of our physical reality, motion becomes a profoundly compelling and dynamic force when utilized within two-dimensional images.

OBJECTIVES

The objectives of this assignment involve the development of a series of related designs that utilize collaborative interaction between participants and the use of digital photography to document this activity. The project will also explore a variety of means of creating the illusion of motion on a two-dimensional surface.

MATERIALS

Digital camera; cohorts; a computer; a raster-based drawing program such as Photoshop; color printer; mounting board; rubber cement; pen or utility knife

PROCEDURE, ELECTRONIC AND TRADITIONAL

Finding the Inspiration As a human being, activity and movement define your life and the lives of the people around you. You eat, study, talk, exercise, touch (hug, kiss), do laundry, and make art almost continuously. These activities circumscribe your time and connect you to the lives of others all around you. Choose one of these activities, considering its role in the liveliness, movement, and even commotion of your own daily existence.

Choose a number of objects that relate to your chosen activity. Food, books, clothing, exercise equipment, art supplies, and other people are all possible props for your selected activity. Working with friends or peers, take photographs of you interacting with your props to create interesting visual relationships. Take any additional photographs of the props themselves that you desire. For any items that are particularly cumbersome or unable to be directly accessed (weights, a laundry machine, or your mother), find clear, uncropped, and high-contrast photographic images. These can be scanned onto your disk in preparation for work in the computer lab.

Create a Design Working collaboratively, create a design that has a strong sense of illusionistic motion. This is a digital photomontage problem whose format will be determined by the group as the project develops. Each individual will work with a photograph of themselves that will eventually be combined with the faces of the others in the group to produce a single finished project.

Begin by exchanging your image(s) with those individuals with whom you are collaborating and who are now seated directly around you. **Copy** their photographs onto your disk. Using your own photograph, alter the image utilizing a minimum of three methods that create the illusion of motion (Figures 8.18, 8.19, 8.20, and 8.21, color insert). Strive to create a unified and exciting visual solution. As you work, create formal, visual relationships to the images of those people with whom you are working. When completed, these images will be abutting (touching) your own. Utilize parts of their images and/or a sense of motion that will relate to them with the goal of creating one continuous, flowing image when they are printed and juxtaposed (Figure 8.22, color insert). Consider how shape/form relationships can create directional movement within the composition as a whole. Consider that the design must have a sense of ***illusionistic space.*** This may include ***value (Chiaroscuro, atmospheric perspective,*** or ***gradation), drawing systems (linear perspective or isometric projection), transparency (penetrating shapes and equivocal space),*** and/or ***curving and bending lines.*** Consideration must also be given to the use of ***balance,***

rhythm, grouping principles, harmony, and ***variety*** in order to unify the completed design. A vast number of design elements including ***line, shape, texture, value, color,*** and ***pattern*** are available to be utilized within your work. You may invent (draw) forms within the program or import any scanned images or information desired. Don't fall back on codified, established ways of creating design solutions: strive for innovative solutions. In addition, thought needs to be given to the implications of open and closed formats, scale and vertical placement in conjunction with your design (Figure 8.22, color insert).

Finally, you must work with the concept of collaboration. This is a group project and all members must work with the processes of critique and analyzation, subordinating their own desires to facilitate the success of the group. When you have completed your design, **Print** one color copy of your own work. Consider having the whole group utilize the same printer so that color preferences are the same in each image.

Over the course of the project, efforts should be made at different intervals to print out a black-and-white copy of the developing images and physically juxtapose them within the classroom. Drawing and notes can be made directly onto these prints, which can then be carried back into the lab and used to edit the original digital images.

PRESENTATION

Cut out your designs and mount on black, white, or gray board, depending on the needs of the image. Carefully consider what size margins and borders would best serve the image. Individual participants may mount their own images on backing boards with only top and bottom borders. Individuals on the ends of the sequence will need to have a left or right border depending on their position. This will allow the group project to be seen and read as one continuous piece with a consistent, continuous border (Figures 8.23, 8.24, color insert, and Figure 8.25).

DISCUSSION

This project creates an opportunity to work collaboratively within both the studio and computer lab environments. Critique should include the altered perspective that is generated in the physical versus the digital environment. Discussion can also deal with the possibilities for image sources available for digital forms as well as formal issues involving the critical use of ***grouping principles*** in order to achieve ***unity*** between the separate images of several different individuals.

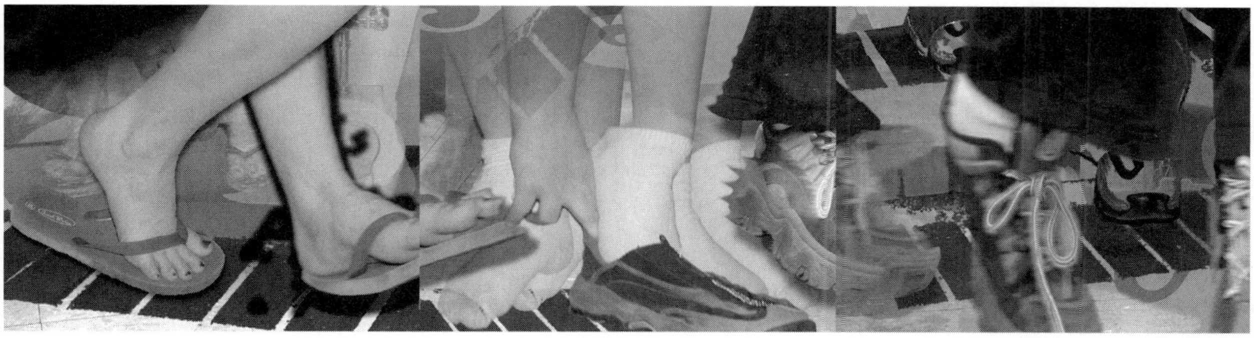

Figure 8.25 *Image by Jaimie Clark, Gretchen Goodhue, and Erin Hart*

CONCLUSION

Now that you have worked your way through the projects in this book, you may have found that technology can be a great timesaver and facilitator. It broadens our horizons and introduces us to new ways of accomplishing our goals. To be useful and productive, however, technology must be directed with both intelligence and integrity. Without a firm foundation and understanding of the elements and principles of design and the accompanying vocabulary, technology alone cannot generate good design. Nor can technology replace the facility and coordination of a trained hand and knowledgeable eye.

This book has presented you with a variety of design projects. It is an anthology, collected and combined from the Two-Dimensional Design classes taught independently by the five authors at Rochester Institute of Technology. The projects chosen for inclusion are those that most closely illustrate the premise of the book. Although inclusive and extensive, the book differs significantly from the comprehensive courses we each teach on-site.

Our curriculum is organic and fluid, continually modified and enhanced in light of the ongoing changes in technology and culture. We hope that you have found our experiences to be a useful bridge to your own exploration and use of current digital media.

GLOSSARY

Abstraction The simplification of form

Accents Relatively small areas of emphasis utilized to create interest and visual variety

Activity A condition or state of movement

Animate Alive; referencing movement

Animism The belief that natural objects or natural phenomena possess souls–that souls may exist apart from bodies.

Anomaly An irregularity or deviation from the normal or common order, form, or rule within an image. The use of anomaly does not break down the order within a composition, it simply provides variety. The functions of anomaly include:

- Attracting visual interest
- Creating variety and relieving boredom
- Allowing a transformation from one regularity to another
- Breaking down regularity into irregularity

Anomaly can occur in a variety of ways, as follows:

- Anomaly of shape—Utilizing forms that are different in shape from the unit forms within the design
- Anomaly of size—Utilizing various sizes of forms within a design
- Anomaly of color or value—Varying the color or value of a form within an overall design that involves similarity and repetition
- Anomaly of texture—Altering the texture of one or more forms
- Anomaly of position and direction—Dislocating one or more unit forms within a composition

Balance A design principle concerned with the equating of visual forces, emphasis, or happenings. Pictorial balance almost always refers to a horizontal balance between the right and left sides of an image. Because of our sense of gravity we are accustomed to seeing more weight toward the bottom an image, resulting in stability and calm.

Types of balance include

- Approximate or implied symmetry—A type of balance that initially appears to be symmetrical but in fact lacks perfect repetition of form and placement.

- Asymmetrical/Informal—A type of pictorial balance achieved with dissimilar objects that have equal visual weight or equal eye attraction. Asymmetrical balance contributes to compositions that have greater dynamic movement and visual energy than symmetrical composition. Asymmetrical balance is achieved through the use of:
  - Color—Higher intensity color has more emphasis or weight than lower intensity color and thereby can be utilized in smaller quantities against larger areas of more neutral chroma.
  - Eye Direction—Two items of unequal weight can be brought into equilibrium by placing the heavier element on the edge of the format and having it point to the visually lighter element.
  - Position—Two items of unequal weight can be brought into equilibrium by moving the heavier form in toward the center or fulcrum of the image.

- Shape—Complex shapes are more visually compelling than simple shapes and can thus be used at a smaller scale to balance larger simple forms.
- Texture—Any visual texture with a variegated dark and light pattern holds more visual interest than a smooth unmodulated surface. Smaller quantities of texture can thereby balance larger amounts of flat surface.
- Value—Higher value contrast is more visually compelling than lower value contrast and thus can be utilized in smaller amounts to balance larger areas where value contrast is relatively low.
- Weight—Two dissimilar forms can achieve visual balance if their visual weight is equivalent.

- Crystallographic Balance—A type of balance that is achieved when there is equal emphasis over an entire format. This type of balance produces a compositional form known as All-Over Pattern.
- Neutral Balance—A type of balance achieved by the random arrangement of elements that have equal emphasis. Neutral balance creates art that is inactive and lacks emphasis or contrast.
- Radial/Rotational Symmetry—A type of balance that is achieved when visual elements are mirrored or moved around a central point.
- Symmetrical/Formal/Bilateral Balance—A type of pictorial balance in which all forms are mirrored on either side of a central vertical axis. Symmetrical balance contributes to the creation of quiet, static, rigid, and stable compositions.
- Translational Symmetry—A one-dimensional symmetry in which elements are repeated at equally spaced intervals along a directional path.
- Visual Asymmetry—A type of asymmetrical balance that occurs when variation in terms of color, value placement, texture, etc. is introduced into a physically symmetrical pattern.

Chaos A condition or state of confusion and disorder

Collaboration A practice of working with others to create visual art work. Collaboration depends on dialogic, interactive, and interdependent processes.

Collage A process of gluing materials and forms onto a supporting surface

Color Optical sensations produced by the various wavelengths of visible light (electromagnetic energy), which form a narrow band on the known spectrum of radiant energy. Color is a function of light and is only perceived when light is present (thus there is no color at night).

Color categories include:

- Primary Colors—Those that stand alone and cannot be obtained by mixing any other colors together. Primary colors in pigments are red, yellow, and blue, and primary hues in light are red, blue, and green.
- Secondary Colors—Colors that are obtained by mixing two primaries together—orange, green and violet.
- Tertiary Colors—Hues that are obtained by mixing a primary with a secondary color—red-orange, yellow-orange, yellow-green, blue-green, blue-purple, and red-purple

Color contrasts include:

- Contrast of Hue—A type of contrast created through the juxtaposition of differing hues. The intensity of this contrast diminishes as the hues utilized are distanced from the three primaries. It is most effective with pure, undiluted colors.
- Contrast of Intensity—A type of contrast created by the juxtaposition of colors of varying strength. This type of contrast is most effective when utilized as a variation of chroma (color strength) when dealing with a single hue or closely related hues. When hues are widely varied, other types of contrast are more evident and become predominant. The value of this type of contrast lies in its ability to make a few colors do many things.

- Contrast of Values—A type of contrast created through the juxtaposition of colors of differing values. Low-value contrasts between colors increase the sense of discord, while strong-value contrasts between colors deaden the chroma. Contrast of value also impacts the appearance of the boundary between colors. Boundaries appear to be "harder" when there is a greater contrast of values between two areas of color and, conversely, boundaries appear softer when value contrast is reduced.

Color, Cultural Associations Some colors have associated means within a specific cultural context. Symbolic color has played an important role as an identifier of importance that creates recognition in both literate and illiterate members of society, especially in terms of religious figures and ceremonies.

Color, Emotional Associations Some colors have associations strongly related to emotions. Many of these may also need to be understood relative to specific cultural contexts.

Color, Formal Qualities

- Hue—Refers to the location of a color on the spectrum of visible light, and to its name. Hue also refers to the relationship of a color to those in its mixture, especially to the primaries.
- Temperature—The warmth or coolness of a color
  - Cool Colors—A group of colors including blue, green, and purple and their tertiaries, that produce the physical impression of coolness by visually triggering a decrease in circulation. Dimensionally, these colors appear to contract and recede into space.
  - Warm Colors—A group of colors including red, orange, and yellow and their tertiaries, that produce the physical sensation of warmth by visually triggering an increase in blood pressure. Dimensionally, these colors appear to emerge, expand, or advance into space.
- Saturation/Intensity—The purity or brilliance of a hue or its relative brightness or dullness. Saturation is the *hue* intensity of a color.
  - High Intensity/Saturated—Color that is pure, vivid, unmodulated by black, grays, or white
  - Low Intensity/Unsaturated—Color that is dull, grayed with black, gray, white, or a complement
- Value—The lightness or darkness of a hue; The *light* intensity of a color
  - Chromatic Value—The lightness or darkness of a color
  - Tints—Light values of colors, achieved either by adding white (opaque media) or by adding water (transparent media, where the paper functions as white) to a color.
  - Shades—Dark values of a color, achieved either by adding black or the complement to a color. As with pure value or achromatic value, value in color is relative, i.e., its perception is based on its context or surroundings.
  - Inherent Value of Colors—The value of a color, pure and unmixed, relative to other colors. On a scale with black being ten and white being zero the pure spectral colors can be numbered as follows:

    10 Black

    9 Violet

    8 Blue

    7

    6 Green/Red

    5

    4 Orange

    3 Yellow

    2

    1

    0 White

- Local Value—The actual value as it is perceived in the visual world. Value keys—High, middle, low, full range and Tenebrism also apply to ranges of color.

Color Harmony A relationship between colors that produces a pleasing interaction involving visual balance and symmetry of forces.

Harmonic Color Schemes

- Harmony of adjacents/Analogous colors—A harmonious grouping of colors that includes any three colors next to each other on the color wheel
- Harmony of opposites/ complements/dyads—A harmonious chord produced by two diametrically opposed colors on the color wheel
- Harmony of split complements—A harmonious grouping produced by a single color and the two colors that fall immediately to the left and right of its complement
- Harmony of triads—A harmonious grouping produced by three colors that fall on the corners of any equilateral or isosceles triangle placed within the color wheel
- Harmony of tetrads—A harmonious grouping produced by four colors that fall on the corners of any square or rectangle placed within the color wheel
- Harmony of a dominant hue—A harmonious grouping that is produced when all colors involved have a common hue in their mixture and that hue predominates within the image or form
- Harmony of a single hue/Monochromatic color—A harmonious grouping that is produced when all colors are differing values of a single hue

Color, Physical Qualities The eye, optic tract, and centers of vision in the brain translate electromagnetic energy, which is light, into electrochemical energy. This transformation takes place through the rods and cones, which are the photoreceptors in the retina. The electrochemical energy then moves through the nervous system as encoded impulses, which are received and interpreted by the sight centers of the brain. These centers transform a multitude of stimuli into meaningful precepts, thus ordering, abstracting, and translating optical data.

Color, Psychological Qualities Refers to the reservoir of experience and memory, influenced by habit and cultural persuasions that affects how we individually and uniquely perceive color

Color Systems

- Additive System—A system of colors created by mixing colors that come from light. A mixture of primary hues in this system results in the creation of white light.
- Subtractive System—A system of colors created by the interaction of material substances called pigments and light. Pigments reflect approximately the same color as is seen in the band of the same name in the spectrum of visible light. The mixture of primary pigments in certain proportions results in the creation of black.

Color Tonality Refers to the dominance of a single color or the visual importance of a hue that seems to pervade the entire color structure despite the presence of other colors

Color Wheel A two-dimensional model developed by Sir Isaac Newton in 1624, whereby the progression of hues in the visible spectrum of white light is presented in circular format

Communication The exchange of thoughts or messages with other people through speech, signals, writing, or visual images. The effectiveness of communication is based on some common information or knowledge, as verbal communication is dependent on knowledge of a common language. Communication is one of the primary functions of art and is generated through the development of an idea or concept.

Composition The formal arrangement of visual elements to create a structured and organized whole. Compositions may be Static, having stability and little motion, or Dynamic, having a great deal of movement and activity.

- Closed Compositions—Compositions in which all forms exist completely within the borders of the format. They are considered to be less active images because all information regarding forms is visible.

- Open Compositions—Compositions in which forms are cropped by the edge of the format. Open compositions are considered to be more active because of the cognitive processes involved in completing those forms that are cropped. They are also seen to involve a greater sense of space and movement as they suggest a continuation of space beyond the edges of the format.

Concepts Those ideas or notions that guide or explain meaning, philosophical or intellectual context, emotional perception and qualitative relationship within an artwork

Content The meaning or significance contained within any visual image as distinguished from its form. Content is the result of combining idea and communication.

- Emotional Content—A type of content that evokes an emotional feeling or response to a work of art. Emotional content involves the communication of an idea visually as a feeling. As basic emotions are universally shared despite cultural, educational, or experiential differences, emotional content has the potential of being widely recognized and understood.
- Intellectual Content—A type of content that involves an intellectual response to the visual or visual–verbal communication of an idea. Intellectual content is dependent on a common knowledge and language that is understood by a desired audience. This type of content incorporates the use of symbols and symbolic language.
- Unintentional Content—A type of content that results from natural visual phenomenon found in visual form. Content is supplied as a result of an individual's personal observations, experience, and imagination.
- Intentional Content—Content that is the result of an earnest desire to communicate a specific idea through a visual or visual–verbal expression.

Context The situation surrounding an element, form, activity or an event that influences and dictates its function and activity

Contour defining the outer edges of a form

Craftsmanship A skill, proficiency, expertness, or technical excellence in the utilization of materials

Cropping The cutting off or elimination of portions of a visual form

Design a plan; a combination of visual elements whose organization has been structured into a unified whole

Directional Forces Within The Format Acting as both a shape and a field in which a composition will operate, the format is an integral part of an image. Different portions of this visual field exert themselves in a variety of ways on a composition.

- Perpendicular forces—A rectangular picture plane creates vertical and horizontal movement along its edges. Any mark or line placed on a page is either a repeat of the format borders or a counterpoint to it. Points of intersection at the corners terminate the perpendicular tensions, hold down the format, and draw the viewer's eye to the corners of the format.
- The edges of the format create a strong visual pull that increases the visual tension of forms as they approach the perimeter.
- The bottom of the format seems to visually contain more weight because of our perception of gravity. Objects placed near the bottom of the format are influenced by this perception and appear to be visually heavier than objects placed farther up on the format.
- The right side of the format holds more power and weight because of our visual tendency to scan from the left to the right and our method of reading from the left to the right. Forms placed along the right side of an image have more visual power than those placed along the left side.
- The center of an image is the most potent area of the design and objects placed at this location have greater visual impact or force.

Directional Forces Within Shapes Refers to the sense of movement within individual shapes and forms. Shapes may have major directional movement, which is the backbone of the shape, and minor directional movement, which involves the outside positive/negative qualities of the contour. These movements together and between shapes reinforce each other by creating points of visual tension. Directional forces also refer to the sense of movement of forms through space and within the general composition.

Dominance The condition of influence or control, surpassing all others in power and importance, within a visual image or form.

Diptych A set of two panels, side by side bearing images, carvings or pictures.

Distortion Stretching or otherwise deforming a shape, changing it from its original presentation

Dynamic Full of life; expressive; showing evidence of movement or change

Elements Those forms that can be manipulated within visual images, such as point, line, shape, value, texture and color.

Equivocal Space An ambiguous spatial pattern created through the use of transparency, in which multiple forms occupy the same space

Figure/Ground Reversal A composition whose positive and negative spaces are visually equivalent and not readily distinguishable

Focal Point The visual center of an image that is utilized to direct and/or attract the eye. The focal point may be a specific element or a general area of a design or composition. Focal points are achieved by creating conditions wherein one form or group of forms is emphasized over another. Focal points may be created by conditions of contrast including:

1. Simple versus complex
2. Direction of form: Change from normal
3. Motion versus stasis/clarity versus diffusion/in-focus/versus out-of-focus
4. Type of form: Identical versus changed
5. Contrast of texture
6. Contrast of values
7. Color Emphasis

Focal points may also be created by altering and emphasizing form position within the composition. These include:

1. Isolation
2. Foreground versus background: Size of form
3. Centering the form on the page

Form A three-dimensional element perceived through the synthesis of its visual characteristics, structure, and unifying components

Format An integral part of a design, the format defines the shape of the two-dimensional surface on which a design is created and the outer edges of the picture plane

Gestalt A German word, roughly translated to mean "form" or "thing" and encompassing ideas of configuration, structure, and wholeness. Gestalt theories, established by psychological studies begun in the early 1900s, delineated our predisposition to view images as complete entities rather than the sum of individual parts. Visual, conceptual, and formal phenomenon associated with gestalt theory include the perception of figure and ground, the perception of symbolic form, and the establishment of identity in regard to visual forms.

Gesture a pose that conveys expression

Grid A network of horizontal and perpendicular lines

Grouping Principles A group of design principles that utilize methods of relating forms within a composition so as to achieve unity. They include:

- Closure—A relationship created between elements that are arranged or aligned to create other recognizable entities. Visual phenomenon in which we close or finish a visual form given only a small part of the actual visual information available.
- Continuation—A relationship between elements based on the continuation of a line, edge, or direction from one form to another
- Proximity—A relationship between elements based on their relative nearness
- Repetition—Form relationships based on the repetition of a visual element such as color, shape, texture, direction, angle, etc.
- Similarity—Form relationships based on similarity of color, value, texture, size, shape, sameness of direction

Harmony The pleasing interaction or combination of elements in a whole based on likeness or similarity

Hierarchy The graded arrangement of elements or forms according to importance or quality

Icon A symbolic image or representation. The creation of icons is dependent on a commitment to a charged idea that precipitates some kind of worship or reverence and reflects an effort to emphasize a fixed attitude. Icons are not primarily committed to conveying information or creating an aesthetic statement and are not necessarily objectified in a finished piece, though there must always be an object.

Iconic An image that has symbolic content or meaning that is conveyed through explicit symbols which are understood by the artist and are intended to impart specific meaning to the viewer

Iconography The study of the total meaning of a work of art. Iconography goes beyond the subject matter of an art object, considering it within its total cultural context and examining it as an expression of the world view of its maker. Iconography is the study of the form and content of a work of art and how the formal qualities combine to convey meaning. Traditionally, especially with religious art, iconography has been concerned with the interpretation of symbols that conveyed specific meanings in particular times and places, even though those meanings may since have been altered or eradicated.

Idea A thought or knowledge that exists in the mind, potentially or actually, as a product of mental activity. Visualization is the result of an idea not an idea in itself.

Ideogram A written symbol which directly represents an idea or object.

Illusion of Space The implied representation of three-dimensional space on a two-dimensional plane

Inanimate Without life; static forms

Interval A space that occurs between elements or forms. Intervals include:

- Alternating Interval—A type of organization in which the spacing between forms reoccurs in units that vary in size
- Progressive Interval—A type of arrangement in which the spaces between forms change in size in a progressive, gradational manner
- Regular Interval—A type of organization in which the space between elements reoccurs and is a consistent size

Isometric Perspective a spatial representation based on non-converging parallel lines on the two-dimensional picture plane.

Light Electromagnetic radiation that is visible to the human eye and facilitates vision

Line A two-dimensional element of design, created by the movement of a point across a plane. Categories of line include:

- Actual—Lines that exist visually
- Implied—Lines that are formed by the eye connecting separate forms
- Psychic—Lines that are created by emotional feelings, without any physical evidence of their existence

Emotional Associations of Line can convey emotional, visual, and even physical movement within two- and three-dimensional forms. These effects may be best understood when referenced by the movement lines in the environment around us, such as

- Curved Line—Found along the edges of many organic forms in nature. They are also found in the movement of liquids, such as the path of a river and the paths of erosion. Animals tend to utilize repetitive movements in nature, creating curved paths within their environments that include the flight patterns of birds and walked paths in woods and fields. These occurrences indicate the more dynamic and active nature of curved lines, which are thought of as being lyrical, sensual, and flowing.
- Diagonal Lines—Found along the edges of mountains and volcanoes, and in the paths of lightning, they are logically associated with action and energy. The presence of these types of lines and the alignment of forms along diagonal paths creates a much greater level of motion and activity.
- Horizontal Lines—Found on the horizon, in architectural forms, in the movement of waves, and in the sleeping posture of people and many animals. They are therein associated with quiet, calm, and stasis. Lines and aligned forms that move along horizontal paths reference these associations and can lend quiet, calm, and static qualities to the compositions in which they function.
- Vertical Lines—Found in trees, architectural elements and the path of growth of many living things. Quiet, strong, and stable, their association with growth makes them a slightly more dynamic linear form than horizontal lines.

Functions of line include:

- Lines define shape and form through outline and contour
- Lines define edge
- Lines create positive and negative space
- Lines create a sense of direction
- As lines are not found in nature, they are a visual abstraction, functioning as artistic shorthand and mediating the spaces between actual forms and their two-dimensional equivalents

Qualities of line include:

- Direction—Lines can move horizontally, vertically, diagonally, or along curved paths
- Weight—Lines can vary in terms of thickness or thinness
- Value—Lines can vary in terms of their lightness or darkness
- Texture—Lines can vary in terms of the tactile quality they convey, created by subtle movement and variations in their form

Lines may be categorized in a variety of ways that reference their sources in the surrounding environments and the ways in which they are created, such as

- Freehand—Lines drawn without mechanical aids
- Geometric—Lines that reference those found in geometric forms, usually involving hard-edged and/or angled lines.
- Mechanical—Lines drawn with mechanical tools such as a compass or ruler
- Signatory—Lines with a unique, handmade quality that reflects the personal response of an individual artist to the object of his or her vision
- Organic—Lines that reference those found in nature, usually involving curved or flowing lines

Where line is found

- Where two different values meet
- Where two surfaces meet
- Where two surfaces intersect

Luminosity the relative brightness of something; emitting or reflecting a glowing light

Motif An element that is used repetitively within a design pattern

Movement A transition of position from one place to another

Negative Space The background or unfilled space within an image that serves as the surface on which figures are presented. This space is also known as ground within a two-dimensional composition.

Non-Objective There is no evidence of recognizable subject matter in the image; the image may be comprised of textures, colors, invented shapes without reference to actual objects

Neutrality A condition of being in the middle without activity, emphasis, or direction toward any one activity, form, or side

Objective Recognizable subject matter is evident in the image

Order A logical or comprehensible arrangement of separate elements or groups of elements within a design. Order involves the organization of forms within a design through the use of focal points and grouping principles. Types of order include:

- Complex—A type of order that involves many systems and subsystems within a larger composition, with their own focal points and elements. These sub-systems function both independently and as parts of the whole.
- Simple—A type of order that involves a system with elements that move toward a single focal point
- Random—A type of order that involves a scattering of forms to create a visual equality of position that subsumes everything into a single system.

Palette a grouping of colors organized around an intentional effect

Paradigm A model or belief system that can reference the organization and creation of information, approaches to process, or various ways of working

Pattern A repetitive design consisting of a coherent, systematic visual structure in which unit forms or motifs are precisely repeated. Pattern is created through the use of rhythm, repetition, and alternating pauses. Types of patterns include:

- Regular—A pattern utilizing a single motif that does not vary in size or orientation
- Irregular—A pattern utilizing a single motif that does vary in size and movement
- Combined—A pattern that utilizes a number of different motifs
- Slip Reflection—A pattern structure in which every row or column of motifs is moved half a unit up or down as they progress across the structure
- Slipped-Middle—A pattern structure in which every other row or column of motif is moved down one half-step
- Counterchange—A simple grid system in which shapes and/or colors reverse across vertical or horizontal axes
- Run Together—A pattern structure in which motifs bleed together visually

Perception Of Space Our understanding of space is dependent on sensory processes involving vision.

- Binocular Vision—Our vision consists of two different views or images, one from each eye (bi = two and ocular = eye) that are merged within the brain through a process called Stereopsis. Developed as a survival technique to estimate distances for nearby activities, Stereopsis is most effective within 12–15 feet and ceases to function at about 1,200 feet.
- Monocular Depth Cues—Visual cues for assessing depth without dependence on binocular vision, i.e. having two eyes. These cues reinforce the information developed through binocular vision but function independently. They provide the primary means for evaluating intermediate to far distances and creating spatial illusion on a two-dimensional plane.
- Aerial or Atmospheric Perspective—The use of value and/or color to show depth. This is a naturally occurring phenomenon, visible in daylight, in which value

progressively decreases, colors neutralize and become a bit bluer, and contours soften as forms move away from the viewer.

- Chiaroscuro—Gradations of value that move over a three-dimensional object or surface, mimicking the movement of light and shadow across the surface of similar forms
- Density/Texture Gradient Cue—A gradual transition of textures, in which coarse textures advance spatially and fine textures recede
- Figure–Ground Reversal—A compositional phenomenon in which quantities and placement of light and dark values are visually perceived as being equivalent, denying the formation of positive and negative space and flattening the image
- Gradation—A gradual transition of values from light to dark through a series of small measured steps. Values move toward or away from the viewer along the path of the gradient, depending on the surrounding value relationships.
- Linear Perspective—The art or theory of representing three-dimensional objects on a flat surface in such a way as to give the appearance of depth and distance. This drawing system is one of the most common indicators of spatial depth in representational art.
  - One-Point Perspective—A system used to represent an object from the viewpoint of having only one of its three dimensions receding from the picture plane
  - Two-Point Perspective—A system used to represent an object from the viewpoint of having two of its three dimensions receding from the picture plane
  - The Horizon Line—The physical, environmental place where the earth meets the sky and your eye level or the distance of your eyes from the ground plane. Eye level determines the height at which you will actually see the horizon.
  - Curving and Bending Line Spatial Depth—The illusion that edges are moving away from the viewer when they travel on curved or diagonal paths. Our memory stores images or forms, as they would be seen frontally, reinforcing horizontal and vertical contours. When lines curve or bend away from these perceived horizontals and verticals, a spatial phenomenon occurs that is interpreted by our brains as an indication of depth.
- Overlapping—Objects partially covered by other objects are perceived as being underneath or farther away than those covering them
- Size—Multiple forms appearing in a variety of sizes create the illusion of depth because objects appear to get smaller as they move away
- Vertical Location—Objects placed up or down within the picture plane will appear to move forward and back in space. This is a cultural tradition that involves the division of the format into three horizontal bands, as follows:
  - Foreground—The bottom of the format that contains forms closest to the viewer
  - Middle Ground—The central portion of the format that contains forms mid-distance from the viewer
  - Background—The top portion of picture plane that contains forms farthest from the viewer

Permanent That which is fixed and inalterable and lasts indefinitely

Picture Plane

1. The frontal surface of a page or canvas
2. An invisible plane, perpendicular to the line of vision, on which information from the visual world is projected before being transferred to the surface of an image

Plane A level or flat surface

Point A determined location in space

Portraiture The pictorial representation of a person

Positive Space The space within an image that appears closest to the viewer and is occupied or filled by forms sitting on a background. This space is also known as figure within a two-dimensional composition.

Principles The rules that govern the movement and manipulation of elements within a composition so as to achieve unity.

Proportion The relative relationships of the size of parts to a whole. The comparison of one thing to another in terms of magnitudes, quantity or degrees.

- Arithmetic Proportions—A proportional relationship where the difference between the actual lengths of elements remains constant. For example, 1 : 2 : 3 : 4 : 5. The actual difference between each of these numbers (lengths, widths, heights) remains the same.
- Geometric Proportions—A proportional relationship where the ratio between elements remains constant. For example, the lengths of elements would be in geometric proportion if the ratio remained **1/2**: 1/2: 1/4 : 1/8 : 1/16.
- The Golden Ratio/Golden Section/Golden Mean/Golden Proportion/Divine Proportion—A mathematical proportion resulting from the search by philosophers, mathematicians, scientists and artists to identify in nature a numerical standard which when translated into human endeavors would assure perfection of form, harmonious balance, and beauty. It involves a proportional relationship between divisions within a large rectangle and the rectangle itself. (See Figure 4.3 in Chapter 4).
- Harmonic Proportions—A proportional relationship where the difference of the inverses of elements must remain constant. For example, 1 : 1/2 : 1/3 : 1/4 : 1/5. The difference between the inverses of each of these numbers (1,2,3,4,5) is equivalent (1).

Random Occurring without a definite aim or pattern

Raster A digital image that is composed of pixels that are structured in a grid and are assigned a specific location and color value.

Remnant A surviving vestige of a former time or condition

Rhythm Movement that is created by the regular repetition or orderly recurrence of visual, auditory, or physical elements. Rhythm consists of a regular succession of strong and weak that creates pause and emphasis within a visual image.

Scale The relative size of a visual element in relation to its actual size

Self Communication A type of communication utilized by an artist to determine

- Audience—To whom it is to be communicated
- Content—What is to be communicated
- Form—How it is to be communicated

Self-Portraiture A pictorial representation of the artist

Semiotics The study of relationships between signs and symbols and what they represent in terms of both content and meaning. Semiotics incorporates the study of signs, symbols, and symbolism through their roots in philosophy and the study of linguistics in reference to the origin and location of meaning within language.

Sequence A series of related stationary images or forms used one after another in a particular order to communicate the passage of time, the occurrence of change, or the action of motion

Shape A two-dimensional element of design that is identified by its contour edge and sense of position on the picture plane. It may be defined by line, value, texture, or color and emerge from our environment, our languages, and our imaginations.

Shape Relationships Within compositions, individual forms can relate in a variety of ways that create visual tension, spatial illusion, and conceptual connections.

- Abutting—The relationship created between forms that touch and adjoin at contours

- Coinciding—The relationship between overlapping forms that fit exactly over one another so that one is obscured from vision and there appears to be only one form visible
- Detachment—The relationship formed between shapes that do not touch. Detachment is modified by proximity between forms.
- Interlocking—A form relationship in which elements fit together in a manner similar to that of puzzle pieces
- Intersection—A relationship between two overlapping elements where only the actual area of overlap is made visible
- Mutual Tension—A relationship between forms in which their orientation creates a sense of visual tension that pulls them toward each other
- Overlapping—A form relationship created when one element partially covers another. The partially covered element is considered to be underneath and thereby creates the illusion or reality of space.
- Penetrating—A form relationship created by overlapping shapes that appear to be transparent and are thus visible in their entirety
- Subtracting—The use of a shape or form to cut away a portion of another element
- Suggesting a Continuous Whole—A form relationship between separate elements in which they are connected by the perception that they are parts of larger forms that have been eliminated from the visual field. This relationship is dependent on the use of the gestalt principle of closure.
- Union—Joining two forms through overlapping so that they become one, leaving the original parts indistinguishable

Shapes Types Shapes may be categorized in a variety of ways that reference their sources in the surrounding environment and the ways in which they are created.

- Geometric—Shapes that are created by mathematical laws
- Implied—Shapes suggested by a discontinuous contour
- Invented or Non-Objective—Shapes that are fabricated or made up
- Organic—Shapes that are derived from living organisms and nature
- Stylized—Basic and simplified shapes derived from known forms
- Complex—Those shapes with a large number of structural features, which can only be understood after a period of study
- Simple—Those shapes with a small number of structural features which can be understood immediately

Sign Something that suggests or indicates the presence or existence of a fact, condition, or quality that is not immediately evident. Signs may take the form of an action or gesture used to convey an idea, desire, information, or a command.

Simplification The paring down to essential elements

Space The intuitive three-dimensional field of our everyday experience

Stasis A condition or state of motionlessness

Stroboscopic Motion The sense of motion created when objects of similar size or shape are placed in different positions, in a progressive manner. This type of motion analyzes the path of movement by allowing only small intervals between the steps of an action. This effect is often achieved through the use of a Stroboscope, an instrument that can view, calibrate, balance, or in general adjust moving objects by making them appear stationary, especially with pulsed illumination or mechanical devices that periodically interrupt vision.

Structure An underlying division of compositional space that predetermines the placement and internal relationships of elements in a design. Structural lines are lines that define the compositional structure being utilized in a design. Structural lines may be

- Active—Structural lines that divide space and interact with forms by touching them
- Inactive—Structural lines that are conceptual; they guide form placement but don't interact with forms

- Invisible—Structural lines that are invisible
- Visible—Structural lines that exist as actual, visible lines

Types of structures include:

- Formal—A design structure in which rigid mathematical lines divide the space into regular intervals or units. Types of formal structures include
  - Gradational—A type of structure in which spatial divisions change in an orderly way through changes in size, position, or direction
  - Multiple Repetitive System—A type of structure that utilizes more than one type of structural subdivision
  - Radiational—A type of structure that involves repeated forms revolving regularly around a common center. Types of radiational structures include
    - Centrifugal—A type of structure in which straight structural lines radiate from the center of the composition. All angles formed by the structural lines are equivalent.
    - Concentric—A type of structure in which divisions of space are placed one inside of the other in regular layers around a central point
    - Centripetal—A type of structure in which sequences of bent or curved lines move from the corners or edges toward the center
  - Repetitive—A type of structure that gives equal space and placement to each of its forms
- Informal—A design structure in which the division of space and organization of elements is free and without formal limitations
- Semiformal—A design structure that appears to have visual regularity but in fact contains asymmetry in terms of the division of space or placement within the format

Style A distinctive visual characteristic attributed to a particular person, region, philosophy, or time period. Types of style include:

- Personal Style—A distinctive visual or philosophic attribute of an individual.
- Cultural Style—A distinctive visual characteristic attributed to a culture.
- Historical Style—A distinctive visual characteristic attributed to a particular period in time.
- Philosophical Style—A distinctive visual characteristic attributed to a common way of realizing subject matter.

Subject The main focus of an image

Subordination A situation of subservience to the control or power of another element or form

Symbol An image that represents or becomes a surrogate for something other than itself. Symbols evoke a range of associations, by pointing indirectly to meaning.

Tensions Refers to the forces within and between shapes and with the conceptual connections that the subject suggests to the viewer.

Texture An element of visual artwork that refers to the surface quality of objects and gives key information about materials and media. Within visual art forms, texture may be actual, referring to sensations perceived by touch, or visual. Texture is an element mediated by visual distance—textures may appear to smooth out when viewed from a distance and textures that are invisible to the naked eye may be revealed through enlargement (microscopic photographs). Visual textures may be broadly defined by the processes through which they are produced and integrated into an image.

Categories of texture include:

- Actual or Local Texture—The actual surface texture of an object from the world of our experiences. Actual textures involve the application of any substance or material to the surface of a work of art to create a texture that may actually be touched. Techniques that create actual texture are:

   - Assemblage—The creation of texture through the attachment of any dimensional material onto a supporting sculptural or relief surface, by any means (glue, nails, wire, rope, etc.)
   - Collage-Papier Colle—Textures created by pasting paper to the picture plane
   - Crossover Textures—Involves the use of both an actual surface and a means of transferring its texture onto a two-dimensional plane. Techniques that create crossover textures are
     - Rubbings or Frottage—Textures created by placing a sheet of paper over a textured form and rubbing the surface of the paper with a pencil, crayon, or similar medium. This type of technique involves both actual texture and simulated texture.
     - Transfers—Visual textures created by the actual transfer of an image from one surface to another. A printed surface is coated with a solvent and then laid face down onto the surface of a sheet of paper. The back is then rubbed with an implement to complete the transfer. Marks created through the rubbing process may become another element of the textured surface.
   - Impasto—The use of built-up media to create a surface texture, which may actually be felt with the hand
- Interpretive or Invented Textures—Involves the creation of visual textures for which there are no visual references. Invented textures Involves the application of paint, ink, or pencil to a two-dimensional surface to symbolize a textured surface.
- Simulated Texture or *Trompe L'oeil*—Involves the creation of visual texture through the imitation of real textures. Simulated textures involve the application of paint, ink, or pencil to a two-dimensional surface to mimic an observed surface.
- Typography Texture—Type functions as both gestalt and texture within printed images. When reduced scale diminishes or eliminates the legibility of typography, it becomes texture, seen as a surface of small forms and variable values.
- Photomontage—A collage technique involving the use of photographs to create a textured surface
- Decorative Texture—Texture that decorates a shape and to which it is subordinate
- Mechanical Texture—Texture obtained by special mechanical means such as a photographic grain or screen pattern or that created by typography or computer graphics. Mechanical texture is not subordinate to the forms to which it is applied.
- Spontaneous Texture—Texture that produces and generates shape as an element or by product of its creation

Time A non-spatial continuum in which events progress in an irreversible succession from the past through the present and into the future. In visual artwork, the suggestion of time is inseparable from the illusion of movement and the occurrence of change.

Transient That which is transitory or fleeting and passes away with time

Transparency The relationship created between two forms that overlap and are both seen in their entirety. Transparency involves materials that possess physical attributes that allow light to travel through their surfaces.

Triptych A set of three panels bearing images, carvings or pictures, etc.

Type Printed characters associated with language

Typography The art of printing with type

Unit of Repetition A single element or group of elements that can be used repeatedly to create a pattern.

Unity A principle of design that involves the arrangements of parts or elements into a unified whole. Unity is achieved through the interaction of harmony and variety within a design.

Value An element of visual art involving gradations from light to dark regardless of color. Value can be determined only when seen in relation to its visual environment, i.e. through comparison and context. With three-dimensional reality and illusion, value is determined by the actual color of an object and by the degree of light that strikes it.

Functions of value include:

- Value can describe light hitting a form to create the illusion of volume. This system is called Chiaroscuro. "Chiaro" translated means clear and we understand it to mean light. "Oscuro" translated means obscure and we understand it to mean dark.
- Value can describe the structure or planar makeup of an object
- Value can describe the weight or sense of the gravity in all objects in actual life
- Value can be used to describe space/depth
  - Greater contrast pushes forms farther apart in space.
  - Less contrast pulls forms closer together in space.
  - Gradations in value can provide a sense of depth in two different ways:
    - Gradation—The gradational movement of values from light in the foreground to dark in the background. Gradation usually involves a situation that utilizes artificial or directed lighting.
    - Achromatic Value—Refers to a range of grays from white to black without any color in their mixture.
    - Atmospheric/Aerial Value Effects—A gradational movement of values from dark in the foreground to light in the background.
- Gradations or the directional movement of value (light to dark) can create rhythmic eye movement.
- Value can create the illusion of transparency.
- Value can organize a composition.
- Value can lend expressive power to a drawing and reveal an emotional response to a form or a composition.
- Value can be used objectively as well as subjectively.
- Value can create emphasis through its use in focal points and greatest value contrasts.
- Value can create spatial unity through its use in creating balance and direction.

Qualities of value include:

- Darker Values—Visually heavier than lighter ones, with an increased feeling of density and energy. Dark values contract in terms of size and movement through space.
- Light Values—Visually lighter than dark values and appear to expand and inflate outward from the source
- Neutral Gray—A mixture of black and white which absorbs and reflects light equally

Value Keys Groups of values that determine the amount of variation in light and darks used in a composition. Value keys can lend expressive power and reveal an emotional response to a form or a composition.

- Accents—Small areas of contrasting emphasis within the larger Keys. An accent in a high key is black, in a low key is white, in a middle key is white and/or black, and with tenebrism or high contrast is middle gray.
- Full Range—A group that includes all of the values from white to black. This is the group of values that we most anticipate seeing in many artworks.
- High Key—A range of light values from white to medium gray. These values are often associated with quiet, calm, and optimistic feelings and situations.
- Low Key—A group of dark values from medium gray to black. Dark values are associated with ominous, threatening, sad, somber, depressing, and mysterious circumstances.
- Middle Key—The narrow range of medium value grays. These values are associated with neutrality and stasis.
- Tenebrism—A group that includes very light and very dark values with no middle grays. High contrast of values lends theatricality and drama to visual form.

Variety A quality of diversity that is achieved through the use of unexpected and contrasting visual and conceptual elements from those found in the dominant visual structure

Vector A digital image that is composed of lines and curves that are defined by mathematical objects called vectors.

Vista A distant view along a particular passage or from a specific point-of-view.

Visual Communication A way of expressing ideas visually

Visual Field The expanse of a format that can be taken in at one time

Visual Narrative The telling of a story through visual images

Volume The space that is found within a three-dimensional form

INDEX

Note: all page numbers that are **bold** indicate an illustration.

S

T

U

V

W